Beyond The Rose

JoAnn Flanery

Elderberry Press
OAKLAND

Elderberry Press, Inc.
1393 Old Homestead Drive
Oakland Or 97462
Tel: 541.459.6043
email: editor@elderberrypress.com
Our books are available from your favorite bookseller.

Library of Congress Cataloging-in-Publication Data:
Beyond The Rose/JoAnn Flanery
ISBN: 978-1-930859-65-4 [soft cover]
1. Romance—fiction.
2. Mystery—fiction.
3. Romantic Intrigue—fiction.
4. Genealogy & Family History—fiction.
5. Birth Mother—fiction.
6. Reunited Family Members—fiction.
7. Grieving—fiction.
8. Drama—fiction.
I. Title

Printed in the USA.

MORE BOOKS BY JOANN FLANERY

Accepting the Unacceptable Alone

Parenting a Parent

Simple Fun Ways of Living Naturally

CONTENTS

INTRODUCTION

Hello once again. For those of you who don't have a clue as to who I am I will give you a quick run-down. My life has had many challenges. My husband died unexpectedly thirty-one years ago, and I was left to take care of our handicapped daughter Christine on my own. We had to move away from supportive family and friends in Michigan to Flagstaff, Arizona to get the special services she needed. Time to live happily ever after? Nope, I guess life decided I needed even more challenges, I fought and survived three breast cancers, took care of my mother who had dementia, and tried to face the unacceptable fact that I was alone. All the details are in my first two books.

Beyond the Rose is my first fictional novel and to be honest out of all the books I have written this was the most fun. It was an amazing experience, the characters themselves seemed to take over and all I had to do was write down what they wanted to say. Strange I know.

This is the story of Sydney Armstrong, a beautiful accomplished lawyer who after the death of her parents decided she needed a change and moved to Michigan from Atlanta, Georgia. Her father's last words hinted at a mystery that she was determined to solve. What she found was a new family, a lasting love and finally the answers she had been seeking. There are many unpredictable twists and turns, some sexy and fun and some very surprising and shocking and I hope you like it.

Enjoy!

Just a quick note, all the characters in this book are pure fiction dreamed up by me. The cities that are mentioned that the characters are connected with are also fictional. Granted Atlanta, Georgia, Detroit, Michigan and Cleveland, Ohio are listed, but only for directional purposes. So if I made up someone who has the same name I am sorry.

DEDICATION

This book is dedicated to my editor David St. John.

Dave left this earth on November 2, 2013 and is sorely missed by everyone who knew him. I have never known a person who truly lived each day to the fullest but Dave did. He found the good in all things. He was an accomplished learned man and author himself and from his many years of experience shared his knowledge with his authors. The best advice he gave me was to "Show the reader what is going on in the story, not tell them– put yourself in the scene and enjoy the adventure." Most of all I admired him for what he stood for, honesty. When I first started with him I read his biography on line and one sentence really struck me, he "Guides writers toward a goal they may not be able to see." And through that guidance and his teaching he inspired me to write the books that I have this one in particular. He told me from the start that I should write a novel and now that I have it makes me so sad that he will not be able to read it. Goodbye Dave, thank you for putting up with me and for being such a special person. I miss you.

–1–

FATHER

"Father it's me Sydney can I come in? Father are you all right, please open the door? Please please let me in."

Panic was setting in, something's wrong. "GRETCHEN GRETCHEN HELP ME!" A minute later she came flying down the stairs.

"What happened I could hear you screaming all the way from the third floor? Take a breath you are as pale as a sheet."

"It's Father, I found the dogs barking and scratching frantically at the office door and have been knocking and knocking but he won't answer me, do you have a key to this door?" Gretchen ran her hand over the top of the door fame, grabbed the key and handed it to me.

My hands were shaking so badly I dropped it twice; finally I turned the lock and entered. "Father I am sorry to disturb you but when you didn't answer my calls I was concerned." No response came so I slowly went through the dimly lit room to his desk. He was sitting in his chair with his head back, the light on his desk cast a strange eerie shadow across his face and I knew immediately something was very wrong. I looked toward the door where Gretchen was waiting and yelled at her to call 911. Gently I touched my father's arm, "I am here Father, I will help you, please talk to me."

There was a slight gurgling sound as he tried to speak but I could not make out what he was saying. Then with what seemed like a great effort, "Sydney… look… beyond… the… rose," and he was gone.

Just before the blackness swept over me I heard the sirens. The next thing I remember was a paramedic kneeling beside me and nearby Gretchen was sobbing, "What happened?"

"Miss Armstrong you passed out," said the man who was holding my hand. "I am sorry but your father has died, there was nothing we could do for him. Are you well enough to get up? We will transport him to the hospital now."

I couldn't move, this was a horrible dream and soon I would wake up and everything would be fine, but deep in my soul I knew the truth. Did he really say 'look beyond the rose' and if so what did it mean? I can't think about that now I just can't.

I can't believe he is gone. I can't believe he is gone. My father Charles Emerson Armstrong is dead, how can it be I have never seen him with even a cold. He was only sixty years old. My father would never be old enough to die he was too stubborn and had no time for such a thing. What could have happened? Why, why, why now, my mother has only been gone for three months, and now Father too?

"Sydney honey, are you all right… Sydney?"

"Sorry Gretchen I was just lost somewhere. Honestly I don't know if I am all right or not, how could this have happened, I feel awful?"

Gretchen put her arm around me, "Of course you do after the trauma you have suffered, but you will get through this. Just give yourself time. Now get up, you have been huddled in that chair since we returned from the funeral, you must get something to eat. You haven't had a bite or slept since it… happened. Besides, Mr. Edgeworth will be here soon to read the will."

"Have the newspaper reporters left yet? I told them my lawyer would make a statement later this afternoon, why can't they leave me alone?"

"You know perfectly well why young lady, your father was a very important man and as usual they want every detail of what happened. Every move your father made was news."

Yes, every move the famous Atlanta criminal lawyer made was news. He only took on the most challenging cases and when he entered the courtroom he dominated it, just with his presence. In cross examination he did not mess around with flowery speeches, every word he spoke meant something. The courtroom was always packed when he was trying a case, and the press followed him everywhere.

"Give me just one more minute. Could you please make me a sandwich, I will join you soon. Stop giving me that look I promise I will at least try to eat it, but just to get you off my back."

Poor Gretchen, she has had to put up with so much from me. I know she loves me very much and has been almost more of a mother to me than my own. She was my mother's best friend and has lived with us since I was born, so I was told. Her title is housekeeper but she is my friend, confidant, and the glue that has held our family together–I truly love her. But somehow I felt like there was something she was not telling me, some secret I guess I am not supposed to know. Once in a while I would see her and my father deep in conversation but as soon as they saw me they seemed almost alarmed and stopped.

I guess I ate the sandwich but what it contained I have no idea. The doorbell was ringing and Gretchen bent over and gave me a quick kiss on the cheek, straightened her spine and made a face, we both knew who was there–Mr. Simon Edgeworth. The time had come to muster up what strength I had left and face my father's law partner.

A wave of nausea spread over me as I entered my father's office, I had not been in that room since….. Swallowing deeply I walked over to greet the lawyer. He rose and slowly walked toward me. If I hadn't been so un-nerved I would have laughed, here was Ichabod Crane in person straight from Sleepy Hollow. Very tall and very thin and when he walked his body was as straight as a ram rod but his legs seemed to have a mind of their own. With each step his knee floated upward, like being manipulated by a puppeteer's string then landed too far from his body which seemed to lunge forward to catch up. His hair was very short and slightly grey on the sides and what looked like a dark mop plopped on top– never sure if this was planned or a hair piece. But it was always his eyes that un-nerved me, dark as coal and so close together they seemed attached to his beaked thin nose. Those eyes missed nothing, they penetrated right through you. No wonder he was also so good at his job.

"Sydney, I am sorry for your loss he was a great man," he said as he took my hand. Then he sat down in "the" chair, my father's chair. How dare he, no one but my father ever sat in that chair. As a child I thought of it as a throne, where my father conducted business with so many important and newsworthy clients. Even the room itself fascinated me, perhaps because as a child I was never allowed to even enter his sanctuary. The walls were completely covered in a deep rich cherry wood paneling, except for the one that was all shelves where he kept his law books. Dark maroon velvet curtains seemed to envelop all light that tried to enter, and a thick maroon carpet lined the floor to muffle any sound or conversation. The desk was mammoth and intricately carved but the dominate feature was the huge black leather chair–His throne.

He picked up a sheet of paper, "I received the coroner's report this morning, your father died of a stroke. He was under so much pressure even he could not stop it from affecting his health. Sydney, are you all right you are very pale?"

"Yes, I am sorry, please continue." I lied of course I was not all right, you stupid man.

"As you know you are the only survivor on both sides of your family and are entitled to by law the entire estate left by your father. It includes this house and all its contents, the cars, the monies, and the estate in Michigan that belonged to your mother's family. I have drawn up all the papers including the information on the Michigan house. Here is everything you will need including the keys."

I took the envelope and decided this would be a good time to ask him a few questions that have been bothering me for a long time. "Mr. Edgeworth I have not spoken to anyone about this but something is bothering me, when I found my father he was still alive and told me to 'look beyond the rose'. Do you have any idea what he meant?"

The man turned even paler than he normally was but seemed to get his control back quickly. "My dear he was probably just mumbling and didn't know what he was saying. I know nothing about what he said."

Somehow I doubted that big time but decided to change the subject. "I am sorry but I know so little about the house in Michigan except my parents went there occasionally on trips. I don't even know much about either side of my family could you please give me some information? All I do know is that Father was an only child and that my mother had three sister's whom I assume have passed away. I do not even know their names or anything about them."

"Your mother did have three sisters two of which married. One died along with her child in childbirth and the other of pneumonia shortly after her son was killed in a car accident. As to the third..." Obviously the lawyer was unprepared for my questions and seemed to be quite uneasy. "Sydney, your father wrote you a letter the morning that he died and had it delivered to me that day. He said he knew he did not have long to live and wanted you to know some important information. Perhaps some of your questions will be answered." He handed me the envelope but I was almost afraid to touch it, what was in there?

Then Ichabod seemed to have drifted off and his face softened as he said, "I can't get over how much you resemble your mother." Immediately he seemed to regret that statement, straighten his spine and turned one last time to me, "I am going out now to speak to the press and hopefully that will satisfy them for the time being. If there is anything you need Sydney please contact me. Good day."

With that he left. What did he mean when he said I resembled my mother, she was short, stocky and had bright red hair and blue eyes. I am 5'7" tall and slim with long dark hair and very pale green eyes. Perhaps he meant in spirit, we were both driven by our emotions. This is too much to think about now I will talk to Gretchen about it later. Finally the tears that had been threatening to come for the last week came, sobbing tears for myself and my mother and father. My legs could no longer support me and I slowly slipped to the floor. "Help me, someone please help me." At that moment Gretchen entered the room and knelt down beside me held me close, she whispered how much she loved me and that she was there and we would get through this together. We cried and held each other, no more words were necessary.

Gretchen was once again trying to get some food into me and I was surprised that I actually wanted to eat, I was hungry. Then it hit me, "Where are the girls, I haven't seen them all day?"

"I thought it best to keep them outside with so much going on, but I will get them now." With that she left and headed for the back door. Within a minute my two wonderful dogs came charging in and I was covered with kisses and soft fur from head to toe. This is what I needed and I couldn't help but laugh as Gretchen tried in vain to peel them off of me. She finally gave up and joined in the fun.

That night as I was lying in bed trying again in vain to sleep the thunderstorm that had been threatening all day attacked in full force, the wind and rain pounded against the windows as the lightening sent eerie flashes to every corner of my room. Even the poor old house seemed to creek and moan at the assault. Perfect, let's add a little more drama to a miserable day. Poor Lilly and Sammy were terrified and jumped into bed with me at the first crack of thunder, or I should say on top of me.

My girls have been with me through everything and I will never forget our first meeting, about three years ago on a night just like this. Gretchen and I were sitting out on the covered old back porch watching Mother Nature at her best when all of a sudden I heard some soft whining and two little wet heads popped up from the side of the porch. I have always loved dogs but my parents decided with our life style it would not be a good idea to have dogs running all over the house with important people coming in and out all day. But that night something strange and wonderful happened. My father appeared on the porch to ask Gretchen something and saw the drenched puppies staring up at us. He told Gretchen to get some towels and food as he opened the porch door and let them in. The dogs immediately began licking his hand and curled up at his feet. My very firm practical father was hooked immediately, and I just sat there in total disbelief. He told me to try to find out where they belonged but if I cannot then I may keep them if I like, but they must be kept out of the way. So many times I have wondered how such a miracle could happen and all I could come up with is that maybe he had a dog as a small boy. I will never know.

Of course my puppies grew at amazing speed, Lilly turned out to be a Cocker Spaniel, a light honey color with fur as soft as a cloud. She is always on the go and wants to check out everything. Sammy- Samantha is a Golden Retriever mix and the biggest softie on the planet, slightly skittish but always up for fun with her little friend. They have been my constant companions since day one. Gretchen told me one day that they somehow got into my father's office and she peeked in to see them jumping all over him and he actually let them and bent over to receive their mounds of kisses.

As the storm progressed my thoughts drifted back to my parents. My mother, Elizabeth Marie Everett was a very kind person but always involved in some kind of charity project or playing hostess to the many guests we had. I always felt like I was in the way, and though she did try at times to help with my childhood problems she didn't really seem to listen. Gretchen became my go to. I guess I loved my mother but wanted more from her than she had the time to give. As I think about all this I realize that she didn't even seem to show affection for her husband, my father. Perhaps that was happening in their private moments, but to me they seemed like roommates though I am here. They even slept in different rooms, strange none of this occurred to me until now.

My father was just that, a father, not a daddy or even a dad. How I wished I had a daddy when I was growing up like my friends did. He was stern and very proper, I never saw him in anything but a suit, shirt and tie. Once in a while I found him staring at me with what seemed like affection, though he rarely showed any. At times it seemed like he couldn't even look at me. So strange but I did feel a bond between us and did slightly look like him with my height and dark hair, though his was changing to a distinguished grey. His eyes were brown though and I do wonder where I got my unusual pale green ones, probably a distant relative. He seemed proud of me when I got my law degree but of course it was overshadowed by the tremendous crowds and news reporters who followed him everywhere. Even the newspaper showed only one picture of the two of us, the rest were of him and underneath, Daughter takes after Atlanta's finest. He did give me a beautiful large heart shaped single diamond pendant, which I will always cherish. I had to just accept that this was the way things were, and be content to love him the way he was, which was after all him. Deep down I knew he loved me but for some reason he almost seemed afraid to show it.

The next day shown clear and bright but my mood stayed where it was. The girls and I took a long walk back of the house so as not to have to see the reporters who had not given up yet. We stopped at the gazebo and I admired the beautiful flowers that covered most of the garden. It was so peaceful and you could barely hear the traffic off in the distance. The grass was so inviting I decided to lie down, which of course was a signal for an attack of kisses from my girls. We rolled and played for some time until Gretchen found us. "Sydney I am getting so many flowers and phone calls from your father's clients and friends, what should I do? Thank you notes have to be written and I am afraid that is up to you."

The spell was broken, back to real life. We followed Gretchen back into the house and as she started to make coffee I began writing the notes. This is going to take a long time as there were over three hundred already. She gave me a homemade cupcake to go with the coffee and that helped a little but after a couple hours my hand was cramped and I needed a break. "That is it for today, I am tired. Gretchen something is really bothering me and I need your answers or advice."

"Ok fire away, I will do my best," she said as she put away the last of the clean dishes.

"When Mr. Edgeworth was here he told me he couldn't believe how much I resembled my mother, what do you make of it?" I jumped at the sound of glass breaking, "Gretchen what happened are you all right?"

"Yes…I…am…fine," she said very slowly, "I just dropped a

glass. I wonder why he said that? You were very much alike as far as trying to help people–that must be it."

She was truly shaken up and since that never happens to Gretchen I was alarmed. "What is it, tell me? Also many times Father has looked at me strangely and I wonder if it has anything to do with the way I look. Maybe I look more like him than I thought."

"It is all coincidence I am sure my girl, nothing to be concerned about." She was back to being herself yet I was sure she had some answers. Just then the phone rang and Gretchen looked almost relieved as she grabbed for it. Ok something is going on but obviously I am not going to get any further with her right now so it was time to change the subject when she got off the phone.

"Do you think I ought to continue with my law practice as it is? I think I would like a change, criminal law just isn't for me, and I don't think it ever was. I want to help the people who really need help and have few to turn to. I have thought a lot about Elder Law and Special Needs, do you think that would be a field I could do some good in?"

"I sure do," said Gretchen as she sat down across from me, "You have always had a soft spot for both, remember when you volunteered at the assisted living home and participated in the Special Olympics? I have never seen you so happy. You have a boundless amount of compassion and that is what is needed."

"I don't think Father would approve, but I will talk to him…" My hands went up to my face and once again the tears began to fall. "Oh God he is dead, he is dead," I screamed. The chair tipped over as I jumped up and headed for the door, all I could think about was running away, running as far as my legs would take me–away from this house, my thoughts, my fears. Finally I had to stop, I could go no further. I yelled at my father for leaving me and at God for taking him away, but when the storm in my soul passed peace replaced the anger and I realized that I had finally accepted what had happened. I knew right then that I was going to be all right in time.

Gretchen let me go, she always seemed to know when to

follow and when I needed to do something myself. When I returned she just smiled at me and I nodded my head. What would I do without my dear friend, she is truly remarkable.

That night as I was lying in bed I started thinking about Gretchen, my Gretchen. It's funny but I never really thought about her appearance, she is always just Gretchen, and while not a beauty queen she is very pretty and I remember as a child I loved to pat her round tummy. She was and is not fat just a little rounded. "More of me to love," she used to say. Compared to me she is quite short, probably about five feet four inches with reddish brown short soft curly hair, but it is her spirit that I love the most, she can sure pack a wallop when she wants to. Her tongue is sharp and at times I don't think she even plans out what she is going to say it just comes out. She has truly devoted herself to my father and me though I know she is a nurse. I wonder if she ever regrets her decision to come here.

–2–

THE MOVE

Almost a year has passed, the reporters finally gave up months ago, and I am now an Elder Law and Special Needs attorney. Our lives are back into a normal routine and it is time to think about the future.

"Sydney are you going to stay here in this house or move on?" Gretchen asked me one morning as we were eating breakfast. I told her I had been thinking a lot about it.

"This house is way too big for us and there are too many memories. I think it is time for me to get out of here and start a new life. I love my attic apartment but except for the years I spent in college and law school I have not been on my own. This place is so dark and gloomy, there are eight bedrooms for heaven's sake, and the maintenance is ridiculous. I love historic homes but enough is enough. Have you too thought about all this?"

"Yes I have but I have no place to go, I wouldn't know where to start. I would have to find another job and at my age that would be a challenge, but the thought of leaving you is too much to bear. I need you as much as you need me my dear girl."

"Gretchen Jane Blanchard you are not that old, is it fifty-nine? There has got to be a way of staying together. Come with me, I have enough money to keep us well fed for the rest of our lives and I too could not imagine even for a minute being away from you. Please think about it."

"Thank you Sydney I will." She turned away quickly as the first tear slid down her face.

That night I was putting some clothes away and found the envelope Mr. Edgeworth had given me. At the time I was not ready to read it and did not care at all about the house in Michigan.

Now I was curious and at least wanted to know where it was in Michigan.

The girls and I cuddled around the fireplace as I opened the envelope. The keys spilled out immediately and when my hand touched them I felt something strange. Maybe it was just the past reaching out to the now but a calming sensation spread through my body. Now anxious to read all about the house I began at the beginning. The house was built in 1881 and was always lived in by the Everett family (my mother's family). Good heavens I had no idea it was so old, in my mind I thought maybe about fifty years old. It is on the shore of Lake Huron– wow I have always wanted to live near water. There are twenty acres of land with a guest cottage on the grounds. I was starting to think this is quite a large place. The girls would have a ball running all over. The last Everett sister died recently but left the house twenty-eight years ago and only came back for quick visits, the house has remained empty. That must have been my mother.

The grounds have been maintained by a local neighbor named Eli McGregor and his family, who receive a yearly compensation. His address and phone number was listed. The rest of the papers were legal things, which I was glad I actually understood.

The next morning Gretchen was in the kitchen preparing breakfast when I arrived. She took one look at me and said, "Something has happened you are glowing, what's up?"

"How would you like to live in Michigan on the shore of Lake Huron?"

"What in the world are you talking about?" she asked as she poured us both a cup of coffee.

"Last night I finally read the information Mr. Edgeworth gave me about my mother's family home. Gretchen it is on twenty acres and there is even a guest house. I know this sounds strange but I think I HAVE to move there. It is a feeling, like something or someone wants me to be there, I am so excited."

"Whoa girl, this is a big commitment, Atlanta is your home your friends are here you have no one there. It would be completely starting over. Let's get packing."

She flew into my arms and we laughed and cried at the same time. "You will come with me, really?" I asked in amazement.

"Of course, someone needs to watch over you. So what do we do first?"

I stood there looking around our old large kitchen; this for me was the heart of this home it is where Gretchen and I solved all the world's problems. "Sell this old mausoleum that's what we do. I think it will go quickly, people will be curious as it is the great ones former home. Sorry Father. We also will need to decide what we want to keep and then have an estate sale or auction. I will need to contact Mr. Edgeworth and quit my practice for the time being. Oh how exciting, I feel truly alive for the first time in so long!"

"One thing at a time girl, take a breath. An old friend of mine is one of Atlanta's best real estate agents and I will give her a call this morning. I am sure she can guide us though the whole process, she will be ecstatic to have it as her top listing."

Our house went up for sale on January 24th and sold on the 27th, which must have been some kind of record. Never did I think the house would sell that fast. We had to be out in sixty days and all of a sudden I was in a panic. Mr. Edgeworth came through big time for us and contacted a local auction house to take care of the furniture. Gretchen and I went around and picked out what we wanted to take with us but with all the wonderful treasurers there were very few things that I just had to keep, besides my mother's jewelry. She wore a single rose around her neck for as long as I can remember and when I found it I decided it was time that I did too.

The owner of the auction house came by the next week and started making a list of the items that were going to be put up. I knew nothing about where they came from or who made them but thankfully he did. Every once in a while I would hear a cry of excitement, "A Chippendale," worth so and so. The actual catalog took another couple weeks. We were down to only one month until we had to be out of here.

There were packed boxes everywhere and my poor girls had to spend way too much time banished to the back yard. They would get confused and excited and between Gretchen and me we had more than enough of that. Thank goodness Mr. Edgeworth took care of my father's office and the paperwork still left.

The time was getting close and I felt I had to go visit my parent's graves one more time before we left. The grand monument stood out prominently in the centuries old cemetery. It was very ornate of course with numerous carvings of angels. I knelt down in front of my mother's grave and said a short prayer then began to talk to her like I had never done before. I thanked her for all she had done for me and told her I was doing all right and soon would be living in her old home in Michigan. Uneasiness was creeping in, "Mother, Gretchen is moving with me, she has been such a comfort. You know she will take good care of me. I am very excited about the move and pray you are too. I love you, be happy."

Next to my father's grave. "Father, it is me Sydney, I just wanted to tell you that Gretchen and I will be moving to Michigan very soon. I am sorry but I had to sell our house, it is just too big for me. Believe it or not it sold in only three days. I got a very good price and was glad I could understand all the legal things that were involved. I am now an Elder Law and Special Needs attorney, I wish I could have had your advice on this. For now I am putting my practice on hold until we get settled. I know you loved me Father and I love you too. Goodbye and be happy."

"Gretchen I'm home, get the coffee poured and cut me a piece of cake, I will be down after I change my clothes. Gretchen, are you here?" Usually I get a 'what took you so long or I am not your servant' but there was nothing. I went down the long hall to the kitchen and found her sitting at the table with her hands over her eyes. "What is it, what's happened, are you sick?" I asked as I put an arm over her shoulder.

She looked up at me with such a sad expression, "I have had some bad news my older sister Louise in Ohio just called and said she needs heart surgery in a week and because of my nursing background wants me to come and take care of her while she recovers. Sydney I have to go."

"Of course you do. Don't worry about anything, everything

is all set up for our trip and all you have to do is buy a plane ticket–it looks like we will all be leaving about the same time. The girls and I will go to Michigan and when your sister has recovered you can join us then. Come on Gretchen things just happen sometimes, the main thing we need to be concerned with is your sister's health."

"But how will I get there you know very well I can't drive?"

"No big deal you worrywart, I will come and get you, it is not that far. We can take all your things with us and all you will have to do is decide what bedroom you want and move in. Besides it will give me a chance to spiff things up before you get there. The old place has been empty for twenty-eight years and I am sure will at least need a good dusting. Now get yourself up and get me a piece of cake."

"I am not your servant, get it yourself," she said with a sheepish grin.

Things were back to normal and while I was a little unnerved about traveling all that way alone and having no idea what to expect when I got there, deep down I was sure everything would be fine.

The following week was nuts, the auction went well and as much as I would have liked to have seen it, the auctioneer thought my presence would be distracting because of "who" I am. Almost everything sold but what didn't went to an upscale consignment shop. Mr. Edgeworth called to wish us well and said he had contacted the caretakers of the house and told them we would be arriving soon. The cleaners finished their work yesterday just before Gretchen left for Ohio. The poor thing apologized the entire way to the airport promising she would call daily. When we got there she suddenly had a terrified look on her face, "Everything is packed, what are you going to sleep on tonight?" To be honest it never occurred to me.

"My bed is still there I will just cuddle up in my sleeping bag." There was a big groan from my dear friend as she hugged me tightly and headed for security.

That night I decided it was time to read the letter from my father, that he wrote the day he died. A new life was beginning and I wanted the past left where it belonged and to be honest I forgot I even had it until I was cleaning out some old papers. There is no way I could have read it right after he died, but even now I was almost afraid to see what was in it. I had made peace with my father and prayed there was nothing that should have been taken care of long ago.

The envelope had his bold unmistakable script. To my daughter Sydney Rose Armstrong.

To my daughter Sydney,

My time here on this earth is very limited and soon I will die but before I go I need to tell you some things that should have been spoken of years ago. I know I have been hard on you over the years and pushed you probably too far but I wanted you to be able to stand on your own two feet and be strong. As you know I am not a demonstrative man but I hope you knew I have loved you in the only way I knew how, I also loved your mother very deeply. You are a strong sensible woman and I am proud of your achievements. I know whatever you do you will succeed.

I learned at an early age what it meant to be strong. Your grandparents, John and Stella Armstrong, my parents, were good people but very poor and I had to work to help support our family while going to school. It made me determined to achieve something bigger. I decided to become a lawyer but had to pay for everything myself and fought hard to get to my goal. The only thing that meant anything to me except my parents was a sickly stray dog that I found in a dumpster. I brought it home but with so little food in our house I had to give up some of mine for the dog. Your girls as you call them meant a great deal to me though I thought it inappropriate to acknowledge it. Now I am sorry I did not tell you. I am so sorry for so many things.

I have meant to discuss your law career with you but now there is no time. I do believe you should reconsider criminal law and pursue a field that helps the helpless. It is an honorable thing to get into and I know you would succeed because of your compassion for others.

Sydney there is something that has been withheld from you and I wish I could tell you and explain why it happened but I cannot. I promised your mother even in death that I would not reveal this. You can always trust and rely on Gretchen but she too cannot tell you exactly what you will want to know. Please do not mention this to her as I know it will be so hard on her and she has served our family well as a trusted friend. I know how inquisitive you are and am sure in time you will go to Michigan; your answers lie there in that house.

Your father,

Charles Emerson Armstrong

There are no words to express how I felt after reading the letter, my emotions were running wild. I knew there were words left unsaid but now I still had to find out what they are. For the first time ever my father was open with his feelings and what his background was. How he must have struggled. I am so happy that he was proud of me and that he thought I would do well in just what I am doing now with my career. Yes he did push me hard but because of that I am the person I am today and I am so glad I realize that. No wonder he seemed to actually like my girls, his only friend was his dog all those years ago. Now to my moving to Michigan and finding the truth there, what truth, what am I supposed to be looking for? Does this have anything to do with his last words to me 'look beyond the rose'? In a sense I am mad that he did not tell me all there was to tell, but it really did not surprise me that he didn't or couldn't, he was a man of honor and his word meant everything to him. Well if I ever had any doubts about moving they are gone now.

The moving van just left and I am exhausted. The only place to sit down was at the bottom of the grand staircase. As I looked around the entry way to the open door of my father's office, just off to the left of the massive wooden front doors where so many important people came in and out all day, my sadness came by for another visit–so many memories of so many years. When movie stars came Gretchen and I would hide at the top of the stairs and peek down just to get a glimpse of them. Of course Father knew we were there and once the person entered his office he would wave a fist at us then almost smile. My first prom was supposed to be a grand experience but did not turn out quite as my mother had planned. I was supposed to slowly decent the staircase as my date waited below. I was so nervous I missed the last step and wound up sprawled on the floor below. Mother talked constantly about how wonderful it would be when I got married to once again descend on my father's arm, which of course would take place here in this house. Now there will be no descending and no Father to give me support.

I walked through the whole house, remembering, my final descent down the old wooden stairs actually made me shiver. Outside I piled the girls into the back of my van and stood there staring one last time at the house I had grown up in and tried hard to make a permanent memory, as though I could ever forget. This was my Tara from Gone with the Wind, not quite as grand but in my eyes even better. Father said it is an antebellum style. Four large stately columns support the first and second floor porches and railings that extend the full length of the house except for the front door entrance. Such fond memories of sitting out there on warm summer nights, wrapped in the smell of sweet jasmine as my mother and I watched the sun set. The black shutters that trembled in the winds stand out prominently against the white siding, and my mother's pink azaleas across the whole front of the house bring life to the scene. I took a cutting from one of the bushes to start our new garden with as a tribute to my mother, just hope they will grow in Michigan. One last glance up above the third floor to my half round attic window, my haven, where dreams were made and life's battles were won. "Goodbye."

"Ready girls let's get on the road, we have a long way to go."

After a day and a half Gretchen called to see how we were doing. "So far so good, tomorrow morning we should be through Detroit and only about one and a half hours to our destination. No big traffic problems and the weather has been perfect. We didn't hurry and spent extra time when we ate so the girls could get out and run. They are getting a little anxious being cooped up all the time and don't seem to like to travel at night so we stop before it gets dark– fine with me too. I am getting so excited now, sure wish you were here."

"So do I but I am glad I am with Louise too. She made

it through the surgery with flying colors and now the recovery begins. Are you eating right, getting enough sleep? Please be extra careful on the road."

"Yes Mother, sorry couldn't resist." We both laughed. "Ok gotta go Lilly wants her last outing for the night and then we are all going to bed, my love to Louise, and a big hug for you. I will call you when we get there. Goodnight."

"Girls settle down back there, stop jumping around I know you don't like stopping and starting in this awful traffic but barking at the cars is not going to help." Really I didn't blame them it has been a long trip and I too was getting tired. None of us wanted to get into the van that morning. Sammy looked up at me as though to say, "You are kidding right?" It made me laugh as I hugged her and gave her a shove.

We were finally heading up the coastline of Lake Huron. Already I loved Michigan. The peaceful little towns we passed through were charming,

We were getting close now, a little more than half way up to the top of Michigan's thumb area, I thought I had better look for the landmarks Mr. Edgeworth told me about–go through the town of Sylerville, ok this must be it, three miles then start looking for a mass of trees on the right hand side of the road. A mass of trees? There were a mass of trees everywhere. Wait, I think this might be it. I slowed down to a crawl and looked for a mail box with the numbers 5401. There it is. I turned right and was immediately confronted with a massive black iron gate almost totally covered with vines. The girls were going nuts as I got out of the car and headed for the gate. It opened reluctantly with a good push. As I turned to go back to the van I saw a sign off to the side THE ROSE established 1881. The hair on the back of my neck stood up and I felt weak, THE ROSE could this be what my father was talking about? I touched the rose necklace around my neck, what is going on? Enough get back in the van and get this whole thing started, I told myself.

–3–

THE HOUSE

We followed the narrow driveway lined with tall full trees and took a curve to the left and there it was, below us our new home. I stopped the van and tried to take it all in from our viewpoint some distance above. The house was still a little distance away but I was totally overwhelmed, it was huge. This is an estate, the grounds were well manicured but they looked like they went on forever–not a square, more long and narrow. So far it seemed from where we were to be totally fence in and lined with trees so thick it looked like a bunch of tall soldiers standing at attention– our guards. The cottage was a little distance from the back of the house, set slightly to the right so as to get a view of the water. The view was spectacular and it appeared the house took full advantage of it.

As we got closer to the cottage I realized that this was not just a cottage it was a cute little one story house dotted with gingerbread. It was painted white but looked like it needed a new coat. There were dark green shutters on each of the windows and what looked like roses completely surrounding the whole thing. Poor things needed a good weeding and pruning. A bright red door greeted you at the front with a tattered flag trying hard to fly next to it. A little bench sat just at the entrance in the dark green that again could use some paint.

As we passed the side of the big house and drove into the curved front driveway I could see that it needed a lot of love. I got out of the van to get a really good look at the old place. It was a true Victorian painted white I think at one time, but after so many years of neglect and the harsh great lakes weather the wooden siding had been almost stripped clean. It could easily pass for a haunted house or at least the cousin of one from the movies. The shutters were hanging by a thread and the large porch that extended completely around the left side and front of the house definitely needed repairs, as did the railings and gingerbread at the top of the thin posts. The only thing that did not seem to need repair was the angled roof above the porch, but since I know nothing about that kind of thing it will have to be checked out. The entry way had a peaked roof, again with gingerbread, instead of an angled one so it would stand out I assume, and there were steps and railing going down the walkway.

On the left side inside the porch area was a very large five sided turret that went from the porch up beyond the third floor with windows in all the angles and its roof was peaked like a cone. On the right side it looked like a large three sided turret that again went from the ground floor to the third, with windows on all sides all the way up–just a peaked roof was on top that had a little round window under it. The whole structure looked like there were a bunch of different sections stuck together forming a very unique house.

The girls were going crazy so I opened the door and let them out. For a minute they just stood there staring at me, "Go girls run have fun." There took off at lightning speed running all over the place barking. I grabbed for my camera to take a picture of my first house. Time to see what is inside. I carefully climbed the steps for fear they would crumble but thankfully did not. With key in hand I opened the creaking door. The past jumped out to greet me, it smelled musty and with years of neglect the dust was everywhere, but all this was mine and I was so excited. "Hello house my name is Sydney and I am going to make you all better." Suddenly I heard a whine and turned around to see two nosey little pouches standing at the open door. "Come on in girls this is going to be our new home." Cautiously they made their way in, Sammy sneezed and Lilly almost hid behind her friend. "Come on it is all right," I said as they slowly made their way toward me. Then the jumping and licking started and I knew all was well.

"Shall we explore?" The almost circular foyer was large and

a staircase across the room to my right went straight up part way then angled to the left for the rest of the way. Next to the staircase was what I assume was the parlor with the curved front wall from the turret all covered with windows. Beyond that was the dining room with a very large bay window and massive table. An archway led into the kitchen which had been updated slightly and thank goodness had appliances. It was still very old but looked functional. Mr. Edgeworth said he would call ahead and have all the utilities turned on, good thing because it never entered my mind. At the end of the kitchen was a breakfast room with a round table and chairs and more windows all around, then to the right was what I would call a mud room that had a door leading out to the back yard. It was a good sized room and I wondered if it was an addition as it had a washer and dryer. Back to the foyer I went. Just to my left were double glass French doors leading into what must have been the music room as there was a baby grand piano in the center and a large harp in the corner by the windows. Really it was more of a turret room with all the different angled walls and windows. A small bathroom was beyond that which I am sure was probably a large closet at one time. Just down the hall was a larger room, probably the family living room with a large welcoming fireplace, across from that was an archway that led back to the kitchen. Yikes this was a huge place.

The girls had had enough exploring and headed for the door. "Go on run and play I will be out soon." And they were off.

Cautiously I went up the staircase to check out the second floor. There were four large bedrooms and a bathroom, all took advantage of the turrets and had wonderful large panoramic windows looking out at the lake or the grounds.

The third floor had one very large bedroom that extended pretty much the whole length of the front of the house but with the way the roof was peaked it was definitely not all useable space. One more bedroom was in the back which again was quite large and had the crazy peaked ceilings. There were storage areas under the eaves also plus a door with steps leading up that I assume was the attic at the end of the hallway. I will wait to explore that later.

Good heavens six bedrooms! I had better get busy and find a man and start having a houseful of kids to fill this place up.

I went out to the van to get my old clothes and saw a tall heavy set man coming across the yard with a slight limp. As he got nearer I noticed he was older and had deep wrinkles on his tanned face as well as a strange confused smile.

"Rose? It's me Eli, I am so glad you came home. They told me you was dead, why did they tell me that?"

I was totally unnerved, "Hello my name is Sydney you must be Mr. McGregor who keeps up this property. You have done a wonderful job."

The poor man looked so confused, "Rose they told me you was dead," he said after he lowered himself slowly down into one of the lawn chairs never taking his eyes off me. "You have been dead for so long how come you back?"

"I'm sorry but you must have me mixed up with someone else," I tried to say calmly but was anything but.

Just then an older woman came out from behind the trees, "Eli, I have been looking for you my dear."

When she got close she reached out her hand for mine, "Hello Sydney I am Edith McGregor Eli's wife, we have been expecting you, welcome. We are your closest neighbor just beyond that clump of trees; a gate was put in so we could do the work needed here. My son works with his father to keep your place looking the way it should. We do not go into the house but I am sure it needs some work and I would be more than happy to help you clean it up."

"It is nice to meet you Mrs. McGregor," I said as I took her hand. "How very thoughtful of you to come by, I feel at home already and am sure I will need some help soon. It is nice to know I have a neighbor close by." The girls finally came over to see what was happening and went right up to the couple, sensing they needed to use their best manners I guess because they just sat down and waited to be petted, which began at once.

"What wonderful dogs you have Sydney, so sweet and loving."

"I do hope their barking will not be a problem for you?" I said with truly great hope.

"Not in the least," the woman said and smiled, "We love dogs and have three of our own. Here I brought you some dinner, I am sure you have nothing and are probably too tired to go out and get some. Have you anything for the dogs?" she asked as she handed me the basket of food.

"Yes thank you I brought some with me. What a kind gesture, thank you so much."

The entire time Mr. McGregor continued to stare at me and I was getting quite uncomfortable. "Eli we must let this poor girl get settled it will be getting dark in just a few hours." With that and a wave they were gone.

I watched them disappear into the trees and decided I had better figure out where we were going to spend our first night. But first I got the azalea cutting I had taken from the old house and planted it next to the front porch. I hope in time it will grow and be a permanent reminder of my mother and our old life. I grabbed a few things from the van and decided the house was way too dirty to stay in now so I walked over to the cottage, hoping it was more livable. It was a charming little place with basically one room that had a bed at one end and a huge fireplace at the other and a small kitchen in between plus a small bedroom and bath off the main room. There were sheets over the furniture and of course dust but all in all it shouldn't take too long to get it cleaned up for at least the night. I opened all the windows, found some rags and got sheets for the bed from the van, plus my pillow and blankets and started cleaning. An hour later we were ready to move in–tomorrow I would do a more thorough job. The girls were still running all over the place so I yelled to them that it was time to eat. I started a fire in the old fireplace to get the chill out of the room and we ate our dinner. Mrs. McGregor's potato salad, muffins, fried chicken and large piece of apple pie were delicious and I was starving.

I gave Gretchen a quick call. She was happy we arrived safely and said her sister is doing well. Then I got my motherly advice, "Get lots of rest don't do too much in one day." I told her I would call with more details tomorrow. It was only eight o'clock but all of a sudden I was exhausted, what a day. The girls curled up by the fireplace and I headed for the bed. Thank you God for such a special day.

The next morning I was amazed to find I had slept in until after nine o'clock, I am always up by seven. I stretched and pulled the covers up over my ears. It was chilly in here. The girls started stirring as I lit a new fire in the fireplace. It didn't take long for the room to warm up and I jumped into the shower, time to start the day. No more city clothes for me, I dug out my blue jeans and a cabled sweater, and wrapped my long hair in a single braid. I was ready for a long work day but first I had better eat a few of those tasty looking muffins left by my neighbor that I was too full to eat last night. I knew I would have to go into town so I could get my coffee there.

The list of things I was going to need to get in town kept growing, cleaning supplies, food–thank goodness the refrigerator worked when I plugged it in last night. The girls were chasing each other all over the yard and when I was ready to go I opened the back hatch of the van and told them to get in. They came over but I could see their hesitation about getting back in.

"Don't worry you silly things we are just going to town, I promise it won't take long, now please get in." It took another lecture but they finally did. Since I wasn't sure if the whole property was truly fenced I didn't want to leave them here by themselves.

Sylerville is my idea of a perfect little small town, ancient buildings housing unique little tourist shops lined the main street that at the end dipped far down to the harbor where many boats were moored off the long dock. A sailboat glided by as if on cue making the scene complete.

In the small grocery store I was greeted by a nice woman named Susan. She was slightly taller than I was with beautiful long blond hair, and about my age. I introduced myself and said I was living in the old Everett house.

"Oh are you a relative, I had heard that the sister's had all passed on? Think I did hear something about someone coming though, sorry you are going to have to get used to small town living where everyone wants to know everything," she said and smiled.

"Yes they have, I am the last of the Everett family, my mother Elizabeth passed away almost a year and a half ago and left it to me. After my father too died I decided it was time to escape from all the craziness that goes on in Atlanta and start a new life here. It will be a nice change."

"Atlanta huh, wait a minute, Armstrong, are you Charles Armstrong's daughter? I saw him in action one time in Savannah, he was really something."

"Yes that's me; I am a lawyer too but have put my practice on hold for the time being. I think it is going to take every bit of energy I have to clean up that wonderful old house."

She looked concerned, "Heavens are you going to do it all yourself, it must be a mess after all these years?"

I took a deep breath, "The inside yes but I know I am going to have to find someone to help me with the outside. Do you have some contractors or good handy men here in town? Here let me help you pack up those groceries."

She fumbled through an over-stuffed drawer for a pencil. "Let me write a couple names down for you, good men, I know they would be glad to help, not much work around here lately."

"Thanks Susan, it was so nice to meet you, you have been a big help."

As I turned to leave she said, "Oh wait one minute here comes my grandmother I would like you to meet her." A small elderly woman with bright blue eyes and silver hair walked slowly up to her granddaughter. "Grandmother this is Sydney Armstrong she is going to be living in the Everett home from now on, this is my grandmother Mrs. Mildred Burnett."

The woman looked up at me with a charming smile on her face which soon faded as she put her glasses on, "Rose is that you, I thought you were dead." I almost fainted, here it was again who in the world is Rose?

"Mrs. Burnett my middle name is Rose but I am Sydney," I said almost too loudly.

"Grandmother would you please go get David, it is time for his lessons? Thanks."

"I am sorry Sydney my grandmother gets confused sometimes," she said as she poured me a cup of coffee and popped the lid on. "Here, this should help you get started, good luck."

With a wave to Susan I left. There is a lot of work to do and I am not going to waste time trying to figure out who Rose is now.

Back at the cottage I unloaded the groceries and decided to take a walk around the property to be sure it is fenced in. Then I will hopefully be able to get some things done.

The girls and I had such fun, they would run ahead and then stop and wait for me to catch up. It took quite a while but I was pleased to see that there was a fence, all but at the water's edge. Of course I had to spend a few minutes sitting on the sand and staring at the water. Water makes me happy and calm and I love it. There is even a dock, maybe I can get a boat someday.

As Gretchen would say if she were here, 'Move it girl'.

Since we were going to be staying in the cottage until the house is clean I thought I had better get started there. The floors got a good scrubbing, the rugs and curtains were shook out, dishes rewashed, and the whole place got a good airing. It was only about an hour before I needed to make dinner so I spent the time down by the water. The gentle sound of lapping water onto the shore was so relaxing, too relaxing as it turned out, I fell asleep. Thank goodness the girls found me and we walked up the hill to the cottage and had our dinner.

Gretchen called just as I finished, "So tell me all, what is the house like, did you get into town yet?" She went and on and on. By the time I "told all" I was exhausted and said I would call her tomorrow. I decided not to say anything about the Rose thing as there really wasn't much to say, yet.

The next morning was gloomy; it rained off and on and was quite cool. Perfect for cleaning I guess. So up I went, through the creaky door and into what I think was probably the parlor. I took the sheets off the furniture and was a little surprised at how nice the classic furniture really was. Thank goodness I brought a vacuum cleaner with me and began the process of vacuuming all the pieces. They came out quite nice and I wondered if I should keep them or start fresh with new ones. This is something I can decide later, next were the floors. Even though they were wood I decided that it was smarter to vacuum them instead of using a broom and spreading the dust everywhere. They still need washing and a good waxing but not right now. I cleaned the windows and took the lace curtains down and that was it for this room now. It was already brighter in there despite the cloudy day.

One thing that stuck me while cleaning were the beautiful old quilts that hung in almost every room. I have quilted in the past but nothing as intricate as these. Those sisters were talented ladies and I spent a great deal of time looking at each one. They will definitely stay but are going to need some cleaning. There were also old samplers with tiny stitches and wordings delicately made with many colors though through the years have faded to a muted tone, still magnificent. Each had a different flower on them, one with a daisy, then a rose, violet, and finally forget-me-nots. Someday I am going to have to find out how to clean these.

Checking on the girls seemed like a good idea so I went out on the porch. They came running up, drenched but having a great time. Both got a drink from their bowls and headed out once more. I sat on the porch for a little while just staring out at the lake watching the lightning as it came across the water. Whoa time to get the girls and get back to the cottage before the storm hits.

They both got a good toweling off and were told to stay in front of the fireplace until dry. Funny they actually seemed to understand but were not happy about all the booming that was going on outside. Dinner, a call to Gretchen, and to bed early seems to be our routine now and that is just what we did.

The next few days went pretty much the same, cleaning, cleaning, and cleaning. Progress was being made but I was still only a little more than half done on the main floor, there were two more to go. I suppose if I hadn't spent so much time examining all the wonderful antique pieces in each room things would have progressed faster but I just had to do it. Even the windows exited me, I don't know if they are original to the house or not but they are old. The glass is slightly wavy and seems to have some bubbles mixed in. The ceiling lightings are all very old too, mostly brass and it is obvious that back in their day had been oil but were converted to electric in time. Some were actually chandeliers with crystal droppings. Many wall sconces also hung throughout the rooms.

One of my favorite pieces was a monster grandfather's clock that stood in the foyer. I looked it over to see if I could figure out how to start it up, if it worked the same as the one we had back home, luckily it did. The chiming reverberated throughout the whole house every fifteen minutes and I loved it. It was like an awaking, bringing life to a very sleepy house. I am sure I will do a little remodeling but for now all I wanted to do was get it clean and livable.

A week has passed and the time had come for a well-deserved break. The main floor was finally done, floors polished and all. I decided to go over and visit the McGregor's and take them some of the cookie I baked last night along with their basket. It took a little doing but I finally found the little gate that was totally covered in vines that led to their property.

As I walked across the yard toward the house I was greeted by their dogs with a lot of barking and jumping. I guess Mrs. McGregor heard the commotion and came out to see what was going on. She waved, "Is that you Sydney?"

"Yes it is," I said as she got closer.

She smiled and gave me a big hug, "How nice to see you, I wanted to come over but knew you were busy and I didn't want to disturb you. How are things going, are you settling in?"

"It is good to see you too. I am sorry I should have come over earlier to return your basket and thank you again for your wonderful food." I said as I handed her the basket. "Last night I got ambitious and baked some cookies I hope you like them. I am not a great cook but I try."

"How very thoughtful of you my dear, I am sure we will," she said as she took my arm and led me over to a grouping of lawn chairs. "Please sit down you must be exhausted."

I pulled up a chair, "Yes I am but I have made good progress, the bottom floor is done as much as it can be for now and I decided today is my day off." I looked up toward the house, painted a crisp white; it had three floors and a huge wrap around porch where many chairs were waiting to be sat on. "What a beautiful old home you have, it looks like a picture out of a magazine ad for seaside living," I said and truly meant it.

"I am glad you like it, our family like yours has been here for a very long time. We raised our five children here and now only Daniel lives with us. He is a contractor and travels all over the state building houses and uses our home as a base. Truly I think he just wants to be near the water, the heck with us," she said and giggled. "Eli has begun to forget things and gets easily confused and Daniel has been a great help. I think he has some dementia but is too stubborn to get tested. Give me a second, I just made a pitcher of lemonade, let me get you some," she said as she headed the short distance to the house.

"Thank you this is wonderful but you didn't have to go to any trouble for me. Mrs. McGregor, do you think Daniel would be willing to help me restore the outside of my house? I asked Susan at the grocery store for some names of handymen here in town but haven't had a chance to check it out yet. I would bet his name is on there."

She brushed a lock of hair off her face and smiled, "My hair doesn't like the wind today, Susan is a dear thing she will make you a good friend. She has a little boy named David and lives with her grandmother—very old school but a lovely lady. Susan's husband died a year ago in a boating accident and she has had to manage the store and her family on her own. And to your question about Daniel, yes I am sure he would be more than glad to help you out. He is over on the western side of the state now but will return in a couple weeks, I will speak to him then and have him stop by to see you."

"That would be so nice thank you, I look forward to it. Oh oh my dogs are barking at your dogs, maybe I had better get going and settle the whole group down. Please stop by anytime I have enjoyed talking with you," I said as I got up from my chair. "One more thing, would you mind if I introduced my dogs to yours, it might help in the future?"

She got up too, "Good idea. Please do come again anytime." Another hug followed and I headed for the gate.

Once the gate opened all five dogs began their barking and sniffing but things went well, how nice Lilly and Sammy have some new friends. Next time I will ask Mrs. McGregor if they can come over for a visit.

Just as I got through the trees I saw the moving van pull up to the house and ran the rest of the way. The girls took off like a shot, barking like crazy. Oh great I had almost forgotten about them and had no plans of where I wanted everything to be put. Not a big problem though as there was not that much, most of it was Gretchen's. I put the girls into the music room and shut the door and went out to get this going. The driver was standing there staring at the house, "Miss Armstrong do you really live in this old place it sure needs a lot of work?" he asked as the other man came over too.

I laughed, "Well we are not in here yet we are living in the cottage behind the house until I can get this one fixed up."

"Good luck you will need it," he said as he headed for the van.

I did the best I could with placement but knew things would have to be moved later on.

After only an hour they were done and on their way.

The next day I was back to work, this time on the second floor. Now seemed like a good time to pick out my bedroom. I checked all four but the one in the front with the turret, above the dining room seemed to speak to me. I love sunlight and this room was packed with it plus there was an amazing view of the lake. Someone else must have thought so too as there was a telescope on a stand by the window. A comfy looking stuffed chair with an ottoman sat next to a beautiful white marble fireplace across the room from the big old brass bed. There was plenty of room for the dog beds so we were set. Suddenly I realized that there were many fireplaces in this house, besides having a radiator in every room. I am sure in the past the whole place was warmed by the fireplaces. I better get them cleaned before we use them.

My room got cleaned and I still had most of the afternoon free so I got my bike off the van and headed for the front gate. Of course the dogs saw me and followed me up. I told them I was going for a little ride and would be back very soon. Sad little faces stared back at me but I couldn't take them this time. I rode along for about a mile then spotted a yard sale, my passion. The woman running the thing came over and asked if I needed any help. "No thank you I am just filling my addiction."

She laughed and said she hadn't seen me before up here so I explained why I was here and where I was living. "My, I have always wanted to see what is behind that old front gate though I have heard that no one has lived there for many years," she said as she picked up a couple things that had fallen to the ground.

"Well as soon as I can get rid of all the dust I think I will have a party and invite the whole area so I can get to know everyone."

"What a great idea, please include me. Oh by the way my name is Elaine so nice to meet you" she said as she extended her hand.

"Nice to meet you too Elaine, my name is Sydney. Sorry I had better get going it looks like it is going to rain at any minute. You do get a lot of rain here don't you?"

She looked up to the sky, "Yes this is the spring and we do, as well as large storms and tornadoes with the temperature changes."

"Tornadoes, oh dear I sure hope we don't get any this year. Time to go, take care. Bye."

Now I wished I had not gone as far as I did the rain was starting and the wind was picking up, also the sky had turned an almost green color—time to get peddling.

My poor dogs were just where I left them at the gate and a real storm was brewing so I yelled at them over the sound of the wind and told them to go home now. We all headed for the cottage at record speed, and I was so thankful when we got in and were safe. This was a bad storm and getting worse, and I was truly getting scared. I heard a siren way off in the distance and panic set in; oh my God could this be a tornado? I closed all the shutters and the girls and I went under the kitchen table. They were shaking almost as much as I was. Then it happened, the lights went out, the wind was so loud and strong I could hear nothing else, both dogs were literally on top of me trembling violently. Suddenly the wind stopped and an eerie silence followed. I held my breath, something is wrong I can feel it, then it sounded like a train was right outside our door. Oh please God help us please. The cottage was shaking and things were falling off the walls. Thank heavens it was over soon but we stayed where we were for a long time afterwards.

Finally mustering up what courage I had left and went to the door, opened it and stepped outside, it was still raining and I could hear a little thunder but I think it is done. I took just a minute more to look around. The yard was a mess, trees down everywhere but the house was still there, though I couldn't see my van, and where was my bike? I didn't even think to bring it in when we got here. The flag and bench outside the door were gone too. Later I found the bench over by the gate to the McGregor's. I went back in and I got some candles in a drawer and placed them around the room, stoked up the fireplace and we just sat there. "Ok girls we are not going out until tomorrow, we are safe and that is all I care about. Tomorrow we will check things out."

I don't think I slept at all that night and when the sun started creeping in behind the shutters I was so relieved and got up. Still no lights but at the moment I didn't care.

"Come on girls let's go out and see what's left of our place." The cottage held up very well but all the shingles on the roof were gone, plus there was a little damage to the wooden siding and shutters. The grounds were a big mess, more trees were down than I realized, it looked like a battle zone as they were scattered all over the place. We walked up to the house and except for some of the shutters being gone, and some porch railing ripped away the old girl looked all right. A large tree only missed the side of the house by about a foot and my van was pushed a ways down the hill.

Boy was I glad I had my cellphone and that it was actually working, because it was ringing like crazy. It was Edith McGregor and she sounded awful. "Sydney are you all right, I have been so worried? I heard on our battery radio this morning that the tornado was coming straight at us but just before it hit our shoreline it turned about three miles south before it touched land. Sylerville got hit hard. I pray Susan and her family are all right."

I felt sick to my stomach, "Oh my God, I hope she is all right too. Yes we are fine but I sure was scared, I have never been through one before. Are you sure you are all right too? The house and cottage have minor damage but my van is half way down the hill. The whole grounds are a terrible mess," I said as the tears started finally coming.

"Eli will check things out later, I am so thankful we exchanged phone numbers when you came by. Wait one second here comes Eli, what is it dear?" I heard her say but could not hear her husband. "Do you have a bike Sydney?"

"Well I did why?"

"Eli found one in our yard, and I would bet it is yours but it has some damage to the front wheel. He will bring it over when he checks your place out. I need to go now but please call me if you need anything."

"Thank you so much, it is so comforting to know you are close. Goodbye."

I called Gretchen when we got back to the cottage. "Hi guess what we did yesterday, went through a tornado," I said as my voice cracked.

"Oh my God are you all right?" she sounded really alarmed.

"Settle down, I wasn't even going to tell you because I knew you would go nuts, we are shook up but fine, our property could use a little clean up though and my van got shoved over, plus my bike is visiting my neighbor. Other than that everything is going well." Then I told her about my progress with the house.

"You are doing too much, just like I knew you would, love you," she said and hung up.

Mr. McGregor did come over later in the afternoon. He

wandered all over the property and came back to the house to give me a report. He took his hat off and brushed the sweat off his brow, "Rose, I'm going to be needin' to get some help cleaning up all these trees. I can fix the lil' damage to the cottage and the house myself but am a goin' to get a roofer in to check out the big house and also put new shingles on the cottage, I can't do no climbing anymore myself. I fix your bike when I have a chance. Before I leave I will get your van back up here," which he did as soon as I gave him the keys. It did take a little doing though. I know I should have tried it myself but with my luck I would have wound up going the rest of the way down and into the water.

He came over and handed me back my keys and I told him how grateful I was and said anything he can do to clean things up would be wonderful. "Maybe the wood from the trees can be cut up to burn in the fireplaces this winter. Say hi to your wife for me," and he left. So I am Rose now, the poor man has decided I guess. Well I have been called worse and I don't see any reason to confuse him any further. I wish Gretchen would get here so we could figure out who Rose is; this is getting stranger by the minute. I wonder if she was a housekeeper here many years ago. Enough enough, I am not getting anywhere.

True to his word Mr. McGregor's team showed up the next day. Because of all the noise and chain saws I kept the girls inside the house with me during the day. They kept running from window to window so as not to miss a thing and were not at all happy with me.

This was a good opportunity for me to do more cleaning and I pretty much finished the second floor. It was not too bad to begin with as each bedroom had little furniture. Sometime I will decorate.

The men left about five and I let the girls go out to run until dinner. I spent my quiet time sitting on the steps of the front porch admiring the view. It was quite breezy but that added to my enjoyment of the whole scene, the lakes waves were "performing" beautifully and I saw a large ship far out in the distance. It seemed to be hardly moving but before too long it disappeared. I wondered where it was going. As I stood up to go make dinner my back side stuck to a splinter in the old wood, time to get some rocking chairs out here.

This morning I decided to go to Sylerville to check on Susan. It has been on my mind and I need to see if I can help her in any way. The road was still littered with debris but passable, how sad that such a beautiful quiet little area had to go through something as awful as a tornado. The police stopped me about a block from the main street and asked if I was a local or tourist. I told him and asked if I could go to the grocery store. He said the whole town is still a mess and nothing is open and I am going to have to either turn around or go down the road. I felt sick as I just turned around. Later I will call Mrs. McGregor and see if she knows anything about Susan and her family.

When I got to our gate I just didn't feel like going in so I went on to see if Elaine, from the garage sale was home. She was out in the front yard raking up the debris left from the storm. I pulled over and rolled down my window, "Hi Elaine its Sydney, remember me from a few days ago?"

She came over to the van, "Hi Sydney it's good to see you, it's been a hard few days and I would love some company if you have some time."

I told her I had just been down to Sylerville and was stopped by the police. "I met Susan at the grocery store and was concerned about her and wanted to see if she was all right. When I got close a policeman stopped me and said the road was closed and they were only letting emergency workers into the town. I assume you know her, have you heard anything?"

"Yes, she called me later in the day and said that she had heard tornado watches were all over the area so she closed up the store and headed south with her family to her brothers. We take these watches very seriously here. Thank goodness for that."

"Good I am very relieved. Did you get much damage?" I asked as I looked toward her house.

"No only minor things, the shingles were blow off of the house and we lost a lot of trees plus the yard is a mess. These old homes have been here for over a hundred years and I am sure have withstood many a big storm. What about you?"

I told her that we had about the same problems and that the McGregor's next door were going to do the heavy stuff for which I was truly grateful. "Do you know them?"

"Oh yes, Edith and my mother were very close," she said as she picked up the rake again.

"Pease let me help you, do you have another rake?" She pointed to one resting against the fence. I watched her for a moment and was amazed that such a little thing could do so much. We were quite a match, she is petite with curly blond hair and I am tall with dark long hair. Then I got to work.

"You don't have to do that but I sure would appreciate it, I have been at this for so long and am getting tired."

We worked for probably about an hour and a half and finally Elaine said, "Enough I need a rest," she said and went up on the porch and lowered herself into a rocking chair. "Please sit down and I will get you some lemonade or water whichever you like."

"That would be great but let me help," and we headed into the house. "What a wonderfully cozy home you have Elaine, do you have children the house looks spotless?"

She looked a little sad, "Yes three girls, but thank goodness they are visiting my parents down south of Detroit for the week, they weren't here when the storm hit, but I miss them so much. My husband is with them so I was on my own and more than a little scared, though I heard we up north here didn't get the full force of the storm. Bill, my husband called right away and said they would be home immediately but later called back after finding out the road along the coastline was closed. Since it is really the only way to get here directly he couldn't come, but this morning he told me they should be able to get here tomorrow."

"Wasn't it odd that you and I were talking about tornadoes when I left that day, maybe we were being warned I just don't know, but boy did I hightail it down the road and got there only minutes before the stupid thing hit?"

"You know when you left I broke all speed records to get the yard sale goodies into the garage instead of just putting a tarp over the whole thing like I would normally do. I think you may be right, we WERE warned," she said as she hugged her arms close to her body. "Have you ever visited here before you moved, somehow you look familiar?"

"No but my parents used to come to the old house on little getaways. We all lived in Atlanta and when my father died about a year ago I was told the house was now mine as it belonged to my mother's side of the family and I was the last survivor. I needed to start a new life and here I am."

She got up and started putting the glasses into the dishwasher, "Are you married Sydney, do you have children?"

"No but I was thinking I had better find a man and get going with children as I am twenty-eight and will totally rattle around by myself in that huge house if I don't."

We both laughed and it felt so good. I told her I should get going as my dogs are going to jump the fence and start looking for me soon if I don't get back there. Again we laughed.

As we left the house I noticed the rocking chair that she had sat in earlier, "Elaine this is a beautiful chair, I need some for my porch. Where did you buy it?"

She smiled and said, "Bill made this, he does them on the side to make a little extra money."

"Well sign me up for six, if he can find the time." She said she knew he would be very pleased to make some for me; he already had quite a few done in his workshop in the garage.

Elaine came over and gave me a big hug and thanked me for helping her. "You are welcome here anytime Sydney." I told her to stop by my house too whenever she could. Then I left feeling so much better, I found a friend and was really starting to get to know the people in my new life.

The following week went well, the last of the mess was cleaned up outside, the house was clean except for the attic and I was feeling quite proud of myself as I sat on my front steps staring at the lake. Just then a small truck pulled up and a man got out. "Sydney?" he asked.

I got up from my perch and again caught my pants on the jagged wood, "Yes, can I help you?"

"Hi I am Bill Elaine's husband, looks like I got here just in time before you ruined all your clothes," he said then smiled. "I have your rocking chairs, six right?"

He was a nice looking man with big blue eyes and a mop of blond hair that I am sure never stayed in place, but it was his smile that really got to me, so genuine. I could tell right away that he was a good man.

"Yes, my goodness you are fast how wonderful!"

"As soon as I got home Elaine told me you had come over and admired the chair and helped her with some of the cleanup. I am truly grateful to you for keeping her company when I couldn't be there; I was so worried about her when I heard about the tornado. You have won a friend in both of us."

"Thank you I feel the same. Now let me see my new treasurers," I said and headed for the truck. They were absolutely beautiful and I told him that. "How did you get them done so fast?"

He lifted them one by one out of his truck and said, "Well I had five done already and the sixth only needed to be stained."

We got them up on the porch and they looked so homey and comfortable that I had to sit down right away. I looked up at Bill, "How sad that these poor beautiful chairs have to share their space with a crumbled down porch. Now I am getting anxious for Daniel McGregor to get home, his folks said he would probably be able to help me get the house back to her grandeur."

"He is a good contractor and I know he will do it proud," said Bill as he turned to leave. I paid him for the chairs and thanked him for such speedy delivery again.

He smiled and gave me a quick bow, "At your service my lady."

"You are a nut sir, get back on your charger and go back to your kingdom." One last smile from both of us and he was gone. Yes this is really my new home with my new adopted families. I am blessed.

—4—

DANIEL

About three days later I decided since the weather was getting warmer I would go down to my beach and sit in the sun for a little while. I love the feel of sand in my toes and the sun on my face. I was "lounging" on my back taking the whole thing in when all of a sudden a shadow covered my head and I sat up quickly. A man with a huge smile was standing over me.

"Sydney I assume?" he said still smiling.

"Yes, who are you?" I asked as I started brushing the sand off on my clothes and out of my hair.

"My name is Daniel McGregor I live next door. My folks said I should come over and meet you and see what you need done to your house," he said as he sat down next to me. "Beautiful day isn't it?"

"Yes it is, sorry I have been looking forward to you getting back and am now surprised that you actually are." Oh man was that lame, Sydney put yourself together and stop sounding like an idiot I thought to myself. "That didn't come out right I meant I have wanted to get started with the house but was disappointed that I had to wait for you to return to see if you were actually interested." Better Sydney.

He picked up a handful of sand and let it slide through his fingers. "I have been interested in bringing this wonderful old house back to the way it should be since I was a kid, and then even more so when I became a contractor. Let's go up and take a good look shall we?" He reached for my hand to help me up and I took it without thought. It has been a long time since I have "been in the company" of a very handsome man and this one seemed quite special. He was tall and muscular with light almost blond hair and "normal" green eyes, not like my very light colored ones, lots of smile lines on his tanned face so I assume he is a happy person. Probably my age or a little older I am never good at guessing ages.

We walked up the hill together and headed for the house. He said he would check it out completely tomorrow but for now he just wanted to get a quick look up close. Right then the girls came charging across the yard and landed right at Daniels feet with their adoring faces looking straight up at him. "Daniel I would like you to meet my girls, this is Samantha–Sammy, "Sammy shake hands with Daniel," which of course she did right on cue. "Lilly I want you to meet Daniel, shake his hand please," and again she did plus gave him a lick on the hand. "Ok you have been accepted now they will almost leave you alone but be prepared they are full of kisses." With that he got down on his knees and the girls were all over him. He laughed and laughed, this one is a keeper I thought.

"Sorry, go on girls go play," I said a little embarrassed. "They aren't usually that affectionate with new people.'

"No problem I love dogs, we have three, but I bet you have met them already."

"Yes and they are so cute, they seem to like my girls too–they met at the gate."

We both laughed and Daniel started making mental notes I assume of what he was seeing with the house. "Of course it needs a lot of paint; you might want to start figuring out what colors you want. Are you going to give it many colors, like the old painted ladies of the past, or basic colors with one or two others for trim?"

Since I really had not thought much about it I told him I wasn't sure but no painted lady, it just doesn't seem to fit with where it is.

He said he thought that best too and suggested maybe a weathered grey/green with cream trim on the gingerbread, porch railing and posts, and around the windows then maybe another color for accent plus for the front door.

"That sounds great! What would you think about eggplant for the accent?"

He thought for a moment and said, "Why don't we get the grey/green and cream on and then experiment on the accent?"

"Good idea, what about black or charcoal for the shutters?"

"Perfect." Now that that was settled he moved on. "I will get up on the roof to check out the shingles but I am pretty sure they haven't been repaired or replaced in many years. When do you want to start?"

"Yesterday," I said then gave him a huge smile.

He wrote something quickly on his paper and said, "Ok Sydney, I will get the supplies we need and get my crew and we will be back in a couple days. Do you want to help?"

"Of course I do," and with a wave he was off.

I was so excited I could hardly stand it finally my beauty was going to be a beauty again.

That night my dreams drifted to Daniel and I woke up feeling very excited, he is something special and I saw it right away. Slow down girl I told myself you have only been with him for a about an hour, and for all you know he could be married with six kids. Burst bubble and I got up and started the day. I took my coffee up to the house and sat on one of my new rocking chairs and just once again stared at the lake. It was so calm it looked like glass reflecting the sun and sky. A flock of birds flew noisily overhead and I saw two large ships way out in the distance. I was happy and content.

Later in the day I decided to go north to a larger small town that Mrs. McGregor said had a grocery store as I still can't get into Sylerville, though I have heard they are making progress on the destruction. This time I took the girls and they were more than ready to jump in for a ride. The coastline was magnificent, and we had a great little journey.

Thumb Harbor is a little bigger than Sylerville and not as touristy. I decided to wander a little and see what stores they had, good there is the grocery store better go in just before we leave. To my surprise they had a general store. The inside was all wood paneled from many years ago with beams that had wonderful antiques hanging from them. Anything you could want was in there, candles, soaps, toys, fancy jellies, some clothes, yarns, fabrics and so much more. In the corner was an old pot- bellied stove that looked like it had been used often with little benches surrounding it. Even the smell was wonderful with a blend of old wood and candles.

First I went over to the fabrics and thought about buying some to make a quilt. I had not done one in years but I already have a house full now. Darn. Then I saw some artist canvases and grabbed three. I brought my acrylic paints and brushes with me but was afraid the canvases would get ruined in the move. Now I can paint again and what a wonderful place to do it. One more thing, how about some yarn to make an afghan or something? I am not the greatest knitter but I do know how and it would be fun to sit in my outside rocker and knit or by the fire in the cottage. I brought some scented soaps and candles, canvases, knitting needles and yarn up to the check out.

The ladies there were elderly and very friendly. "Hello my name is Mable, welcome to our store." I introduced myself and asked her if she had any directions for making an afghan. She said I really don't need any, "Just figure out how long and wide you want it to be and get going in a simple knit and purl stitch." I told her that is about my speed and thanked her for the hint. "Sydney, if you find you would like to branch out and do something different the area hospital needs knitted hats for their newborn babies, we all make them. Here is our pattern, very simple to follow and fun to do. You can always come back if you get stuck and we will be happy to help you." I thanked her and said I would be back. I could hear the girls barking so I went to the grocery store and got what we needed then we headed home.

The next morning I went up to the house again with my coffee, this was now my ritual and I heard people talking and turned around to see a group of men coming out of the woods. It was Daniel and his crew. I was so excited I jumped up and spilled my coffee all over my jeans.

"Good morning Sydney, did we have a little accident?" he asked as he looked down at my pants.

"Yes WE did so what's it to ya?" I said followed by a huge grin and probably some red cheeks. "So what do I do?"

"First off we put the chairs into the house, and sometime I would like a tour of this place what ya say?"

Of course I said yes but warned him that although clean it needed some decorating–I got a big, "No problem."

The crew was already scraping the porch rails and floor. "Want to do some scraping, not much fun but has to be? Guys this is the owner Sydney, she is our free labor for the day." They all waved and smiled.

He gave me a scraper and I went to work. Just before my arm fell off I decided I would get up and see what else was going on. Daniel was talking to one of the men and turned when he saw me. "Copping out already?" he asked and smiled. He was kidding I knew so I too smiled.

"Nope, just taking a break until I can feel my arm again, how are things going?"

He said progress was being made but the whole house needs to be scrapped and that is going to take some time. He headed for the ladder and said he was going to go up and check out the roof.

I watched from below as he went higher and higher. "Be careful up there," I yelled.

"Thanks didn't know you cared," he said as he turned slightly and made a face.

Back down on the earth he called me over, "It is a mess up there, probably aided by the storm, but you need a whole new roof."

"Great just add it to the stash." Somehow I think this whole thing is going to cost more than if I had bought a new house. I thanked Father for leaving me enough money for all this. I was more determined than ever to make this MY home, a new start for it and me.

My poor girls were banished to long leashes at the cottage during the day and were not happy. At night they got to run so I didn't feel too guilty.

One afternoon just before it was quitting time Daniel came over to where I was sitting on the hill, "Sydney do you like fish?"

I looked up at him, "Yes I had a goldfish named Moby Dick when I was a kid, does that count?"

He sat down next to me, "Well not really unless you ate him." We both started laughing. "I meant do you like to eat fish, there is a wonderful little place in Thumb Harbor and I am starving, would you like to go with me?"

"I would love to thanks I haven't had a good fish dinner since we got here. Do I have to change my clothes or do they cater to dirty people with ripped jeans?"

He looked down at his clothes and smiled, "Well if they do we would both fit in perfectly. How about I pick you up in about an hour, it's up to you what you wear though it might be smart if you put a patch on the jeans, much classier."

"Great I'll see you then," I said as I got myself up and headed for the cottage.

A date, I guess anyway, how fun and with Daniel. I took a quick shower and put on a pair of pale green slacks and matching sweater and I was set. I love this outfit, it sets off my eyes.

Within a couple minutes Daniel appeared at the front door. "You look great but I do miss the holey pants," he said as the girls began jumping all over him. "Better get going the fish are waiting, hold down the fort girls," he said and we were off.

The drive was beautiful again and I told him I was just in Thumb Harbor recently for the first time. The restaurant was small and cozy and there was even a fireplace, we got a table near the window over-looking the lake. "So what do you think, like it?" he asked as he picked up the menu.

"Yes I do, you sure know how to pick um."

"So who are you going to eat tonight?" We both ordered the small mouth bass, a salad, and iced tea.

As we waited I looked around at my surroundings. The tables had checkered blue tablecloths with bright white cloth napkins and a candle lit the lantern in the center of the table. The walls held nautical pictures, an anchor, and ships portholes. Very cozy, very romantic. I glanced out at the harbor and the light from the moon shining down on the water was truly magical. I unknowingly sighed and of course Daniel picked it up, "You look so relaxed and happy, I hope it's from the company."

"Yes of course it is, but I can't remember being in such a perfect spot for a very long time. So much has happened in such a short amount of time I think I finally feel grounded, secure, and right where I belong."

Right then our dinner came and we talked as we ate about the progress on the house. He said, "The scraping is taking longer than I had expected mostly because we had to stop so the roofers could do their thing and we are a little behind. Then there is priming and painting and anything else that might come up."

"I'm sorry do you have another job you have to go to soon?" I held my breath, please no please my heart whispered.

He looked out at the water, "No I am here for the summer, I always spend at least two months at home to help out. I don't know if you are aware of it but my dad has the beginning of dementia I am sure and Mom needs me. Besides we all need to get away don't we? Would you like to go out on the deck and stare at the stars while we finish our tea?"

We were alone as we sat in two very comfortable padded chairs out in the darkness, the only light came from the restaurant and the moon.

"Tell me about yourself Sydney," he said in almost a whisper. "Where have you been, what do you do for a living, did you have a nice childhood, everything, I want to know everything?"

"Boy, are you going to be disappointed," I said wishing I had some exciting things to say. "Well I think you know I am from Atlanta, I have lived there my whole life with my parents. It was always a grownup atmosphere because of my father's profession. I was an only child and had to find my own fun. Gretchen, our housekeeper and my girls were my only true friends. Oh I had friends in school but they never seemed to want to come over and play. As to making a living, I am a lawyer first into criminal law and now in Elder Law and Special Needs. I have always had a soft spot for people who need help but are ignored. There is a real need. I put aside my career when I decided to move up here and hope someday to get back at it. About a year before we moved my father died suddenly, only three months after my mother, and I was the one that found him," my voice cracked and all of a sudden it all came back. "I'm sorry but it was very traumatic. My father was a dynamic personality but didn't seem to know how to be a father, I know he loved me but sometimes I just wished he would have shown it. My mother was busy too with charities and helping the poor and in many ways Gretchen was more of a mother to me. She is in Ohio now taking care of her sister who had to have surgery she will be joining us before too long I hope. When I found out that my mother had left me this house I jumped at it, the time had come for me to have my own home away from so many memories. I am so thankful I came this is where I was meant to be. Oh, I am so sorry Daniel I really got carried away, more than you needed to know I am sure. I haven't let myself think about all this in a long time."

He put his hand over mine, "Thank you for sharing it with me, you are quite a remarkable woman Sydney Armstrong. Wait a minute are you Charles Armstrong's daughter, the lawyer that was always in the paper about some big case?"

"Guilty sir," I said with a bitter smile he could not see.

"You know I saw pictures of you on television after his death, trying to hurry into your house. It must have been awful trying to avoid all the publicity and I bet it lasted for a long time."

"Yes way too long I am afraid. Enough about me, tell me about you, your hopes and dreams."

He looked directly at me, "Very basic I am afraid, as a kid I was always building something so it seemed like a good idea to become a contractor when I grew up. Honestly I love every minute of it. I would guess Mom told you about all my siblings and being the youngest of five boys our house was always a busy place. We had a happy childhood here running around and doing all things concerning the water. I am the only one who has not yet married, all my brothers have children and with them and their wives we are quite a group when we get together. July 4th is our big once a year gathering and I hope you can meet everyone then. As to my dreams all I want is to find the perfect woman have a bunch of children and live happily ever after, as corny as that sounds. I love the simple life and plan to do my best to keep it."

This one is definitely for me, now to convince him. "Daniel thank you."

"For what?" he asked as he leaned forward.

"For just being who you are, an honest sensitive man who loves his life and his family and is not afraid to say it."

With that we sat in silence still holding hands in the darkness covered by a huge blanket of stars. It was a true beginning and a night I will remember forever.

As soon as I opened my eyes the next morning I could hear the crew busy at work. They got there early as it was only eight now. I got up, showered, dressed and packed a big batch of cinnamon rolls and mugs in a basket. The girls got put out on their leashes and I grabbed a big thermos of coffee plus the basket and head for the house. "Good morning everyone, I brought you some goodies for your breaks," I said as I put the basket on the porch and laid out the mugs and coffee. "Homemade," I yelled.

I took about three seconds for the men to charge over. Daniel was the first, he got his coffee and roll and motioned with his head for me to follow him. "Thank you so much this was such a nice thing to do. When did you have time to bake these?"

"Yesterday afternoon when you went out to get more primer."

"Thank you also for last night I really had a fun time, I hope we can do it again soon," he said.

"No I thank you, I really enjoyed myself. Anytime you feel the need to eat a fish call me." I turned to go and Daniel asked if I was leaving. "Only for a minute, I am starting a new fun project and want to get my supplies," I said as I made my way back to the cottage.

I gathered up my box of paints and brushes, an easel, and rag and headed back to the house. I set everything up at the top of the hill leading down to the lake. The view was perfect and I was going to paint it, hopefully. "Well if it isn't Ms. Picasso," Daniel said as he watched me get set up. "You didn't tell me you were an artist too."

"Maybe because I'm not, I just like giving it my best and find it very rewarding if I get lucky. What a perfect place to make a lasting memory. Go be busy and finish up my house."

"Aren't you going to help us today?" he yelled.

"Nope, you are just going to have to try to do it on your own, if you get stuck call." The next thing I knew I got hit in the arm with a dirt ball.

It was almost noon when I stopped. My back was sore and I needed to move around. A quick look at the house to see the men priming the wood I guess. They were painting but it just looked wet, no color. It was a gorgeous day and I headed down to the beach. I decided to walk the shoreline at the water's edge to see how far I could get. It was pretty rocky and my bare feet were not impressed after only about a hundred feet so I headed back. As I passed the McGregor's I looked up and saw Mrs. McGregor sitting in the yard knitting. I yelled a quick "HI" and she waved back, just then I stepped on a piece of glass and let out a cry. I had no idea she could move so fast, she was down there in a second.

She bent down and looked at my foot, "Oh my dear you are bleeding badly. Here let me help you sit down."

"Please don't fuss I am sure I can make it home." But the pain had really set in, there was blood everywhere and I was starting to get concerned.

"Stay here I will get some help."

Then I heard it, boy that woman has a good pair of lungs, "DANIEL DANIEL COME QUICK!" I was sure he would not be able to hear but within seconds he was running down the beach.

"Good heavens what happened here, did my mother beat you up?" Poor Mrs. McGregor looked mortified.

"Daniel McGregor you are awful, of course she didn't beat me up, I am a klutz and stepped on a piece of glass. Can you help me back to my house so I can fix it up?"

He took my hand and started to help me up, "Can you walk? No, ok," with that he picked me up and carried me back down the beach, up the hill, and to the work site. All the men gathered around, are you all right I heard over and over. "Bob get the first aid kit soap and a bucket of water and bring it to me please," he asked.

"Don't try to be brave yell if you want to you have a bad cut and this is going to hurt."

"Yes Doctor."

He rolled his eyes around and got to work. "Yikes!" I yelled.

"Can't you do better than that?" he asked.

"Oh yes but I have found swearing doesn't do much good and

makes me sound like a truck driver which I am not."

"Could've fooled me. Ok you are done, as done as I can do. If this gets infected you are going to have to go to a doctor. Check on it daily and change the bandage."

"Yes sir. Really thank you Daniel you are my knight in shining armor charging down to help a fair maiden."

With that he roared with laughter and went back to work. The other men seemed to get a kick out of it too and kept bowing to him and waving sticks like a sword. Poor Daniel must have been so embarrassed.

I was hungry so I hobbled my way back to the cottage and got something to eat. Then decided to lie down for a while and put my foot up which helped the throbbing. I slept for about an hour until I heard the girls barking and then a knock on the door. "Come in," I called from my bed. It was Daniel with my painting goodies.

"I don't think you are going to need these for the rest of the day," he said as he put it all in the corner. "How are you feeling?"

"Well I am sore but hopefully all right. Thanks for bringing my stuff back."

He reached into his pocket and pulled out a card, "If you need anything here is my cellphone number, call me promise?"

"Thank you yes I promise I will." He was gone and I thought about how fortunate I was that he was there when I hurt myself, but then I am sure his mother would have helped.

The next morning I was hurting less and tired of lying in bed so I got my coffee and a ball of yarn with needles and headed slowly for the house, still limping but at least I was moving. "So how are you doing this morning, boy what some people will do just to get out of a little work," Daniel said as he pulled one of my rockers out of the house and down to the drive so I could sit. "Are you going to sit there all day knitting like a little old lady or do you want to be the supervisor? Don't let it go to your head it is only for the day."

"You know I think I can do both if I try real hard, though I did leave my old lady spectacles in the cottage," I said as I gave him my toothless smile. Big smile and a lot of head shaking and he was off to work. Once in a while I would yell at him and say that he wasn't doing whatever according to the plans. He actually rolled up another dirt ball and threatened to throw it at me. It was a fun time but I hope I haven't been too big of a pain.

Deciding my supervising career was over I left about three and was almost back to the cottage when Mrs. McGregor found me. "How are you doing my dear, you had me pretty scared? Daniel told me he fixed you up, are you in much pain?'

"Thank you no just sore, but I don't know why I didn't see the glass. I am klutz by nature so sometimes I do stupid stuff," I said and made a goofy smile. She laughed and told me to go in and rest and to call her if I needed anything. After a big hug she turned to leave.

"Mrs. McGregor?"

She turned around, "First off we are friends and my name is Edith so please skip the formal stuff. Do you need something?"

"No Edith," I said with a grin, "I just wanted to thank you for caring about me and for being such a dear friend, you made me feel so welcome on my first day here and it meant so much."

Her eyes welled up with tears, "I feel very close to you Sydney and I have from the start, it is like I have found a daughter. We will always be there for you. Goodbye now."

I was overwhelmed, I too felt like I had found a family after losing my own but until this moment I don't think I realized it. They have all been so kind.

Just about dinner time there was a knock on the door. When I opened it there stood Daniel with two big bags of take-out food. "Just thought you might be hungry I got some hamburgers, French fries and shakes. Can I come in?"

"Of course what a nice thing to do I am famished and Sammy just won't get dinner started." I peeled the girls off of him and told them to go sit by the fireplace, which they actually did but watched every move we made. Daniel told me to stay in my chair as he gave the girls their food and put ours out on the table, got out glasses and all and announced dinner was ready. "My goodness good sir you must have spent hours preparing this magnificent feast," I said as we dug in. "Really it tastes wonderful thanks so much." After dinner we sat in the overstuffed chairs on either side of the fireplace with the dogs at our feet and just talked.

"What in the world did you and my mom talk about this afternoon? She said she stopped by to see how you were doing and when she got home all she did was talk about you and how sweet you are. I really believe she loves you already."

"Well to be honest I feel the same way. She is a very dear person I wish I had had that kind of caring from my own mother, though I know she did her best. You are a very fortunate man to have a mother like her."

He smiled and seemed to have drifted off to a lost memory, "Yes I know how lucky I am, she is an amazing woman." We sat in contented silence each lost in our own thoughts.

All of a sudden Daniel looked at his watch, "Eleven o'clock. Sorry I have to get going I had no idea it was so late, it has been so nice and I thank you, but I have to go to work early tomorrow, my supervisor is a stickler for promptness," he said with a wink, patted the dogs and he was gone.

The next morning I again hobbled up to the house. Daniel was there and came over, "Aren't you feeling well, you don't look so hot?"

"Honestly I don't feel so good and I think I have a fever. Is there a doctor nearby I think my foot may be infected it doesn't look hot either?"

"Wait here I will get my truck, Dr. Winters is only about a mile away," he said as he hurried off.

"Stop, can't you just tell me where he is and I can go by myself."

"No way girl, get in."

Dr. Winters was very close and he got me right in. The infection was just starting so he treated it and gave me an antibiotic then put his arm around my shoulder and assured me I would be fine in a day or two. Such a nice man, an old fashioned hometown doctor that actually makes house calls I learned, amazing, so different from a big city where I probably couldn't get in to see a doctor for a week!

Daniel seemed relieved and we went back to the house. "What would you like me to take out for dinner tonight I want you to stay off that foot? I am so sorry I should have brought you something that first night too."

"Surprise me," I said with the best smile I could muster. "No worries that first night the girls shared their food with me, only kidding, stop looking so alarmed." Then I smiled.

We had a repeat of the night before but this time we had Chinese. Daniel left promptly at eleven and I was so grateful for his help and told him so.

The doctor was right by the end of the next day I was feeling much better. The antibiotic did the trick. So the following day I was back in my supervisor position.

"You look great kid, feeling good now?" Daniel asked as soon as he saw me coming.

"Yes and thanks again for all the TLC." As I looked up at the house I was amazed the grey/green paint was about a fourth of the way done and looked fantastic. "Oh I love it, the perfect color don't you think? You are a good paint picker outer."

"Yes it really looks good. It won't be more than three or four days and it should be all done. Then we can decide on an accent color to finish it off. My gosh you almost look sad, what's up?"

"To be honest it has been so nice having you and your guys here I think I will be lonely when you are all gone."

He looked at me in such a gentle way as he said, "You are not going to get rid of me that easily girl."

Daniel did not come that night but in a way I was glad it gave me some time to think about "us", is there really an us? I am not quite sure. He is a very kind man and maybe he was just being nice to help me so much, maybe he feels sorry for me. I feel something very special for him, something I have never felt before with any of my old boyfriends. Could he be THE one, yes he could, there is no doubt in my mind.

The next morning I was back to my painting on the hill. The picture was almost done and it came out quite good. Daniel stopped by and watched for a couple minutes, "You have real talent girl the picture is beautiful you really captured the water and waves." I was thrilled and thanked him. "You are going to have to branch out around the area there are some wonderful old lighthouses that I am sure would be more than glad to sit for you," he said smiling once more. "Have you ever thought of selling your work, there are many shows over the summer in town, at least there have been we will have to wait and see about this year because of the storm damage?"

"Sir you flatter me, thank you. Have you been into Sylerville, how are things going?"

"No but I hear things are progressing", he said as he picked up a wildflower and stuck it in my hair. "There now you look like a woman of the earth."

"I have been called a lot of things but not a woman of the earth, I know you are teasing me but I like it," and I did.

"Daniel would you like to come over for dinner tonight, I am not the greatest cook but I do make a mean roast beef, payback for all the food you have brought to me. Say six o'clock?"

He said he would love to and then went back to work, while I finished my painting.

We had a lovely evening, and thankfully the dinner turned out very well. As we were sitting by the fire I asked him if he knew a woman named Rose, and told him about my father's last words, how his father thinks I am Rose, this estate is called The Rose, and Mr. Edgeworth my father's law partner commented that I resemble my mother but we look nothing alike. "Many other people here in town think I look like a Rose too. Oh and my middle name is Rose. I am getting a little freaked out about all this."

He looked a little bewildered and said he had only seen my mother once when she came over to get something from his mother. "My father gets confused easily so I wouldn't think too much of that, but it is quite a coincidence isn't it? Wait a minute, do you know what your mother's sister's names were, do you suppose there is a Rose and you might resemble her? I do agree you do not look like your mother."

"No I don't know the sister's names. It could be that one of them was named Rose and I have heard of women who look like other member of their families but not necessarily their parents, but no I think it must be something else. When my friend Gretchen gets here I will talk to her about it too, she seems to know everything about my family."

"When is she coming, didn't you say she was helping her sister?"

"Yes she is but there hasn't been anything said about when she can leave as yet. Sorry to bring this whole thing up but it is starting to drive me nuts."

The time has come I am going to find out who Rose is, but where do I start? Maybe Mrs. McGregor, oh Edith, might have some information so I decided to go over for a visit the next morning. I gathered up my knitting and headed for the woods. When I got there she was in her usual spot under a big tree in a glider rocker with her feet propped up. As I got closer I yelled, "HI would you like some company?"

"Oh my yes, come on over, grab that chair," She said as she pointed to one close by. "Are you knitting too Sydney, personally I can't sit down without picking mine up, guess I am addicted?"

This lovely lady, and she is just that, is cute as a button with her round pink cheeks and curly almost white hair which blew gently in a little breeze then seemed to go right back down where it belonged. She is not that old, probably in her late sixties and the only real lines on her face are just happy smile lines around her eyes. She is obviously a happy woman.

After explaining I was anything but a great knitter I did tell her that I love doing it and am trying for an afghan. "I got my yarn in Thumb Harbor at the general store, and met the nice ladies that own it."

Edith got out a loose skein of yarn and started making it into a ball, "Yes I get my yarn there too and they have been friends of mine for years. They have run the store for a long time and their husbands are still sailors, I don't think they will ever retire it is in their blood I guess. Would you like some lemonade?"

I told her I would get it but she said to stay put with that injured foot of mine. Then if like magic Daniel appeared out of the woods, covered from head to toe in paint.

"Well I see my two ladies are pretending to be old and knitting their day away," he said with an impish grin. Edith threw a ball of yarn at him which he caught and we all started to laugh. Honestly I don't think I have ever laughed as much as with these people in my whole life. How wonderful!

He looked down at himself and said, "Guess who was in the wrong place at the wrong time? Think I had better go in and get cleaned up."

"Honey, will you please bring out the pitcher of lemonade and a couple glasses when you come back out? Thanks. He has been the perfect son," my friend said with great pride I could actually see. "He has always been a true delight. I just wish he would find the right girl and settle down and give me a bunch more grandchildren but honestly I don't know if he has the time, as sad as that sounds, he is so busy with work." Look in your backyard, she's sitting right there I thought.

"Have you ever been married Sydney?" she asked as her eyebrows went up slightly.

I told her no, "I had one serious relationship but it got too complicated and I had to end it, plus my father did not like him and that was a big problem."

"Fathers can be a problem sometimes with their daughter's dates, I know mine was," she said with a grimace. "No one seemed to meet up with his standards but finally he approved of my Eli and things have been wonderful ever since. I think Daniel told me your father was a lawyer and that you are too. How exciting that must be for you. What field are you in?"

"At first I practiced criminal law but now I am into Elder Law and Special Needs, they need help more than others, and I have quite a bit of experience volunteering in nursing homes and with the Special Olympics. My practice is on hold for the time being there is so much to be done here now. I'll tell you a little secret I really don't miss it yet," and until that moment I didn't realize it.

"Sydney, I hope I will not embarrass you but I really would like to tell you what a beautiful girl you are, inside and out. Eli even mentioned it one time, I wish my skin was as smooth and flawless but I guess that is the price I pay for getting older."

I didn't quite know what to say, "Edith what a lovely thing to say thank you. I think all women need to hear that once in a while whether it is true or not," and I gave her a big smile. "Now Mrs.

McGregor I too have a compliment for you. Your skin is beautiful and I noticed it right away, those little lines are your badge of courage, you earned each one of them by being the caring sensitive dear thing that you are. I hope I look half as good as you when I get to be your age. I really mean it!" and I went over and gave her a hug.

She hugged me back and said, "What a dear you are, so do you think these two lovely ladies should continue to knit or go out partying?" I laughed so hard I thought I was going to fall over in my chair.

Just then I looked up and saw Daniel heading toward us with a sandwich hanging out of his mouth and a pitcher and glasses in his hands. "mmmmcnmdm," he said as he put the lemonade down on the small table by his mother, "sorry I couldn't figure out how to carry all this and still get my lunch. So what are two laughing about?"

"First off you look like a goof," then Edith simply said, "It is girl thing Son. Now leave us be and get back to work."

He saluted her, bowed to me and took off across the yard.

We sat there in silence for a couple minutes then I said, "Edith, something has been puzzling me for a long time and was hoping maybe you could help me with it?"

She set her knitting aside and gave me her full attention, "I will do my best what is it dear?"

Again I told my story about the Rose thing. "I mentioned all this to Daniel and he doesn't know either. Do you have any ideas?"

"Wow that is really something, we have been here forever, I came as a bride many years ago and the only Rose I know of was your mother's sister. She was a beautiful woman, and yes you do look a little like her with your dark hair but that was a long time ago and I hardly remember her. Even back then I only saw her a few times she must have died almost thirty years ago, about the time your mother moved to Atlanta. I didn't even know she was dead but heard that she went away and must have passed on while gone. I'm sorry but that is the best I can do, does it help any?"

My heart was beating too fast and I took a minute to take a deep breath, "Thank you I think maybe things are starting to come together. At least I have a start. This whole thing seems to be centered around my mother's sister though I have no idea how. It gives me a lot to think about."

Finally I told her how much I have enjoyed myself but I had better get going and got up from my chair. She came over and gave me her special hug and said that if she thought of anything else she would let me know. "Please come back and knit with me anytime, goodbye."

My girls were waiting for me at the gate and we had a race back to the house which ended in me tripping and landing and being covered with dogs. It was so much fun but unfortunately Daniel saw the whole thing and stood there with his arms crossed shaking his head. "The only good thing I saw was you running which means your foot is much better, the rest well not too pretty," and he turned away. Lucky for me there is an abundance of dirt everywhere which makes great balls in a hurry, I rolled one up and let it go, bingo, right in the smart guys back. Then I started laughing and literally could not stop. Payback. He came over, picked me up and just stood there staring at me, then looked around and silenced my laughing with a kiss–nowhere near a brotherly kiss. I was shocked but immediately responded. When he let me go he too seemed shocked and said, "Sorry I don't know what made me do that."

"I'm not," I said serious now as the girls and I walked away. Let him figure out what made him do it and let me try to get my equilibrium back.

That night I could not sleep my thoughts kept going back Daniel and our kiss. Maybe I shouldn't have said "I'm not" was I too forward, but it just came out. We have had such fun kidding each other and I hope I didn't blow it. Enough, I need some air. I got up and put my jeans and a sweatshirt on and headed for the door. "Go back to sleep girls I will be back soon." It was two-thirty, how ridiculous to be wandering around at this time.

The moon was bright and I could see my way across the yard, but the shadows cast by the house were very deep and dark and a little scary. I made my way to the beach and sat down by the water hugging my legs tightly to my chest. What did I do, what am I going to do about Daniel I thought? Just then I heard someone walking along the beach and jumped up and started running up the hill.

"Sydney, is that you? What in the world are you doing down here at this time of the night?"

I stopped and turned around, breathless, "I could ask you the same question."

"Come on down and sit with me, we need to talk."

He took my hand and said, "I am sorry for what happened but yet I'm not you just looked so beautiful with dirt on your face and your hair full of leaves I just couldn't help myself. I care very deeply for you Sydney and I felt something the first time we met. You are so full of life and such fun, it was like a dream come true, but it also scared me. Every time I find someone I have come to care about they back off and leave. It hurts and I was worried it would happen again if I showed you how I felt. I didn't want to ruin the fun friendship we have. I don't know if this is love but it is darn close even after knowing you for such a short time. I don't know if there is a time schedule for falling in love, like a year and then you know for sure. But I do remember something my mother once said to me about love. She said, 'Love is really quite simple whether it takes a year or a minute. It is when you can look at each other and without words say I love you or when you can touch their pain from across the room. It is when you know your soul would die without that person by your side. Love is all'."

"That is the most beautiful thing I have ever heard," I said wiping the tears from my eyes.

Daniel put his arm around me and held me close. "What do we do now, I too care very much for you and have been happier than I have ever been but I want us to be like we always have been is this going to change things?" I asked.

He didn't speak for a couple minutes then, "I won't let it change anything in fact I think it will make it even better, are you game?"

Now the tears were really rolling, I looked up at him and said, "Yes," as he bent down and kissed my forehead then my nose, and finally my lips. Then we lied back in the sand and just held each other.

We must have fallen asleep because when I opened my eyes we were still in each other's arms but the sun was out and I could hear the workers off in the distance. "Daniel wake up it is morning your guys are coming."

He jumped up, gave me a quick kiss and headed up the hill. When he got to the top he turned with a huge smile on his face and said, "Well, this is going to be an interesting day, get me some coffee will you?"

"Will do, but stop looking so happy the guys will think you are up to something you nut."

I don't think I have ever been so happy; we are going to give this a try. I have always believed that if something was meant to be it will be, and boy this sure had better be one of those times and I headed back to the cottage. I made some coffee and grabbed some muffins and mugs and headed back up to the house. "Free coffee, get it while it's hot," I yelled when I got there. Everyone scrambled.

I had a cup myself then decided it would be a good idea to go back and take a good shower to try to get all the sand out of my hair and get this day going. It is time to back to Sylerville and see if I can find Susan.

The town was still under construction and being cleaned up but thankfully I could get in. I parked on the road about a block from the main street and walked to the grocery store, there were so many trucks and such I didn't want to get in the way. Susan was there cleaning but stopped when she saw me. "Sydney how wonderful to see you," she said as she put down her broom and came over.

"It is good to see you too, I was so worried about you and your family but Elaine told me you got out in time before the storm hit. I am so glad, your building appears to be all right but you still have a lot of cleaning up to do in here."

She took a deep breath, "Yes all of the windows got blown out and the wind threw everything everywhere, thank goodness this old brick building held up, all but the roof, heaven knows where it is now. The disaster people called and told me what was what, and as soon as they could get in some roofers came. I decided to wait for a while before coming back so I have only been in here for about two weeks. From what I can see we were one of the lucky ones, so many stores collapsed and everyone has to start over. The dock was completely destroyed and a new one is almost finished. As you can see almost all the trees were uprooted. It was awful Sydney really awful but I am so thankful I listened to my heart and got out of here. My grandmother is still quite shaken but all right though she will not come back. David, my son, wants to help but there is too much glass everywhere. The windows were replaced only about a month ago."

"Here let me give you a hand," I said as I picked up another broom. "We had a lot of damage to the yard but the house and cottage only got a little. In fact the big house is almost renovated if you can believe."

"Really who did you finally find to do it?"

"Daniel McGregor and he has done a wonderful job, he and his crew have worked very hard. I can't wait to move in."

Susan and I worked for about two hours and she said she had to get going back to her brothers to take David to the doctor, I guess he's had a cold for a long time and she wants to get it checked out. "So thank you so much for all the help. When I make a little more progress I will come over and see you," she said as she gave me a hug.

"That would be great, please let me know if you need more help. Here is my cellphone number, don't hesitate to call. Goodbye."

Wow and I thought my construction zone was a mess, she has got a long way to go and I think I had better make more frequent visits. I did go back a couple times a week until it was all cleaned up.

When I got back home I was greeted with, "Well Sydney the time have come, we will be finished with the painting tomorrow and we still need an accent color, do you still want to go with the eggplant?"

"What do you think you are the pro? I do like it but am not quite sure."

Magically he produced a small can of paint and took off the lid, "Eggplant my dear, maybe we could give it a quick try," he said. So we both got a brush and did just a small section. "Like it?"

"Yes, what about you?"

"Looks good to me but I think we are going to need a little more paint than just this sample can. I will get some in the morning," he said as he put the lid back on.

Right then a car pulled up, who in the world I thought. "Josh, oh my gosh is that you?" and I ran over and hugged him.

He hugged me back and gave me a big kiss, "So how are you girl you look amazing? Simon told me you had moved up here and my grandparents said they had heard about a woman moving into this old house so I put two and two together and decided to see if it was you. Good heavens I have missed you, why didn't you call before you left?"

"Oh Josh I wanted to but things got so complicated toward the end with the move and all. Thank you for the flowers you sent after Father died, I did try to call you but your secretary said you were out of town on a case. So tell me what are you doing up here, are you going to be staying for a while?"

"My grandparents are just a few miles down from Sylerville and I usually come up for a couple weeks in the summer, I told you about them but I guess you forgot, bad girl," and he laughed. "We have a lot of catching up to do, how about I pick you up later and we can get some dinner?"

"That would be great; oh I would like you to meet someone, Josh this is Daniel McGregor, Daniel this is Josh Sorenson an old friend of mine."

They shook hands, "Nice to meet you Daniel, looks like you are busy so I won't keep you. I'll see you later Sydney," and he gave me another hug then left.

Daniel turned around and headed back to the house and didn't say a word. I followed him, "Boy what a surprise, Josh and I have been friends for a long time and it really was good to see him."

"So you two are close huh?" he said with a strange look on his face.

"Yes we are, I met him through my practice and we worked on a couple cases together. Many nights we would grab a late dinner after work, he practically lived at our house and was one of the few friends I had that my father approved of–probably because of their law interests. So where were we, again I do love the eggplant and can't wait to see what it looks like all done."

"It's getting a little late maybe you should get going and fix yourself up for your date," and he walked away.

Ok what is going on I thought everything was fine until Josh showed up? Good heavens maybe Daniel thought Josh and I were more than friends, oh oh. Well tomorrow I will explain, tonight I am going to have a good time.

We had a lot of fun getting caught up. "This Daniel, is he more than your contractor Sydney?" Josh asked as we ate our dinner.

"Yes he is, for the first time in my life I am in love. He is so special and makes me so happy; you know I think he may love me too. I am so lucky."

"I am very happy for you girl, you deserve some happiness, can I come over tomorrow and pester you?"

"Of course you nut."

When we got back he hugged me and said he had a wonderful time. I was not tired yet so I thought I would go down to the beach and enjoy the beautiful night. I sat for about an hour then as I got up to leave I saw Daniel coming down the beach. "HI," I yelled, "come on over and keep me company."

"So your date left huh, did you have a good time?"

I leaned back on the sand, "Yes it was a lot of fun, so what are you doing wandering around in the night, looking for mermaids?" and I smiled.

"No, I had better get back, I'll see you tomorrow," and he left.

"Daniel get back here, what is the matter with you?"

He stopped and looked back at me, "I thought we were going to give this a try between us but obviously there is something between you and Josh. Goodnight."

I jumped up and went after him, "Daniel you are so wrong, now get back here and let me explain a few things to you." He just kept walking, "Fine, just go, run away," and I headed up to the cottage.

I decided not to go up to the house the next day, let him stew a little, I think he is jealous, good serves him right. Josh showed up and we took a drive down to his grandparents. They were also right on the water and had a huge old house like mine. They were delightful people and I enjoyed our visit. I told them about my renovations on the house and how happy I am to be living here.

His grandmother said she would love to have me come back and visit them anytime and I think I will. I did go back several times. We stopped for dinner in Port Shores before heading back, it was such a nice day but I couldn't stop thinking about Daniel and told Josh what had happened. "I think he is jealous Sydney, want me to talk to him?"

"You know what maybe I do, but he doesn't deserve it. Come on back tomorrow and maybe we can straighten this thing out."

He did come back and Daniel was working. I called to him and he came over to where we were standing. "Nice to see you again Daniel, can I have a minute of your time?"

"Sorry I am right in the middle of something, how about later, are you going to be here for a while?"

"Yes, o.k."

"See what I am talking about, well after all, suddenly this tall dark and very handsome man appears at my doorstep, kisses me and takes me away for the day right after we had decided to hopefully move our relationship forward. He needs to talk to us right now."

I yelled, "Daniel McGregor get over here now, no excuses." I got a not so great look but he did come over.

He stood there with his arms crossed, "So what do you want?"

"Please sit down here Josh wants to tell you something." We all sat down.

Josh pulled out a picture of himself and Ken Bronson, "This is my partner Ken, we have been together for five years, Daniel I am gay. Sydney has been my dear friend and supporter for a long time and I love her dearly, when I first came out she was the only one to accept me for who I am and I will always be grateful to her. She got me my first job at her father's law firm and because he too accepted me I was able to start my own practice. So my man, I too care for her, like you do, only in a different way. I hope we too can be friends," and he held out his hand. Daniel took it and apologized to both of us.

"You are welcome here anytime Josh, I feel like an idiot." Josh said he would see us tomorrow. I hugged him and he left.

"Sydney forgive me, I really am an idiot, but all I could think about was here we go again, I found someone I really cared about and boom she was gone. I am so sorry."

"So am I," and I started to walk away.

"Wait, where are you going? Can't we talk about this?"

I turned, "Daniel you don't trust me, you jumped to conclusions and were not even willing to listen when I tried to explain, you basically ran away. I need to do some serious thinking about all this," and I left.

When I got back to the cottage I lied down on the bed and cried. How can we move forward if he doesn't trust me, is he going to get upset every time I talk to a man? I honestly don't know if I can risk this. The hours passed and I knew I needed to get away from this whole thing for a while to think, I can't do it when he is around.

I called Edith, "Hi it's Sydney. I have a gigantic favor to ask of you, could my girls come over and visit you for a couple days, I need to get away for a little while?"

She didn't say anything for a second, "Of course my dear, are you all right?"

"To be honest right now I don't really know I have a lot to think about."

"Where are you going to go?"

"Honestly I don't know, are you sure it is all right with the girls?"

"Yes of course, they are so good. But honey, can't I help you, you sound so strange?"

I started to cry, "Dear Edith maybe when I get back and have figured things out. If you don't mind I will let them into your yard early tomorrow morning and leave their food in a bag by the gate."

"Oh Sydney you don't have to leave their food, we have plenty but please let me help you, please don't cry. I love you."

"I love you too, I am sorry if I have upset you. Goodbye for now."

I packed a bag and went to sleep.

The next morning at dawn I let the girls into the McGregor's yard along with the bag of food and told them to be good, I would be back soon, got in my van and left. I had no idea where I was going but it felt good to be going somewhere. I drove down the coast to Port Shores and decided I had better get some breakfast. As I ate I looked out on the lake, then I heard, "Sydney what are you doing down here at this hour?" It was Josh.

"I ran away from home," and tried to smile. "Daniel and I are having some problems and I needed to get away and think."

He sat down next to me, "Is this my fault?"

I put my hand over his, "No dear friend, it is just that Daniel doesn't seem to trust me, he wouldn't listen when I tried to explain about the close friendship you and I have. He just jumped to conclusions and honestly I don't know if I want to continue with the relationship that we have. Is he going to be jealous of every man I meet or know? Right now I need to take some time to figure out this whole thing."

"So where are you going?"

I started to cry, "Oh Josh I don't know."

"Well I do, you are coming home to my grandparents with me, remember the little guest house on the beach, well you are welcome to stay there for as long as you want. Where are your girls?"

"They are visiting the McGregor's next door. Since I had no idea where I was going I didn't think it would be smart to take them with me."

He told me to finish my breakfast and we left. "Thank you Josh I would love to stay with you but please don't think you have to entertain me, I just need to sit on the beach and work this all out. Do you think your grandparents will mind?"

"Not in the least they were very taken with you when you came for a visit, and guess what Ken is here now too, I know he would love to see you."

I visited with everyone for about an hour then Ken and Josh took me down to the guest house. It was charming, one room with a little kitchen, a couple big chairs and a bed. Perfect. I thanked them and they left. I was to come up to the house anytime, but they would leave me alone down there.

I decided to call Edith, I know she was concerned. "Hi it's me Sydney; I just wanted you to know I am down the coast at a friend's house. I will call you when I get back."

"Oh Sydney, what in the world happened, Daniel is a mess? I

thought he was going to go nuts when he found out you were gone. He looks so lost and honestly scared. Can I give him a message from you?"

"I'm sorry Edith but not now, he needs to do some thinking just like I do. Thank you for caring about me, I love you. Goodbye for now."

I spent the rest of the day on the beach, just staring at the water trying to find the answers I needed. Josh called at dinner time and asked if I would like to join them. "Yes thank you I would," and I walked up to the house.

They all seemed so concerned and I thought maybe I had better tell them a little about what was going on. "I am so sorry to invade you all but I have some problems with a man I have been seeing, I thought we were perfect for each other then something happened and now I am not too sure. I can't tell you how much I appreciate you letting me stay here for a couple days."

Josh's grandmother, Mrs. Sorenson is such a dear, "Sydney I am so sorry, if you need to talk we are all here for you," and she gave me a hug. "You know sometimes when you truly love someone with all your heart you do stupid stuff," and she smiled. "It is not that you take the person for granted, it is just the thought of losing them that makes you do the stupid stuff, if that makes any sense. It sounds to me like you both love each other very much and maybe it is smart sometimes to shake things up to really see how much you do care."

"Oh my thank you Mrs. Sorenson, that does make sense, but he got jealous of Josh when he came to see me and wouldn't even listen when I tried to explain about our special friendship. Is he always going to be jealous of any man I talk to or have known?"

"Ah now this all makes sense, this grandson of mine is very handsome and is such a special person, no wonder your man got jealous. No I don't think he will continue to be jealous, from what I can tell you two are still pretty early in your relationship, maybe he just needs to feel secure and know you are not going to leave him."

"Grandma you are embarrassing me, I love you," said Josh. "I owe Sydney so much and she is truly so dear to me, but I feel awful that I started all this."

"Josh, things happened for a reason and once Sydney takes a little time to think this out I am sure things will work out fine." She looked at me and smiled.

I was overcome with emotion, "You all are really something else. Thank you so much. I think I will go back to the guest house and get some sleep now; I do feel so much better."

The next day I stayed on the beach and things finally started to come together. Daniel has had several broken relationships and I think he was scared that this one was going to end too. Yes we all do stupid stuff when we are in love. There is no doubt in my mind that he does love me or he wouldn't have reacted the way he did. There is no way I am going to lose him for any reason.

The next morning I went up to the house and told everyone I was going to leave today and go back home. "There are no words to thank you all for being so kind to me and helping me figure this whole thing out. I would love to come back and visit sometime without tears," and I smiled. I gave them all big hugs and said if they were anywhere near my place to please stop by. "Josh, please keep in touch I have missed you so much," and I hugged him again. "Goodbye."

I was nervous as I pulled up to the house. The painting was almost done, though I thought it would be completed by now. I decided to go over and get my girls, plus I needed one of Edith's hugs. As soon as I got to the gate all the dogs were all over me and Edith was out there under her tree. "Oh Sydney I am so glad to see you." She got up and hugged me big time. "The girls have been wonderful but I know they missed you, we all did. Are you feeling better?"

"Yes and I am so sorry I worried you. Is Daniel here we need to talk?"

"No he and Eli went into town; they should be back any time now. Oh my, he is really a mess; I have never seen him so upset."

"Please tell him to come over when he can, and thank you so much for taking care of my girls. I am going to go home now I am really tired" and I hugged her.

I sat on the porch of the house and saw Daniel come through the woods. As he got closer I was shocked, he looked awful.

I stood up and walked over to him. "Hi big fella have you got any hugs for this girl, she sure could use one?" He just stood there then grabbed me and I did wonder if he was ever going to let go.

"Oh Syd, my Syd I am so sorry, my God these past couple days have been so horrible. Are we all right? What can I do to make up for all this?"

"Just promise that you will trust me, I told you I wanted to move forward with our relationship and you need to believe that I meant it, you are the only man in my life. Now do you think you can do that?"

He kissed me like never before, "Oh I have been such a fool, sometimes it is hard for me to realize that someone as wonderful as you could actually care that much about me."

"I don't know about the wonderful part but I sure do care, very much, I guess I wouldn't have gone semi nuts if I didn't. Now, how about tomorrow we finish up this house, by the way have you got any more kisses you would like to share?"

That night as I lied in bed I thanked God that all was well again. I hope we can just go on like we were. Then I fell asleep.

First thing the next morning the phone started ringing, it was Gretchen. "Hi there sweetie how are things going, how is Louise? When can you come? Guess who showed up for a visit, Josh."

"Hi yourself Sydney, things are going very well and I should be there in less than a month now. Can't wait I miss you so much. My goodness it must have been a surprise to see Josh, how is he doing? I always liked and admired him."

I decided not to mention anything about Daniel until she gets here so I concentrated on the house. "It will be all done tomorrow if you can believe it. Oh Gretchen it looks so wonderful, a rebirth. I hope all the sisters who lived here are watching from above and are happy for me. We have so much to talk about. I could not be happier with my new life, everything is perfect. Can you believe I am painting again, and also knitting an afghan, which will probably take five years to complete? Josh is fine and still with Ken, he is visiting his grandparents who live just down the coast from here. We have had a lot of fun catching up."

"Slow down girl don't tell me everything I want a few surprises."

"Oh you will get a few I promise," I said. "You take care too and hopefully I will see you soon. Love you. Bye."

The next morning I was up at the house before the guys even got there, with more muffins, donuts, and two pots of hot coffee. This was their last day and I wanted them to know how much I appreciated all their work. I was still sad though that they were all leaving, no more Daniel first thing in the morning and the last thing in the afternoon. 'HI!" I yelled when I saw them come through the trees, "The good fairies have left a treat for you over there," I said as I pointed to the work table. Many smiles followed as they poured their drinks.

"Good morning sunshine," said Daniel as he poked me in the back. "Sleep well?"

"Yes thanks. Did you bring the paint?"

"Boy you sure have a one track mind, don't you, not even a good morning?"

"Good morning, did you bring the paint, how was that?"

He whipped a can of paint out from behind his back and set it down on the ground at my feet. "Your paint Madame, grab a brush and we can get started, AFTER I get some coffee."

The more we painted the more I loved it, but I should have warned Daniel that I am a good painter but usually get more on me than what I am painting and this was no exception. It was everywhere, even in my hair but I could have cared less.

"Are you trying to look like a rock star with streaks of purple in your hair or did the good fairy that left us the goodies have his way with you? You are a mess girl."

"So what do you want good painting or a perfect person, who by the way is free labor, spotlessly clean?" I asked with my hands on my hips and a stubborn look on my face.

He picked up his brush and planted a dab of paint on my nose and said I need just a touch more to make it complete. I held up my brush, aiming for his head and said, "Don't tempt me." Then we both laughed.

Josh came by but only to say goodbye, there was some kind of emergency at the office and he had to fly back tonight. "I hope to be able to come back later in the summer, will let you know if I can. It was so nice to see you again, and also meet you Daniel, hold onto this girl she is a gem," and he hugged me and headed for the car. Then he whispered, "Is everything ok again?" I smiled and said yes and thanked him again.

"I am going to miss him; he has more courage than I ever will."

By a little after three o'clock the house was done. I stood there and cried it looked spectacular. The guys were packing up their equipment and I quickly grabbed my camera. "I have only one more favor to ask of you all, I am going to take a picture of the house and I would love it if you could all stand in front of it. After all you made this wonderful old house become a home with your many talents and a whole lot of hard work. Thank you from the bottom of my heart, you have been fun to have around and I will miss you all." Without even a grumble the men did what I asked and I took the picture.

Daniel came up to me afterwards, "That was such a nice thing to do, the guys are really touched. You really spoiled them."

"Well they deserve the praise they worked miracles. By the way if anyone is interested in celebrating tonight meet me on the porch at seven-thirty and I promise he won't be sorry. Stop with the look, I baked a cake and need some help eating it, what a dirty mind you have Mr. McGregor." With that they all left and I headed home.

Tonight I decided to do it up right, it was a celebration after all, my house was done and I was going to meet the man responsible, plus we were back together again. So, I slipped into my "vamp" dress–long black tight silk with a plunging neckline, added a little extra makeup and piled my hair up on my head. Long thin gold earrings were the final touch and I was ready. I put the cake in a large basket with plates and forks grabbed a bottle of Champaign and two glasses and up I went.

Daniel must have gotten there a little early and saw me coming. Though it was dusk I could clearly see that he was surprised and a little more than impressed. "No one told me this was a formal affair, you look spectacular! WOW!"

"Well this is a big day for me and I never get to dress up so I went for it," I said as I handed him the bottle. "Besides if I am going to be the lady of this manor I had better look the part. Come sit with me on the porch. Oh, thanks for getting the rockers back out I forgot all about them," I said as I sat down.

I cut the cake as he opened the bottle. "This is really good Sydney you did yourself proud."

"Thank you sir, now all we need is a little music and things will be perfect."

He went down to the end of the porch, "Your wish is my command my lady, one of the guys left his boom box here that has a radio. I am sure we can find something appropriate," which we did. "May I have this dance?" he asked with a slight bow.

I took his hand and was in his arms. We glided across the "ballroom" in the moonlight. It was magic and I felt like I was in a wonderful dream. "Thank you Daniel for making this night so perfect."

"No thank you lovely one, you make me so happy."

"It is midnight Daniel and unless you want me to turn into a pumpkin right before your eyes I had better hurry home. Will I see you tomorrow?" I asked trying to sound coy.

"You bet you will but get going before I forget that I am a gentleman."

Bright and early the next morning I headed for the house. Somewhere while cleaning I came across some gardening tools and now that the house looks so wonderful I have to start cleaning up all the rose bushes that surround it. Thank goodness Mother taught me how to prune in our garden.

Goodness some of the roses are actually starting to bloom, I know it is June already but after so many years of neglect I didn't give them much hope. Maybe they have been doing this for a while but I was so focused on the house itself I didn't pay attention.

It is going to be a nice warm day I thought as I searched for the tools, bingo there they are in that big old basket in the mud room. So out I went. It felt so good to get my hands into the soil, I used to love to help Mother in Atlanta but it has been a long time. I was so glad I had gotten mulch from Thumb Harbor on my last visit, hoping to do exactly what I am going to do now.

I clipped and pruned for a couple hours then got out the thermos I brought and went up on the porch to rest a little. The waves from the lake were getting stronger and the sound they made was wonderful. I love to lie in bed at night and listen to their "music".

Back to work girl if you stay here much longer you won't leave I thought. Ok I was about half done and all of a sudden my father's last words came back, 'look beyond the rose' and it startled me. Here I was deep into the roses but there was nothing beyond them but the house. Could that be one of my clues? Maybe but I couldn't figure out how. Could the house itself hold my answers? Well if it does I guess I am going to have to look carefully but for now I want to finish this.

It took another couple hours but I did finish. The only thing I forgot was to put on sun screen and my arms looked pretty red, and I am sure the rest of me does too, why did I wear my skimpy swim suit top? What a dummy!

Just then Daniel appeared at the side of the house. "Wow you have been a busy girl the flowers look wonderful but you are as red as a beet. Love the top you are almost wearing," and he smiled big.

"Yea I know I guess I just forgot the sunscreen as this is our first really warm day. So what's up?" I said as I gingerly got up from my kneeling position. "My knees are not happy with me right now."

He started laughing and asked if I wanted to have a picnic on the beach tonight for dinner. "Nothing fancy I will bring everything."

"Are you going to cook?" I asked looking skeptical.

"Have no fear I will get something from Thumb Harbor. Is six-thirty all right?"

"That would be great, I love picnics. Now let me get a shower and put some lotion on my poor skin. See you at six-thirty," and I left.

When I got to the top of the hill that night I couldn't believe my eyes, what lay below was magical, there were probably thirty lighted candles poking out of the sand and a huge blanket with china plates, a centerpiece of another candle, and a wine bottle next to tons of food. "Good heavens," I said as I walked down the hill,

"I have never been to a picnic like this before you really know how to do things up right. I am totally impressed sir!"

"That was my intention my lady, please come and sit down and the feast will begin. I tried to get some jugglers and merry men to play for us but they were all booked up so I guess we are just going to have to make do with this," and he pulled out a guitar.

"I love guitar music could you play me something please?"

"Your wish is my command, I take requests got any?"

"Nope surprise me." And he began with "Greensleaves", and I was in heaven. I just sat there mesmerized, and when he finished, "Oh Daniel that is one of my favorite songs, you sang it so beautifully and are truly talented." I bent over and gave him a kiss, "Thank you so much. You are spoiling me rotten."

"Good now grab a chicken leg and let's eat."

It was a beautiful night. We ate, laughed and had a wonderful time. The setting was perfect, the moon was full and the water gently lapped up on shore made a soothing rhythmic sound which completed the picture. What a very special man I am sitting next to I thought, so kind and gentle and to think he may be falling in love with me.

"You look so healthy tonight," he said with a smile. "Horrible sunburns become you."

I gently rubbed my sore arms, "You're lucky I even showed up with clothes on, everything hurts."

"You could just have come naked and it wouldn't have bothered me one bit," he said with a snicker.

"I am sure it wouldn't you nasty old thing. By the way I brought down some lotion would you please rub it on my back I can't reach it, can you even see my back, and I undid my straps?"

"Your wish is my command, and yes I can see it, is this upper part all that got burned?"

"No, pretty much my whole back got it; can I trust you to be a good little boy if I let you do the whole thing?"

"All I can say is I will try." I got an evil little look. Down went the zipper. "Your skin is so soft, does that feel good?"

I was getting a little excited and said in a whisper, "Yes, thanks."

Then his hands moved to my sides and brushed my breasts, "That is not my back you goose."

"Just wanted to be sure I got it all. Want me to do your chest too, it is red?"

"Nice try, now zip me back up."

He did but I guess decided I needed as few kisses back there first. "Anytime you need anything rubbed I am your man."

He was looking out onto the lake as I cuddled up next to him. "I have a boat maybe we could go for a ride before too long. We could cruise along the shore and you could see how really big this lake is. Would you like that?"

"I would like that very much I think I am part fish as I love to be in it or on top of it."

Daniel was still staring at the lake, "Do you know much about Lake Huron Sydney, if not you should go to the library and find out it is very interesting."

I told him I had thought about it and would do it soon.

The evening passed too quickly and I was starting to fall asleep on Daniels shoulder. "My dear you have a busy day go home and get some rest, I will see you tomorrow," he said as he helped me up and gave me a kiss.

–5–

THE DISCOVERY

Today I am going to check out the attic in the house, with any luck maybe I can find out more about this aunt of mine named Rose and see if she is the one that looks like me. The attic was at the end of the long hallway on the third floor. As I touched the knob I got a strange sensation and didn't know if it was good or bad. The door was a little stuck but with a quick bump I got it open, and of course it creaked. I turned on the light which was just a bulb hanging from the ceiling. The stage was set for a spooky haunted attic like in the movies, spider webs and all. But I was so surprised that the attic itself was lit reasonably well with the two quite large round windows on each side. I had to be a little careful because of the pitched ceilings but all I wanted do is just stand there and stare at a room full of the past, my families past. There were old trunks, furniture, clothes, and heaven knows what else. This is going to be such fun and I couldn't wait to get started.

A large trunk sat at my feet and I opened that first. It contained what I assumed was a wedding dress, very ornate with lots of buttons and lace. Faded but appeared in decent shape. Got me wondering whose it was. There were shoes in the bottom and undergarments as well as hankies and a lace shawl. Onward, I closed the lid and went deeper into the room. The furniture was very old but seemed to be all right. I would check it out later. There were so many trunks I didn't know which one to look into next. Several contained photo albums which again I will check out and take downstairs. Then I saw a bible on top of an old chest. It turned out to be a family bible and I was so excited when I opened the first page and saw all the names. This is definitely going downstairs. There were racks and racks of clothes all very old. Boy this would have been great to discover when I was a little girl–dress up. If someday I have a little girl this will be a fun place for us to play. Hat boxes were everywhere filed with wonderfully old fancy hats and sometimes gloves. Ornate mirrors hung on the walls along with pictures. Everything was totally covered in dust and I pretty much sneezed my way through the room. I gathered up the things I wanted to take down and decided that all I was going to do up here was dust. The past needs to stay right where it is for future generations to discover. I will come back and continue my adventure another time. Though a particularly sweet little rocking chair is going to be put somewhere in the house below.

I put all my treasurers in the parlor and picked up one of photo albums. Then sat in a comfortable chair by the windows and opened the first page, amazed that the photos were still pretty much visible but very yellowed. My very early family greeted me for the first time, such stoic gentlemen and demure sedate woman stared back at me. Always the man was in the big chair and the woman behind him with a hand on his shoulder. Some had children gathered around too. Most had names but some didn't. No one was smiling and I really wondered why, were their lives so hard that there was nothing to smile about or were they told not to. I have no idea. These pictures were portraits not action ones. I went through two more books which were slightly more up to date then I hit the jackpot. My first picture in the book was of Susannah holding baby Elizabeth in 1943. Then Elizabeth with baby Ophelia in 1945, and finally Ophelia holding baby Rose in 1956. Then there was a group photo of the four sister's in1954. Susannah had golden blond hair, Elizabeth had her curly red hair, Ophelia had a combination of the two, and little Rose had dark hair. A family picture was not dated but was probably taken shortly after the last one of the four girls. So these people were my grandparents. My grandmother Leona was very pretty with a beautiful flawless completion and curly red hair while my grandfather Thomas had dark hair and was tall and thin. All were smiling and seemed very happy. So this is Rose with the dark hair. Suddenly I was almost afraid to continue and find out what she looked like when she got older, but I did. It was hard to really tell what she looked like with all the action shots of the girls, they never seemed to look directly into the camera. As the girls grew older there were not as many pictures but in the last book I saw HER but HER was ME. I thought I was going to faint. It was a graduation from college picture and even though she had red eyes from the camera I could clearly see her. No wonder all these people think I am Rose come back from the dead.

I shut the book and leaned back in my chair as I tried to figure this whole thing out. Ok the logical explanation is that for some reason I turned out to look like my aunt instead of my mother, makes sense, but then why did Mr. Edgeworth say I resembled my mother. Maybe he was just mixed up and meant to say my aunt. There that must be it. But what is the big mystery, so what if I look like my Aunt Rose what does that have to do with Father's last words of 'look beyond the rose?' Does that mean I have to look beyond Rose, so what could be there, she was Rose my mother's sister that has to be all. Looks like I have trying to find something that really wasn't there in the first place. In a way I am disappointed but also relieved now I think I can put it aside and just live my happy life.

Just as I got up to put the books away it hit me, the sister's names, if you mix them up they spell ROSE–Rose, Ophelia, Susannah, and Elizabeth. That is how this place got its name, Rose House. How sweet, I wonder if it ever had a name before the girls came along. Maybe each sister planted their own rose bushes on each birthday or something. I can't wait to tell Daniel.

Then I saw the Bible but decided to wait on that, I had had enough for one day. Besides it was I am sure just the dates born and when they died. I do wonder why all my aunts died reasonably young though but that will be something I hope to discover later.

It was only noon so I thought I would go into Thumb Harbor

and treat myself to some lunch then go to the library and look up Lake Huron, as Daniel had suggested. First I had better clean up a bit I was full of dust and cobwebs.

As always it was a beautiful drive. There were quite a few more people wandering around the town, probably tourists I thought it is that time of year. I found a cute little café and went in. The room was full but lucky for me a man left right when I entered so I got a table by the window which overlooked the water. I sat down and looked around at my surrounding, bright red and white stripped walls were covered completely with pictures of boats and the lake. Along with an anchor, ships steering wheel and many more ships items–very nautical and nice. Lunch was so good, a big cob salad with a crusty roll and iced tea. Perfect. It was fun to watch the children down on the beach swimming and playing in the sand. One little boy was burying his sister, I assume, in the sand and both were laughing like crazy, while Mom soaked up the sun close by. When I left I saw a man selling ice cream cones and decided this would make a perfect ending to my meal. I got a mint chocolate chip double dip and did some window shopping as I explored the little town. Again like Sylerville there were ancient brick buildings and lots of little tourist shops, a florist, barber shop, the general store and finally the library. I sat outside under a big maple tree and finished my cone then headed in.

It was small but very cozy and I asked the gal at the desk for a good book on Lake Huron. She took me over to a rack full of them and pulled out one, "I think this is the best one." I sat down and began my learning adventure.

The melted ice from the last ice age formed this lake as well as the other four great lakes, the book said. I didn't know that. It was the first great lake to be discovered by the white man, who were French and named it Wyandot after the Indians who lived there. Lake Huron is part of the St. Lawrence Seaway, where large ships pass carrying limestone and grain from April to late December. It is connected to Lake Michigan by the Straits of Mackinac and the two lakes combined are the world's largest fresh water lake at 45,300 miles. Yikes, again

I did not know that. Lake Huron itself is the second largest great lake and fifth largest fresh water lake on earth, and has the longest shoreline of all the great lakes. There have been more than 1000 shipwrecks on Lake Huron and some are still underwater. Its length is 206 miles, breadth is 183 miles, and has a depth of 750 feet.

It was a fascinating discovery and I am so glad I went but it was getting a little late and I wanted to get home and play with the girls. Things have been so busy I am afraid they may feel a little neglected. We spent the rest of the afternoon chasing each other all over the massive yard and it was such fun. Finally it was time to make dinner, but just before I went in I laid down on the ground, which is always a signal for the dogs to "attack", which of course they did. They were all over me and I couldn't stop laughing. All of a sudden I heard, "Can I play too?" and Daniel lied down next to me. The girls went wild slobbering and jumping all over us both.

Finally they took off across the yard and I headed in, "I'm going to start dinner, only spaghetti but do you want some? I also handed him a towel, "Slobber clean up," I said.

"Sounds great, I'll give you a hand," he said as he followed me in. "What can I do?"

I got out an onion and asked him to cut it up. "When you are done could you please set the table? I have the sauce all made so all that is left is warming it up and starting the pasta. I will do the salad in a minute. Don't give me that, the woman is a slave driver look, you asked what you could do."

After dinner we sat outside in some lawn chairs talking. "Daniel I think it is time for me to redecorate the house inside, the outside looks so grand so should the inside but I don't know where to start. Sometime would you go through with me and give me your advice?"

"Sure but I don't know how much help I am going to be, how about tomorrow morning?"

"That would be great thanks." I was thinking if I could con him into helping then I would be able to see him more. Tricky.

The sun was setting and the sky was a million shades of

red and oranges. It was so special, then I remembered I did not tell him I went to the library. "Guess what I did this this afternoon, I went to Thumb Harbor and treated myself to lunch then wandered the streets a little and wound up at the library. I took your advice and checked out Lake Huron. Truly I was amazed at how much I didn't know. Have you lived here your whole life?" I asked.

'Yep, born and bred why?"

"Nothing just curious, it is such a beautiful place to live."

We sat there for a little while longer and Daniel said he was getting tired, big night last night, "Think I will head home, thanks for the dinner it was great!" He kissed me goodbye and was off.

The next morning we started our tour of the house with the parlor. The photo albums were still there and I realized I had not told him about my discoveries. "Before we get any deeper I want to show you something," I said as a reached for the album. I found the graduation picture of Rose and showed it to him.

"Oh I see you brought an album from home, is that when you graduated from law school? You were a knock out even then, but too bad your beautiful eyes are red."

Again I felt a little queasy, "Daniel that is my Aunt Rose, not me."

"My God Sydney, you look exactly like her. It's amazing!"

"I have to say it gave me quite a start when I saw it too." Then I told him about my theories; "I don't think it is that big of a deal that we look alike, just a coincidence, some kind of genetic thing." I also told him about the sister's names spelling out rose, thus the name of the house. "I am sure Mr. Edgeworth was just confused when he said I resembled my mother. So what is the big mystery of what my father said before he died? With all this I really don't think there ever was one. No wonder some of the people here in town got such a shock when they saw me and thought I was Rose back from the dead." Phew I was out of breath from talking so fast.

Daniel sat there for a minute absorbing what I said, "You

know you may be right about all this, now can you just go on and not worry about it anymore? Good."

The book got put away and I picked up my note pad and off we went through the house. I did not want to touch any of the beautiful wood trims and molding but was wondering if I should paint all the ceilings and crown moldings up there white so as not to break up the height of the ceiling. Daniel agreed.

"Are you going to keep the wallpaper or get it down and paint?" he asked and he looked at the walls.

"This poor wallpaper, really it needs either a good bath or get ripped off. It is too old looking but I don't know if I should get new paper or just paint it all. I don't want to change the integrity of the house but it sure needs brightening up, this whole place is too dark and gloomy. I wish I knew more about old homes like this."

"Well how about some paper and some paint, all new?" said the very wise ole guy.

I went over and gave him a huge hug, "That's it why I keep you around, aren't you the clever one."

"Well for more hugs like that I will do a little researching on interior design," he said laughing. "How's about another one just to get me more inspired?"

"Later, I want you to keep your mind where it belongs for now."

We finally figured out what walls were going to get what. "Ok what is the theme of it all, Victoria, seaside, anything but modern, the house would never forgive me?"

He rubbed his cheek contemplating I am sure but he did look very studious. "It is my learned opinion that again we decide individually what room needs what, like the parlor should be very formal and that should also go into the dining room to an extent. Now do I get another hug?"

"You bet you do professor, and maybe even a kiss if you take kisses from your student."

"I will make an exception this time, get over here."

This time through we decided what colors and styles would go where and I was bursting with excitement. "You know the only problem with all this is that I have to get someone in here to help me at least get all this paper down. I have done it before but nearly every room has it and I will be stuck in this house until the snow flies," I said with my most pitiful expression.

He pretended like he hadn't heard a thing for a minute or two. "Ok when do we start, you do realize this is going to cost you big in hugs and kisses. Just want to make that clear from the start."

"Oh my, the price I have to pay to get help these days, I guess I can sacrifice for the good of the house." With that he came at me like a raging bull and I took off for the kitchen, thank goodness the whole place was open from room to room or I would have been trapped. The sneaky bugger turned suddenly and headed me off straight on and tackled me. We both wound up on the floor, out of breath and laughing our heads off. "What am I going to do with you?"

"I have good idea," and he grabbed me. Our kisses were becoming more intense and leading to much more passion, then all of a sudden he said, "I think we had better get up and do something before this gets more serious, what would happen if Mom and Dad popped in for a visit and saw us down here on the floor in the dining room?"

"I wish we weren't right but I guess you are."

We sat holding each other on the floor. "Sydney, I will admit that I have had a couple relationships that I thought were serious but they were not love, it was just sex. I have never told a woman that I love her. After what my mother told me about the meaning of real love I vowed that from that moment on I was going to wait until I knew for sure that I truly did love the woman. Then share the ultimate love with her as my wife forever."

It was hard for me to speak but I finally said, "Daniel, you are the most expressive honest person I have ever met, it is so rare for a man to be so open. I admire you so much. To me I want a man who is my friend first, no complications no playing games just two people sharing their lives and having a good time, then see what develops. I have dated many men and did care about one in particular but I did not love him, the only thing we shared was a good friendship and a kiss at the end of a date. To be honest I have never been in love. Maybe I just didn't have, or make the time to give a relationship a chance with all my schooling and career. I too feel love and sex are very different, sex is too easy, giving yourself completely is a commitment, sharing forever something so special. Love, true love is precious and rare."

There was so much emotion between us I could hardly breathe. Finally Daniel smiled and helped me up then kissed my nose, "You are truly one of a kind and I am so glad. Can I come over for dinner tonight?"

"You are a true nut, so romantic always thinking about food. Of course you can, but beware I told the girls you are an ax murderer so you will probably get attacked."

"So what else is new?" Again with his wonderful smile.

As always we had a nice evening but Daniel left early, he said he had a bunch of meetings tomorrow with the city about new building codes and then is getting together with his crew to discuss what he learned through dinner, so he probably won't be over.

The next morning I called Edith and asked her where I could get some wallpaper for the house. "You are going to have to go to a larger city, there is nothing up here," she told me. "Probably down the coast to Port Shores, it's about a forty-five minute drive."

"Thanks, hey how would you like to get out of there for a while and come with me, I could use your advice on what to pick?"

"I would love that I haven't been anywhere in quite a while, I will treat us to lunch."

"How about today, it is still early?" She sounded excited and so was I. "Great, I will be right over."

I had forgotten how much fun it can be to go shopping with a friend, we chatted happily the whole way down. Port Shores was really quite a large city, lots of traffic and lots of stores. I was glad Edith knew her way around because I was totally lost. We arrived at the paint and wallpaper store and I was overwhelmed with all the choices. "Edith you had better call Eli and tell him you won't be home for at least a week this is going to take some time." We both laughed and she patted me on the arm for support.

I pulled out a list of the rooms I wanted to paper then asked her where I should start? "Why not go from front to back so the wallpaper will lead from room to room. Are you going to do it all in Victorian?"

"You know I have been thinking, I love traditional furniture but not sure if it would fit in a Victorian house. Do you think I could mix the two types of furniture? I do want to brighten up the place. I love the way you have done yours in the seaside style with the pastel colors but your house is like an old large farmhouse, and mine sure isn't. I think it is important to keep the integrity of the house but traditional is so much more comfy and cozy and I hope someday that this will be MY OWN family home. So what do you think?"

She seemed to think about it for a couple minutes then said, "My dear you can do anything you want that makes you feel comfortable, after all it is your home. So blend the two together and brighten the place up with the wallpaper and color of furniture, rugs, and the like."

The sales gal came over and asked if we needed any help. I told her what was going on and she said she deals with this a lot as there are so many older homes along the coast. She pulled out a few large books and suggested if I want say a blue and white traditional stripe why not make it a little fancier than just a clean cut stripe, that would fit in with the house yet give it a lightness. Perfect and we got to work.

The parlor paper will have a more formal look, so we started with more Victorian. I found a paper that had cranberry and light blue flowers with pale green leaves on a cream background. "Then I could put a solid cream area rug on the floor so the room won't seem too busy. That would flow into the dining room with this pale blue and light cream stripe that has a very thin, almost pencil thin edge of the cranberry between each stripe. The kitchen beyond will be painted in pale blue." I had thought of the cream again but the cupboards are all white and it would look washed out.

The music room is going to just be painted a pale green. The family living room has some wood wainscoting half way up that will be a cream color. The top half will have a muted pale green stripe wallpaper, the same green as in the music room, and a simple flower border at the ceiling. I almost forgot about the foyer, "What do you think Edith, paper or paint?"

"How about just a large Victorian style border at the top then painted cream or light gold walls below? That should make a statement, as they say," and she gave me her best lady of the manor hand wave. I started to laugh and couldn't stop.

"You have the grand lady of the manor wave down perfect, you should graduate to queen." Then she started laughing, and I am sure the salesperson thought we were nuts. "Before we start on the upstairs how about we break for lunch, my eyes are trying to pop out of their sockets and my brain has turned to mush?"

"Good idea, I know just the place and it is just down the street, we can walk there," she told me.

It was a delightful little restaurant that looked like it catered to women as it was painted a light pink with pale green accents. Also they had mostly salads and fancy desserts. We both got a mixed fruit salad with different kinds of nuts that turned out to be enough for about three meals but it was wonderful. There was a bread basket with homemade muffins and little chunks of warm bread and fresh butter. It took some doing because we were both stuffed but I convinced Edith to share a piece of their homemade cheesecake with strawberries on top for dessert. It was all so much fun, we giggled and laughed and shared a very special time.

Before we went back to work we wandered, or as Edith said we waddled down the street to check out the shops because we were so full. They had everything you could want and someday I am going to come back and really spend some time here. It was almost fun to be back in a larger town though I sure wouldn't want to live there again.

We finally got back to the wallpaper store and picked out the bedroom papers for the second floor. One room is going to be a light feminine flowered paper in different shades of pastel colors and another in more blue and white tones but no flowers. I wanted to leave one room just painted pale blue, just in case someday I have a baby boy. My room will have a pale blue background with soft cranberry and cream larger flowers. Each room will be different and special. I decided not to do anything with the third floor now, if it gets to the point of actually using the rooms it can be done then.

Our very patient sales gal wrote everything down and said she thinks it would be smart to send someone out there to measure to be sure we order the right amount of paper. "Are you going to do it yourself?" she asked.

"Well I am going to try but in case it gets to be too much do you have someone I can call on to finish it?"

"Yes just give me a call." Then she told me all the things I was going to need, like a putty knife to smooth it out, roller for the seams, wallpaper paste, razor blades, and on and on. "After everything is measured it will take about a week to get the paper in, we will call you as soon as it comes. Do you want to get some paint while you are here? It would help get things started and you might not feel up to it after you finish the wallpapering?"

I looked at Edith who was nodding her head. "Yes that is a good idea all I need is the pale green and blue and something for the foyer that is ecofriendly and doesn't smell too bad." I looked at the border we chose and picked a light creamy gold that matched the background. The gal mixed up my choices and told me what brushes I would need and we were done.

"Someone will contact you soon about the measuring," she said as we left.

"Time to go home I guess," I said to Edith, "it has been a long day and I don't know about you but I am tired."

"Me too but it sure was fun, I would love to come back with you to pick up the wallpaper, it is so good to get out of the house for a change."

That evening after the girls and I had just finished our dinners and I was cleaning up my cellphone rang, probably Gretchen I thought, but it was Edith. "Sydney is Daniel with you I have been trying to get ahold of him but he is not answering and I have left many messages to come home quickly?" She was sobbing so hard I could hardly understand her.

"No, what's happened you sound awful?"

"It's Eli he has gone crazy, he is shouting, swearing, throwing things, and doesn't seem to know who I am, please help me please."

"I will be there in a minute," I said as hung up and ran for the door.

I ran as fast as I could through the yard and to the gate then up to their house. Edith was just outside the door when I got there. It was hard to speak as I was so out of breath but I hugged her quickly, "Go back into the room and sit in a chair by the window and watch for Daniel, when he comes do not let him come into the room, tell him to stay in the hall. Then I want you to just sit there and knit, be calm and don't say a word. You will have to trust me in what I am going to say I have had a lot of experience with people who have dementia, which this could be as you said you think he might have some. Now go." I followed and when I got there Eli was still yelling and throwing books. Edith did as I told her to but looked terrified.

I saw Daniel arrive and run for the house out of the corner of my eye and Edith got up slowly to go to him. Then she returned and I walked over to Eli.

"Hello Eli," I said in a very calm voice, "it is me Sydney… Rose…from next door I came over to see if Edith could help me with my knitting, is she here?"

"No." he screamed at me. "I don't know where she is, why aint' she here?"

"Well if you don't mind I would like to wait for her, it would be nice to visit with you we haven't had much time to talk since I got here," I said as I got a little closer to him. I reached up to his hand that held the book, "Here let me put that down for you."

"No."

"All right then how about we sit here on the couch I have wanted to tell you how much I admire you for the way you have taken such good care of our property all these years."

He seemed to still be confused but I could tell some of the tension was leaving him as the book fell from his hand. "You have a real talent for landscaping and maybe someday you can give me some hints," I smiled then told him I was no good at it. Then I took his hand gently and did not say anything more for a couple minutes to try to give him a little time to process what I have been saying. "I am your friend Eli," again I smiled, "and very proud of it, can I help, you seem a little angry?"

"Mad, I mad at me, I wish I knew more, I hate these damn books, too many words, too late to learn more." and he started to cry.

"Eli it is never too late." and I put my arm around his shoulder, "I admire you for wanting to improve yourself and we are all here to help you, you are loved, you are safe."

"But I forget things and scared."

"We all forget things sir, and get confused, I know I sure do," I said and made a crocked smile. "Think about it, for many years you have been storing things in your mind and it is packed full, maybe your brain just doesn't think it is important to bring up that information right then. Who cares if you have to take a little more time to find the right words or remember something? It does not matter at all, you are you and that is why the people who know you love you."

"Do you love me?"

"Yes I do you are a very special man."

The storm was over and I was totally exhausted but I think I helped a little. Just as I was about to get up he hugged me and started to cry again. "Thank you...Sydney." I cried too as we hugged each other in quiet peace.

Finally I got up and took both his hands and helped him up too. "I think it is time for you to get some sleep dear friend." Then he looked over at Edith and seemed to see her for the first time who was crying too but his time tears of joy because she was smiling.

As he headed for the door he said, "Are you coming my dear?" She got up and then Daniel appeared in the door.

"Daniel help your mom and dad get up to bed they are very tired. I am going to leave now but will come back tomorrow morning." He tried to say something but seemed too choked up. I just squeezed his arm as I went past him and left.

As I walked across the dimly lit yard to my own I felt exhausted but happy, I think I helped at least for now. When I got home the girls were very glad to see me but seemed to sense I had been through a lot so when I put my pajamas on and got into bed they jumped up and snuggled next to me. Just their warmth and presence was all I needed right then and we all fell fast asleep.

First thing the next morning we were awakened by a knock on the door. I jumped up and opened the door, it was Daniel. "Damn you even look good with your hair all over the place and in you jammies," he said trying to make light. "Can I come in?'

"Of course but what are you doing up so early."

He looked at his watch, "It is ten o' clock."

"Oh goodness I really slept in. Let's get some coffee going."

Then he grabbed me and gave me a huge hug, "Sydney I have never seen anything like what you did last night for my father, there will never be enough words to tell you grateful we all are to you. How did you know just what to do?"

I grabbed for my robe and put it on as I said, "When I switched over to elder law I knew I would probably have to deal with people who have Alzheimer's and dementia so I took a bunch of classes, thank God. My first time using it to this extent was last night and I was terrified I would say the wrong thing, but somehow I kicked into professional mode and it just happened. Your father is a dear dear man and it hurt me so much to see him so distressed. No wonder he was throwing the books, he was very angry that he couldn't read them as well as he wanted to. I think it would be smart to get some help for him on that, yet not make him think they are actually doing it, which can be tricky–if I can help with that let me know. Also I think you should contact his doctor and tell him what happened. Maybe he could just stop by saying something like I haven't seen you in a while and just wanted to check up on you. He should be aware because I do think it is dementia. There are medications that he can take to slow the process but I have a lot of print outs that might help you and your family. I know right where they are, here. You and your mother read these carefully, I hope they help. Dementia is a very nasty disease for those that have it and the loved ones that are taking care of them. It is usually a slow process but you don't know how long he has had it. Be prepared, you are going to have to have patience like never before."

"My word, if I didn't know how much I cared for you before I sure do now, more than ever, you are something else."

We drank our coffee in silence then I got up and started making some breakfast. "Want some? Ok but don't think you can just show up every morning and expect me to give you free eggs," I said as I got out the fry pan.

When we finished I told him to get out so I could get cleaned up. "I will be over as soon as I can, how about a morning kiss for the cook?" Then he left.

About an hour later I was at their door and Edith hugged me so hard I could hardly breathe. "What a great greeting," I said with a big smile. "How was your night?"

We sat down and the couch and Edith smiled and said, "We slept so good for the first time in a long time and this morning Eli is Eli again. We talked a little about what happened and he actually wants to go see Dr. Winters, I think the whole thing really scared him. You were so warm and comforting to him and I love you even more than I did for just that. You truly are my daughter Sydney. Thank you so much for all you did!"

"Oh stop you are going to make me cry again, I love you too, you are my family now." Just then Eli appeared in the door.

He looked a little embarrassed but said, "Hello thank you for help last night, I just got confused and angry but you made me feel better," and being a man of few words he left.

We talked for about another hour then, "Edith I am going to go now but read the print outs I gave to Daniel I think they might help you all. If you ever need me anytime please call," I said as I got another crushing hug.

Later that morning I got a call from the wallpaper store, a man would be here tomorrow at nine o' clock if that is all right. "Yes, that is fine thank you," I said surprised they would be coming so soon.

He did come and spend almost two hours measuring and writing things down. His name is Ted and I would guess he is about as old as Daniel, nice enough looking but there was something about his eyes that bothered me. Just after he finished he commented on there being so much wallpaper to come down, "Are you going to do it yourself?"

"Well I had planned on it but this is very old paper and I am not sure if will come down easily like the newer kind does, do you happened to know?"

"I am also the wallpaper removal man for the store and I can tell you it can be very hard, depending on how many layers of paper there are. Generally in a house of this age there will probably be many. Do you mind if I try a little area say in the parlor near the floor?"

"No, go ahead," I said feeling a little sick to my stomach. I never thought about layers of paper.

He got down and with his finger scrapped up a little of the paper. "It looks like about three layers. You are going to have to do a lot of spraying with hot water and scraping. Then the new stuff has to be put back up. This is going to be a big job. If you decide you want some help give me a call," he said as he handed me his card. "I can have several men in here to give me a hand and we should be able to do it all in maybe two or three weeks, depending on what we run up against." Then he gave me a quote and said he would give the measurements to the store owner and they will call me when it comes in.

After he left I started thinking about all this, the price was a little high but it sure would save me a lot of effort, and what if by the time I finally got it all off I was too exhausted to put the new paper up and the poor walls just sat there for God knows how long? It could be a very long time before I could move in and I really would like to do that soon. Hopefully while the new paper is being put up I could live in there but again it would be a wreck and everything would have to be put away at night so the girls could come in. I am going to think about this very seriously.

I did think and finally called the store and asked if Ted, the measuring guy could remove all the wallpaper in the house. I explained that he talked to me about it when he came and gave me a quote. "I will speak to him, no wait a minute he just walked in let me ask him now. Ted said he would be happy to do it and is not busy right now so he could start as early as tomorrow at say nine o'clock if that is all right with you."

I was so surprised, "Yes that would be great I look forward to it thank you." We hung up and I did a little spin around the room, this is wonderful everything is working out so well and so fast.

I called Edith with the good news and she was excited too, "That is great Sydney I was worried about you having to do all that work by yourself."

"Well to be honest I asked Daniel if he would help and he said yes but I have felt guilty ever since. Maybe he will help with putting the new stuff up if he doesn't have to take the other stuff down. You did a good job with him Edith he is a very good man."

"Yes he is and we are so proud of him. It has been so nice to have him here this summer, but I hate it when he leaves in the fall for some new building project somewhere in the state. Oops gotta go my bread is done in the oven. Take care and thanks for letting me know your good news. I really had a good time with you the other day. Bye."

Oh my, I had totally forgotten that Daniel will only be here for the summer, how sad but I guess I am going to have to deal with that when the time comes.

Isn't Daniel going to be surprised when I tell him my good news, hopefully he will come tonight. He did come over and I told him all that has been going on and he said, "Ted is a good man I know him quite well but he sure has a thing for the ladies so be on your guard. Oh he is not going to attack you but I have seen him in action and he is a big flirt."

"Strange, when he was here he was just fine, maybe I am not his type. Thanks for the warning though I will try not to wear my low cut tank tops while he is here." I was only kidding but the look on his face said he was not amused.

He put his arm around me, "Sydney you are a beautiful woman and are here by yourself you need to be careful."

"Daniel I lived in Atlanta forever and worked long hours at my law office and sometimes didn't leave until late at night. My father insisted I take a course in Karate, which led to three more courses, I am not too worried. In other words don't sneak up on me in the dark," I said as I raised my arms ready for battle.

"Ok and thanks for the warning, but still be careful ok? I think I may be spending even more time around here while he is working do you mind?"

"You are kidding right, of course I don't mind, bring your knitting and we can spend our time out in the rockers on the porch."

"You know you really are a very mean woman, why didn't I see this before, now come here and give me a good night kiss."

"Enough kisses, how is your dad doing?"

He pretended to look like a sad little puppy but said, "He is back to his old self but seems a little more relaxed than he was, I think the attack he had shook him up but made him admit to himself that he does have a problem and I think he actually might get some help."

"I am so glad, but I do think that if he tries to improve a bit of his speech difficulty it will give him more peace of mind and hopefully feel better about himself, it seems this has been bothering him for a long time."

True to his word Daniel was over first thing in the morning, only it was a little too first thing. He banged on the door at eight o'clock and I had just gotten out of the shower and dressed, thank goodness, but my hair was soaking and I had no makeup on. "Ok," I said, as I opened the door, "this is the real me, wet hair and au natural, no makeup, turn around and run while you can. Stop grinning and get in here, want some breakfast, yea I know stupid question. Sit down and tell me about your meetings, did you get everything done you wanted to?"

Daniel landed with a thud in what he calls his favorite chair, "Yes I want to eat, and yes I got everything done, and no I am not going to run anywhere though it is quite scary," he said as he dodged the loaf of bread that I threw at him.

"Why are you here so early, Ted won't be here until nine, afraid he will show up early and have his way with me before he even gets into the house?"

He looked quite serious, "No but I think it's smart to have him see me around at all times of the day so he will have a harder time figuring out when to plan his seduction. Now stop chattering and sit down here and eat."

Ted and his crew arrived right on time and seemed surprised to see Daniel there. "How are you doing, I haven't seen you in quite a while, still building houses?" he asked as he shook his hand.

"Yes, and things are picking up finally. I didn't know you did wallpaper removing, last I heard you were a painter."

Ted started getting his supplies off the back of his truck, "Things have been slow for me too that dumb recession really messed things up so I branched out a couple years ago."

Daniel went over to help him and I heard him say, "The guys and I just finished restoring the outside of this old house, now Sydney wants the inside to match. Glad you could help. I will be around so if you need more help just ask."

All I could think was hint hint. Then to top it off he put his arm around me and asked how his family is. Marking his property was all I could think of. Well guess what Daniel I am no one's "property." I went over to Ted and thanked him for coming so soon and asked if he minded if a watched for a little while? As we headed for the house Daniel whispered in my ear, "Stop being so nice." I turned toward him and gave him a look that I hoped would speak volumes, knock it off.

Ted and the men moved the furniture to the center of the room or put it in another room then put plastic tarps over the floor and furniture. All the equipment was ready to go–a steamer, putty knives, rollers, razor blades and many spray bottles–each man took a different room and they began. It turned out that in the parlor and dining room there were four layers of old paper and only three in the music and living room. I was glad I could watch as I might have to do this some time. Daniel just sat on the front porch sulking. As I got out there my cellphone rang, it was Edith, "Hi Sydney is Daniel with you?"

"Yes he is right here do you want to talk to him, is everything all right?" I asked as Daniel looked up at me a little alarmed.

"Oh yes everything is fine, it's just that it is such a beautiful day I decided to have lunch outside and was hoping you two would be able to come over. I know the wallpaper people are there but I am sure they won't need you."

"That sounds wonderful when do you want us? Ok we will be there in an hour. Thanks."

We did go over and it was so nice to sit outside under their huge old maple tree and stare at the lake as we ate, plus of course I loved spending time with Eli and Edith. Eli was quite talkative and it made me so happy. "I am reading a book on grammar, and feel like a kid again. I like it," he said with great pride I could tell by his smile.

"That's wonderful if you need any help call me, not that I am that great at it but maybe between the two of us we can figure it out." That seemed to please him.

"Ok that a deal," he said smiling.

We chatted about all kinds of things and Edith asked Daniel when he was going to put his boat in, "Very soon I hope we are getting toward the end of June and I usually have it out in May. I am going to take my fishy friend here," he said as he looked at me, "out for a spin, she said she loves the water."

"Are you going to enter any of the races this year?" his mother asked.

He seemed to think about for a minute then said, "No I don't think so. Stop looking so sad Dad I know I do it almost every year but not this year. I will think about it a little more though."

"Please tell me about the boat races," I asked as I leaned forward to Daniel.

"Oh it is not that big of a deal the people living along the coastline get together and race from Sylerville up about fifteen miles. Then there is a big picnic afterwards for all the families on the beach. It is usually held on the weekend after the fourth of July. Say Mom are the guys and their families going to be here for the fourth this year it is coming up very soon?"

"I have heard from Steve and Scott and they are coming but Michael and John are still trying to work things out. I guess their kids have so many things going on this year. Wouldn't it be wonderful if we could all be together for a nice long weekend?"

I turned to Edith, "I would love to know more about your son's."

She reached into her pocket and pulled out some pictures she said she had just gotten and was going to show us today. "Here is Steve, he and his wife Michelle have three sons– ten, twelve, and fifteen. They really keep them on their toes. Let's see Steve is thirty- seven, right Eli?" He nodded. "Then this is John, he is a furniture maker and is forty and has one child, Adam who is twelve. His wife Janet didn't get into the picture but she is a stay at home mom. Michael is the oldest he is forty- four and is a foot doctor. He and Lori have four sons. Then Scott is a school teacher in on the western side of the state. Scott and Penny have three boys; he and John are twins so he is forty also. Then came Daniel, he is the youngest, by the way are you thirty-two or thirty-three now dear?"

"Thirty-two Mom," he said and rolled his eyes around.

Now I know where Daniel got his silly little evil eye thing

from, Eli gave me one and asked, "How old are you Sydney? If you tell me I will tell you."

"I am twenty-eight; now let me guess you must be about thirty Eli, with all your energy, though how your kids got older than you I can't imagine."

With that he threw back his head and roared with laughter, "I like you Sydney." We all laughed and had a very nice time.

Daniel said we had better get back to the house and see how they are doing. Really I just wanted to sit there for the rest of the day it was so pleasant but he was right we should check. "Ok but first I am going to get a little mushy so be prepared. Thank you both for such an enjoyable time and of course your wonderful lunch Edith, but most of all thank you for being my family. I love you all."

"Even me?" asked Daniel, and gave me his pitiful puppy look.

I stood up and walked around the table to where Daniel was sitting and rubbed the top of his head, "Especially you," I said looking down at him as adoringly as I could, "I have a soft spot for sweet little puppies who wear pink bows on their heads." Then I took off running like crazy across the lawn. It took about two seconds for the pursuit to begin. I made it half way to the gate before I got tackled and we both wound up face down in the grass. Then he started tickling me and I laughed until my stomach hurt. "You are better stop unless you want to see what I had for lunch." We just laid there laughing and it was so good. I looked up and saw Edith and Eli standing there watching us, both were laughing as Eli held up a napkin that read 10. "Guess we should try out for the Olympics your dad just gave us a 10."

"My folks are crazy about you girl, I hope you know that," he said after we finally got up and headed back.

"Well we are even because I am crazy about them too, I really do love them." I said as I put my hand in his. "This was such a fun afternoon."

Daniel said he left some papers on the table and went back to get them, all of a sudden I heard, "Danny baby is that you?"

BEYOND THE ROSE

as this gorgeous blond came running across the yard. She jumped into his arms and started kissing him, "Oh my I have missed you."

Right then I decided it might be a smart idea to find out what was going on so I slowly made my way back.

Now she was standing in front of him rubbing herself against him and grabbing his butt, "Boy I have missed you, can we go someplace and I will show you how much?"

I sat down next to Edith, "So who is the blond Barbie?"

"Oh God that is Katrina, she and Daniel were a couple at one time, but thankfully not for very long. I had hoped we were done with her."

Eli looked uncomfortable and a little angry, "Good God she is back."

Daniel seemed to be trying his best to peel her off of him but was not having much luck. He turned around and saw me and came over. "Sydney this is Katrina Majors and old friend of mine. Katrina, this is Sydney Armstrong."

"Old friend huh?" and she put her hand under his shirt, "we were a little more than that Danny baby. So this is your new catch of the day huh, you are a lucky girl Sydney, he sure is something else huh especially in bed, he just never seemed to be able to get enough of me," she said as she flipped her long blond hair back.

Edith was furious, "Katrina I think you had better leave, you have caused us all enough grief."

"But Eddie, you know the only reason I left was that I had a new modeling job in LA otherwise I would have a ring on my finger by now. Right Danny?"

I could tell Daniel had had enough and picked her up and threw her over his shoulder and walked down to the beach and tossed her into the water. "Cool off Katrina then get out of here, you my dear are not welcome."

She got up and if looks could kill Daniel would have been dead. "Shit, if you weren't so good in bed I never would have even given you a second look. Good luck Sydney, you are next in line to get dumped." Then she went back to her car.

"My, what a delightful woman," I said, "she sure makes a good first impression, do you supposed I could catch her and knock a few teeth out of her head?"

"Sydney!" said Eli, "didn't know you had it in you, good for you." Daniel just laughed.

I must have blushed but finally said, "Sorry all, but I just remembered that I have seen that delightful creature a long time ago, I guess she forgot too. I happened to open the door when she came to see my father. She wanted him to take her case, something to do with her not getting the dressing room she was promised. I heard her yelling at my father before she even shut the door to his office. He just laughed and escorted her out the door as she was swearing her head off."

"Boy Daniel you sure can pick um. Any more sexy skeletons in your closet I should be aware of?"

"God I hope not, I am really sorry Syd, Mom and Dad too. I thought I had gotten rid of her a long time ago. This was embarrassing."

"Ok let's get back to the house. Again sorry for my outburst it even surprised me."

Edith got up and hugged me, "My dear if I had thought of it I would have offered to do it too." Then she smiled.

On the way back I couldn't help but say a few hundred more little jabs. "So you are king of the bedroom huh my man?" Then I patted his butt and gave it a good grab and started laughing.

"Would be glad to show you my many skills anytime just give me a holler." Of course I hollered. "Boy are you in trouble now," and he picked me up and took me into the woods laid me down in the leaves and started kissing me, then grabbed my bottom, "turn-about is fair play, hum I could get used to this."

"You know maybe it might be a good idea if you showed me your talents later or the workers are going to get a great half time show," I said and giggled.

"You are really a nut my girl."

"You too Danny baby," and I flipped my hair over my shoulder.

"Come on you naughty woman let's get back to the house."

The guys were making some progress but had a long way to go. I was wondering just how long but I guess it is one of those it takes as long as it takes things.

The next morning I got on my grubbiest clothes and grabbed the brushes and blue paint and headed for the house. The guys were already there and I asked Ted if it was all right if I started painting in the kitchen, would that interfere with his work. No, good. The color was perfect and I was so excited. It surprised me that I had made so much progress in the couple hours I worked so I decided to take a little break and go out on the porch. It was a cloudy day but no rain yet but still the view of the lake was wonderful. Just then Daniel appeared on the steps. He gave me a long thorough look, "My you didn't have to dress up for me, how stunning you look, though I think you should button up your shirt a couple more toward the top you sexy thing."

"Sit down and shut your mouth, I have been painting the kitchen, guess what color?" Then I unbuttoned one more button.

"Blue, unless your fancy jeans were used the last time you painted. Let me go see" and he reached for my shirt and redid the button. "Not smart to get the workers all turned on my girl."

He stood there looking all around, "You know you are doing a great job I love the color, keep up the good work." In other words I don't want to paint. Fine with me I am having a great time. He said he had another meeting to go to and left.

By noon the room was done and I stood there staring at it for a long time, very proud of myself. I hope my relatives are looking down and are proud of me too. Tomorrow I will put the next coat on.

In just under two weeks Ted and his crew had worked wonders and were done with the first floor, so I was able to paint the music room and foyer as well and they looked so clean and renewed. I told him how pleased I was that things were moving along so quickly and said I knew he used to do a lot of painting but is he still at it? "Yes do you need more done?"

"Well the ceilings are so high and I have no idea how I would be able to paint them, all of them need it plus the crown moldings up there, could you do that too when you are done?"

"Sure what color? Just off white would be good."

"Perfect thanks, one more thing off my list."

My cellphone started ringing and it was Daniel, "Tomorrow is Saturday how about we go for a boat ride? I just got the old girl in today."

"Thanks I would love that." Oh boy a day of just having fun.

Right after Daniels call my phone rang again. It was Mr. Edgeworth and I was really surprised I hadn't heard from him since our move. "Hello Sydney, I hope you are well and you have adjusted to your new surroundings. I just wanted to tell you that your father's estate has settled and that I will be depositing a sizeable check in your account on Monday."

"Thank you, it will come in very handy right now. The money I got from the sale of the old house is helping with my renovations on this house, but the way things are going I might need some more. The outside is done and a crew is working on the inside now, we have been living in the cottage. It has been a lot of work but the house looks wonderful. If you like I can send you a picture, and yes I have adjusted well and made many new friends. I do feel right at home here."

"I am pleased and would appreciate a picture, I haven't seen the place in many years but it did need a lot of work then. Please do call me if you need anything. Goodbye."

What a stuffy man, I thought to myself. He needs to get out and have some fun but I don't think he even knows how to spell the word or what it means.

Well the rain that had been trying valiantly to fall did the next morning so we decided to wait until the next day to go boating. We were both disappointed.

"Oh Daniel what a beautiful boat what is it about fifteen feet?" I asked as he helped me aboard.

"Think that is about right, glad you like her. If you are

good little girl I will let you steer later. Here put on your life jacket."

He revved up the engine and we were off. What a thrill to be flying across the water, it has been a long time since I have been out in any boat. The weather was perfect as we cruised along the thumb area. There were wonderful lighthouses and many people out on their beaches who always waived at us as we passed by. What fun.

"Want to steer?" he said as he motioned me over.

"Oh I am not too sure," I said from the back of the boat, "what if I ram into a tree or something?"

He rolled his eyes around and said, "How can you hit a tree out here on the lake you goose?"

"Well when I hit the shore there is bound to be a tree close by." I said almost kidding.

"Ok so at least come up here, I will guide your hands and you can at least help a little. But be careful walking up."

I gave him a mock salute and said, "Aye aye my caption." It turned out to be quite fun and I did try it by myself about a minute and a half. "Think I will let you drive, could you please put up your tarp thing, I'm hot? Thanks that's better."

A short time later he turned off the engine, "How about some lunch I am getting hungry, Mom packed one for us?"

I was more than ready too and it was delicious. We just floated around and watched the other boats that passed us by. Then Daniel asked if I wanted to do a little fishing. "Don't we need a license?" I asked as I got my legs out of the water.

"Yes but I have a family one so if we get caught just say you are my wife or sister, you can choose," he said with an evil smile.

"Thanks brother, let's fish." We did and I flipped my legs back over the railing. All of a sudden my line went crazy and I felt like I was going to get pulled into the water, "Daniel help I got a big one."

"Wow you sure do, reel him in, here let me help. Get your legs out of the water or he might pull you right over."

I hoped he was kidding but the longer I reeled the harder

it got. Finally the biggest fish I have ever seen almost jumped into the boat. "What is it?" I asked as I rubbed my sore arms.

"It's a Lake Trout the biggest one I have ever seen. Good going you are a true fisher lady to land this monster. Guess what I am going to cook you for dinner for maybe the next week? How about we ask Mom and Dad to come and join their kids?" Another silly grin, "What do you want to do now?"

"Go home, I'm pooped."

That night we had a big cookout on the beach and Eli and Edith did join us. I was a little late getting down there as I fell asleep after all the sun and surf. Just as I was leaving I thought it would be fun to make up two slings from scarves and put my sore arms in and give everyone a good laugh. I was not disappointed they took one look and roared. Daniel did the honors and MY trout was delicious. It was a fun night. Just as we were getting ready to go home Edith got a phone call. "You sound upset Michael what is wrong, oh my, well Daniel is right here you can speak to him now," she said as she gave him the phone.

"What's up, you're kidding? I will come down tomorrow and check it out. You're welcome see you then," and he hung up. 'They are getting water in their basement from the ceiling above but can't figure out where it is coming from so I will have to go down and check it out."

After the folks left Daniel gave me a kiss and said he would get back as soon as he could. "I'll miss you." I told him to be careful and I would miss him too.

About three days later I got a call that my wallpaper was in and Edith and I headed down to   Port Shores. I put the boxes in the van and asked Edith if there were any furniture stores here. "I would like to just see what is available when everything is done, are you game?"

"Sure, about three I think, but first could we get some lunch I am hungry?"

"Of course sorry I haven't been paying attention to the time." This time we went to a restaurant that Edith said had wonderful cooked on the grill hamburgers. The place was packed with people but it only took about ten minutes before we got our table. Very interesting décor, like out of the old west, with the servers dressed up, even a chuck wagon held the salad bar.

After we ordered I asked Edith if she had heard from Daniel, "Well he called just before we left and said he hopes to be back tomorrow, it turned out the water leak was coming from the roof and he had to fix it by himself though it was more work than he had expected. Oh he said to say HI to you, I'm sorry I forgot all about it."

"No problem. I hope they bring our food soon, my stomach is starting to growl from smelling the burgers cooking." Almost immediately we had our meal and it was delicious. "We have to come back here again, this really is the best hamburger I have ever had, thanks for bringing us here Edith."

"You are welcome, now, how about we wear some of this off and check out some furniture?" and we both got up.

We hit all three stores and I was very pleased with what I saw, it shouldn't be too hard to get what I want when the time is right.

The next morning I couldn't wait to take my new paper up to the house. Maybe I could even start so I brought my supplies also. The guys were already there and I went up first to check on them. Ted smiled when he saw me and I told him I got the new paper. "By the way," he asked, "do you have a ladder tall enough to get up to the ceiling?"

Good heavens I didn't even think about that, "I am going to have to look around and see if there is one." Luckily there was off the back of the cottage. I dragged it up and into the house and set it in the parlor just as Ted came down the stairs.

"You should have asked me to get it, I am sure the thing is very heavy, they made stuff to last forever way back," he said as he went over to it, "this should do fine. I will be here for another few days so if you decide to start and need help just call."

"Thanks so much I will." He is such a nice guy I don't know why Daniel is so concerned. Well I do now. The guys all left at about four and Ted stayed on to finish what he was doing. I was out on the porch enjoying the view and he asked if he could sit down. "Sure, you guys are really doing a good job it sure saved me a lot of time."

"Since you are pretty new here would you like to go out to dinner some night and I could show you some sights?"

The alarm bells started to go off in my head, it sounded innocent enough but something told me to be very careful. "Daniel and I are seeing each other and I don't think that would be a good idea but thank you."

"Well as the old saying goes, 'what he doesn't know can't hurt him' so let's set up a day."

I got up to leave and he grabbed my arm, "Come on honey let's have some fun. We have this big house all to ourselves and like it or not you are going in there with me now," and he tried to kiss me.

I started hitting him as he reached for my blouse and started ripping the buttons open. "Oh how beautiful," he said as he stared at me, "I love you Sydney let me show you how much. I don't want to hurt you stop fighting," then he started putting his hands all over me.

I still can't believe what happened next; I kicked him in the shins, punched him in the throat and flipped him over all in seconds. I turned and looked down at my feet where Ted was sprawled out then I ran screaming at my girls to follow me. They came running barking like crazy. I made it to the gate, too afraid to look back and see if Ted was following me, got through and ran. I saw Edith and Eli out on their patio and started screaming, "HELP PLEASE HELP ME PLEASE!"

They came running, Eli got to me first and I fell into his arms. "Oh God help me he is going to get me, HELP ME PLEASE!" Edith caught up and cried out when she saw my clothes were torn. Just then I heard Daniel.

"Hey where is everyone I am home?"

"Daniel," I said almost in a whisper then I fell to the ground sobbing.

Edith screamed at him, "DANIEL GET DOWN HERE

HURRY SOMETHING HAS HAPPENED TO SYDNEY!" I looked up and saw him running then I fainted.

He was kneeling down beside me, 'Sydney honey wake up please wake up." I grabbed him and held on with all my might.

"My God what happened to you?" I guess he just realized my clothes were torn and took off his shirt and put it on me.

Edith told him to carry me up to the house, which he did and laid me down on the couch. I was screaming, "Please don't let him get me, over and over. Stop it don't touch me. Daniel where are you help me…."

Edith said to call Dr. Winters now. Eli did and told us he would be right over. "Edith my chest hurts," she opened Daniels shirt and started to cry.

"My dear you are scratched up pretty bad, now just rest."

She covered me with a blanket and held me tight, "The doctor will be here soon."

I could hear Daniel in the background, he sounded hysterical. "Dad what happened?" Then he went over to me and took my hand. "I am here Syd you are safe."

Right then Dr. Winters came. Since no one knew what happened they couldn't tell him and right then neither could I. I felt so strange, I could hear and see everything that was going on but I couldn't respond. He came over to me and took my hand, "Hi Sydney it is Dr. Winters, do you think you can tell me what happened? Edith she has had a bad shock, something very serious happened to her tonight, let's just stay with her and reassure her that all is well and give her time to tell us."

Edith pulled back the blanket that was covering me. "Look at this."

I heard him gasp, and then Daniel and Eli ran over and looked too, "Oh my God!" they both said.

"She has been attacked," said the doctor, "and with the condition of her clothes I would say this was I hope only an attempted rape. Call the police now." Eli started swearing and got up and phoned.

Then he cried, "Edith, my dear are you all right?" I guess she fainted and Dr. Winters went over to help her.

"Folks I am going to stay here until we find out what happened. Please sit down and try to relax, Sydney will tell us when she can."

"Daniel," I whispered, "are you there?"

"Oh Syd, I am here my love." Then I guess he realized what he had just said and looked over at everyone. "Ok I said it; it is true I love this woman."

"Daniel, it was Ted. He... he told me he wanted to have some fun... and said like it or not he was going to take me... into the house. When I refused he... grabbed...me... started ripping my blouse...like he was...frantic. Oh God help me, don't let him hurt me please help me! Stop it Ted stop it!"

"Syd relax you can tell us later." Daniel said.

"No I have to tell, he stared at my chest and said ...how... beautiful ...and that he loved me...and wanted to...show...me how...much... he...didn't want...to hurt me. I was not to... fight him, and then he started touching me... all...over. Daniel, I was so scared and I felt so sick to my stomach. I was... desperate so I used Karate to get him...off me. I kicked him in the shins, punched him...in the throat... then flipped him over. Then I ran for the... gate and...called for Eli and Edith. Oh God I was so scared...he would run after me. Hold me please. Did you say you love...me?" All of a sudden I started shaking violently and sobbing. Dr. Winters said he was going to give me a sedative but said it might not work very well because I was so upset. Then he just sat there and held my hand.

Daniel looked furious, "I am going to kill that man!"

"Daniel, we are here and we heard everything." Daniel went over to the men and shook their hands and thanked them both for coming so quickly. I was told later that they were policeman and Daniel knew both of them. He motioned for them to sit down. The officer named Mark said there had been another complaint against Ted from a woman who had contracted him to so some painting for her but she never filed actual charges. "I wonder how many others there have been that never called us?"

"Mark, I have known Ted for a long time and never saw this

side of him, though I know he likes the ladies. I just thought he was a harmless flirt. I feel awful that I didn't see this coming and put Sydney in danger. What do we do now?"

The officer asked us to go to the station and file a formal complaint tomorrow then they would start investigating. "Tonight we are leaving a man here on the grounds. When you return I want you all to stay here, let your dog's run free if Ted decides to come the dogs will let you know. Of course call us if anything else happens. I do not think you are in real danger but I don't know, just be careful," he said as he shook his head. "Better yet it might be a good idea to have all the dogs in the house tonight just in case."

Mark came over to me and said, "Sydney I am so sorry but thankful you are all right, do not worry we will get him." And they left.

"Edith, Sydney is going to need to stay here with you all for a few days at least and I think she should go to bed now and try to get some sleep. I will go up with you and treat her chest wounds," said the doctor.

Daniel picked me up and asked which room he could put me in, "Go to Michaels." He gently laid me down on the bed then kissed me on the cheek and left. "Wait Daniel, honey Sydney is going to need something to sleep in do you have a clean T shirt, it would be soft and not hurt her scratches." He left and came back with one. "Now go."

Edith removed my torn shirt then covered me the best she could with a sheet. Dr. Winters washed the cuts and dressed them then helped Edith get the T shirt on me. "I am going to leave now but if you need me tonight just call. Sydney you are a brave girl, you are safe now so try to sleep," and he patted my hand.

"Thank you Doctor," I said and shut my eyes.

My dreams were terrifying Ted was attacking me over and over and I started screaming. All of a sudden Daniel was there, "Syd Syd, are you all right?"

"Oh I am sorry I didn't know I had screamed out loud I was dreaming and Ted was attacking me again," and I started to cry.

Then Eli and Edith were there too. Again I said I was sorry for waking everyone up. "I am so scared that he is going to come in here and get me."

"Mom can I please sit in here tonight with Syd, maybe that would help?" asked Daniel.

She looked a little uneasy but said yes, "No funny stuff got it, Sydney would that be all right with you?"

"Yes and don't worry I won't seduce him," then I smiled. Everyone looked relieved.

"She is coming out of this thank goodness," said Edith, "Ok you two get some sleep," and she kissed us both.

My dreams continued and I woke up again a couple times but it did help that Daniel was always there. When I woke up in the morning he was lying next to me on top of the covers holding me close. Just then Edith popped her head in and saw us. Daniel was still asleep and I looked over at her and smiled, pointed to him and whispered, "Not my doing, I have no idea when he came up here."

"Daniel wake up," said his mother. He did and looked a little surprised at the whole situation.

"Mom I didn't do anything, Sydney was screaming again and I just sat on the edge of the bed then I guess I laid back and fell asleep. Sorry."

She smiled and told him to get up. He sat up and gave me a quick kiss, "Next time you want to seduce me you had better plan it more carefully and not do it with my mom in the next room."

I wacked him on the arm and smiled. "So you are going to blame this whole thing on me huh, get out of my bed you naught boy."

Edith just stood there with a huge grin on her face. None of us saw Eli behind Edith, "What in the world is going on?" he asked.

"Nothing special Dad, Mom found me in Sydney's bed and I was just explaining that in the night Sydney decided to seduce me and I fought it, but she finally won. Really I will explain later."

"Does anyone mind if I have a say in all this?" I asked. "The only person I want in my room now is Edith, everyone else out."

When they left Edith came over and hugged me. "How are you feeling my dear? We were so worried about you last night."

"My chest is very sore and my dreams were awful but mentally I am doing much better. I am sorry about Daniel being in the bed but really I didn't even know he was there. Edith did he really tell me he loved me or was I just so messed up I thought he did?"

"Yes he did Sydney, and I know he meant it, I have seen the way he looks at you and have known for a long time. I think it is wonderful. So tell me how do YOU feel about him, if I may ask?"

I smiled and took her hand, "Edith I have loved him since the first day I met him, he gives me such joy and is such a nut. We have not said anything to each other about this but one day he told me what you had said about how precious love really is and he said because of that he wants to only share that kind of love with the one woman he spends the rest of his life with. I know I shouldn't be telling you all this but your words made a huge impression on him and I think you should know that."

There were tears in her eyes, "Oh Sydney thank you for sharing this with me, sometimes it is hard for a mother to know if she has made a difference. I will never tell him what you said I promise. Is there something else, you look a little uneasy?"

I decided I needed to confide in her, "Edith I do need to talk about something quite personal, I hope you don't mind, but I have no mother but you, do you mind?"

"Of course not, I am so proud to know that you really do think of me as your mother."

"Last night when Ted attacked me it was even more traumatic than everyone thought it was for me. You see I have never made love to a man; I have never even been in love until now with Daniel. And when Ted attacked me all I could think about was if he raped me he would be my first and that terrified me. I only wanted to give myself completely to the man I love, my husband. And the thought of being forced was too much I..." Then I started to cry.

She held me tight and said I was so special, "There are not many women left that feel the way you do. You are really something else Sydney and I am proud you chose me as your mother. Now when are you going to tell my Daniel how you feel about him?"

"When the time is right I will know. I do wonder if he just said it to me because he was so concerned last night, I am not too sure."

Edith got up and said she would help me get dressed then, "Oh no my dear he does love you I have no doubts." Then she smiled and kissed my cheek. "Hey you have nothing to wear, do you mind just wearing Daniels T shirt until we can get some clothes from the cottage, you do look cute in it?"

"A little casual but it does feel good on my chest. You know what I am hungry could you please get me a muffin or something?"

"I can do better than that come downstairs and I will make us all breakfast, but you are not to help just keep me company."

The men were already down there and Daniel took one look at me in his T shirt and of course had a comment, "My goodness you sure fill out that shirt better than I ever could," and got a look from his mom. "Well she does, so how are you this morning girl, you look tired but much better, probably because you got to sleep with me."

My turn, "Daniel you are really awful. After breakfast could you please go down and get me some real clothes?"

The breakfast tasted wonderful and I thanked Edith. "I just don't know how to thank you all for what you did for me. If you hadn't been there I just don't what would have happened, I..." and the tears started up once again. "I'm sorry I guess I am still shook up."

After we ate I gave Daniel a list of the things I wanted at the cottage and he said he would go right down and get them. "Want your knitting too?"

"Yes good idea thanks."

Mark appeared just then; he was out on the patio and knocked on the window. Eli let him in, "Any news yet, did you catch the bastard?"

"Sorry but not yet, we will keep a man here until we do though. How are you feeling this morning Sydney, I am so sorry this had to happen?" I told him I was better and thanked him. Daniel said he was going to go down to the cottage in a minute and asked him to come so they could talk more.

"Oh could you please lock up the house I left everything open, and put the rockers inside for safe keeping? If Ted comes back for revenge I..."

When the two men got back they looked very upset. Eli asked what happened and Daniel told me to go out on the patio and get some sun and visit with the dogs for a minute. "No way buster what is going on?"

Daniel looked at Mark, "All right tell her."

"Sydney when we got to the door Ted had written 'I love you Sydney, I miss you' on it in paint."

The room started spinning and I grabbed for the edge of the table. "Get him Mark, get him quick" and I sat down. Edith looked sick and put her arm around me.

Right then my cellphone rang; I was surprised as I didn't even know the phone was in the room. I picked it up and must have turned pale because Daniel jumped for the phone. "Who is this?" he demanded.

Daniel was really shook up, "It was Ted, he said 'you might as well give up old boy, Sydney is mine' then he hung up."

Mark looked angry, "Sydney what did he say to you?" everyone looked concerned.

"He told me that he would be coming for me soon," and I started to cry. "How did he get my cellphone number Mark, how? Wait I remember one day when I was painting I left it in the front hall that must have been it. Oh my God what's next, I can't stand this I thought he would be a million miles away by now."

"That's it I am calling the state police," said Mark. Now

we are also going to have a man in the house at all times too. Sydney I don't think he is going to try to hurt you but he does want to take you away with him, you are to keep this house locked up tight, and no one is to leave, do you understand?" We all nodded.

A week has passed and we are all going nuts just sitting around. "Daniel I think we had better call the wallpaper place and tell them what has happened," I did and the owner answered and I explained the whole thing from the start of buying the wallpaper and that Ted had agreed to paint my ceilings then to what happened with him. There was a short silence on the other end then Mr. Osborn, the owner said he was shocked, they have never had anything like this happened to them and wanted somehow to make it up to me. I told him that was not necessary but he went on.

"How much more work did Ted have to do?" he asked me. "Well I promise we will get someone there to finish it and also paint your ceilings at no charge. It is the least we can do, I am so very sorry." Just as we were saying goodbye and I thanked him he said, "If any of us sees Ted we too will call the police."

I walked to the door with Mark, "I know this is nuts but do you think I could go down on the beach and sit by myself for just a few minutes to clear my head?"

He looked worried and said, "Only if you have a guard with you at all times and even then I don't think it is a good idea."

"Please I promise to be very careful the dogs could be there too."

"It is against my better judgment but only for five minutes."

He called for the guard and said he would be waiting on the patio and we went down. The girls were running around nearby and it was good to see them having fun. It felt so good to just sit and relax by myself and stare at the beautiful lake, the wind had picked up and the water got choppy. My man said it is time to go back and I turned to say something and he was on the ground. The next thing I knew I was being dragged over the rocks and into the trees, my mouth was covered with an odd smelling cloth and I could hardly breathe, then I heard him,

"You are mine now Sydney we will be so happy together," and then there was nothing but blackness. When I opened my eyes Eli had my head in his lap and Mark was kneeling beside me, I could see Daniel running like crazy across the yard followed by Edith.

"It was Ted wasn't it?" I said through mounds of tears.

"Yes, now please try to relax and tell me what happened," Mark asked as he held my hand. I told him what I could remember. "Are you sure you all right Sydney?"

"Good God what happened I heard gun shots?" asked Daniel trying to catch his breath. "Sydney are you hurt what happened?"

Mark stood up, "It was Ted. I told Sydney she could come down here for five minutes with a guard. She conned me into it. All of a sudden I saw the dogs come charging down the hill and I ran over to see what was happening. Then I saw the guard on the ground. The dogs were biting Ted's legs as he tried to drag Sydney away. I drew out my gun but was afraid I would hit her so when he let her go and dove into the water I started shooting. I don't know if I got him or not because he was underwater. Could someone please call for an ambulance for Tom over there?"

I tried to get up but was too dizzy so Daniel picked me up and carried me up to the house, and laid me down on the couch, again.

Mark said he had left the two men down at the beach to try to find Ted. I assume there was no sign of him because one officer came back up after about an hour and said they needed more help so he called back the state police.

Before Mark left he reminded us that a man would be outside the house all night and also one inside the house.

We were all in shock to say the least and I just couldn't stop shaking. Daniel never left my side nor did Edith except for getting us some hot tea and later lunch. We were all exhausted and Eli thought maybe we should call Dr. Winters to check me out. I told him I was all right just very shook up and whate Ted had put on the cloth to cover my face must have left little dizzy. "All I need is to have you all here with me. How can I thank you and the police?"

"Please don't think about it now, you are safe and that's all that matters," said Daniel, "and I think this may be finally over."

I decided I wanted to lie down for a while and stood up with Daniels help. He let out a cry, "Syd the back of your shirt is covered in blood." Edith came over and pulled my shirt up.

"Oh my you are really banged up it must have happened when you got dragged over the rocks on the beach. Doesn't it hurt?"

"Yes I guess it does and so do my legs but it didn't seem that important right now." Daniel helped me up to my room and Edith said she would fix me up and went out to get the first aid kit.

Daniel stood in the doorway with a silly little smile on his face, "If you need any help getting out of your clothes or just someone to sleep with give me a yell."

"Oh you will be the first person I call, now get out of here you goof."

Edith got all the cuts washed and bandaged then helped me into another shirt and told me to get some rest. At about five she came back and asked if I wanted some dinner.

"You know I feel so much better that would be great thank you, I guess I did actually sleep." She helped me get down the stairs where everyone was waiting. Even Mark was there. He asked how I was doing and I told him I have a bunch of cuts and bruises but am all right. Then he told us they are going to start dragging the lake in the morning if they don't find Ted today and his men will be down there all night.

"Daniel I think this is over, he has probably drowned. I will keep you posted," with that Mark turned to leave.

"Mark is it all right if I go outside for just a little while I want to thank the dogs for saving me?'

"Yes there are so many people out there you will be fine."

"I will go with her," said Daniel.

The minute I walked out the back door all five dogs were all over me. I bought them treats and hugged each one separately and thanked them. Though they had no idea what I was saying they knew I loved them all.

That night as I lied in bed thinking about all that had gone on I suddenly realized that I had not heard from Gretchen in several days. I will call her tomorrow and confess everything. She needs to know what has gone on. I had expected her to be here before now, hope nothing is wrong. I finally fell asleep with the sound of rain gently tapping at my window.

The next morning was gloomy and damp. No rain but the grass was very wet. My back and legs were still sore but I was in better spirits. At about ten o'clock the doorbell rang and I got it, it was Mark. He looked very tired and said he had been up all night. "Please sit down let me get you some coffee, you'd better take that wet coat off and get warmed up." As I handed him the steaming cup he asked if anyone else was here. "Oh they are around somewhere want me to get them?"

"No, that really isn't necessary, Sydney we found Ted's body early this morning almost down to Sylerville harbor, he drowned from what we can tell but there will be an autopsy. They did see a bruise on his head; he could have hit it when he dove into the water." He reached for an envelope on the couch next to him, "Here," he said as he handed it to me, "I think these belong to you. We found them on Ted."

I was almost afraid to open it. Ted must have gone into the cottage when we were gone. To my horror there was an almost ruined laminated picture of me and my family, a pink comb, small bracelet, and a pair of my stockings. "Oh Mark, how awful, he really was a sick man. I am sorry his life had to end the way it did but... I am glad that all this is over and we can get back to living again." I took a deep breath, "Please thank all the men who helped and a special thanks to you."

"You are welcome. The men have all left now so you are free to go out wherever you want. I never welcomed you to our little community so I will do it now. We are so pleased to have you here, I hope this incident hasn't changed how you feel about Sylerville, I was told by Daniel that you are very happy here and have made many friends."

"Thank you and no nothing has changed as far as my feeling for this wonderful little town. This is where I belong and plan to raise a family and stay forever. I hope we get to see you again under better circumstances. Please stop by anytime. If you are married bring your wife."

"I will do that and thank YOU."

He got up and put his jacket back on, "I need to get back now. Please do something good for yourself today and say goodbye to the rest of the family. Goodbye."

When everyone was gathered at lunch I told them about Ted and how kind Mark had been. I also told them that he brought an envelope with some of my things in it that were found on Ted.

"What was in it?" asked Eli.

I just couldn't tell them in detail so I said, "Just a few personal items he must have gotten from the cottage. Now I will thank you all, as I thanked him, you have been so supportive and strong and I am so happy to be even a little part of such a special family. My family life was complicated and it has been so wonderful to see what it can be. I don't see how I could have gotten through this without each one of you, though I still feel so bad that you had to be a part of it all. So thank you I love you all."

"Sydney I wanted to wait until this was all over before I asked you something," said Eli. "Where did you learn to do Karate, wow I am so proud of you for what you did to Ted? I know I shouldn't even bring this up but I have been so curious."

"Eli it's all right," and I explained about the classes I took. "Really now that I think about it I am amazed that it actually worked, I have never had to use it before."

Edith smiled, "Next time I go for a walk in the woods I want you with me."

Of course Daniel had to say something too, "Well folks you don't have to worry about me anymore, as long as Syd is by my side I will be safe, right slugger?"

"But my dear man, who is going to protect you from me?"

We all got a good laugh.

That evening everyone seemed to be doing something separately so I decided I was going to call Gretchen, with all that has been going on I just didn't have the time. The girls and I went up to my room and built a little fire in the fireplace, it was still damp from the rain the night before and it felt so cozy.

Gretchen answered right away, "Guess who?" I said. How are you I haven't heard anything in a while and have been involved in so many things I couldn't get to you?"

"Sydney I am so glad to hear from you, yes things are crazy here too. Louise had a set back and has been in and out of the hospital. She fell down the front steps and is in a leg cast. Oh my gosh I miss you tell me everything."

I hesitated but, "Ok I want you to know everything is fine but..."

Gretchen interrupted, "I hate it when you start out like that it means something awful has happened, give it to me straight."

"Remember you asked, Gretchen there is no other way to tell you this but to just say it. I got attacked by the man who was stripping the wallpaper, he, he tired...to rape me. Believe it or not I finally got to use my Karate on him and really let him have it. Then I ran next door to the McGregor's. The doctor and the police were called, oh God I was so terrified and except for some deep scratches on my chest I was not harmed. It all ended when the man came back and tried to abduct me, but the dogs saved me, Gretch the man jumped into the lake and drown. It has really been a mess around here that is why I haven't called."

"Oh my God girl, are you all right? You should have called me I would have come right away. This would not have happened if I had been there I would have strangled him before he had a chance to die. I am sure there is more so spill it."

"Now to the good part, guess what I have found the man I want to spend the rest of my life with. His name is Daniel McGregor and he lives next door, his family has been the caretakers for the house for a long time. He is a building contractor and is the one that finished my house. We have had a wonderful summer and though I love him, I have since we first met, have not said so, he did the night I got attacked but I am not sure if he was just shook up or not but I do think he loves me too. I know what you are going to say so don't, we haven't known each other long enough but how long is long enough? He is so much fun and we are always kidding around. His family has adopted me and they are so very special. Daniel lives with them during the summer then travels around the state to do his building for the rest of the year. They have all been so supportive of me and I love them very much. Gretchen my life is so full and I am very happy."

"Wow for once I don't know what to say but will give it a try. Sydney I am so happy for you, you deserve the best and Daniel seems to fit the bill. It makes me feel better knowing that you have people who care about you, but does that mean you don't need me anymore?" she said as her voice cracked a little.

"Stop it you idiot, of course I need you, you are my Gretchen and these past few months have been so hard for me without you here. I love you and miss you very much."

We talked for just a little while longer then she said she had to get Louise ready for bed. "I love you too my sweet girl and as soon as I can I will get there. Please be careful. Bye."

I stayed at the house for another couple days then decided it was time to go back to the cottage. Edith looked concerned but I assured her that it was safe now. "It has been so nice to have you here I hate to see you go, but I do understand," she said as she got up from the table and gave me a hug, "but you do need to have some breakfast first."

"Of course I will, but we all need to get back to our normal routines now that everything has settled down. I need to really concentrate on the house now and get the wallpaper up so we can move in."

Daniel got up and pulled a chair out for me and as I sat down he looked me straight in the eye and said, "So you are going to climb up the ladder and hang the wallpaper up at the ceiling by yourself huh?"

Oops I hadn't thought about that, "Well maybe some handsome strong man wouldn't mind coming to my rescue, humm?" We all laughed

"Of course I will help you, you nut" and if on cue my phone rang.

"Miss Armstrong this is Edward Osborn from Osborn's Wallpaper Plus. We have found some skilled men who will come out to finish the work you need done and would like to send them whenever you are ready. I did read what happened to Ted in the paper, and again am so sorry for all you went through."

"That would be wonderful, whenever they want to come is fine with me. By the way what should we do with Ted's equipment I assume it is still here?"

"We will take it away if you want. How about I send the men first thing tomorrow morning, would that work for you?"

I was getting excited and said, "Yes that would be perfect, again thank you so much for doing this," and we hung up.

"Guess what that was the wallpaper place and they are sending a crew out tomorrow to finish up what Ted left undone, isn't that great? So Mr. Tall, Blond, and Handsome want to follow me home and get to work?"

Again I thanked Eli and Edith for everything and after breakfast we went back to the cottage. Bless his heart Eli had gone over and repainted the door and I was so relieved. I went into the bathroom to change into my grubbies and almost immediately there was a knock on the door, "Can I help I am really good getting people dressed," then a slight pause, "and getting them undressed?"

"Nice try, cool off I will be out in a minute." When I opened the door he kissed me and we went up to the house.

Daniel gathered up Teds stuff and put it out back and then we started. We had finished the parlor the last time we were here so we started on the dining room. Edith had given us a bag of cinnamon rolls and a thermos of coffee so after a couple hours we took a break and sat out on the porch and ate our treat. "It is so beautiful here," I said with a big sigh, "I can't wait to move in." Daniel was unusually quiet and I asked him if he was all right.

"You know sometimes I think we all forget how important it is to just live, live in the now, enjoy what we have and be thankful for it. These past days have really got me thinking. We all take too much for granted, we do need to stop and smell the roses as they say." He took my hand and squeezed it. "When I realized I could have lost you I…, there are no words to express how I felt, but meet me on the beach tonight at about six and I will try to tell you. I will bring a picnic dinner."

I was so overwhelmed with what he had said I too didn't know what to say, he is such a gentle wonderful man and the love I felt for him that moment was almost too much to bear. "I would love to sir, thank you, thank you for everything." And I leaned over and gave him a big kiss. "You are really something you know that?"

"Of course I do," he said and smiled, "now let's finish up the room."

We did finish and went our separate ways at about four-thirty. "Go home and get glamorous for our beachside dinner my dear and I will see you soon." With that and a kiss he left.

I sat there for just a minute more and watched him as he walked across the yard. He is so right we do need to be grateful for what we have every single day. Then I went home.

I showered and did my hair and makeup with great care I wanted to look extra nice for him tonight. The vamp dress had done its thing already so this time I chose a coral colored sundress that was quite plain but had great lines and showed off my figure well. I found a bottle of good wine that I had brought with me from Atlanta and decided it would be perfect for tonight.

As I headed for the beach there was just a slight cooling breeze coming from the lake almost calling me to come and enjoy a very special night.

Daniel was waiting for me and he looked quite grand in a pale green shirt with cream colored pants. All I could think of was handsome he looked. "My you look very handsome sir," I said. "Flowers for me, how sweet?"

"Back at ya girl, you look like a Caribbean princess with your dark hair and coral dress." He took a flower from the bouquet he was holding and put it in my hair. "Now you are complete."

We sat down on the blanket and stared at the view for a couple minutes, "Are you hungry?" he asked, "or would you like a glass of wine first?"

"Wine then dinner I just want to take in this view a little longer. Oh I see you have a fire ready to go, how nice could we start it now, the breeze is a little cool?"

After we finished dinner I guess Mother Nature thought we needed just a little more to look at so she told the sun to do something extra special. The sunset was the most beautiful I had ever seen." Daniel look at that," I said as I pointed to the sky.

He turned around and was just as excited as I was, "Wow that is fantastic look at the brightness of the colors."

Then he turned to me and took my hand, "Sydney Rose Armstrong, I know we have not known each other for a very long time but I knew the minute I met you that you were the one for me. You are the most beautiful woman I have ever met outside and inside and have made my life so fun and exciting, I never know what to expect from you and I love it. You are the woman I have been waiting for for such a long time and I love with all my heart. Will you do me the great honor of becoming my wife?"

I was numb, could this really be happening? I looked at him with tears running down my cheeks and said, "Oh Daniel..., I too have loved you from the very start, you make me so happy, and fill my heart with such joy every single day. You are such a special man and I feel so proud that you chose me. Of course I will marry you, my love."

He pulled me into his arms and kissed me almost frantically, "Oh my God can this really be happening, I was so afraid you would say it is too soon, or worse that you didn't feel the same. Do you have any idea what a wonderful life we are going to have?" Then he kissed me over and over again.

"Whoa boy, breathing is something I am used to doing quite regularly and if you don't stop kissing me for a least a few seconds we will never make it to the alter," I said as I started to kiss him back. "Who cares, breathing is over rated anyway. Oh I am so happy I love you so much," which led to more kissing. "Do your folks know anything about all this?"

He smiled and said, "Yes my love, I told them all about it over a month ago when I was sure how I felt. Of course Dad said to give it a little time and not rush you but Mom said to go for it immediately. They had a little battle of words but will be so happy when I tell them. They didn't know I was going to ask you tonight, so it will be a happy surprise."

All of my dreams have come true I am going to be his wife and was overcome with emotion. "So what do we do now?" I asked.

He took out a small box from his pocket and opened it as he reached for my hand, "This is our beginning," he said as he placed the ring on my finger and then kissed it.

I stared at the ring; it was absolutely gorgeous. The diamond was huge and stood out prominently in the center and there were two smaller ones on each side. I just couldn't take my eyes off of it. "Oh my, this is the most beautiful thing I had ever seen, I love it, and I love you," again the kissing started. "Good heavens you are spoiling me rotten."

"Well get used to it, I intend to spend the rest of my life doing just that."

I looked up at him and said, "Daniel all I need is you, I really mean it, well and maybe a little food too."

"You are something else Sydney. Hey how many kids do you want, could we live here at your house, what about…"

"Slow down boy, first I want about twenty kids, and of course we can live here at the house, after all you made it good again and it is only fair. So did I scare you enough so you will go screaming into the night?"

He seemed to be thinking about what I said then, "Twenty huh, well we had better get started no time to waste," again the evil smile. "Ok ok we can wait a little longer but I was thinking about four or five, could you be happy with just that many? Twenty, really?"

I pretended to be disappointed but said, "Well I guess that would be all right. No really that is the number I had in mind. I love children and with a father like you they can't be anything but great. Goodness I am so excited!"

We talked for hours and finally I said I need to get some sleep the guys are coming tomorrow. "I just hope I don't wake up and find this whole wonderful night was a dream."

"Have no fear my love, I will ask you again tomorrow, just don't forget the answer is yes," he said and helped me up. "Hey I have a fun idea, how about we go wake up Mom and Dad and tell them the good news?"

"Oh I would love that, they need some good news for a change and I need to tell my family and since they are it let's go." We got into the house and Daniel went up to their bedroom and knocked on the door while I waited downstairs.

I could hear him knocking; "Sorry to wake you but I have some wonderful news come on down."

It was only a very short time before the two sleepy looking people came down the stairs, "What up Son?" asked Eli.

"Well Dad, Mom I have made it almost legal, Sydney is going to truly be a part of our family. I asked her to marry me and believe it or not she said yes right away, can you believe it?" He took my hand and showed them the ring.

Edith started crying and gave me one of her special crushing hugs then winked at me. Eli wiped the tears off his cheek in his manly way and did the same. "Welcome my daughter." he said with great emotion. "If we could a picked a wife for Daniel it would have been you. The ring is beautiful Son, you did good."

Poor Edith could not stop crying, "Do you have a date yet?" she finally got out.

"No and honestly I didn't even think about it," said Daniel as he looked at me.

"Don't look at me I am still in happy land and am trying to figure out what my name is. We can talk about that when I land back on earth again. Time for me to go home and get some sleep, though I doubt I will sleep at all, but I do have to try. So I will say goodnight and we can talk more tomorrow. Daniel will you walk me home please?'

Hand in hand we walked or should I say I floated back to the cottage. Daniel held me close when we got to the door, "I hate this I don't want to leave you for even a minute. Hopefully before long I won't have to. Goodnight my love."

The next morning I woke up, amazed that I actually did sleep, got breakfast and dressed and went up the house with my coffee. I decided to just wait there for the workers. The sun caught the glow of my ring and it gave me a little shiver, I still couldn't believe all that happened was real. I am going to marry the man that I love and he actually loves me too. I have to call Gretchen today and tell her. Then it hit me, I have to wait for her to get here before we can get married. There is no way I would do it without her, besides she would kill me–no way to start out.

I could hear Daniel singing a happy song before I even saw him. The girls saw him too and almost knocked him over with their greeting. "Go sit down you silly girls so I can talk to your mom," he said as he tried to peel them off. He stood at the end of the porch with a huge smile on his face, "Did we really get engaged last night or was it a fantastic dream?" he asked.

"Well unless we had the same dream I guess it is true. Do you have any kisses left from last night to share with me," I said as I got up and ran to him. He caught me up in his arms and held me tight, kissed me on the nose then put me back down. "You know I think I had better show you what a kiss is, I think we have a different idea," and I planted a big one on him.

"Shameful woman, kissing a man in public, what would the birds say if they saw us?"

"Who cares let them get their own mates or whatever it is."

The crew came right on time and I showed them where the wallpaper was that had to be removed upstairs then asked if would be all right if we continued hanging the new paper downstairs. A nice man named Paul, said that was fine but they would be more than happy to help us with it once they are done upstairs and painted all the ceilings. "Mr. Osborn told me to tell you it is the least they can do and it will cost you nothing more. Looks like you have a ways to go," he said and smiled.

"Oh my, that would be wonderful he is such a kind man." Right away I went in and told Daniel the good news.

He was as happy as I was, "But, I think we had better do what we can until they are done, it's only fair." Of course he was right so we got back to work.

Because of the open doorways and windows the paper went up quite quickly and we were done about one o'clock. "How about I make us some lunch and bring it up so we can eat it on the porch?" I asked Daniel from the doorway.

"Good idea, the guys are breaking for lunch too. I'll come down and help you as soon as I wash off my hands."

So we were all out there. These workers were so nice, especially Paul the supervisor I guess. He was probably in his fifties and told us that his daughter just had her first baby, a boy and they named him after his grandpa. He was so proud you could see it in his face. "My wife and I will be going down this weekend to see him, I hope you don't mind me not being here, but the crew will come."

"No problem," Daniel said, "I am amazed you will actually have anyone here on the weekend. This should all be done very soon and we are very happy. Thank you."

The crew went back to work and Daniel and I went in to admire the work we did that morning. "So what do you think Daniel, do you like the paper color and design? After all this is even more important now because you will be living here too. Sorry I had no idea when I picked this out. We can change it if you like."

He stood back and looked at the parlor and the dining room and said they matched, "Yes I do like it. What is going to happen in the family living room?"

I went over to the box of wallpaper and took out the pale green stripe, "This is it, like it?"

"Yep it is good, now what about OUR bedroom?" Again I went over and brought it out.

"This is pretty feminine Daniel you really might want to change it. I just wanted it to be light and bright."

He seemed to be trying to make up his mind and said, "I'll tell you what if you are willing to compromise and give me a big stuffed chair in say that darker shade of blue or green solid color, and maybe some darker furniture I will let you keep the paper. Deal?"

"Deal, want to shake on it?" I asked.

"Sure but there is something else I would like to do more," he was back to the evil grin thing.

"Mr. McGregor the best I can do is a kiss for now. So here…"

–6–

ROSE

As we were leaving I passed the quilts and samplers that were taken off the walls when we were preparing to take down the wallpaper. "Daniel look at these, I think they were made by my Aunt Rose and I would like to clean them but I don't know how. Do you think your mom might know?"

He took one of the samplers and said it wouldn't hurt to ask her. "She is expecting us anyway; oh I forgot Mom wants us for dinner tonight, sorry–ok with you? We could bring them over then."

"Bad boy for not telling me but it sounds great. I'll go back and get cleaned up and meet you over there. Would you mind taking them with you when you go? Ok thanks see you soon," and I left.

Eli and Edith were very glad to see me, as always, and said it is such a nice night why don't we sit outside until dinner is cooked. Daniel excused himself and went in and got the four samplers, "Thought this would a good time for you to show Mom these," he said as he laid them on the round table.

I picked them up and brought them over to Edith, then sat down and one by one showed her. "These were on the walls in the house and it looks like they were made by my Aunt Rose but they are so dirty I can't make out much of what is on them. Do you know how I can clean them without ruining them?"

She examined them and said she has only done a few of these and can't guarantee that her method would work but if I am game we could give it a try. "Let's take this one into the kitchen now and give it a try, we still have an hour before dinner and I am curious too what is written on this." First she vacuumed it, cleaned the sink and filled it with cold water, then added a little mild detergent that had no dyes or perfumes in it. She put in the sampler and swished it around, "Let's set the table and let it soak for about ten minutes." Then she drained the water and added fresh several times until the soap was gone. "Hand me that clean white towel please Sydney," she asked as she took the sampler out of the water. "Lay it open, thanks. Now we just gently put it on, but first a quick peek. You know I think it got most of the dirt off, we will know when it is dry." She rolled the piece into the towel and then took it out and laid it out on another towel at the end of her counter. "Now we wait. Let's go back out with the men."

The dinner was wonderful and we sat for a long time talking about us getting married. "Daniel I thought of something this afternoon, we can't get married until my friend Gretchen gets here. As I told you she practically raised me even with my mother there, she and I very close. I am going to call her tonight and tell her our good news and start pushing for an arrival date. I hope you understand, until I met you she was all I had."

"Of course but if she was here right now when would you want the wedding to be?" he asked. "We haven't even talked about if we want a large wedding with lots of people or a small one with family and friends. What do you think?"

"As far as when, yesterday would be a good day. Gosh I just don't know this all happened so fast. What do YOU want Daniel?"

"Weddings are for the bride but if I had a choice I would love to get married right here in our backyard with the people we really care about there to help us celebrate. But this is all for us and we need to think about it don't we?"

I was so choked up I could hardly speak, "Daniel what you just described is exactly what I have always wanted. If my father were alive it would have had to be a grand production with reporters and the whole thing. I know he would not have even consulted with me. My mother always wanted me and my father to descend the grand staircase to make a big impression on those below. But now I have no father so I can't…wait a minute," I said as I walked over to Eli and sat down on the couch by him, "Eli you are my father now will you give me away? I know it is a lot to ask and a little unconventional but it would mean the world to me!"

I have never seen a man look so surprised, he just sat there staring at me, "Sydney you are truly my daughter and I would be proud to give you away," he said in perfect English, then he hugged me and gave me a kiss on the cheek. I kissed him back and thanked him over and over.

"It will make my day perfect. I want Gretchen to be my maid of honor and you Edith as my bridesmaid, if you would. This bride is going to pay for the whole thing, it is only right and I know my father would want it that way, so no arguments even if you hadn't planned on arguing anyway." I smiled at everyone, who were all in tears by this time. "Hey this is supposed to be a happy time no more tears, only the bride is allowed to cry."

Edith dried her eyes and said she would love to have the wedding here but couldn't she just make the cake? I almost said no but I do know that she wants to be a part of it all so I agreed. "That would be wonderful but I don't want you to go to too much trouble, I want you to be able to enjoy every moment of it, not running all over. My goodness there is so much to plan I will need your help with that for sure. Ok?"

It was such a fun evening and when it was time to go Edith reminded me of the sampler. "Just take it with you and let it dry overnight then let me know how we did."

Daniel came with me and again we walked across the yard to the gate but talked the whole time. "Sydney that was such a kind thing you did asking my dad to give you away and I am so happy that we want the same thing for our wedding, it is going to be so special. You are truly my love and I thank God you agreed to become my wife. I promise you will never be sorry."

The following morning Daniel came early for breakfast, which seems to be a given now. I was scrambling the eggs and he asked, "Hey girl what is this?" I turned around.

"Oh that is one of the samplers your mom helped me clean last night, it has been drying overnight." I almost forgot about it. Hopefully it will be easier to read now that it is dry but the stitching is quite small. Check it out for me will you?"

"Sydney put down that spoon and come over here, now," he said sounding serious.

"My goodness what is it give me a minute?"

"No come here NOW!"

I was getting worried and walked over. Daniel was standing there looking as white as a sheet, "Look beyond the rose," he said as he handed it to me.

I grabbed the edge of the counter for support, "What did you say?"

"I said look beyond the rose."

I literally jumped back not willing to even get close to the fabric. "Daniel do you realize what you just said, remember my father's last words to me and how concerned I was about what it meant? Do I want to know, I am scared?"

He came over to me, "Brace yourself my love you are in for a big shock," and put his arm around me. "You have to look."

I was shaking as he put the sampler in my hand. Almost hidden beyond the single rose were small stitches but I could read it. It was a family tree with the names of my mother and my aunts, their husbands and their children. Rose Anne Everett and Charles Emerson Armstrong married 1981 and below it connected with a long thin line was Sydney Rose. I grabbed Daniels arm and slid to the floor.

When I opened my eyes Daniel was kneeling beside me, "Oh Syd are you all right, you scared me to death?"

"What happened I don't rememb…oh my God?" I just laid there staring at the ceiling and repeated over and over, "No, no, no it can't be it can't be."

He helped me up and sat me down in a chair. "Syd we will work this out I promise, here have a drink of water. Please try to relax I am here I will help you. Do you want me to call my mom?"

"Maybe in a little while but not now, I am so confused, it's like my whole life has been a lie, why didn't they tell me why why? How do I even start to figure this out?"

He held me so tight it hurt but I didn't care. "Thank heavens you were here, I need to go out and run, I have to do something or I will go nuts. Just stay here and let me go." I did run like I have never done before and when I could go no further I started screaming at my father, the woman I thought was my mother, at God. Totally exhausted I slowly went back to the cottage and fell into Daniels arms. "I feel better now just very tired."

He picked me up and laid me on the bed, "Take a little rest, I will be here."

"Please lie down with me." He did and we held onto each other as I fell asleep.

When I woke up I felt a lot better and was now just mad. "Daniel what could have happened that my mothe…aunt pretended to be my mother and what happened to Rose. I guess maybe she died and Elizabeth took over, but why would that have to be kept a secret, why didn't my father tell me, why in his letter to me did he say even in death he could not revel this, which I am sure is what he was talking about. Well he did tell me to come here and my questions would be answered, that one I am sure of but now there are so many more. Boy am I mad at everyone right now except you. Goodness I don't know what I would have done without you here. Thank you love," I said as cuddled closer to him.

"Ok let's take this one step at a time. First you need to get up and get something to eat, don't give me that look, you need some brain food. I will start over with the eggs and you stay put. No more questions, got it?"

"Now," he said as he put the plate in front of me, "you are going to eat every bite of this, if you don't I will have to get violent and spank you."

"You'd like that wouldn't you," I said then gave him an almost smile.

"That's my girl, but for your information you bet I would, now eat."

After breakfast Daniel found a pad of paper and pen and we sat at the table, "Let's write all this down, maybe if we see it on paper it will help. Try to start at the beginning if there is one."

"Well, let's see. For some reason I have not felt like I had a bond with Elizabeth like I did with my father. She was there but not so much for me, she was so busy with fund raisers and the like. It was Gretchen who helped me through whatever I needed. Though now as I think about it, after Father died I told her what he had said and also Mr. Edgeworth's comment about how much I resembled my mother. I just thought he got mixed up. But Gretchen seemed to get shook up, which is not like her. Do you suppose she knew about this and was also sworn to secrecy by Rose? I knew she was my mother's best friend as she told me so many times, but now that I think about it Gretchen and Elizabeth didn't act like best friends, so I guess she was referring to Rose."

"Sounds like they could have," he said as he reached out and poured us some more coffee. "I think we are starting to get somewhere, go on."

I took a minute to figure out what could be next, "No wonder everyone who knew Rose thought I was her, my word I look exactly like my mother. I did think it was quite a coincidence but would never have thought of this. Hey, maybe that is why my father used to look at me strangely at times, he was seeing my mother and I get the feeling he loved her very much, come to think of it he said so in his letter but I thought he was referring to Elizabeth. I assume she did die so it must have been very hard on him. Do you suppose she died when I was very young and that is why Elizabeth took over, it makes sense?"

"Good going, keep it up."

I took a deep breath, "But there is still the question of why they didn't tell me, I am sure it would have been hard on me but I know I would have been all right in time. The mystery of looking beyond the rose was my father's way of trying to help me find out the truth, but again why the big cover up? I am sure he wanted me to find out though. Oh Daniel he was such a staunch man, so proper, so cold at times but he did say he loved me in the end, but why couldn't he actually be a dad instead of a father. I have sometimes wondered if he named me Sydney because he wanted a boy. He also told me in the end how proud he was of me when I got my law degree, again why didn't he say so at the time. I have thought of all this many times and just figured that is way he was but it hurt. To be honest I don't know how I feel about him now. Maybe when all this is done I will know. How about we stop for a while my mind is tired?"

"Very good suggestion," Daniel said as he got up and pulled me up too. "Let's go see how the workers are doing at the house. I am so proud of you Sydney you are doing so well with all this after such a shock."

I gave him a kiss and said, "I have found when something major happens I have to start planning or figuring things out right away, feeling sorry for myself accomplishes nothing. But I may collapse later, so keep your arms open. Oh would you please call your folks and see if we could come over later, I would like their opinion on all this as they knew my aunts, maybe they heard or saw something that they have forgotten about?"

The guys were working hard and progress was being made so we decided to go to the McGregor's. Just as we were walking out of the door I suddenly remembered the bible that I found in the attic, maybe that will help us. We sat out on the porch and I opened it up. There on the first page were all the family records from way way back. Again I found what was on the sampler. I put the bible back and grabbed the photo album and we left.

"What a lovely surprise to see you here so early," said Edith. "Sit down and have a cup of coffee, Eli they are here," she called. "So what's up, you look awfully tired Sydney?"

"Edith I am so sorry but I have just learned something quite shocking and I really need your advice. I hate to ask for your help again after what we have just gone through but I need it."

Daniel held onto my hand for support, "Do you remember me telling you about my concern for my Aunt Rose? Remember also the sampler you cleaned for me last night. Well this morning it was dry and it had all four sisters listed plus their husbands and children. Here look at this," I said as I handed it to her.

Edith gasped, "Oh Sydney what a shock that must have been. But now after the things you told me it almost makes sense." She handed it to Eli who looked just as shocked as she was.

"Yes it was a terrible shock and I don't think I would have

even started to recover at all if it wasn't for this wonderful man sitting next to me." I smiled at Daniel.

"Eli you were the first one to really start me wondering what was going on when we first met, you called me Rose. It's no wonder as I found an old picture of her and I look exactly like her, which was a little unnerving. Here I brought it with me."

Edith was clearly surprised, "Oh my gosh you do look just like her. Why haven't I seen that, but it was so long ago?"

"Do either of you remember anything that might help me find out what happened, I guess she died, but how and when, obviously it was after I was born? Oh there are so many questions I have even about Elizabeth."

"This is something I am going to have to think about, we will talk it over and let you know, as of right now I can't think of a thing, can you dear?" Eli shook his head. "To change the subject, how are things going at the house?"

Daniel told them that they are doing a good job and quite fast, it shouldn't take too long for them to be done. "Did Sydney tell you that they offered at no extra charge to help us finish the wallpapers too? Great huh!"

"Yes that is good news, Sydney I am sorry but I have a dentist's appointment in half an hour and I need to get going. I will say goodbye for now but I promise to think hard about your situation."

We decided to leave too. "Daniel," I said as we were walking home, "do you think it would do any good to go to the city offices and see if there are any death records or something that might help us? Also I wonder where the family plot is, what cemetery?"

"There is only one cemetery here in town; do you want to go check it out now?"

"I sure do if you have the time."

It was a pretty little cemetery; very old with wildflowers everywhere all surrounded by a black wrought iron fence. We started our search and had pretty much given up when I saw a small area off to the side that was very overgrown and the head stone was almost completely covered in vines. "Look over there!"

There it was the whole little area was for my family. "My goodness they go back over one hundred and fifty years." I saw Ophelia and her family, and Susannah, but there was no Rose. Elizabeth was buried in Atlanta in the Armstrong's plot. "So what do you make of this, if she is dead where is she? I am afraid this is the end of the line."

"I have a friend in town that takes care of the records, when we get back I will call him and see if he can help us," Daniel said as we left. We did and there was nothing but he did find my birth certificate.

"Oh my gosh I never even thought about that. But wait I was born in Atlanta how could he have a copy of my birth certificate unless…, Daniel I was born here, I must have been."

"Haven't you ever seen your birth certificate?" he asked looking surprised.

"Come to think of it I haven't my father kept it, which from what we just found out makes sense. Boy this keeps getting more and more complicated doesn't it? I am going to have to get over to Sylerville and get a copy for myself."

"The time has come to call Gretchen and see what I can get out of her, though I have a feeling this is going to be tough."

That night I did call. "Gretchen I have had some shocking news," and I told her what and how I found out. "I have a feeling you know something about this and for some reason have not told me. Please tell me what happened, I promise I won't get upset, but I HAVE to know it all. I should tell you that I put us on speaker phone as Daniel is here with me I want him to hear this first hand because we are getting married, he asked me two nights ago. We can talk about that in a minute."

"Hi Gretchen this is Daniel, I can't wait to meet you. I just want you to know that I love her with all my heart. Sorry Sydney, please continue."

"Hi to you too Daniel. Oh my child, I was afraid this would happen some day and I was going to explain it all when I got there. I hate to do it on the phone but I can tell you are very upset. About six months after you were born your mother Rose got very sick. Your father took her to every specialist he could find but none were of any help. Then he heard about a clinic in Norway that seemed to be treating what symptoms your mother had, so he made an appointment and she left. She would not let your father go; she wanted him to stay with you. I was living with them at the time to help her. She was so worried and sure she was going to die so she signed some papers divorcing your father so he would be free if she did die, but told her lawyer to only give them to your father if she did. That never made sense to me because if she died he would be automatically free. We kept in touch regularly as best we could and she seemed to be improving and was planning to come home. Then she stopped writing I heard nothing from her and neither did your father. The last thing I heard was that she was heading to the airport and the bus she was traveling in went over a cliff and there were no survivors." She stopped for a minute as she was crying so hard. "Oh Syd it was so awful for your father and I, he was served the divorce papers shortly after it along with a letter from her explaining why she did this. He was in a terrible state and couldn't figure out why as they loved each other so much. I told him that it was because she loved him so much that she did this, she thought if something did happened to her it would get very complicated considering she was in a foreign country and also if he remarried. She never would have done it if she had come home. He decided to go back to Atlanta, and have his practice there where he was from originally and bring you with him but he knew he could not take care of you by himself. We all sat around and tried to figure out what to do. Elizabeth said she would go back with him and take care of his daughter, you, and Charles was very grateful but said they needed to marry or people would talk. I agreed to come too and help them both."

"Oh Sydney you were such a beautiful little thing, you looked like your mother from the start and unfortunately or otherwise your father saw it too. He told me many times he couldn't get over the resemblance, but it did hurt him too. If you ever doubted how your father felt about you forget it he loved you with all his heart but being the man that he was it was difficult to show you."

"But Gretchen, why didn't you or Father tell me what happened? I know I would have been upset but I am sure I would have accepted it."

"Sorry I forgot to tell you that before your mother left she sat us all down and made us promise that if anything happened to her we were not ever to tell you if your father remarried. His new wife would have brought you up as her own and she was afraid it would hurt both of you very much and possibly change your relationship. How she thought that far ahead is beyond me. All she wanted was for you Sydney to have a wonderful life with no complications and to be loved. Your father and I honored her wishes and so many times I wished I could have said something to you and so did he. Ok as long as all this has come out I think it is full confession time."

"Oh God there is more," I said feeling alarmed.

"Nothing disastrous my dear and I think you're going to be very pleased. For some reason it just didn't seem to be that important to tell you but I was also born in Sylerville, your mom and I met in elementary school and remained best of friends. I used to play at her, no your house so I know it very well, in fact when I was helping your parents I lived in the cottage. I never went back there after your mother died but now more than ever I want to be home again to stay. So many coincidences huh?"

I was literally sobbing at this point even Daniel was having a hard time keeping himself together. "You are really a stinker, you know that, all this time I have been trying to describe the house and you said nothing. Well you will have a shock when you see what my Daniel has done with it. Just for that you get no pictures you are going to have to wait and see it for yourself. We will have both come home you dear thing, how wonderful! Oh Gretch thank you so much for telling me everything, I know this was so hard for you but I love you even more for it. Now we have to get you back here so I can get married and you can be my maid of honor, after all who else would I ask, you have truly been my mother from the beginning."

"ME oh my how wonderful, bless you my dear. Give that

man of yours a big hug for me, and you Daniel a little warning if you hurt her in any way be prepared I will shoot you, I am a good shot don't make me have to show you." Then she laughed and said, "Get some sleep I love you both. Good night."

Daniel just sat there, "Boy she is really something isn't she, I can see why you love her so much, I do too and I have never met her. So how do you feel love, did you get some peace of mind?"

"Yes I think I did, they did what they did for love and they both did love me. I think it is time to let them both rest in peace and for me to accept what happened and move on. Imagine, I was born here in Sylerville just like you, that makes me a local," I said with a great deal of pride, "no wonder I feel so right at home."

After Daniel left I laid in bed thinking for a long time and looked up to heaven and told my father that I understood everything and that I loved him for loving my mother and me so much. I promise I will make you proud. Then I talked to Rose, my mother who I did not even know. "Thanks Mom for caring so much about me, I wish I had known you but now I almost think I do. I love you." What a day it has been from such trauma to understanding and acceptance.

The next week was spent working on the house and by Saturday everything was finished and the men left. I spent the rest of the day just going from room to room admiring each one. This is now officially my home and I can finally move in. With Edith and Eli's help we were able to get my few things moved in and by Monday morning all was done and the girls and I are now living there. The only thing left is ordering some new furniture and Edith and I will go back to Port Shores sometime this week, really I hope Daniel will come too.

That first night turned out to be quite special, besides the fact that we were finally there. Just as I was getting into bed I heard something outside under my window, a guitar. Good heavens I thought what in the world. I opened the window wider and looked down, there guitar in hand was my nutty love. He gave me a little bow and said it is only fitting that the lady of the manor got serenaded her first night by her suitor. Then he started playing and singing "Jeremiah was a bull frog", I laughed so hard I thought I was going to fall out of the window. "My sir you are so romantic what a lovely song, it touched me deeply. You do play so beautifully and look so handsome silhouetted against the moonlight. Now if you plan on scaling these walls to get up here and ravage me I must warn you the guard dogs are on duty tonight and will attack you for sure." I blew him a kiss, "Go home you silly wonderful man I love you."

He looked up at me and slumped over, "My lady I feel rejected for sure but be on guard I have the key to the castle, sleep well if you can." Then he blew me a kiss back and was gone.

I was still laughing when I got into bed, good heavens I love that man.

As it turned out all four of us went shopping the next day and as I went over to the van Daniel poked me, "So how was your first night in the castle, anything special happen?"

"Yes as a matter of fact, there was a frog outside my window singing away but I finally yelled at him and he left." He picked me up and just about threw me into the van.

"A frog huh?" Then he leaned in and kissed me. "I love you too, my lady." It was the start of a very fun day. Poor Edith and Eli had no idea what was going on but I guess since we laughed just about the whole way there they figured all was well. I was so glad Daniel went, after all he has to live with it all too. Thank goodness he seemed to like my choices so things went smoothly.

When we got back to the house Edith pulled me aside, "Sydney I know I am being nosey and you don't have to tell me but what is the frog thing?"

I couldn't help but laugh. "Edith last night Daniel came over and serenaded me under my window, then he started singing the song "Jeramiah was a bull frog". I truly almost fell out of the window laughing. Not the most popular serenade song which made it even funnier. Oh please don't tell him that I told you."

"Have no fear my dear, what a funny nut he really is, I love it and him."

"Me too."

Daniel and I were sitting on the porch early one morning, it was a beautiful day and I said, "Honey, why don't you call your dad and see if he wants to go fishing, you two haven't spent much time together with all that has been going on and I know he would love it, you too?"

"What a great idea, I will call now."

They did go out and both got sunburned but brought back some fish for another bonfire on the beach for dinner. "Thanks for thinking of this love, though I should have," Daniel said as we all left, "we both had a great time."

Tomorrow is the 4th of July and I will be spending it at the McGregor's. Daniel told me all his brothers and their families will be there. "They are all excited to meet you. It is going to be a fun day!"

He came over to get me about nine the next morning. It was going to be a very hot day so he said to bring my swim suit. I decided to wear shorts and a top and hoped I wouldn't be out of place. No problem we all wore them. One by one I met everyone, you could tell all the guys were brothers, they looked so much alike. I got along well with them and their wives and we played games, threw balls, and swam the entire day. Edith really did a wonderful job with the food. I went in to help her get everything out to the yard and quickly told her about my call to Gretchen and that I actually was born here. She was so pleased that everything worked out so well. "How sad though that you will never know your mother."

When it started to get dark all the guys built a raging bonfire on the beach and we all sang songs and roasted marshmallows. The Japanese lanterns were lit in the trees and we could see most of the fireworks from Sylerville. We had a great time.

I thought it would be a good idea for me to stay home the next day and let them have their family time together. That lasted maybe an hour and Daniel came over to find out where I was. I told him I should stay here but he wouldn't hear of it, everyone has been asking where you are. "Besides there is a good chance I will get to see you in your swim suit again, woman you have no idea what strength it took for me not to attack you right there in front of everyone."

I smiled sweetly and said, "If the truth be told you were in grave danger too. Now let me go up to my room and put my suit on under my clothes. A few minutes later I yelled, "Daniel I am stuck will you please come up here?"

I could hear him thundering up the stairs to my room, "Where are you?"

"In the bathroom."

He peeked his head in, "What's up?" He started laughing, "Syd did you know that your hair is stuck in your swim top tie?"

"Dah, help me please."

He got that silly little evil look on his face, "Be glad to my dear but I am going to have to undo that string thing and I can't be responsible for what might happen."

I started to laugh, "I will take my chances now get to it." It did take a couple minutes for him to get the thing undone and my hair out of it and of course in the meantime I was topless and try as I might I could not cover myself up.

The dummy just stood there and stared at me, "You do realize I am going to have to ravage you now?"

"Ravage away but make it quick we have to get over there," by this time I was laughing like a crazy person.

"My dear I will almost spare you this time but not completely, I have tried to be patient but this is too good to pass up, your first ravage in the bathroom how romantic." The "ravage" only lasted a couple minutes and he tied me back together again.

"My sir you are truly a talented ravager, did you learn how to do it in school? Ravage 101."

"Watch it girl or I will show you what else I learned from a couple more classes."

As we were walking through the yard he turned to me and said, "Syd we have got to get married very soon or I will have to spend my life in a cold shower. Oh by the way va-va-va-voom and he took off running."

I was laughing so hard I could hardly move, "I am going to tell your mother on you," I yelled.

I was so glad I went, we had such fun. The brothers took

their kids out for an afternoon of fishing while the girls sat down on the beach enjoying the sun. Janet asked me what I did for a living and I told her I am a lawyer, "I decided to put my career on hold for now with all the work that we have been doing with the house. I would love to have you come over sometime and see what a wonderful job Daniel did on it. The inside is done too but I am waiting for some new furniture to arrive. I have no idea what I am going to do with the old stuff, it's beautiful but dark and I am trying to lighten up the place."

Penny said she couldn't believe that Daniel had finally found someone, "I was sure he was going to be a bachelor forever. He is a good man Sydney, which I am sure you know."

"Oh my yes, we have had some challenging things going on here lately and he has been so supportive, besides he's a nut, and I am very partial to nuts." We all laughed.

Edith came over and asked what we were laughing at, we told her and she laughed too. "Can I join you ladies? It is hot but a beautiful day, I heard we may get a storm tonight but for now it is perfect. Look, Josh caught something, he sure looks excited. All the kids love fishing, just like their fathers and grandpa."

A little later Daniel came over and whispered, "You do know you have fingerprints all over your chest don't you?" I looked down of course, but naturally there was nothing and give him a smack in the head.

"What am I going to do with you?"

"I have an idea." Another smack followed. "But Syd we are engaged I don't think anyone would be too surprised it I threw you on the ground and made love to you."

"Somehow I think they would be now control yourself but it does sound like fun."

We did have a pretty big storm that night but I felt cozy and protected in our big house.

The next morning was a little gloomy but we all gathered outside as usual. Lori asked if we could all go over to my house and see the improvements. It must have looked like a mob scene with all of us trooping over but it sure was fun. Everyone was so impressed with what Daniel had done and he got the usual back pats, or should I say slaps from his brother's. The girls were especially taken with the new interior. "Didn't you say you have new furniture coming soon?" Sandra asked.

"Yes next week and I can hardly wait. Then it truly will be done, which I am sure will make Daniel just as happy as I am, he has worked very hard inside and out."

"So you did wallpaper too, how versatile you are little brother," said John. Daniel gave him a hit on the head and that started them all roughhousing."

Edith spoke up loud and clear, "Children please remember your manners," which got everyone howling with laughter. The guys all picked her up and carried her back to their house. Of course she protested but laughed the whole way. What a fun loving family I am getting into, I thought.

The next day everyone left, I felt so sad as we had had such a good time and now it is back to whatever. I decided to go over and see Edith she must feel sad too with them all gone. She looked tired and said, "You know it is always so much fun to have them here but I hate to admit that it is pretty hectic and I am pooped, that sounds awful doesn't it?"

"No it doesn't, as much as you love them you aren't used to so many people going in and out all day, I am sure it is a lot of work."

Somehow we got to talking about careers and she asked, "Have you thought any more about getting a practice of your own, this town could sure use you?" she asked.

"To be honest I haven't thought anything about it, there has been so much going on with the house and all but maybe after the wedding and we get into a normal routine I could at least do some work out of the house. Not much but something."

Edith got up from her chair and came over to sit with me on the couch. "You know I volunteer once in a while at the assisted living home just north of Thumb Harbor, it is a very nice place with nice people. I do hear them talking about making out wills but are afraid it costs too much and they might get someone who would take advantage of them. If you do decided to get back into it all maybe you could start there and help those people."

"That is a wonderful idea, I practice Elder Law and Special Needs and that is the perfect place to start I think. Thank you for telling me about it. Maybe when I am ready you could come with me and introduce me around to everyone. That might put them at ease rather than a total stranger coming in. It would probably be a good idea if I had a short lecture where I could explain a few things and then if they are interested I could help each individually."

I got up to leave and Edith said, "Oh say, I just remembered I need to go to the assisted living home tomorrow and drop off some things for the craft woman, would you like to come and just see the place?"

"Thank you I would love that, how about I treat you to lunch afterwards?"

"Now that is a deal, come on over about eleven o'clock."

We drove along the coast and it was so nice to not have to drive for a change, just sit back and enjoy the coastline and the view. "I will never get tired of this view, it is even more beautiful this morning after the rain, have you lived here your whole life Edith?"

"No my father was an insurance man and we moved around a lot, I was born in Indiana. I met Eli through a mutual friend after we wound up here, my families last move. I will never forget the first time I saw him, he was so handsome and strong and his smile blew me away, as the kids say today," she said then smiled. "He is everything to me Sydney."

We sat in silence for a few minutes then Edith said, "Here we are." She pulled into a circular drive to the front entrance and we got out. "Lovely area isn't it?"

"Yes it really is I am so glad I came." We walked into the lobby where several ladies were sitting and talking, all said hi to us and Edith introduced me. I had thought they would be quite old but many were in their fifties and seemed to be well up on what was going on. They may just have a disability and can't walk. I know I am going to like coming here, I can just feel it. Edith dropped off the box of crafts and Rebecca, the manager, told us we are welcome anytime, the people would love to have more visitors.

"Many of them have no families and some get no company. It is so sad but sometimes this can happen. All they want is for someone to listen to them, someone to just care, sometimes I wonder how I would feel if I were alone and sitting here all day," said the woman.

"Do they all have their own rooms or apartments?" I asked.

"Some live on their own and some share with a roommate. We serve three meals a day but they have a little efficiency kitchen with a microwave and a two burner stove plus an apartment sized fridge. so if they want to cook a little something they can. We have a beautiful patio out back where they can sit and watch the lake and the birds. There are physical, speech, and occupational therapists who come in once a week to help those that need it. Also there are people who come in every two weeks to entertain them with songs or play instruments, also we have travel lectures. I love working here it is so rewarding. Sydney, if you find you have the time please come back you won't be sorry."

"Thank you so much, my friend Edith has told me that there may be a need for someone to help these people make out wills or trusts. I am an elder law attorney. But now that I have been here I really want to come back and just volunteer then later when I start up my practice again maybe I can help them that way too. This is a very special place. It makes me feel good to know there are still people in this world who really care and try to make other's lives rewarding."

On the way to Thumb Harbor I thanked Edith for letting me come, "What a wonderful place I am really so touched and impressed, somehow I have got to find the time to volunteer there at least once a week."

"I knew you would feel just like I do and I know they would love to have you. Daniel will be very happy, I conned him into being Santa one year and he loved it."

Daniel came over for dinner that night and I told him about our trip. He was pleased but concerned that I was spreading myself to thin, "We do have a wedding to plan and hopefully that will happen very soon. Let's take a walk down to the beach it is such a beautiful night, I heard that there are going to be shooting stars."

Once again Mother Nature gave us a great show, every few seconds the stars streaked across the clear sky. "Amazing isn't it?" I said as I snuggled closer to him.

"They only slightly compare to you my love, I can't wait to start our lives together and get started having your twenty kids."

"Really love that was almost a joke, four or five will be plenty. I so hope we get a mixture of boys and girls though, do boys run in your family?" I asked– "considering your family circumstances."

"Brace yourself, they do, we haven't had girls born in probably fifty years, do you want to call this whole thing off before we get started, now is your chance RUN."

I got up to leave as a joke but the look on Daniels face stopped me cold. "You big dummy I was only kidding you are stuck with me longer than forever. Besides boys are great, you are a boy, and to have four or five of you running around would be wonderful."

He pulled me down and hugged me furiously, "Please don't ever kid about leaving me I couldn't bear it." Then we kissed and I knew it would lead to much more but at that moment I didn't care. "Syd we have to stop we have waited this long and I want our first time together to be in a fantastic place not a sand box."

I bopped him in the head and laughed so hard I thought I would throw up. "Oh my God you are too much; we are going to have such a fun life. Now be a good little boy and sit up and watch the rest of the sky show with me."

He moved and let out a cry, "Oh I twisted my back."

"Here let me help, take off your shirt."

The evil eye thing made an appearance, "Want me to take off my pants too?"

"It's up to you but the shirt should do it."

"What are you going to do to me, something naughty I hope."

I rolled my eyes around, "Lie down on your stomach

carefully, ok now relax you nut." I started massaging his back.

He started groaning, "Oh boy that feels good, how did you learn to do this so good?"

"When I was in college I took a couple classes and this is how I made some extra money, aren't you lucky?"

After a few minutes he asked, "Do you do whole body massages too?"

"Yep, but maybe we had better save that for when we are married as it is better if you are naked."

"Gives me something to look forward to" and he flipped over and started kissing me. "Though if you think it would help I guess I wouldn't mind taking all my clothes off now after all if it would be for the good of my poor poor back."

I smacked him on the arm, "Somehow my dear I have a feeling that if you took all your clothes off you would be thinking of other things besides your back, now get up you bad boy."

"You're no fun."

When I got home I got a call from Gretchen, she said she will be able to come out here on August eleventh. I told her I will be there with bells on. Oh I can't wait!

Two days later a big truck pulled up with our furniture. I was so excited! I told the men where each piece went and then called Daniel, who came right over.

"Wow everything looks wonderful, I am so glad we got the old pieces that we didn't want put up in the attic before they came. Syd it looks like a totally different house. The parlor looks quite formal but that is the way they are supposed to look. I like the mixture of old and new lighter colored furniture."

"Come see the dining room, do you like how it all came out?" I asked, as I ran my hand over the new table. "The other one was so heavy looking but this is better I think. I am glad I saved the lace curtains for both the parlor and here, again mixing the old and new. The music room didn't need much but I am glad we saved the old high back chair by the harp. I think most of our living is going to be in the back family living room and am so glad you thought this room should be more casual with comfortable over- stuffed chairs and couch. The dark greens and tan colors you picked out are perfect."

Daniel was heading up the stairs to check out the bedrooms. "I see you left one room with only blue paint," he said, "any special reason?"

"Yes as a matter of fact, that is where our son will live, though when I decided on that I had no idea there was even a chance of that happening."

He put his arm around me, "You bet there's a chance."

Our room only got a larger dresser and Daniels stuffed chair by the fireplace and my stuffed chair which was a smaller version of his was on the other side. "Now we can sit here on cold winter nights and read by the fire," I said.

"OR we could just jump in that nice big bed and get warm," he said as he went over to try it out.

"You really have a one track mind don't you sir?" I said as I jumped in and landed on top of him, but quickly rolled over and out.

"That mister is what we females refer to as a tease."

He laid there looking dejected and shaking his head, "You are a very mean woman and I guess I am just going to have to get used to being turned down," he said then sighed deeply.

"Not for long," I said as I ran down the stairs.

When we got into the kitchen I pointed to what looked like a door in the floor. "What do you think this is I found it when I washed the rug that was over it? Do you suppose it is a dungeon and there are skeletons down there?"

He went over to it and lifted the lid and looked down. "This is a cellar I guess let's go and see." He went down but I was only brave enough to go a few steps and peeked, basements are not my thing, I think I have seen too many scary movies.

"What's down there?"

"Just a bunch of old preserves and boxes, it actually has a dirt floor, come see. If there is another tornado we will all have to come down here so you might as well try it now."

"Tell ya what when the tornado comes I will think about it more seriously now come on up let's get some food."

Then I remembered Gretchen's call, "Guess what we can set

a date for the wedding, Gretchen called and she will ready to come on the eleventh. She doesn't drive so I am going down to get her. Let's start thinking about a date."

"How about August 29th?"

"Fine by me, yea it is set."

After we ate I said, "Daniel, do you remember Josh? Well I got a couple letters from him and wrote him back about us getting married. He is very excited for us. I thought I had better ask you if you minded if I continued to write him, really he is such a good friend. Actually I would love to invite him and Ken to the party we briefly talked about having after we get married for our friends. What do you think about all this?"

"Of course you can write him and I don't see any reason why we can't invite them both to our party. I still feel so bad about the way I acted when he was here; he did seem to be a very nice man. I am so proud of you for sticking up for him my love."

"Thanks I am glad you understand."

Later in the afternoon I went over to visit Edith. She was in her usual spot under the tree in the yard. "Hi!" I yelled as I got closer.

She turned and saw me, "Hi yourself, come on over. So what are you up to today?"

"I got a call last night from my friend Gretchen and she finally told me she will be coming here on the eleventh. We decided the wedding is going to be on the 29th, how does that sound to you? Good, now I think we had better get planning this wedding, are you up to it now?"

She smiled so big, "You bet I am I haven't been able to plan my other son's weddings so now that I have a daughter I can help with it, where do you want to start?"

"Well I know this is going to sound odd but I want the wedding to be friendly, a celebration of the love Daniel and I feel for each other, with only family and very good friends. This is a very serious thing we are about to do but it should be relaxed and fun too. Daniel and I talked about maybe having a big party later on and invite everyone else. Oh course anything we plan I will consult Daniel on. Anyway, how about the flowers, your yard is so full and beautiful now I don't think we need to bring in any extra. I was thinking that it would be fun if we had the actual ceremony under your arbor over there," I said as I pointed to the white painted arbor that was covered in vines and creeping flowers. "What do you think?"

"That would be perfect very romantic and the family could sit in front of it. We are going to have to get a bunch of chairs though, and music. I think just a small grouping of musicians to play softly in the background during the ceremony then play something maybe more lively for dancing afterwards at the reception. Good I am glad you agree."

"Do you know of a caterer here in town?"

"A good friend of mine does it out of her house and if you wouldn't mind I would love to ask her, she needs the business right now," Edith said.

"Perfect, now what do we serve? I would like to keep it simple but nice, any ideas?"

Edith said, "How about some fancy horderves, punch and drinks and of course the cake, that way we don't have to set up tables, they can just grab what they want and sit in the chairs. Seems a little friendlier and would allow them to circulate easier?"

"You're good woman, I like that. We will have to go over to your friends soon and see what she thinks. I will let you decided what you want to do with the cake so it will be a surprise. Please don't make it too hard, I want you to be able to enjoy every minute of all this."

She leaned over and took my hand, "You are such a considerate person my dear."

"I just had a thought, I have to go down to Ohio to pick up Gretchen, maybe I could look for my dress down there, they have a lot of stores."

Edith was nodding her head, "Unless you want to travel farther in the state you will not find anything near here. Besides it will be a lot of fun for you and her to pick it out together."

"What a great idea, I will let her know I will be spending two or three days down there before we return. By the way did I tell you she is from Sylerville originally, born and breed?"

"No you didn't, what is her last name?" she asked getting excited.

"Blanchard do you know the family?"

"I sure do, wow what a coincidence. I can't wait to meet her and thank her for being so kind to you. So, it looks like we have things pretty much planned out. All we need to do is order some flowers for your bouquet, set up the food, get the chairs, order the invitations, and pray the weather cooperates. I don't know about you but I am tired already." And we both laughed. "Let me start things going and I will let you know how I do. The invitations should be done quickly as there won't be that many."

I got up and put my arms around her, "Thank you so much, you are so special to me. Hey I almost forgot I called the gal at the assisted living home and am going to go and volunteer tomorrow, do you want to come too?"

"Sure would I am scheduled there tomorrow also. I usually only stay until lunch as the people take napes afterwards and there isn't much to do. Is that all right with you?"

"Yes, that will give me some time to do a few things here. Shall I pick you up at nine? Good. I brought my knitting so can I stay and keep you company for a little while longer?"

"You bet it is such a beautiful day I think I will just stay out here." So we just chatted away and had a good time.

That night I told Daniel all about our plans and he thought they were fine, all but the part about me spending a few days in Ohio. "But love don't you want me to be the bell of the wedding in a spectacular dress? Who knows maybe I will find one the first day."

"Of course but I don't want you gone for even a minute just to get it. Absence makes the heart grow fonder is a bunch of rubbish."

"Oh I am going with your mother to the assisted living home tomorrow for my first morning of volunteering, I can't wait it should be so fun."

The next morning when we got to the home we were greeted again by the staff. "What would you like me to do?" I asked.

Edith just went to her favorite person and they started talking.

Miss Brown, Rebecca, said to just go over and talk to whoever I want and go from there.

I looked around and saw the woman I learned a little about on our first trip sitting by herself looking out the window. "Hello, my name is Sydney, may I sit down."

"Of course dear, my name is Rae, do you live near here Cindy?" she asked. I decided not to correct her this time.

"Yes down the coast a few miles. I was born here but went to Georgia, now I am back and so glad to be here. I noticed that you wear sunglasses even inside, do you have some eye problems?"

"Yes I do, I can't see too well things are a little bleary and I can't make out colors, my doctor is going to do surgery soon to hopefully correct the problem. I can't wait I have had this a long time."

She looked so sad and I felt so sorry for her but she had a strong spirit and seemed to know exactly what was going on. She was a very pretty woman I would guess she is in her late fifties. I assumed because she was sitting in a wheelchair that she couldn't walk.

"Do you have family here Rae?"

She seemed to have left me for a moment and gone back to another time, then "No I used to though, they are all gone now. Are you married Cindy, do you have children?"

"No to both but I am getting married soon and my to be husband just asked me how many children I want and I told him twenty. Of course I was kidding but boy did he give me a look."

She started laughing, "Thank you for that I haven't laughed in a long time. I like you Cindy."

"I like you too Rae," I said as I took her hand. How fun to find a new friend on my first day. "Would you like me to take you outside for a walk around the grounds, it's a beautiful morning?"

"You had better check with Rebecca first so she doesn't think you are kidnapping me," she said with a chuckle, "they are very protective of us here."

I went over to Rebecca and she said that was fine. "You two seem to be hitting it off well, I haven't seen Rae smile let alone laugh in a long time. Thank you Sydney." Then she smiled and put her hand on my arm.

Rae and I went out into the beautiful garden and I told her what colors the flowers were then put her chair under a shady tree, while I pulled up a lawn chair, "It is probably a good idea not to keep you in the sun too long with your eye problems." We just sat there admiring the beautiful gardens and pond and I asked, "Are there fish in there do you know?"

"There are supposed to be and I think there is some fish food near it to feed them with, could we do that please?"

I wheeled her over and found the food and put a cup of it in her lap. "Ok fire away" and she did with great gusto. "Hey slugger you better be careful you don't want to knock them out." We both laughed really good this time. I was having such a good time and it looked like she was too which made me very happy. "Rae can you hear the water from the lake, it sounds so soothing doesn't it?"

"Yes I can hear it from my room. When we go back would you like to see it? I haven't been able to decorate anything but it is comfortable. I live by myself."

"Yes I would like that very much, thank you."

We went in about an hour later and she showed me where her room was. It was a nice clean room with a large window facing the water. "I like this Rae, it is quite homey. Do you like being here at the home?" I asked. "Is there anything I can pick up for you the next time I come?"

"Oh are you going to come again, that would be so nice. You know what I would really like is a new bedspread, this one is so worn out and I love flowers. If it isn't too much trouble could you find something in pinks and purples? I will pay you for it as soon as you come."

"Of course, that is no problem." There was a knock on the door and Rebecca peeked in to say it was lunch time.

I pushed Rae into the dining room and sat down with her for a few minutes as she ate. "The food looks good, and to think you didn't have to fix it, lucky you. If I ever get rich and famous I am going to have a live in chef. I love cooking but hate the clean-up," I told her.

"Me too," she said then laughed.

"I am here with my friend Edith and it is time for us to go but I promise I will come back again very soon Rae. It has been such a pleasure to meet you," I said as I gave her a quick kiss on the cheek. "Be prepared," I whispered, "I am a kisser."

She took my hand and looked up at me, "So am I" and she drew me down and kissed my cheek. "You are a treasure my dear, goodbye for now."

I spoke to Rebecca one more time. "I really like that woman, she is a doll. Oh I asked her if she needed anything and she said she would like a new bedspread, I told her I would get her one. She said she would pay me for it when I returned. Was that all right?"

"Yes that is very kind of you. I am amazed that in just this short time I can see Rae is happier, thank you so much Sydney please come back very soon."

I promised I would and we left. "How about lunch in Thumb Harbor Edith?" I asked as we got closer.

"Good idea I am not ready to go home yet." We went to the cute little café I ate at the first time I came here. I told her about Rae and she was very pleased. "You certainly have a way with people Sydney, I have seen Rae there for years and she never smiled once. All she did was sit there in the window and stare out at the lake. I am so glad you are doing this. I too get great joy out of it."

I did get Rae her bedspread in pink and purple flowers and she loved it then thanked me about a million times. We have become so close in the past few weeks and I have tried hard to see her twice a week. I look forward to it as much as she does I think.

When I got there yesterday she wasn't in her usual spot by the window and I asked Rebecca where she was. She said she had her eye surgery this morning and won't be back for a couple days. "It happened quite quickly, the doctor called and said he had a cancellation so they took her."

"I hope she will be all right and the surgery will be successful, how long before you know?"

"The doctor said it could take a week of her having to wear bandages on both eyes then we will know once they come off. I am going to see her this afternoon is there any message I can give her?"

"Yes tell her the fish are hungry and want her back. She will know what I mean," and I giggled. "Also tell her that I am sorry but I won't be able to come quite as much, I am getting married soon and have a lot of thing to do, plus I have to go down to Ohio and pick up my maid of honor. Rebecca would it be all right if Rae came to my wedding, I have so few friends here and a familiar face would make me happy? I could get someone to pick her up and bring her back?"

"My goodness that is so nice of you, it will give her something to look forward to. If you wouldn't mind, I would be glad to bring her myself and stay for the wedding if that is all right?"

"Of course how wonderful, thank you for thinking of it. I will call you with all the details as soon as I figure it all out. Now what can I do today while I am here?" As it turned out I was the bingo person, and we all had a good time.

On one very hot evening while Daniel and I were sitting on the porch trying in vain to get cooled off he suggested we go for a swim. "Great idea let me get my swim suit on. Do you want to go home and get yours?"

"Nope I will just go in my shorts or au natural."

"Good heavens man what are the fish going to say?" and I went up to change.

It was getting a little dark when we got down there, "Ok girl turn around your soon to be husband is going to strip."

I did what I was told but said, "If you need any help holler." Of course he hollered. I went over and slipped his shirt off then I grabbed his shorts, "I will be so glad when you get to be a big boy and can do more things for yourself." With that he picked me up and threw me into the water. Then he took off his shorts and jumped in after me. "I knew I should have brought a flashlight,"

I said and laughed like crazy.

"Syd you really should get rid of that swimsuit, it feels good to be so free"

"Dream on you silly," and I tossed my suit on the beach.

"Get over here you."

Immediately I started swimming out farther and he followed, when he caught me he said, "Well we are either going to drown or one of us is going to get ravaged again, you choose."

"You know I am leaning toward the ravage but you will still drown, ravaging and treading water at the same time doesn't sound too smart. At least we should get to where we can stand up; ravaging is not recommended in ten feet of water, from what I read. You do realize what this is going to lead to don't you?" I asked.

"Yep."

Then I started to laugh, "So mister how do you propose we do this seems a little complicated to me? Maybe I could swim on my back and you could jump on top but then we would both sink and drown any ideas? Plus it is pitch-black and you might miss me."

"I think you have a point, how about we get out of the water?" and he picked me up and plopped me on the sand. "Love your outfit by the way."

That did it we both just laid there laughing, "Better luck next time you goose," and I kissed him.

Then we heard, "Sydney, Daniel are you down there?"

"Oh God its Dad, quick put yourself against me and slide down a little, stop giggling, and I will wrap us up in the blanket. It's so dark he won't see. Hi Dad it was so hot we decided to take a swim."

He started looking around, "So where is Sydney?"

"Ah, she is close by. So what's up?"

This was too good to pass up so I started kissing his chest and running my fingers over his back then down to his bottom and grabbed it and he let out a little yelp.

"Are you ok Son?"

"Yes just a little spasm in my leg."

"I called but you didn't answer your cell, just wondering if you have time tomorrow to help me with the dock?"

"Sure."

"Well good night Son," then a little laugh as he started to walk away, "good night Sydney."

"Good night Eli."

Everything was pretty much set for the wedding, Edith did a great job and I did my best to help. Almost a week before I was going down to pick up Gretchen I got a call from Rebecca at the assisted living home. "Sydney I know how busy you are but is there any way you could come up here tomorrow morning? Rae is going to get her bandages off and she asked me to call you and see if you could be there when she does. She is scared and I think she needs your support as her friend."

"Of course I will, she is my friend too, what time? Ok I will be there."

That night I told Daniel what was going on and he said he was so proud of me for helping that woman. "She is something very special love, and I care very much for her. So I won't see you until tomorrow afternoon. Be good you naughty boy," that got me a lot of head shaking but a smile too.

The next morning I was a little nervous for Rae, "Please God let her be able to see, please." The doctor was already there and I sat down by Rae and held her hand as he began removing the bandages, first one then the other. Rae was told to open her eyes but said she was scared. "Come on Rae, I want to see those pretty eyes of yours," I said.

What followed was a true miracle and I don't think I will ever get over it, it changed my life completely. Rae did open her eyes and what I saw made me jump back. She blinked a few times then turned to me, "Oh my God can it be," she said as she looked at me. "Sydney is that you, it can't be it just can't be?"

Rebecca stood there with her mouth open, repeating over and over, "Oh my God, oh my God, Rae you and Sydney look exactly alike and you both have the same eyes. I have never seen anyone with that color and now you both have it."

I was sobbing, "Rose oh my God is that you, Rose, my MOTHER?"

Rebecca grabbed for me as I started to faint, "Sydney no don't faint take a deep breath. That is Rae, not Rose."

But Rose interrupted, "No Rebecca my name is not Rae it is Rose Anne Everett–RAE, and Sydney IS my daughter but she didn't even know I was alive until this moment."

"Mama oh Mama," I cried as I clung to her. "Please tell me what happened where have you been? I just recently found out about the secret that Father and Gretchen have kept all these years but they both thought you were dead. But first I have to call Daniel, he is my fiancé, and he needs to be here with us both now."

I did call, "Daniel please come up to the assisted living home I need you, I am fine but very shook up, a miracle has happened and I want you to be a part of it. Come now."

Daniel came running in and saw us clinging together, first he looked at me then at her then looked again. "Daniel I would like you to meet my mother, Mom this is Daniel McGregor."

Another, "Oh my God," but from him this time, "Rose is it really you, of course it is, you and Syd look exactly alike? Boy have we got some talking to do."

Rebecca suggested we all go into the small sitting room off the main living room where we could have some privacy. We just sat there staring at each other, "Mom please tell me what happened."

"Oh Sydney just let me look at you and touch you just a little longer, I have dreamed of this moment for almost thirty years. Never did I ever expect to see you again in person. Where is your father, can I see him, or really should I?"

"Mom Father died of a stroke a little over a year and a half ago. He is the one who told me in a letter that I received after he died that there were things he could not tell me but for me to come here and I would find the answers I needed. His last words to me were 'look beyond the rose'. I had no idea what that meant and it haunted me." Then I told her about the sampler. "Almost a year after he died I almost felt compelled to come, like somehow I HAD TO. Gretchen has been with me since we moved to Atlanta and was going to move up here with me but Louise had to have heart surgery and needed her help. Did you know that Father married Elizabeth to help him take care of me? I know he didn't love her but he couldn't do it alone. She did a lot of charity work and almost took care of me. Oh I know she cared about me but it was Gretchen who was really my mother. Elizabeth died three months before Father in a terrible car accident. Since I was supposedly the last member alive from both families I inherited the house. Daniel and I met when he restored the old house, and Mom it is gorgeous. He also helped me inside and we fell in love. I have never been so happy in my whole life," I said as I reached for his hand. "As I said we are going to be married very soon and next week I am going down to pick up Gretchen so she can be in our wedding and live with us. There is so much more to tell you but please tell me what happened to you."

"Gretchen has been with you, how wonderful. I became sick about six months after you were born, and after months of going to every doctor we could think of your father heard of a clinic in Norway, so I went. I did not want him to come he needed to be with you. I started improving and wanted to get back home, oh I forgot, this is going to sound odd but before I left I gave my lawyer divorce papers, I was afraid I was going to die and if I did things would have been very complicated getting my body back, plus I hoped your father would remarry. I did tell the lawyer not to serve the papers unless I died. It just seemed easier at the time but now I know it was stupid. Whatever, I was on a bus going to the airport and it swerved to miss another car and went over the cliff. Somehow I was thrown free before it hit the water and a nice couple found me. I guess I was badly banged up and hurt my back; they took me back to their home and called the doctor who told them what to do to help me. He was there many times while I was hurt. It was mostly my back that is why I am in this chair, though I can walk just not long distances. Gradually I improved but had no idea who I was or where I came from so I stayed with them. They told me that there were no other survivors of the bus crash. When my memory started to come back I decided to travel back here. Since I had been gone so long I wanted to find out what I had missed in those years so I got some old newspapers and read that Charles had remarried though I did not know it was Elizabeth. It hurt but I didn't think I should reappear and cause a lot of problems for everyone, so I changed my name and became Rae and moved in here. Sylerville had been my home for so long it seemed natural to stay. I found out you had gone back to Atlanta with Charles so I subscribed to the Atlanta paper and of course saw your father very regularly, he really became an important man didn't he? I saw your picture when you graduated from law school with your father. Then I stopped taking the paper because it hurt so much, though I was so very proud of you. Oh I would have done things so much differently now but at the time I was young and didn't know better. All I hoped for all these years is that you were happy and well taken care of. I knew Charles would be a good father to you no matter who he had married."

"Oh Mom I am so sorry you had to go through so much. Well guess what your life is going to change again, you are going to come and live in YOUR house with me, Gretchen, and Daniel and the twenty kids we are going to have. They are going to need a grandmother."

"Twenty kids, are you kidding, they will need more than a grandmother they will need an army!"

"Yes Mom, when I told Daniel he had the same reaction. We are going to try for four or five. So what do you say, will you come and be my mom?"

Rose just sat there crying, "Of course I will my daughter, how wonderful that sounds. But won't I be in the way with all your plans? Daniel am I going to mess things up for you two, after all you will be just married?"

He had been sitting there for so long quietly listening to everything that I almost forgot he was there. "Rose you are so welcome please do come we are both going to need you. Wait til you find out what Sydney is really like, you will love her just as much as I do. She is my life and I promise you, as I have promised her that we are going to have a wonderful life, twenty kids or not," he said then laughed. "I know my parents will be thrilled to see you again, they have adopted Sydney as their own and I must warn you they're not going to give her up, so I guess you are going to have to share her with them. Sydney is a remarkable woman Rose and I am so excited for you to find out why–she is funny, very smart, a martial arts expert, and has me, who could ask for anything more."

"See what I have to put up with Mom maybe between the two of us we can reform him."

"No way my girl, I like him just the way he is, now when do I get to get out of here, yesterday?"

Daniel did his rolling eyes thing and said, "Oh God two of them help me."

"Bless you Daniel, I promise to be a fun mother-in-law."

"Mother-in-law, not on your life you will be my mom too. I am sure my mom will agree that I need more than one at times. He went over and kissed her on the cheek, "Welcome home Mom."

"Wait until Gretchen sees you, she will need heart surgery," I said with a snicker. "Hey I have a great idea, how about coming down to Ohio with me when I pick her up we can surprise her then, boy will we surprise her," I said then smiled big. "I am going to pick out my wedding dress when we are there and you can help. That is something I have always dreamed of. Mom can you climb stairs up to a bedroom?"

"I am not sure about the stairs dear I haven't had to climb, but I am in physical therapy so I will ask. I hope that won't be a problem for you?"

"Not at all we can convert the music room into your bedroom right Daniel?"

"Yep."

"Ok it is all set, I will go and talk to Rebecca and if all goes well we can bring you home NOW, how's that?"

"Sweetheart if you don't mind can we do it tomorrow morning, it will give me a chance to say goodbye to everyone and have a good rest, I am very tired right now, so much has happened. Plus my doctor is going to come back in the morning to check me out then we can go. Do you mind packing me up, can I bring my new bedspread?" she asked with a grin.

"Of course you can bring your new bedspread. Whatever you think best, I will go now and see Rebecca and get it all set up. Oh my I never expected anything like this when I came to volunteer, but I did know right from the start that you were going to be the one I wanted to befriend. Wow this is all so wonderful!"

Rebecca came over as soon as we left the room and I told her that Mom would be leaving tomorrow morning and hoped that wasn't going to be a problem. "Not at all I am so thrilled that this all came about, how wonderful for you all. I guess this means you won't be back. Well I can truly understand. I will get the paperwork together and ready for you. Have a good night and God bless you all."

We both hugged my mom and left. Since we had two cars I followed him. We got back to the house and I motioned for him to come in. "Want some dinner? Why do I even ask, come on in and help me."

"I still can't believe all this," I said as I started making dinner, "my mother is alive and I actually found her here. If I hadn't gone over there with your mother none of this would have happened. It was meant to be I am sure, I don't believe in coincidences, everything happens for a reason."

"It is a true miracle Syd, I can't wait to tell Mom and Dad," he said as he started to set the table.

"Could we not tell them and just invite them over and let them be surprised, or would the shock be too much?"

"I really don't know let's think about it for a little while."

After we finished I realized that we had to fix up the music room as a bedroom tonight so it would be ready for Mom in the morning and told Daniel. "We had better get going don't you think?"

We moved the piano, which was thankfully on wheels down to the living room along with the harp, then went upstairs and got a bed, and finally a dresser. It didn't take too long and we were done, tired but done. The room looked pretty good but needed a chair so I again took one from upstairs. "Oh these French doors are just clear glass, she is going to need some privacy, I guess I could put up a sheet for the time being. She can use the bathroom next door, but it is small, I hope her wheelchair will be able to fit in there."

"Are we done love I am exhausted, how about we call it a night and I will come over for breakfast and we can go get her afterwards?"

"Sounds good to me, thank you for everything, I love you so much," I kissed him and he left.

The girls and I went up to bed right away, whoa I thought, the girls, I hope Mom likes dogs!

That night I felt the need to talk to my father, it had been a long time. "Hello Father it is me Sydney again. You are not going to believe this but guess who I found today, my mother Rose. She is alive and looks wonderful. She didn't die in the accident and came back to Sylerville to live. It is a long story. Now I understand why you sometimes stared at me strangely, we look exactly alike. Daniel and I are going over to pick her up tomorrow and bring her home here to live. You can't imagine what a shock for both of us to find each other. Oh Father I am so happy. Goodnight." Then I slept.

Daniel arrived and we ate, "How was your night?" he asked.

"It took me a little while to get to sleep, but at least I got some. Goodness I am so excited I can't wait to get over there."

Mom was in her room when we got there and Rebecca gave me the papers to sign. "She is like a schoolgirl, so excited I don't think she slept at all. I just can't get over this whole thing it is like a wonderful dream come true. Now go down there and get her," she smiled and gave me a hug.

I knocked on the door and peeked in, "Good morning Mom time for the jail break," I said as I went over and gave her a kiss. Daniel and I packed up her things and headed for my van. She got in quite easily thank goodness, and we put the wheelchair in the back. It made me so sad to think those few boxes were all she had.

When we got to the gates she started to cry, "Oh I have missed this place to much, I am so glad to be home." We drove slowly up to the house and when we stopped in front her crying turned into sobs, "Daniel you are an amazing man, the house looks brand new, it is absolutely beautiful!"

"Wait until you see the inside Rose, Sydney remodeled the whole thing."

We helped her up the few steps and Daniel went to get her chair. "Please take me on a tour I want to see every inch of this. Oh it is so light and I love all the new wallpaper and colors, you have truly made this a new home my daughter, my daughter, how wonderful that sounds."

"Here is your room for now Mom, I hope you like it, you can move upstairs when your back is better."

"It is lovely thank you both for going to such trouble. Oh my, and who have we here?" she said as my girls came flying up to the door.

"I hope you like dogs these are my girls and have been with me for many years. This is Samantha, Sammy, she is very affectionate and I am afraid you will get many slobbery kisses. And over there in Lilly, she is very active and again you can expect many kisses. Girls come over and say hi to your grandma." They stayed by the door checking things out but then charged in and the attack began. "Girls settle down," I said as I peeled them off of her. She was laughing so hard she couldn't even speak.

"I adore dogs and I am sure we are going to be great friends," she said between kisses. "Sometime you are going to tell me how you met these delightful creatures."

"Oh Mom we will be talking for months, there are so many things I want to tell you."

Just then, "Sydney are you home? It's me Edith and Eli is here too we need to ask you..." They stood there like statues, not moving a muscle, Eli was the first to speak, "Rose, my God, is it really you? What in the world is going on?" Daniel went over quickly and put his arms around both of his parents.

"You are not going to believe what happened," he said gently.

"Hello Eli, it is so good to see you and Edith too," Rose said as she held out her arms. Edith started crying and went over and gave her one of her famous crushing hugs. "Sydney can you get us some coffee this is going to take some time and I think we could all use it," and Mom was right.

We went into the living room and Rose began her story. They literally were sitting there with their mouths open. Edith said, "So it was you that Sydney was helping at the assisted living home, didn't you recognize her right away?"

"No because my eyes were so bad, I had to wear sunglasses day and night so she couldn't see my eyes either, but once I had surgery and the bandages were taken off.... Oh I asked the home to call Sydney to see if she could be there when they did, I had grown so found of her I wanted her there because I really was scared. Anyway after I blinked a couple times I could see perfectly and was totally shocked when I looked over and saw my daughter sitting beside me. I knew her immediately, those eyes; I have never seen anyone with the same color as mine. And then it all began."

"It is so good havin' you back Rose, just in time for the wedding," said Eli still quite shaken I could tell.

"Sydney has told me how very kind you have been to her and how much she loves you both and I just want to thank you. I know we will all be a very happy family together."

"Of course Mom will be living with us and my wonderful Daniel agrees completely, we just fixed up the music room for her to stay in until she can use the stairs."

Edith just sat there shaking her head, like she couldn't believe what she was hearing, "And this all just happened yesterday how amazing!"

Everyone stayed on and we talked and talked. Mom finally said, "Sydney would you please call my physical therapist and let him know where I am, here is his number?" she said as she pulled it out of her pocket. "I am scheduled tomorrow. I hope you won't mind him coming here dear."

"Of course not it will be nice to meet him and keep up on your progress, maybe he can give us some ideas to help in between sessions. Oh, did the doctor come by this morning at the home, if so what did he say?"

She smiled brilliantly and said, "He told me I am doing fine, I should have no more problems with my eyes." We all cheered!

I invited everyone to stay for lunch and when we were through Mom asked if she could lie down for a little while, she didn't sleep much last night. She said goodbye and I helped her get settled down. "I put a bell here on your nightstand, if you need anything holler or ring the bell. Can I get you anything else?"

She smiled up at me, "Sydney you have given me everything already I love you, now go talk to your friends."

"Mom last night as I was trying to get to sleep it occurred to me that you might not have a lot of money of your own. Father left me more than I will ever need so I think we should share it. Please let me know if you need any or I could give you an allowance each month," and I giggled. "My little mommy might need an allowance. So what do you think?"

"Sweetheart that is very generous of you, I may need to ask you for some at some point, we can think and talk about this later."

I told her I would see her a little later, "Have a good rest," I said and blew her a kiss.

Edith was saying that she still can't believe all this has happened. "I am so thrilled for you both, hope you won't forget us," she said then gave me a sad little look.

I went over and hugged her, "Oh Edith you silly I love you both and always will, you are still my family, we have just added a new member," and I really meant it.

"If Mom is up to it next week we will go down to Ohio and get Gretchen. It is going to be so much fun; we can all pick out my dress. Please come with us Edith you are more than welcome."

"I would love to but you need some time alone with your mom. It will be fun for me to have your dress a complete surprise. Oh and don't worry we will take care of your girls while you are gone. Now I think it is time for us to leave my dear, thank you for lunch and enjoy your time."

Daniel and I sat out on the porch and talked. "I hope you are not just being nice about having Mom here, is it really all right? I don't want this to change anything between us."

"My dear Sydney, I love your mom already and I truly think this is going to work out so well for all of us. Please don't worry I am as happy as you are in how things turned out."

"Yep I did good when I trapped you," I said and took off across the yard. Once again I got tackled and landed face down in the grass. We had such a good laugh and I was so very happy— there is nothing else I need, I have it all, except of course for the twenty kids.

Four days later Mom and I were on our way to Cleveland. Gretchen had given me instructions on how to get there and it wasn't hard at all. When we arrived I told her to wait in the van and I would give Gretchen some excuse to come out here. I got out and went up to the door and rang the bell. Gretchen opened the door and grabbed me so hard I could hardly breathe, "Oh Syd I have missed you so much" then she planted a bunch of kisses on my cheeks, "come on in and see Louise."

"First could you help me get a couple things out of the van?" I went over to the passenger side, glad that my windows were tinted so she couldn't see in and opened the door.

Gretchen screamed and I had to catch her as she started to fall, "Rose is that you is it really you? I thought you were dead boy have you got a lot of explaining to do, so do you Sydney," she said trying to look stern but it wasn't working the smile came right back. She looked a little surprised as I got the wheelchair out of the back of the van, but I explained that Mom's back got hurt in an accident and this is helping her for now. As soon as Mom got into the chair Gretchen bent down on her knees and held her close for a long time the kissed her cheek, "Oh Rose I have missed you so much."

We went in and again Mom had to explain everything that had happened. "Can you believe Sydney found me at the assisted living home, never in a million years would I have expected that to happen? Now I am going to be able to live with you, Sydney,

Daniel and the girls. This is truly too good to be true. We are all going home."

"Oh ah, one quick thing ladies, the bride, me, needs to pick out a wedding dress while we are here. Are you game?"

Both said together, "We sure are." Then Gretchen said we must stay here with Louise and her family while we look.

"Sweetie we have already made arrangements at that nice hotel just a mile away. I don't want to put you and your family out. Stop shaking your head it is done, so there," I said with my most determined look.

"Rose you have no idea what I have had to put up with all these years with this girl but I am afraid you are starting to find out. We all laughed and Louise came into the room. She too was shocked when she saw Rose but very happy. We talked for hours then Louise told us dinner was ready and of course we were to stay. Afterwards I could see that Mom was tired from the trip so I thanked Louise, gave Gretchen a hug and told them we were going back to the hotel and would pick her up about nine- thirty tomorrow.

I was tired too so we went to bed early. The next morning our adventures began, we went to four shops in town and I finally found the perfect dress at the last one. I went in to try it on and it fit perfectly. It is an ivory color silk organza with different lengths of the thin organza falling gently over the long A- line skirt, with a short train. The top is strapless and has thin strips of beaded lace going up and down over the whole bodice. The back of it has a deep V that goes to my waist. Around the waist is a thick satin ivory ribbon that ties in a bow in the back then cascades down. The woman who helped me into it said she has never seen anything so beautiful it was like it was made for me. I was just about to walk out and yelled, "Grab your tissues ladies here I come."

They both gasped and Gretchen jumped up, "Oh Syd you look spectacular." Mom just sat there crying. I did my model thing and gracefully turned around and around, then gave them the look.

"Isn't it wonderful, I am so excited, now I have to pick out a veil." Again I went with the silk organza; it was so sheer I could hardly feel it. It was held on at the top with a ring of silk ivory colored roses. Perfect. "Wrap it up I am taking this home." The woman asked if I had shoes, I guess flip flops are out this year so I chose a simple heel in ivory satin.

We got back about dinner time and again Louise insisted we stay and eat. We talked for quite a while then headed back. I told Gretchen we would pick her up at eight the next morning. On the way back to the hotel I thanked Mom for being with me, "It meant everything to me. We have missed so much but now is what is important and we have the rest of our lives to make new memories."

We picked up Gretchen and were off. It was a fun trip, the two talked about all the silly stuff they did as kids and even sang their high school song. Of course I had to add a groan or two but only got hit in the head once. Gretchen said she had a confession to make, "Guess what I learned how to drive, with Louise having to go back and forth to the hospital I thought the time had come. I know I should have told you so you didn't have to make this long trip but I would have had to rent a car and that seemed too complicated, I don't have a car of my own. I hope you aren't angry with me."

"Of course not you nut, I think it is wonderful, besides it was so much fun to surprise you with Mom and I needed to go to a big city to find my dress." It only took us four and a half hours and we were at the gates.

Gretchen was practically speechless when she saw the house. As soon as we stopped in front she jumped out, "Oh my Syd this is an amazing transformation, it looks brand new. I love the colors. I can't wait to see what you have done inside." I got out and stood beside her but we had to wait another couple minutes to go in because the girls were in the yard and saw us pull up. They came charging over to me and practically knocked me down, "I missed you too you sweet girls." Then they saw Gretchen and went nuts, no problem with them not remembering her. She got smothered with wet kisses. When the excitement settled down I told them to go lie down while I helped Mom in and sat her down then got her chair. Gretchen followed and immediately went flying all over the place. No tour needed for her. All I heard was wow, amazing, then perfect. "It is so light an airy now you guys really worked your butts off."

"Gretchen," Mom said, "really?"

"Well they did. Sydney have you called Daniel to tell him we have arrived? Well get to it."

He answered on the first ring, "Hi love your harem has returned, yes everything went fine, yes Gretchen was shocked, yes I missed you too now get your handsome self over here."

"He is on his way."

He came charging in the door with a huge grin on his face. "So, my ladies are all home and safe did you have a good trip?"

Gretchen gave him a big smile and asked, "Don't you knock?"

"Nope not when I get a chance to meet Gretchen the Great," he gave her a deep bow then said, "come over here and give me a hug, or am I going to have to come there?" the evil Daniel look was back.

"Good heavens Sydney how do you put up with this man?" and she gave him a huge hug. "Young man we are going to get along very well."

We told him all about our trip and he asked if I found my wedding dress. "Yes but you can't see it until the big day, bad luck you know. Though I do have a little warning, you had better be sure your heart is in good shape because it is going to knock your socks off. By the way everyone here got a hug but me think you could possibly give me one too?"

"I can do better than that," and he kissed me long and hard. "Ladies you had better get used to this we do a lot of kissing around here."

Gretchen looked him straight in the eye and said, "I should hope so." We were all laughing so hard. What a fun family we are going to be.

"Daniel please sit down with Mom while I take Gretchen up to her room." I told her that there are three empty bedrooms left on the second floor and I put the things we had sent from Atlanta into one of them but she can choose which one she wants.

She liked the one I picked out because it was large and overlooked the lake. "I know I am going to be very comfortable here Syd, thank you again, I am so happy to be with you again, it has been so long. I just can't get over that you found your mother and me my dear friend, it is a down-right miracle."

"It really is, to think all the people I love are under one roof now. I am so happy! Let's go down and get some tea."

We found them in deep conversation. "Ok what lies are you telling my mother about me you nasty man?"

He looked up and said, "My dear all I was saying is that I love you with all my heart and she never has to worry." I kissed the top of his head and told them I was going in to make some tea.

Of course Daniel stayed for dinner and we talked about the wedding. "Everything is set, there will only be family and very close friends at the ceremony, then a big party later. It is going to be held in the McGregor's large yard. Mom I asked Eli to give me away, he has been like a father to me and I love him very much, and also I asked Gretchen to be my maid of honor and I know this is a little different but I want you to be my other maid of honor. How can I go wrong with the two of you, it will be a wonderful start to my marriage?"

"Oh Sydney that would be fantastic, get me some tissues I am going to cry."

Daniel got the whole box, "The way things are going you are going to need this."

We all sat out on porch after dinner and surprisingly no one said anything. The view was so beautiful as the sun set and we were all content to just stare at it. Even my girls seemed happy just to sit at our feet. Finally Gretchen broke the silence, "It is so wonderful to be back home again, I had forgotten how gorgeous the sunsets can be, and to be sitting here with the people I love most, is almost too much." She reached over and took Moms hand.

A million stars replaced the red glow and I glanced over at Mom who had fallen asleep. "I think it is time to go to bed."

Daniel gave us all a little kiss and left and I went over to Mom. "Time to get up sleepy head and get into bed," she smiled and I pushed her in. She was back to sleep immediately. Gretchen and I headed upstairs, "If you need anything holler," I said as I gave her a hug. "Sleep well."

I fell asleep right away too it had been a long happy day.

The next day Mom's therapist Peter came at about ten. He was a nice young man and seemed to know what he was doing. He was kind and gentle to her and she responded well and did a good job. I asked him how her progress was coming and he said, "Very well if she does her exercises she should be able to walk again and not have to use her chair very soon." He told me how to do the exercises and after an hour left. I guess he comes once a week. I told Mom how proud I was of her and that I would help her.

We talked practically non top for the next few days, there was so much catching up to do. Then Mom threw me a curve, "Sydney did you and your father have a good relationship?" Gretchen squirmed a little in her chair, sensing what was coming I guess. I tried to soften things a little but there was no way to do it.

"Mom he was a very busy man and spent most of his day with clients or in court, I am sorry but he did not have much time for me." She looked distressed. "But I know he loved me I just don't think he knew how to show it. Honestly I think he loved you so much that whenever he looked at me he saw you that must have been so hard on him. I will show you the letter I got from him after he died, it says a lot. I found him and was with him when he died and it just about did me in. I loved him very much and the following days were very bad for me. Thank God Gretchen was there to help."

"But I wasn't," she said, "and I should have been. I am so sorry, how I wish things could have been different."

"Mom you had no idea what was going on, you did what you had to do, and I think you are the bravest person I know to have sacrificed so much for us. Now please stop and remember we all love you. I believe strongly that things happened for a reason and if they were supposed to be different they would have been."

She sat there trying to absorb it all I guess and finally said, "Charles changed so much after he thought I was gone, I can see that now, he never was so stoic which I assume he was. We had such fun swimming, boating, and just sitting on the beach when we lived here in the beginning. Did you know that we lived here and so did you? When you were born it was the most fantastic thing for us both, he was wonderful with you, carried you everywhere, wanted you to be a part of everything. Oh Sydney he was so proud to have a daughter. In fact he wanted to name you Sydney because we went on our honeymoon to Sydney, Australia, and you were conceived there. He wanted us to always have a reminder of the wonderful time we spent there."

"Thank you for sharing all that, you know I thought he named me Sydney because he wanted a boy, this makes me feel so good. It just blows my mind to think that you both lived here and now I do. No wonder I felt right at home the minute I arrived. Sometimes this whole thing is so hard to absorb."

A couple days later I realized I had not told Mr. Edgeworth anything about what was going on, and since he is my lawyer I thought I had better call him. I did wonder though how much he knew about all this. "Hi Peggy this is Sydney Armstrong, is Mr Edgeworth available?"

"Sydney how nice to hear from you, how are things going? Good, I will get him."

"Hello Sydney, what can I do for you?"

"I hope you have a little time this is going take some." I took a deep breath and began, "Do you remember when I told you my father's last words and how confused I was as to what they meant? Well I found out," then I explained about the sampler. "I was totally shocked to find out Elizabeth was not my real mother and Rose was. I assumed Rose was dead but you are not going to believe this, she is alive, and has been living in Sylerville for almost thirty years." Then I told him the whole story. "She is well but in a wheelchair from the accident in Norway, though she is getting physical therapy and is expected to be able to walk again soon. She is here with me at the house and will stay forever."

"I am very surprised Sydney, I did know that Rose was your mother, your father told me, but I was sworn to secrecy. Your father thought she was dead and so did I what a discovery! Is there anything you need help with?"

"No though legally my house is not really mine it is hers isn't it? So what do we do?"

"I do remember when they married she turned everything she had over to him and though she did divorce him and the house was her family home. Let me recheck a few things and I will get back to you." As it turned out the house was mine after all.

"There is more, I am getting married in less than two weeks to Daniel McGregor. I know it seems like we are rushing things but we are very much in love and decided there was no need to wait. I am very happy, I have it all now, my mom, Daniel, and Gretchen. Oh Gretchen is living here too now. By the way did you get the picture I sent of the house?"

"I am very happy for you and wish you all the best and yes I did get the picture, you did a remarkable job restoring the old place. I am very proud of you, and I know your father would be too. As you know I am not a demonstrative man, as was your father, but I do care for and about you and am always available if you need anything Sydney."

I was overcome, this from a man who was always total business, "Thank you very much that means a lot to me. Goodbye."

Later in the day I told Mom about my call and said, "Mr. Edgeworth is checking into whether the house is mine or yours."

"Is he still there, he must be ancient by this time? You know I used to think he looked like Ichabod Crane. You too, my we are so alike? Oh I completely forgot about anything concerning the house. I did turn over everything to Charles but then I divorced him," she broke down in tears and tried hard to compose herself, "but if it does come out that I do own the house I will immediately turn it over to you. You have brought this place back to life and you are my daughter and I want you to make this home for your family. Besides I will be living here too, so what is the big deal?"

I was choking back the tears too, "Thank you, you know I will love and take care of this house forever, and hopefully my children will too. It makes me feel so good to think that a member of the Everett family will probably always live in this house."

Of course Daniel came over every night for dinner; I think he stayed away during the day so we could have some time to talk. We always had a fun time. I asked my mom who in the family played the harp, "It was me, I took lessons for many years and sometimes we would all gather in the music room and each would play something. Did Elizabeth ever play the piano Sydney? No well she should have she was very good."

"Mom will you play the harp for us now?" I asked.

"Oh my, it has been so many years but I sure will give it a try." She said she needed to sit in a chair and not her wheelchair so Daniel just picked her up and put her in one. It took a little time but when she started playing it was like listening to the angels. I have always enjoyed listening to the harp but this was my mother playing this time and it was magical. When she was done there was complete silence, I think we were all lost in it.

"Oh how wonderful," I exclaimed, "that was so beautiful. You do realize that we are going to expect this every night now. It is so soothing and relaxing, you are so talented."

"You know, I surprised myself as well," she said, "it just seemed to come back so easily."

–7–

THE WEDDING

The countdown was here it was only one more week until the wedding. Edith came over regularly and the poor thing was so worried that something awful was going to happen. She said the caterer woman had everything planned, Daniel asked a friend to take pictures, the Champaign had been bought, the musicians set up, invitations were sent, and Eli had gotten the streamers to decorate the trees with, plus he put the little lights in the trees. She said she has the cake figured out but she must be forgetting something. "Edith I told you not to get upset about all this, now stop, everything is done," I said as I hugged her. "You have done a wonderful job and I am so grateful! Please take this next week to relax, in fact I need to do some knitting to keep myself busy too so how about you come over and sit on our porch for the next few days?"

"You know that really would be nice, I will come thank you." She did and she and Mom had the best time chattering.

Daniel was getting excited we could all see it at dinner that night. "So my almost bride, where do you want to go on our honeymoon?"

"Oh my gosh I haven't even thought about it, where do you want to go?"

"I have always wanted to go to Scotland where my ancestors are from, what do you think?"

"That would be wonderful, oh Daniel what a great choice." Then I looked at Mom and Gretchen. "How can I leave…?"

"Sydney don't even consider it, you and your husband need to have some time together, your mother and I will be just fine here. We will take care of each other and the McGregor's are close by so say YES," said Gretchen in her we are done talking about this way. Mom was nodding too.

"Ok YES" and I ran to him and he picked me up and kissed me. "How very exciting, but it is getting late, can you arrange everything in such a short time?"

The stinker put me down and pulled the plane tickets out of his pocket, "Just took a chance and hoped you would agree. Start packing my girl we leave the night of the wedding."

"Good heavens there are a million things I have to do. I just can't wait. Thank goodness I have my passport but I have to figure out what to bring."

The night before the wedding Daniel made his final appearance, I told him I cannot see him again until the ceremony, "Bad luck you see."

"I guess I can wait but it won't be easy," he said then smiled big. "Good night my love, tomorrow you will be my wife, it just doesn't seem possible." I walked him to the gate and we kissed again and he was gone.

It had been arranged that I would get dressed at the McGregor's so I wouldn't ruin my dress walking across the lawn. The ceremony was at one o'clock and at noon we went over. Mom and Gretchen looked so beautiful. I told them I would go up and get dressed and see them outside later, "I want you to see the bride all done up." This was my time with Edith she was going to help me dress. She has been working so hard and has helped me so much in the past months I wanted to share this with her. My makeup and hair were done already so it was just getting into the dress. I piled my hair up and had soft curls circling the top where my ring of roses was to be put. My earring were a gift from Mom, she wore them on her wedding day. I took the dress out of the bag and we began. First off I put the heart shaped diamond necklace that my father gave me for my graduation on. I wanted him to be a part of this too, and I truly think he will be here. Just then I felt something like a kiss on my cheek. I looked around and of course no one was there. "Father is that you?" I whispered, "yes I am sure thank you for being here, I love you."

She had a full length mirror set up in her room and when I

was dressed I slowly turned around. Edith was truly overcome, "You are the most beautiful bride I have ever seen, the dress is perfect, here let me put your headpiece and veil on. Sydney Daniel is going to faint."

"I sure hope not, Edith I want to promise you that I will do everything in my power to make Daniel happy for the rest of our lives, he is my world and my love. You and Eli have been so supportive and loving to me and there are no words big enough to say thank you."

"No thank you's are needed, we love you very much and I know how much you love our son, but honey why the tears? Are you getting a little nervous?"

"Oh Edith, I am a little nervous but not about the wedding. This is very personal but I do need to talk to you as my mother do you mind?"

"Oh course not, how can I help?"

I wiped the tears away and said, "Do you remember me telling you that I had never made love to a man after Ted attacked me? Well tonight us our wedding night and I am scared I will disappoint Daniel, he knows what he is doing I don't."

"You mean you still haven't…?"

"No… oh my, this is embarrassing, I probably shouldn't have said anything."

She took my hand, "Don't be embarrassed I think it is wonderful. Sydney when two people love each of as much as you do things will come naturally, sharing and giving to each other is the ultimate gesture of that love. I am so touched that you trust me enough with your concerns. Now the time has come for you to get married, let me see that beautiful smile of yours."

"Oh thank you Edith, I love you so much."

At that moment there was a knock on the door. It was Eli, "You girls had better get going it is almost show time."

"Come in Eli." He opened the door and just stood there staring at me.

"Sept for Edith I have never seen a more beautiful bride in all my life," he said as he walked toward me. He put his arm up and I took it and we left the room. It didn't even occur to me but we had to descend the staircase to get out to the yard. I couldn't help but think of Elizabeth, it was her wish.

Mom and Gretchen were waiting at the bottom, both in tears. In unison they said, "You are so beautiful, we love you." Then they left to take their places.

The music started and Eli and I walked over to the archway. All the family was there including my girls who had huge bows around their necks and were sitting next to where Mom and Gretchen would be. The garden was lovely, so serene. But it was my Daniel that took my breath away; he looked so handsome in his formal attire. He looked up and saw me and bowed. He told me later that he was so overcome with love and how beautiful I looked he almost forgot the words he had written for me. Eli took me up to him and put my hand in his, then kissed me on the cheek and said, "I love you Sydney." He patted both of our hands and stood back as Gretchen and Mom WALKED down the aisle.

My mother was walking with the help of Gretchen and she came over to me and whispered, "My gift to you my daughter." Edith followed and went to stand by my other mother's.

"Dearly beloved we are gathered here in the sight of God to join together this man and this woman in holy matrimony... Daniel and Sydney have written their own vows, Daniel will you please begin?"

"Sydney I wrote down what I wanted to say to you but it doesn't seem necessary. My heart knows just what to say. Since the first day I met you I knew you were someday going to be my Sydney. My life is complete now that you are with me, and there is nothing more I could ever want but you. You are as beautiful inside as you are outside. We are going to get through whatever life has in store for us because we will do it together. I promise to love you with all my heart and soul now and forever."

"Sydney will you please say your vows to Daniel now?"

"Daniel, I too knew from the start that we belonged together. You are the man that I love and I promise you that I will be by your side and support and love you no matter what. You have given me such joy and laughter and I can truthfully say I have never been happier. Some day you will be the father of my twenty children and we will tell them all about this day and the love we share for each other and them. Thank you for loving me."

"May I have the rings please? Daniel repeat after me…with this ring I thee wed."

"Sydney please repeat after me…with this ring I thee wed."

"Now by the power vested in me I pronounce you man and wife, Daniel you may kiss your bride." And he did, though maybe a little too passionately but I didn't care.

"Ladies and Gentlemen may I present Mr. and Mrs. Daniel McGregor."

Gretchen gave me my bouquet and we walked down the aisle. When we got to the end I raised my hand and pointed, "Everyone, do you see that beautiful lady sitting over there in the blue dress, she is my mother and I would love to have you meet her. Also the lady next to her is her best friend and mine too Gretchen, please go over and say hi. Thank you."

Then everyone came running to congratulate us. "Twenty children?" was asked many times and I had to admit I exaggerated a little and Daniel kept rolling his eyes all over the place. I told him over and over I was sorry but I couldn't resist. When I could break away I went over to my mom who was finally sitting down.

"Oh Mom what a wonderful surprise gift I hope you are all right?"

"Don't worry dear my therapist said it was all right. After all I didn't want to have to get wheeled down the aisle in that awful chair on your big day. You looked so beautiful and your words were wonderful. He does love you Sydney and I am so happy for you both. Now go mingle with your family."

"One thing mom, as I was putting on the heart necklace Father gave me for my graduation from law school I swear I felt a kiss on my cheek. I know it was him I just know it, it was so wonderful."

"Oh, I just felt the same thing," and she started to cry, "Oh

Charles is it really you, I love you and always will. Thank you for being here with us."

We clung together and cried, even Gretchen was crying. "How perfect!"

When I got myself put back together I looked over at Gretchen, "So how did I do?"

"Well except the twenty children thing you did fine, you just couldn't resist could you, I am glad it made things fun. You are really something else, and I am so proud of you my girl. Where's the food?"

"You stinker you are as bad as Daniel. Go find it yourself. I love you!"

Edith and Eli brought out the cake an hour later and it was magnificent. "Edith I can't believe how talented you are this is a masterpiece," I said to her. It was too, three layers of white icing with pastel colored roses scattered all over as swirled leaves clung to the flowers, simple yet anything but. We cut the cake together and of course I had to do the traditional cake in the face thing when I was feeding Daniel. He took his piece for me and started at me, but backed off at the last second. Thank goodness.

It was a wonderful afternoon, everyone was so happy. The musicians played slow and fast numbers and there was a lot of dancing. Daniel and I had the first one, he held me in his arms and looked deep into my eyes as he quietly sang, "Could I have this dance" (for the rest of my life). Suddenly I felt like there was no one there but us, it was our beginning of forever and I will never forget that moment. What a romantic wonderful thing for him to do. I told him I loved him and to please don't wake me up if this is a dream.

"It is a dream my love, but it will never end."

It started to get darker and the twinkling lights on the trees came on, turning the whole scene into a magical land. Daniel announced that we had to be at the airport in three hours for our flight to London so it was time for us to go. There was one last toast and we went into the house. We changed our clothes and met in the hallway. He took my hand and we went back down to say goodbye to all our guests. I told my girls who had been perfect for the whole thing that they need to be good and we will be back soon, be good to Grandma. I hugged Mom and Gretchen and told them I would keep in touch with my cellphone. Edith and Eli got huge hugs too and lots of thank you's. "Goodbye everyone thank you for making this day so special for us, we love you all." I turned around and threw the bouquet, which my mom caught. And we left.

The flight was long but very smooth. Daniel told the stewardess that we had just gotten married and she announced it on the speaker. Everyone clapped and I was a little embarrassed but wildly happy. When the movie was over and the lights got turned down Daniel lifted up the arm rest between us and pulled me close. "Sweetheart the most wonderful thing happened to me as I was getting dressed for the wedding. I was putting on the necklace my Father gave me for graduation and I felt a kiss on my cheek, I am not kidding, I just know it was him. Also when I told Mom she too got a kiss. It was so special my father gave both his girls a kiss on our special day."

"Oh Sydney what a wonderful thing to happen, I too am sure it was him."

We snuggled and I told him my back was stiff from sitting so long.

"Want me to rub it?" He put his hand on my back and started. "Your sweater is so thick I don't think you are going to get much out of this, I have an idea." He put his hand under my sweater and again started rubbing. "Oops," the silly guy said as my bra hook popped open. "Now I can do a better job." Of course his hands did not stay on my back.

"First I get ravaged in the bathroom, then almost in Lake Huron, and now in an airplane. You are such a romantic," I said as I rolled my eyes around. "Daniel you had better stop, what if someone sees us?"

"My dear I am your husband now and we get to do this plus we are both covered with blankets, we are in the last row, and there is no one else even close to us. Want to make love?"

"Good heavens man," then I whispered, "Yes, but if you don't stop right now I am going to have to attack you and we will be the first people in history to get thrown out of a plane while it is in the air with no parachutes. Not the greatest way to start out a honeymoon."

"You may be right but I am willing to take the chance, let's see we have about three hours to go, if we stop messing around in say two hours we will have plenty of time to get you put back together again. Stop giggling and kiss me."

"I'm curious do women get to ravage too or is there some law that says only men get to?"

He looked almost surprised but had a huge smile on his face as he said, "Ravage away my girl but be careful it could lead to some big problems that will be hard to resolve."

"You may be right," and I giggled again, "ok I will give you a rain check."

We landed in Heathrow airport in London at about eight the next morning. There was a two hour lay-over until we got our flight up to Edinburgh, Scotland and I was hungry, so was Daniel so we got some breakfast in the airport. What a busy place, it was so exciting to see so many people from all over the world in one place. Maybe if we have time we can come back and see the sights of England also.

This flight was spectacular, we were going over land instead of water and the countryside was beautiful. When we got over Scotland all I could see was green, rolling green hills and little dots of small towns. Amazing! After we landed we took a cab to our hotel. "Daniel this is quite a fancy looking place, there is even a door man," I said as he opened the door for us. "I feel like a queen with all this attention." But it was their accents that really got to me I could listen to them all day.

Our luggage was brought up to our suite and the man showed us around the rooms then told us to check out the view from the window and left. We were right on Princess Street and could see the castle above. It was a remarkable sight, so dominant like a giant protector of the city. I guess Daniel must have done a little homework because all of a sudden he sounded like a tour guide, "Did you know that Edinburgh Castle stands on the core of an extinct volcano called Castle Rock? It is the oldest castle in

Scotland, and was occupied in the sixth century. It is a favorite residence of Scottish kings from at least the eleventh century. Stop clapping you nut, I just thought this was interesting," he said and smiled, "Ok you can clap but stop with the silly face lass."

The room was amazing, a gigantic four poster bed was the dominate feature, and off to the right was a cozy sitting room with two large over-stuffed chairs and a coffee table. A large bathroom with a claw foot tub and separate shower plus mounds of fluffy white towels and bathroom accessories was beyond that. It was absolutely grand and I felt like a princess on Princess Street and did a little twirl around the room. Daniel was smiling at me then came over and took me in his arms. We stared at each other and didn't say a word, we both realized that we were finally alone, just the two of us. He picked me up and put me on the bed, "I love you so deeply Sydney and now I can finally show you." In this place of such splendor I truly became his wife.

Much later he turned to me and whispered, "Better than a sandbox huh?" and I burst out laughing. He joined in then asked, "Are you sure this was your first time love, you are really amazing?"

"I think I would have remembered this, beginner's luck I guess–I am a fast learner and you are a great teacher. Really baby I have been worried that I would disappoint you."

"Oh Syd come here," and he pulled me closer. "You don't ever have to worry about that, I have never been happier. You are so precious to me, the king of the bedroom, as you once referred to me has met his queen," and we both laughed. "So how about we try this again, of course just to give you a little more confidence? Stop giggling you sexy thing."

We spend the whole afternoon in each other's arms and all of a sudden Daniel said, "I'm hungry."

I bopped him on the head, "So our whole marriage is going to be controlled by your stomach huh, well I guess I can live with that but it is going to be tough, or I could just run away now."

I started to get up and he pulled me back, "Live with it chick, you are not going anywhere." We hugged and laughed.

"Shower time my husband, care to join me?"

"I would love to but if I do we will never get out of this room and I will die of starvation, oh what the heck."

When we finally got out of the room we found a cute little pub not far from the hotel and got a delicious dinner. Then we walked up and down Princess Street–so many unique little shops and friendly people. As the sun started to go down we sat on a bench and stared up at Edinburgh Castle, it was a truly magnificent sight, "I hope we can take a tour of that place," I said.

"Do you suppose we could get some sleep first, all of a sudden I am exhausted," Daniel said as he started to get up.

"So am I, what a day this has been."

We slept in the next morning and ordered breakfast through room service. The hotel provided thick fluffy bathrobes so we put them on and sat in the sitting room by the window admiring the view as we ate. "This tastes wonderful, so nice not to have to rush and get dressed and then find a place to eat. Boy do I feel pampered."

"Get used to it kid, I plan on keeping you that way." We drank our coffee then he asked where I wanted to go today. "We had better find some brochures and check out what there is to see. Let's get dressed and go down to the lobby."

"I have a better idea," I gave him my best seduction smile, "How about we jump back in bed for say an hour or ten and THEN get dressed and go down to the lobby?"

"Good God I created a monster, ok if we have to." He made it look like it was a big effort to get up and slowly moved over to the bed. I scooted past him and jumped into bed. It took two seconds for him to dive in. "Ok you got me here so what do we do now?"

"Come here and I will demonstrate."

The lobby was full of people when we got down there. The man at the desk gave us a schedule for city tours and made some suggestions. "You might want to rent a car and see the countryside. We even provide picnic lunches for our guests." We went outside and sat on a bench and started looking at everything.

"Wow I hope we have about three months this is going to take some time," I said pointing out places I wanted to see. "How about we start out with a tour of the castle–warning I am a castle nut and will want to see them all?"

"Perfect, let's go back in and sign up for it." I ran back up to our room to get my camera as I was sure I would need it. The view was amazing from the castle in any direction you looked– you could see the whole city from up there. I bought a book on its history and the tour started. The guide said it is over one thousand years old and was at one time a military base and housed prisoners from the many wars between the English and Scots. Because of the tension between the two monarchs nearly all of the wars were centered around the castle and it was under siege almost constantly. The Royal Mile is below the castle and connects it with Holyrood House where the royals used to travel back and forth, thus the name. We got to see the soldier's barracks and so many interesting rooms and areas. I about jumped out of my skin when, at one o'clock I heard a loud bang, like a cannon had gone off, but later found out it was a gun. Right then I decided I needed to see this. The guide took us over and it was not just a handheld gun it was a huge thing that sat on the ground. He said it goes off every day at this time except Sundays so people can check their watches. Originally it was to signal ships at sea.

The castle tour also included lunch and afterwards we went to Sterling Castle. Another gigantic place that we learned was built from 1490 to 1600–the first records of the castle were in 1110. Four of the Scottish kings lived there. It is set on Castle Hill and three sides have steep cliffs, for protection against invaders. I guess there were eight major sieges. It was fun to see all the people there in period costumes and there were a lot of activities that the children could take part in, like dressing in costumes and playing medieval instruments. They really did a good job bringing the past to the present.

Our last visit was to Sir Walter Scott's Abbotsford home, which he bought in 1811. It sits on one hundred acres of land, and while not a palace it was darn close, except this really looked like a home. I guess Abbotsford started out as a farmhouse and Scott built on many additions over the years. We found out that Scott was the youngest son of thirteen children, six died in infancy though. How sad! He was a lawyer and judge plus a novelist, poet and playwright, and became lame from polio in childhood. He was born in 1771 and died in 1882. The house itself was magnificent, so many beautiful stained glass windows, rich paneling, and little cozy nooks. I absolutely loved it! When we were walking through the fantastic grounds we actually saw a peacock sitting on the low branch of a tree. Daniel took my picture by it.

Well for now anyway I am castled out, I am exhausted. Daniel won't admit it but I can tell he is tired too because he asked if it would be all right if we ordered room service in for dinner. It was such a nice evening; we took showers and got into our pajamas, ate dinner and climbed into bed early.

We sat there with all the brochures in front of us and planned our next day. We decided to rent a car and see the countryside. "Hey, I think I had better call the front desk and have them make up a picnic lunch for us." He did and they said it would be ready whenever we are ready. Daniel asked them where to get a car and the desk clerk said they would arrange it for us. Neat!

We got up a little early and called room service for our breakfast. Afterwards Daniel got a evil little smile and said, "Shower time Syd how about we save some time and you join me?"

"Somehow I don't think we are going to save any time, you do realize what that is going to lead to don't you?"

"Yep."

"Who's going to drive," Daniel asked once we finally got down to the lobby and out to the car.

"Not me," I said, "unless you want to die. The thought of driving on the wrong side of the road, right as it may be, does not make me all warm and cozy inside. I have a feeling that if

I went around the corner I would automatically go to the other side where I should belong but don't."

"You lost me on the first curve, get in." The hotel gave us a map of where to go for the best views and explained about stopping for lunch. I guess it is not a good thing to do on someone property so he told us how to do it. It was so much fun to drive wherever we felt like going, the scenery was spectacular everywhere and I loved the cute little cottages that were everywhere.

"Daniel, do we really have to go home? Why don't we just gather up everyone and find a nice manor house and move in? I love it here."

He pulled over and said, "This is one of the lunch spots, want to eat now? As to moving here I think that would be a mistake, then where would we go on vacation?"

"Of course you are right, but this is so beautiful, and yes I am hungry I wonder what they fixed for us?" There were slices of roast beef, cheese, big crusty rolls, potato and macaroni salads, pickles, a bottle of wine, and cheesecake. They included china plates, wine glasses, silverware, cloth napkins, and a linen tablecloth. "Wow now this is a picnic lunch," I said as I grabbed a roll. When we were through we lied down on the grass and stared up at the sky. There was a slight breeze that was the perfect touch to the beauty all around us. "I like being married to you sweetheart, so far this trip has been perfect. I didn't realize how much I needed to get away from everything. I love you so much. Should we get gong now?"

"No need to hurry" and he rolled over and kissed me and started unbuttoning my blouse.

"Daniel not here, what if someone sees us? Maybe there is a law against this or something."

He looked all around, "My dear there is nothing but grass and trees for a far as the eye can see except for that cow over there; I don't think she will turn us in, now hush up and kiss me."

Right in the middle of the whole thing I opened my eyes and our cow friends head was up about two feet from mine. I screamed and Daniel took it the wrong way, "Glad you are enjoying our forbidden lovemaking."

"Open your eyes you nut."

He did and jumped a mile. Then he started laughing and so did I. "Well that took care of that, shoo you nosy thing," he said and hugged me tight. "I think we just made a Hallmark moment Syd something to tell our kids about."

"You have got to be kidding," but I just couldn't stop laughing.

We got back in Edinburgh about four, turned in the car and strolled down through the Princess Gardens then ate dinner, "This has been such a fun day, thank you for bringing me here. I will never forget this wonderful place," I said as we headed back to our room.

I thought I had better call Mom and tell her all was well. She was so excited to hear all that we had done so far. Everyone there was fine, "Have fun."

We decided to plan tomorrow's adventure. "Daniel, I would love to go up to Loch Ness and see if Nessie is around how about we go there? The desk clerk said we could take the train but it's an all day trip."

"I'm game it sounds like fun I haven't been on a train in years."

We did go and had a great day. The train trip was so much fun we got to really see pretty much all of Scotland in luxury. Very comfortable seats and we got special care in first class– back to feeling like a princess.

Unfortunately Nessie did not come when I called but we wandered along the shore of Loch Ness then just sat on the water's edge. The trip home was so special, I felt like we were on the Orient Express. We sat alone in a compartment that was shut off with etched glass doors; the upholstery was red velvet on the high backed seats. It was a steam engine train and I loved to see the smoke coming out. I think I fell asleep the minute Daniel put his arm around me. He only let me sleep for about an hour then woke me up, "Hey there sleepy head you are missing all the scenery."

I yawned and stretched, "Sorry but all of a sudden I was

very tired. Maybe tomorrow we should rest a little and just go shopping. I do want to bring all our family something back with us."

"Sounds like a good idea to me."

That's just what we did. We found some fun things for everyone. Edith got a plaid McGregor shawl, Eli a beret of course in the McGregor plaid, Mom a beautiful white shawl from Ireland, and Gretchen a hat and scarf from Ireland. Daniel thought it would be smart to send all our things back by mail so we didn't have to carry them. "See that is why I married you, you are so smart."

The rest of our time in Scotland was spent being total tourists and went on one more tour, this time to Oxford University, which was gorgeous, Stratford-Upon-Avon, Shakespeare's birth place, Anne Hathaway's cottage before she married Shakespeare. Then a couple more days of shopping and seeing The Palace at Holyrood House, Melrose Abbey, and Loch Lomond. We were scheduled to go back home in four days and Daniel asked if I would like to spend the rest of our time in London. "We could see the sights there and then when it is time to go we would be closer to the airport."

"That is a wonderful idea there are so many things to see and do there. Shall we make arrangements to leave tomorrow? Ok, I will go down and tell the desk clerk."

"You just sit there I will do it, back in a minute," and he left. Again the hotel did it all for us. That night as we lay in bed we went back to all the wonderful things we have seen and places we went. "I will always remember this wonderful country and its kind people; we are definitely going to come back again someday right my love?"

"Yes and I hope soon."

This time we took the train and it was again a beautiful comfortable trip. I was amazed at how fast the train traveled. The hotel had made reservations for us so we were all set. It was a beautiful old hotel again very elegant. The clerk took us up to our room, while another young man carried our bags. Such special service just for us I thought. The room was delightful, again a huge four poster bed with draped velvet curtains. There was even a fireplace with two comfy looking chairs next to it.

When the men left my Daniel once again lifted me into the huge bed. "Shall we give this one a try?"

"You really do have a one track mind my love and I pulled him down next to me."

"Are we always going to be this much in love Daniel?" I asked on the way to dinner.

"No it is going to get stronger and stronger as each year passes" and he kissed my head.

At dinner I told him that while we are here I really want to see the Changing of the Guard at Buckingham Palace and Henry the 8th' Castle, and really as many castles as I can. "Did I tell you I am a history nut, especially when it comes to Henry and the rest of the royals? But Henry is one of my favorites, did you know that he was born in 1491 and only lived fifty-six years?" He was nodding. "Ok smarty did you know he was a wrestler, loved to dance, was crowned at age seventeen, composed songs, and wrote verses and was well educated? "

I could tell I got him on a couple points, but being the man that he was, or really just a man, he wasn't about to admit it and said, "Of course everyone knows that. Anyway we had better get a plan of action going quickly, let's stop at the front desk when we get back maybe they can help us."

They did help and we found out the time for Changing of the Guard and also a tour to take to visit Henry, plus a lot more places we could see.

The next morning we were out early and took the castle tour, Henry was not at home but we did get to see his castle. Good heavens those walls are thick, and even though it was warm outside it was cold in there. All I could think about was those poor women who had to wear fancy gowns, no wonder they didn't live very long. Granted they probably had everything but the kitchen sink under them but still... "Some more trivia Daniel, this palace was one of his seven greater houses, he also had seventeen lesser houses and fourteen medieval ones. When he died he had at least sixty properties, most of which he drew up the plans for. How's that grab you?"

"Grabs me just fine, stop showing off."

The grounds were spectacular around the castle of course, but it was the feeling I had just being there that sent chills up my spine. So much history, in fact the whole country was packed with it. My history nut self was in heaven.

Next on the list was Warwick Castle, our second of three on the castle tour. This one was gorgeous and over one thousand years old. They sure knew how to build them back then. Our guide took a picture of us outside among the gigantic pink rhododendron bushes with the castle in the background. "Honey how about we use this for our Christmas cards this year, if it turns out? We could tell everyone that this is our remodeled house." Inside there was a room that was about the size of three football fields with tapestry as tall as our house and red velvet upholstered gold chairs lining each wall. I got into a little trouble once in a while trying to find out what was down the little roped off stone staircases that seemed to be everywhere.

The guide told us that the castle we were to see next was not available now so we are going to the Tower of London. This place has always fascinated me; again so much violent history is connected to the towers. If you listen carefully you can almost hear the cries of the past. We learned it was built by William the Conqueror as a fortress. It was also a royal residence and palace, the government Treasury and Mint is in there plus the Jewel House, where the Crown Jewels are stored. Elizabeth the first spent some time in the White Tower. Poor girl, I just can't imagine such a thing.

It was time to go, the sun was going down and honestly as much as the place intrigued me I was ready. Our guide told us that we are going to have to wait probably quite a while as our van had broken down. All the other ones are on the road with tourists so we have to wait until one of them can come and pick us up. "So how about we go back in and I will give you a little scarier tour of some of the not seen usual places?" We did and honestly I was getting unnerved, it was dark in there and all he used was a flashlight, I guess to make it scarier–well it sure did.

I decided it would be a good idea to hold onto Daniels arm, no way was I going to get lost in there.

"Syd, you are digging your fingernails into my arm, scared? Don't worry I will protect you from the ghosties that I am sure are in here, too much violence for them not to be. Want to make love?"

"Yes, maybe we could jump into one of cells or dungeons and lay on a rack or something. By the way thanks so much about telling me about the ghosties, sure makes me feel better."

I think I really surprised him, but true to form I got, "Great let me go ask the tour guide which one he thought would be best."

"Don't you dare, now control yourself you goose we will be out of here soon, I hope."

The guide told us we were going to head back toward the main entrance but we still had some time because the rescue bus also broke down. That did it, my nervous system left my body. It turned out that we didn't leave until one o'clock in the morning. We all got special tickets to be able to come back at no extra charge, yea like that's going to happen.

Today is our last full day in London, and it was Daniel's day, he got to choose what we did. First we took a double decker bus to the Changing of the Guard at Buckingham Palace. I got out my handy dandy guide book. "Here's today lesson young man, Buckingham Palace was built in 1702. The Changing of the Guard happens daily May through July and then alternative days after that. It is smart to get there early to get a good vantage point. The guards are not just ceremonial they are infantry soldiers, who also patrol the palace day and night."

I loved every minute of this grand tradition, and when it was over, "Daniel how about we pop in and say HI to the queen while we are here?" When is he ever going to stop with the eye rolling thing?

"Sorry sweetie but the queen is out for the day, the flag is down, maybe next time."

From there we went to the wax museum. There was quite a line waiting but well worth it. Honestly it was a little unnerving, especially the Chamber of Horrors. The wax figures looked so real it was amazing. The guide book said there were over three hundred figures of celebrities, the royals, music stars, super heroes, sports figures, world leaders, and on and on.

Next stop was Covent Garden; it was a shopping center where you could buy many different things. I loved the street entertainers. Onward to Trafalgar Square and we were done.

By the end of the day we were exhausted and I was almost glad we were going home tomorrow. It has been a fantastic honeymoon.

Bright and early the next morning I told Daniel we had better start packing up and he didn't move, "Come on get out of that bed you silly."

"Nope."

"Don't make me come over there and get you," I said in my trying hard to sound tough voice.

"If you want me then you are going to have to come and get me, but I can't be responsible for what might happen."

I slowly made my way over to the bed, when I got close I put out my hand to pull his covers back and he grabbed it and I wound up sprawled across him. "So glad you decided to jump back in I have an idea about something we could do to pass the time before we have to leave."

Our flight left at eleven o'clock and again it was flawless, we slept through most of it. We arrived in Detroit at one- thirty in the afternoon. Thank goodness Daniel remembered where we parked his car and we got in and headed for home. It felt good to be back in Michigan and we talked the whole way about our adventures. "Does the family know when we are supposed to be getting there?" I asked Daniel. "We are only about half an hour away."

"Yep I called Mom from the airport, I am sure they are all waiting at the house."

They were all waiting and it was total chaos, everyone was hugging, kissing, and asking a million questions as the girls jumped all over us. Daniel got the luggage and we all went into the house. "So tell us everything, well almost everything,"

Gretchen said with a little smirk, "we got your package and can't wait to see what's in there."

"Oh just our dirty laundry," said Daniel then laughed. "How about we just sit and relax for a couple minutes, it has been a long day already. Though I do think we should tell them about the night you had to spend in the Tower of London Syd." Now that got some interesting stares all around.

"Stop it you nut, all that happened was that the tour bus broke down and all the other ones were busy during the day, and then the one that was going to rescue us also broke down so we were stuck until very early the next morning. I can say that I do not recommend being in the tower at night, very spooky but a neat experience."

"Yea neat, so how come you grabbed my arm and never let go, huh?"

"Ok I was scared, you happy now?" I asked.

"Yep."

Daniel did his evil eye thing and I knew I was in trouble, and then asked, "Should we tell them about our adventure in the countryside with the cow?"

Everyone looked curious but I gave him a hit in the arm, "If you dare say one word I will never speak to you again," and I am sure I must have turned bright red.

Gretchen just couldn't stay quiet. "So did you get attacked by a cow or something while you were running naked through a field?"

The whole gang yelled, "Gretchen you are awful!"

"Almost," said my soon to be ex-husband.

Eli asked how our flight over was, and of course my husband had to tell him, "Well Dad it was smooth as your back when we started then I guess we went through a storm because on the other side of it there were a couple very big bumps that we seemed to have to go over and over so I had to hold on tightly to Syd but that only lasted a couple hours, very scary."

"I am going to kill you," I said and buried my head in my hands.

Gretchen looked at us, "You know I could probably try to

figure out what you are really talking about but this time I am going to let it go. Wait a minute…, Daniel, really on the plane, two hours?"

A lot of confused looks were passed around, thank goodness. "Drop it please just drop it." I begged then laughed along with Daniel and Gretchen.

I guess he finally decided he was in big trouble and asked if anyone was interested in seeing our dirty laundry in the box we sent, as he went over and got it. Everyone had a great time opening their presents and liked them.

"Really it was a wonderful trip and I can't wait to get the pictures back. We stopped on the way home at the drug store in Sylerville and dropped them off. They said we would get them in a day or two," I said as I kicked off my shoes and leaned back on the couch. "It is good to be home." Lilly and Sammy jumped up next to me and the kissing began, "I missed you too sweet girls."

"We will tell you everything in a minute but how did things go here, any problems?" I asked.

"Nope, unless you want to hear about your girls first meeting with a skunk, interesting but not newsworthy, especially when they decided to pollute the whole house as I was chasing them," said Gretchen with her fingers over her nose.

I couldn't stop laughing I could visualize the whole thing. "I am sorry but glad I wasn't doing the chasing."

"Mom how is the therapy going, are you now running all over the yard?"

"Not quite dear but it should be soon," she said and smiled with pride. "I have been trying extra hard and Gretchen has been a real slave driver."

Daniel finally got a word in, "Mom, Dad how are things at home?"

Eli was the first to answer, "Just fine Son, I am getting some help with my speech and feeling much better." His smile said it all. "Your mother sure missed you guys though, every once in a while she would say, 'Let's go over and see the kids', then make a sad face."

"Well I missed you," said Edith.

We sat there for several hours and finally Mom said, "We should get some dinner, Gretchen put in a roast, anyone hungry?"

It tasted wonderful and afterwards we all went out on the porch to sit and relax. Mom said she needed to talk to us about something and now is a good time, "Sydney, Daniel, Gretchen and I have decided that we should move into the cottage. You need to be alone and it is not like we would be far away."

I was shocked, "But Mom I only just found you I want you here with me. Let me talk to Daniel about this."

"No need to talk to Daniel about this, Daniel says no way," and he looked very serious. "You two are part of my family now too and I want you here as much as Syd does. No more talk it is settled," then he went over and gave them both a hug. "Besides this house is huge and when the twenty kids start coming we will need you badly."

"You are a tyrant Daniel, a nice tyrant, but a tyrant none the less, of course we will stay if you really want us to," said Gretchen as she looked at Mom for approval. She nodded and everyone was happy. "One last thing, don't expect me to get up in the night with twenty kids."

It was such a fun night but I was getting very tired and said it was time for bed, "For me anyway, please stay and talk."

Daniel said he was tired too so we went up.

As we lay in bed I snuggled close to him, "You are such a dear man, how can I ever thank you for how wonderful you have been to my family, I love you so much?"

"I have an idea," he said and smiled.

"Don't you ever have any other ideas than making love?"

"Nope."

A few days later we got our trip pictures back. Everyone gathered around one afternoon to see them. I just about lost it when I saw the picture of our cow, I had no idea we had one. Daniel said he took it just before we left. Oh well it was funny and part of a wonderful honeymoon. They all brought back so many memories. "I need to get a photo book to put these in," I said. That night I asked Daniel if he was going to go away soon and build another house, "I like it when you work close by like you have been doing lately."

"This year I am staying as close to home as I can, I can't imagine being away from you for even a day."

Fall is in the air and the hundreds of maple trees surrounding our property are changing color–the reds and gold's are magnificent. I wish I could enjoy them even more but I think I have a little bug, my stomach has been acting up and I am not amused. I wish I could blame it on eating something while on our trip but it has been a month since we returned. Maybe it is just all the excitement of our masquerade party for Halloween in two weeks, when everyone we know will be coming to celebrate our wedding. Hopefully the weather will cooperate and we can use the large porch too. I had better get thinking about a costume, Daniel said he has his all figured out but won't tell me. I am leaning toward a princess as that is exactly what I feel like. I think I will ask Mom and Gretchen if they will help.

"A princess is perfect Syd. I have a million patterns upstairs, let me go find them, "said Gretchen as she hurried up the stairs. Mom was all excited too and we spent the rest of the day looking though all of them. We finally found a perfect princess one and Gretchen said she would start on it right away. "Do you think that old sewing machine upstairs still works? Let's go up and see. Hurray for our side, it works. Let's move it into my room, now where can we get some material?"

I told her about the country store in Thumb Harbor and the next morning all three of us went over there. We got everything we needed then had lunch at my favorite little café and headed home.

It is finally Halloween and Daniel and I got dressed separately, he stayed in our room and I went down to Mom's so we could surprise each other. Gretchen worked wonders on the dress, it had layers and layers of thin silk with sparkles, the sleeves were puffy and started just at the shoulder. Then all of a sudden I realized we had not thought of a tiara, every princess needs one. Mom told me to wait a minute she had just the thing. She looked through a couple boxes and finally found what she was looking for.

"Sydney this is the tiara I wore when your father and I got married, the veil was attached to the back of it but I took that off. Your hair is already up so I think this will do the trick."

"Oh thank you it IS perfect!" Right then there was a knock on the door, it was Daniel.

"It is almost time for the guests to arrive are you ready yet my love?"

I opened the door and found my prince charming sword and all waiting for me. "How perfect my princess and he bowed and kissed my hand. You look spectacular!"

"So do you my handsome prince."

Edith and Eli were the first to arrive, Eli was Zorro, and Edith was a flapper girl. "You guys look wonderful, go say HI to Marilyn Monroe–Mom, and the pirate–Gretchen, they are in the living room I think. After that there was a steady stream of people coming. Elaine and Bill looked fantastic, she was a sailor and he was an anchor. "It has been so long since I've seen you but I have been busy, you know my husband Daniel?"

"Yes," said Bill. "How are you? Or is that a stupid question, you married a princess," he said then smiled big.

Bill gave me a bow and asked for permission to hug the new bride. Which he did before Daniel could say a thing. "I am so happy for you both."

"Elaine you look adorable, how have you been?"

"Really good thanks, I have wanted to come over but life seems to get in the way of my plans. When did you get married? Oh the house looks wonderful, Daniel did a great job. Let's get together soon ok?"

"I would love that thanks," I said as my mother came over and I introduced her to Elaine.

Elaine stood there staring at the two of us, "Goodness you look alike, but I am sure you get that all the time. Oops Bill is waving, someone else I have to meet I guess. Thanks for inviting us."

Susan and her grandmother came next; they were Laurel and Hardy and looked terrific. "I love your costumes, Mrs. Burnett I have a little surprise for you, stay here a minute. I got Mom and brought her over, "I think this is the Rose you thought I was."

"Rose my goodness it is you, I thought you were dead, my you and your daughter look so much alike. Please tell me what happened."

Susan and I went over to the food trays. "I hope that wasn't too much of a shock for your grandmother, you can imagine what it did to me to find her; I had no idea that she was even my mother until just recently. Believe me it is a very long story, and I am so happy with everything these days. Can you believe Daniel and I got married, I know it was sudden but sometimes love happens that way?"

"You are a lucky girl Sydney he is a good man, which I am sure you know already. When did you get married? I can't thank you enough for all your help after the tornado."

"Susan you are my friend and friends help friends, really I was very glad I could help. We were married at the end of August in the McGregor's yard then went to Scotland for our honeymoon for two weeks. We wanted just family at the ceremony and then have a party for everyone later, which is tonight," I said and giggled.

About a half hour later I looked up and saw our policeman friend Mark and his wife, (he was a civil war soldier and she a southern belle). "My goodness I am so glad you could come, you look fantastic, it is so nice to see you again," I said and truly meant it.

He introduced me to Carol and said I sure look better than the last time he saw me. "I am so thankful everything worked out as it did. I hear you are truly a local and were born right here along with the rest of us. No wonder you fit in so quickly. We can talk more later you have a full house tonight," and they went over to Daniel.

All of a sudden I got poked in the back and turned around, it was Josh and Ken. "Hi Princess Sydney," and he hugged me.

"Can I get a hug too?" asked Ken.

"You bet, oh my gosh I can't believe you were able to come, I am so happy. Let me see we have a Pirate of the Caribbean and

Harry Potter, how clever of you, you look grand. Daniel look who is here."

He came over and shook both of their hands and I introduced Ken.

"It is good to see you, I am so glad you could come, let me introduce you to my family," which he did. He also brought over my mother and again we got the how much I look like her comment.

Gretchen seemed so excited to see them, "Good heavens you two get more handsome every time I see you, now come here and give me a hug. We have sure missed you; Sydney said you were here during the summer, how grand! Isn't it wonderful we are all living here now, I couldn't be happier, please come by anytime you are around here.

"So how are your grandparents? They are so sweet and I do plan on going back to see them again," I said. Daniel gave me a strange look, "I will explain later," I told him. "How are things at work, any new challenging cases?" We talked for quite a while then Daniel told me he was going to make a little speech.

"Friends and family, I just want to thank you for coming here tonight and helping Sydney and I celebrate again our wedding, where are you Syd? Come here." He put his arm around me and said, "I am the luckiest man alive to have found such a wonderful woman and I hope before the night is over you will get to know her too. Again thanks for being here. Now go have fun."

We did have fun, dunking for apples and just plain talking. Gretchen and I decorated everything with scary ghosts, pumpkins, spiders, and lanterns. The evening was cool but we still could go out on the porch, good thing as just about everyone we asked came.

It wasn't until two o'clock that everyone left and I was exhausted. Mom and Gretchen left about eleven thirty. "Daniel it was such a fun night, maybe we can have a BBQ next summer and do it all over again, but for now all I want to do is sleep."

–8–

RYAN

"You have been tired lately haven't you, and how is your stomach doing?" asked Daniel.

I didn't want him to worry so all I said was, "Yes I have been tired but there has been a lot going on probably why my stomach was upset too."

A couple days later after throwing up my breakfast I decided to go see Dr. Winters. I just told everyone I had a few errands to do, so they wouldn't worry.

He seemed glad to see me and asked what was going on. I told him I just got married at the end of August and then we went to Scotland and England, and we also had a party the other night. So I think that is what is going on but I have been very tired and sick to my stomach. "Is there a bug going around, though usually I don't get sick at all? By the way I can't thank you enough for taking care of me after my attack."

"You are welcome I am just thankful you weren't seriously hurt. As to your problems I have a couple ideas but how about we do some blood work, I will get the results in a couple days. Don't worry I don't think there is anything really wrong."

Two days later he called and asked if I could come in. I said I would, "How about now?"

"Good I will see you soon."

I made up another excuse and left. Dr. Winters seemed very happy, "Please sit down Sydney I think I know why you have been feeling like you have. First off when was your last monthly period?"

"Oh my I haven't even thought about that maybe a couple months ago. Sorry I don't keep track of it like I should, I have never been regular it seems to come when it feels like it," and I laughed. "Why is it important, do I have a female problem or something?"

He put his hand over mine, "Yes you do have a something but it is not a problem at least I don't think it is. Sydney you are pregnant, I would say about two months."

My head started spinning, could it be, so soon in our marriage? "Oh Dr. Winters I love you," and gave him a hug, "sorry but I am so happy I don't know what to do! Are you positive, can I tell Daniel?"

"Yes you can I am positive, now go home and knock the socks off your husband, I know he is going to be very happy."

I literally could have floated home without the van. I am going to be a mother, how amazing! Now how and when do I tell Daniel, he has to be the first told then Mom and Gretchen and the rest of the family?

That night I asked Daniel if he wanted to go down to the beach for one last time before it gets too cold. Of course he was willing and I told Mom we would be back soon and left.

"Back to the sandbox huh Syd?" he said as we sat down on the blanket. "This is pretty much where it all began isn't it?"

"Yes it is so I thought this would be a good place for another new beginning."

He looked at me strangely, "Why do you want a divorce or something?" I could hear the concern in his voice.

"Oh my God no you silly man, you are stuck with me longer than forever, remember? You know all the stomach problems I have been having and how tired I have been, well I went to see Dr. Winters and he gave me some startling news, he said..."

"Oh Syd what is it are you sick, tell me?"

"No but you are going to have a new title to add to Son and Husband. It is Dad my love, the first of our twenty children will be born in seven months. I am pregnant, no doubts said Dr. Winters."

He gave out an incredibly loud WHOOP and grabbed me, "Oh my God I love you so much." We both sat there crying but smiling.

I guess his whoop was heard up at the house and Gretchen came flying down the hill, "Is everything all right I heard a strange sound, sorry to butt in but it scared me?"

"Let's go back up to the house and I will tell you, come on sweetheart."

Mom was waiting and looked upset, "Are you two all right?"

"Yes, we are more than all right, should I tell them Syd?"

"Well hurry up man you look like you are going to fly around the room," Gretchen said.

"Might be a good idea if you both sat down first. You are both going to be Grandmothers in about seven months and I am going to be a dad, Sydney is pregnant."

Both women sat there with their mouths open then charged at us, crying and laughing at the same time. "How absolutely wonderful," said my mom, "I am totally overwhelmed!"

"Well I am a lot more than that, do I really get to be a grandma too?" asked Gretchen.

"Of course you do you silly thing, you have known me forever and have been like a mom to me practically from the start, now that I have two, really three including Edith, I am the luckiest girl in the world. Edith, oh Daniel call your folks and get them over here, or we could go there, I don't care they need to know."

He did call and told them he had some really big news and they said they would be right over. Both looked concerned but since we were all smiling I guess they decided everything was all right and smiled too.

"So what's up Son?" Asked Eli and he sat down next to me.

"Mom, Dad do you have room in your hearts for one more Grandchild because ready or not there is one on the way?"

"Oh Daniel, Sydney I am so excited!" said Edith, "are you sure?" And she jumped up and hugged me.

"Yes Mom Sydney went to see Dr. Winters today."

I guess Eli was more shocked than I thought because he was still sitting there with his mouth open, then finally, "Of course we have room, how wonderful, of course it will be a boy." Then he put his arm around me and gave me a quick kiss on the cheek,

"You have made me very happy Daughter."

"Maybe we will break tradition this time Dad, you never know. Honestly I don't care which it is it will be loved like no other baby has ever been."

That night as we lay in bed I put my hand on my tummy, "Oh Daniel this is such a miracle, a baby, and so soon. I just can't believe it. Are you disappointed should we have waited a while?"

He put his hand over mine, "Oh no my love, this baby was conceived out of our love for each other and I am so excited I can hardly stand it. Let's pick out some names."

I laughed so hard, "Isn't it a little early for that this tiny little person to be is probably only about one inch long. Buttttt, why not? Guess we had better start with the boys. How about Daniel, I have always liked that name?"

"You really are a nut, though I have thought about it. But would it get too confusing with another Daniel in the house? Someone would yell Daniel and both of us would come running, though we could use it for a middle name or just call him Danny."

"Ok I think we had better figure this out later it is getting complicated already. How about we sleep on it for now? You know I do think we should go and see Dr. Winters and find out what I am supposed to do and not do. I don't even know if he delivers babies or not or should I see an OBGYN?"

Daniel hugged me very close, "I think that is a good idea but I do know he delivers babies, everyone I know was brought into this world by him including me."

"Good I like him; I will call tomorrow and set up an appointment."

We did go and Dr. Winters said he would be very happy to take care of me. He told us what I should eat and to be sure to get some exercise, then gave us a print out of what to expect as the baby grows. "Here is a prescription for pre natal vitamins, be sure to take them, and I want you to come and see me once a month. I am so happy for you both." Then he looked Daniel straight in the eye and said, "Don't spoil her too much," then laughed, "though I know you will."

"Dr. Winters I have an unusual question to ask you, not long ago I found out I was born here in Sylerville, could you have delivered me?"

"Well why don't we try to find out, what are your parent's names and your birth date? I have a good memory but have delivered a lot of babies. Well look here, yes I did, how about that?" He was really smiling.

"Oh my, that makes me so happy, now you are going to deliver my babies too."

The weather was changing, all the beautiful trees were losing their leaves and it was getting colder. One day I told Daniel that I have never seen snow or been in cold winters. "I don't even have a heavy coat or boots, think we had better go shopping soon." So the next day we took off for Thumb Harbor. There was a small shop that had everything I needed and I was set, let it snow. Really I was looking forward to it I'll bet it is gorgeous.

We got our first snow just before Thanksgiving and I was so excited. I got up that morning and looked out and magically the whole yard had been transformed into a winter wonderland. "Daniel wake up it snowed last night let's go out in it."

"Syd it is seven o'clock in the morning I am sure it will stay there for a little while, come back to bed."

"No way, you can stay there if you want but I am going out now." I got dressed and put my new winter coat and boots on and headed for the front door. It was freezing cold but I didn't care. I just couldn't believe how beautiful it was. The girls were whining at the door so I let them out too. It was so funny, they stood on the porch and looked all around, trying to figure out what was going on I guess, then bravely went down the steps and into the snow. The walked carefully for about a minute then ran all over the place, stopping once in a while to put their noses in the white stuff. "Don't go too far you sillies it is cold, in fact I am going in now come on you can go back out later." I got a no way look and they were off. You are going to be sorry I thought and went back into the house and up to our room. I took off my coat and jumped back into bed and snuggled up to Daniel to get warm.

"Yikes woman you are freezing cold, I know just how to warm you up quick." We stayed in bed for about another hour then got up. "I am hungry," said this man who practically thinks of nothing else, if he is out of bed.

I turned the heat up and started a fire in the kitchen fireplace and it didn't take long to get things warmed up. Gretchen wandered in looking very sleepy. "Didn't you sleep well?" I asked.

"No all I could think about was being a grandma and my girl being pregnant. Oh Syd all of our lives are going to change and it is going to be so much fun, I can't wait."

"Me either, but right now I have a hungry husband on the way down so I am going to get breakfast, want some? Ok get me some eggs will you. Also please call my silly girls and tell them to come in. I got up early and saw the snow and went out for a few minutes and of course the girls followed, they are probably frozen stiff by now. We southerners are not used to the cold you know."

The girls were covered in snow and I told Gretchen I was going to get some towels so I could clean them off. "You finish breakfast I will do it. Come here you wet things let me get you dry. Now go over to the fireplace and get warmed up." She was rewarded with many kisses.

Thanksgiving was wonderful Edith made a feast for all of us. This was the first time we did not bring Mom's wheelchair, the therapist wanted her to walk on her own as much as possible and she did great. I made sure that if she had to go outside there was always someone with her so she wouldn't fall and reinjure herself.

Winter had set in with a vengeance and ice had been added to the snow so even I did not want to go out in it. So we just stayed inside and played games or read.

All of a sudden we all realized that Christmas was coming and no one had any presents so on a nice clear day we all went down to Port Shores. We separated and did our shopping then met back for lunch. We were all excited about what we had bought and glad to just get out for the day. I bought some more yarn, my baby needed a blanket and I was going to give it a try. The afghan was finished but it was far from perfect so I hoped this one would be better now that I had a little experience. Well I guess the other ladies had the same idea because at lunch we all pulled out some blue yarn. "Well I guess this is going to have to be a boy huh?" and we all laughed.

My monthly visits with Dr. Winters were going well and he said I was doing fine. Thank goodness the morning sickness went away pretty quickly so now I was hungry all the time, though I knew I had to be careful of my weight.

Christmas morning Daniel woke up early and asked if we could go down and see if Santa had been there yet. I laughed so hard, my big strong husband was a kid in disguise. I patted him on the head and told him it was too early he had to be a brave little boy just a little longer. He was not amused and said he was awake so what could we do to pass the time. Of course as always he came up with an idea.

There were so many presents under the huge tree in the living room and everything had been decorated to the hilt. Sweet smelling fresh boughs were all over the house with big red bows. We even strung popcorn for the tree and cranberries.

Finally everyone gathered by the tree and we started opening our presents. For four adults we sure didn't act like it. The paper was flying all over the place and there were so many oh's and ah's, it was so much fun. I got Daniel a key chain with a cow on it for fun, plus a heavy winter coat that he needed. He laughed so hard when he saw the cow–"a permanent reminder of our Hallmark moment."

Daniel got me a beautiful gold necklace with a single heart that had to rose embedded in the center. It was amazing and he got a huge hug from me and my mom too. "Where in the world did you get this–how perfect?"

"I got it in Scotland when we went shopping for everyone's presents. I just couldn't believe how perfect it was for you, it pretty much says it all, the rose and your mother are now permanently embedded in your heart." We were all in tears.

"Daniel, if I could have picked a son for myself you would

have been him," Gretchen said as she kissed his cheek. "You and I were picked by this family to be a part of it and I know you are as grateful as I am that they did. There are no words to say how happy I am this Christmas. Ok now that the mushy stuff is over how about breakfast."

"Wait one minute there is still one more gift tucked into the tree," I said as I reached for it. The card just about did me in, To my baby with love from Daddy. I sat there on the floor with the gift held to my heart and tried to speak but there were no words to say. Daniel kissed me and read the card out loud. When I could finally open it I found a sweet little rocking horse with six little hearts on its back each with our initials engraved in tiny little print. I was totally overcome, my dearest husband is amazing. "How in the world did you get this done so quickly," I asked.

"A couple days after we found out that you were pregnant I called a friend of mine who makes special things and told him I wanted it done. Now our baby will have all the people who love him the most right there and every year he can put it on the tree and remember."

Mom was sobbing by this time and really we all were, "Daniel that is the most wonderful thing I have ever heard, how proud I am that you are my son. This has been the best Christmas I have ever had, and I am so very grateful that Sydney found me and brought me back into this wonderful family. When I think about what my Christmas could have been back in that home all by myself I just…I love you all so much."

The whole day was magical, Edith and Eli came over for a big ham feast and I course I had to show them our baby's first gift from Daddy. "You even have our initials in the hearts." cried Edith.

"Of course Mom," said Daniel as he put his arm around her shoulder, "of course."

We sang Christmas carols and Mom played the harp as we sipped eggnog and ate some of Edith's fancy decorated cookies. When it was time for Edith and Eli to go home we discovered that it must have been snowing hard all day because there was about two feet of snow out there. Daniel told them there is no way they are going to trudge through all that, "You are going to stay here tonight."

"But dear we have no pajamas and we don't want to be a bother."

"Between us all we have plenty of pajamas, and even extra toothbrushes, it is settled," said good ole Gretchen. "There is a room all set for you upstairs with even a fireplace too keep you toasty warm, lots better than getting buried in the snow."

"That sound like fun," Eli said. "We will stay and thank you, it has been a perfect Christmas. I don't think Norman Rockwell could have done any better."

We all laughed then talked for about an hour more and headed for bed.

"Thank you my dear husband, I have never been happier in my whole life," I said as I kissed him goodnight. I gave the baby a little pat, "Daniel I think I am getting a little baby bump, here feel."

"You are wow this is exciting. Before long you will be as big as a house."

"Thanks makes me feel so good you dummy, yet it will be great huh?"

New Year's Eve was fun we all got together again and ate, played games and of course watched the big ball fall in New York. Daniel gave me a nice big kiss and the rest of the ladies too, then came over and kissed my belly, "Happy New year little one, you are almost half way here."

One night in the middle of January it was particularly cold and I snuggled up behind Daniel to get warm. "Syd stop poking me, what do you want?"

"I am not poking you, oh my gosh Daniel it is the baby she is kicking." He flipped over and touched my tummy.

"Oh my, he is, hi little one boy you are busy, doing a few pushups in there? Syd this is so great!"

The baby finally settled down but I was wide awake. "That was so wonderful but now what I am too excited to sleep?"

"I have an idea."

"You and your ideas, do you really want to wake her back up you nut?"

He laid there for all of a minute, "Yep."

February was a nasty weather month but we did get out a little. Daniel took Gretchen on a sledding adventure from the front gates to the cottage. It is a decent hill but not exciting enough Gretchen said. I decided it wouldn't be too smart for me to try it too so I was the cheerleader on the sidelines. I did help put faces and twig arms and legs on a snowman and a snow lady and made a bunch of snow angels. I have more than a baby bump now at almost six months and am starting to get more excited about meeting our little one. We decided not to have an ultra sound and be surprised if it was a girl or a boy. Unfortunately we just can't seem to get on the same page with names. I really want the name Daniel in somewhere but not sure if it should be the first name or middle one. He is still fighting me on this but can't come up with something different. For a girl I have always loved Emily, but for whatever we decide on I do hope her middle name can be Rose. Oh well I am sure we will figure it out before too long.

It took a little time but we finally got the nursery all set up. We got a changing table, crib, bassinette, dresser and comfy chair for me. The room is painted blue but Daniel said we can add pink stripes or something if it a girl. It is right next door to our room so that makes me feel good. I got striped blue and white curtains and I painted a mural of animals on the walls–a giraffe, hippo, elephant, monkey and birds, all with tall grasses at the bottom and a blue sky with white fluffy clouds. It really came out well and Daniel loved it. Along the way I picked up a few things for the baby to wear and we were pretty much set.

March showed some hope that spring was on its way and I was very glad, I haven't been able to exercise that much because of our bad weather. By April spring was in full bloom and I was so happy, big but happy, only about a month to go. "You made it kid you are as big as a house," said my wonderfully supportive husband. He really has been I thought. He has pampered me so much and it really has been fun. Now I just want to be a mom quickly, I am tired of trying so hard to get out of a chair, and feel like I wobble instead of walk.

In the second week of April Edith surprised us with a baby shower, all my sisters-in-law were there, Susan, Elaine, a few neighbors and friends of Edith. Of course Mom and Gretchen came too. I was so shocked when we went in; we were supposed to be there just for lunch. The baby got some wonderful things, and Edith made a delicious lunch. We played a few games then just sat and talked. I just couldn't get over how tiny the clothes were and that my baby would be wearing them before too long.

It is May Day and the rain is still coming down, it is starting to get to me as this is the third day of the constant downpours, so I picked up a book and sat by the fireplace. For some reason I couldn't get comfortable, I had been having cramps all morning and they weren't letting up, in fact they were getting worse. Since I have been constipated for a couple days I just figured that was it. I got up to make some tea and all of a sudden the cramps became intense and didn't stop. I leaned against the sink and yelled, "DANIEL HELP HURRY HELP ME," and I doubled over.

He came running, and so did Mom and Gretchen, "What is it Sydney?" asked Daniel. "Are you sick?"

"No I think it's the baby, oh God I hurt call for an ambulance I think it is coming now."

Gretchen picked up the phone and started dialing while Daniel helped me to a chair, "How long has this been going on?" he asked looking very concerned.

"Since I got up but I thought I was just constipated, ohhhhhhh it is awful."

"I will yell at you later right now just breathe deeply and try to relax."

Gretchen was as white as a sheet, "The ambulance can't come for a while the roads are flooded so I called Dr. Winters and he is stuck at the hospital for the same reason. Looks like I am going to have to play midwife. Stop looking at me like that Daniel, I am a nurse and have assisted and actually delivered three babies on my own. Bring her into her mother's room NOW!"

He picked me up and carried me in. Then Gretchen told Mom she needed her help and get a sheet and a bunch of towels.

By this time I was screaming, "Get this baby out of me NOW!"

"Daniel I think you have better get out of here and let us handle this," said Gretchen

He kissed me and left but said he would be right outside the door.

Gretchen examined me and said we still have a little while to go but it won't be too long. "Hang on honey, grab your mom's hand that will help and breathe deeply in and out, that's a girl, keep it up."

About an hour later Gretchen said, "It is show time honey, time to push and I do mean PUSH, give it everything you got."

"DANIEL," I screamed, "COME HERE AND HELP ME PLEASE!"

He popped his head in and Gretchen nodded. "Hold her hand and Rose hold her legs, now Syd PUSH. Good girl I can see its head, one more PUSH. This is the last one PUSH!"

Daniel gripped my hand tightly and all of a sudden there he was our little son, screaming his brains out. Gretchen held him up and asked Daniel to cut the cord, which he did. Then she wrapped him in a towel and laid him on my chest. I was so overwhelmed, "Hi sweet baby I am your mommy and that guy up there looking pale as a ghost is your daddy." Daniel kissed me and then the baby.

"I have never seen anything like that, what a miracle. Syd you did great, I am so proud of you. I can't believe I actually got to be here," he said as the tears fell down his cheeks.

"Daniel I think you had better sit down you don't look so good," said Mom with a smile. "Oh Sydney you did so well I too am very proud of you and thankful I could be here." Then she hugged me and kissed my baby's head.

Then we heard the sirens, the ambulance was finally here. Mom let them in and showed them where we were. "Looks like we got here a little late how did it all go? The baby looks good and so does Mom, very tired but all right. Let's go to the hospital and we will get you both checked out. Dr. Winters is waiting for us there." They loaded us in and of course Daniel came too.

"Thank you Gretchen," Daniel yelled "you have got a big hug coming."

On the trip I started to cry, "Oh Daniel he is so beautiful he looks just like you. He is finally here can you believe? Boy am I tired, no one told me it would be like trying to pass a bowling ball." Then we both laughed.

When we got there I told Daniel to call his folks and tell them the baby has come. He did and said they heard the ambulance and panicked and ran over and Mom told them. "They are very excited and wanted to come to the hospital but I told them to just wait until tomorrow."

The nurse said the baby and I are doing fine he weighs seven pounds one ounce. "The doctor wants you two to stay the night just to be sure all is well, though I am sure it is. You have been through a lot and need to rest for a while, are you going to breast feed. Good, then let me tell you a little about how to do it, also about the care of your baby." Just then Dr. Winters came in.

"So you just couldn't wait for me huh?" he said as he took my hand. "You did very well Sydney and your baby boy is fine I just checked him out. He sure has a good set of lungs. You two can go home in the morning. I will stop by every day and check up on you. Oh here he comes; he will be with you here in the room tonight. Daniel go home in a little while you too have been through a lot today."

"Thank you Doctor, "Daniel said as he shook his hand. I feel like I was in labor too, a man thing I guess," and they both laughed. Then he put our son in Daniels arms. "Hi little one I am your daddy and I love you so much," and he kissed his head. "Of Syd he is so beautiful I just can't get over it, my son."

It was late when I finally convinced Daniel to go home. He looked so tired but didn't want to leave us. "Sweetie we have forever to stare at him now go downstairs I am sure your dad is here by now so go home and sleep. We will see you in the morning."

He told me later that Gretchen and Mom were waiting up. After being assured all was well they all went to bed. Gretchen got her big hug and a kiss too and both got about a hundred thank you's.

The time had come and we were heading home. Everyone was at the door when we arrived. Eli was the first to speak, "Well hello my little man I'm yer grandpa. Sydney you really are amazing." He kissed me on the cheek and his smile was literally dazzling.

"Sydney may I hold him?" it was Edith. I gently gave him to his grandma and she looked so happy. "Yes he is beautiful, another boy, how grand. We kinda like them around here," she said with a giggle, "have you picked out a name yet?

Daniel and I looked at each other, "Good heavens Syd we haven't, how about Ryan Daniel McGregor?"

"Perfect, very Scotch."

Mom was next in line to hold him, "A Grandson am I old enough to have one?" she asked with a huge smile, "you bet. I am so proud of you Sydney and you too Daniel for being there for the birth and not fainting," then she smiled at Daniel and gave him a wink.

"Gretchen is going to get a metal for this," said Daniel. "You did a wonderful job and we both thank you so much. I don't know what would have happened if you hadn't been here."

Gretchen gave us all a confident look then said, "Aw shucks birthin' babies ain't notta big deal." Then she asked to hold him. "Welcome my little man, you are so lucky you have so many people who will love you forever, but no one is going to love you as much as old Gretchen."

I was getting very tired and wanted to lie down, "Do you all mind if I rest a little on Mom's bed I am really tired? The baby can stay but I will bet he will be asleep soon too."

Everyone promised to let him sleep if he does, and though I had big doubts that they would I went to bed. Daniel came in with me and held me close as I went to sleep. "I love you" was all I heard.

A couple hours later I woke up and it took me a minute to

remember what had happened. I went out and there was the whole gang standing over my sleeping baby. Daniel must have gone up and got his bassinette and brought it down. "Hi, have you all been standing there this whole time?" I bent over and gave my little one a kiss then said, "Someone had better make some food around here I haven't eaten in weeks, at least it seems that way."

All of a sudden we all realized that we had not eaten breakfast, I guess we were all too excited and in the hospital they hadn't served it before we left–Daniel got there practically at dawn. Gretchen went in and made us breakfast and it tasted so good. I was so glad to be home. My good little boy waited to wake up until we had finished. "No everyone sit down, my turn." We just sat there staring at each other, "Hi pumpkin I am your mommy, you are such a special little person and your daddy and I love you so much. We are going to have so much fun. How about a snack, are you hungry?" I pulled up my shirt and he started sucking and I was in heaven, women have been doing this since the beginning of time and now so am I.

Just then Daniel came in to see how we were doing. He just stared at us with tears in his eyes, "This is so beautiful." When Ryan fell asleep he gently lifted him back into his little bed and said he would change him. It was so cute he got the diaper, opened it up and just stood there. "Ah how do I do this?" and he smiled.

"Well love I learned last night, not hard just get the ole one off and slide the new one up and on, then attach the sides. Bingo!"

Our first night was a little challenging. We put the bassinette in our bedroom next to my side of the bed so it would be easier to pick him up and feed him. Last night I found out that about every three hours he needed to be changed and fed. I was glad Dr. Winters warned me about that and also said he will be up about sixteen or seventeen hours a day. It seemed like I just got to sleep and Ryan was awake again. Tonight the second time I got up with him just changing him and feeding him didn't seem enough so I sat in the rocking chair by the fireplace and sang to him. That worked well. My loving husband slept through all but one of the wake-ups. "Syd, Ryan is crying I guess he is hungry." That was the best I got. By morning I looked like the walking dead, Ryan and I were up four times. At seven I decided to take him downstairs just in case Mr. Wonderful wanted to sleep in. I was so tempted to put Ryan right next to him and walk away but was scared he would roll over.

After the feeding I took him on a tour of the downstairs. I am sure he liked everything but he didn't say a word. Despite no sleep I still marveled at this beautiful little person, my son. We sat down and I snuggled him up to my chest. "Dear God thank you for this child I promise to take care of him forever, I love him so much."

My girls came over to see what was going on I guess. "Sweet things this is your new little brother, you have to be very gentle with him, ok?' Sammy peeked her head over and gave him a lick on his leg and then so did Lilly. "Thank you, now go sit down."

Just then Mr. Wonderful came bounding down the stairs, "Hi you two, our first night went a lot better than I expected it to, I feel great."

The best I could do is glare at him, then, "I hope the good fairies that got up and fed, rocked, and changed him four times didn't disturb you."

Oh boy what a look I got, "You mean I slept through it all, I am so sorry, you must be exhausted."

"Ya think? Don't forget buster that I did this last night in the hospital by myself too. To be fair you did wake up once to tell me he was crying, I was so grateful as I didn't hear him," another glare. "Tonight you can breast feed and change him. It is only fair."

"I would if I could you nut," and I really think he meant it.

I handed him Ryan and said I need coffee badly, I have many months to catch up on when I couldn't drink it, and I headed for the kitchen.

I heard Gretchen come down and of course stop and say good morning to Ryan and Daniel. "You guys did a good job last night, I only heard him once."

"Ah I think it would be wise not to tell Syd that, SHE was the one up four times last night and I was the one who slept. Don't look at me like that Syd already has. Guess I am a sound sleeper."

"Ya think?" I yelled from the kitchen.

"Good morning little mom, I see you survived the night, and your knight in shining armor slept through it all," said Gretchen as she went over to set the table. "Men" and she shook her head.

That got me laughing, "You are truly one of a kind Gretch, thank goodness. I am starving how about we make some French toast for a change, and please hand me a mug, I am in desperate need of coffee. How do new mothers survive on so little sleep, maybe I could just put him up to my breast and let him take what he needs when he wakes up and I could sleep?" She gave me a horrifying look, "Ok ok I was only kidding and you know it."

She came over and patted my head, "You are doing just fine my girl, I do know a few little tips I have heard from other Mom's to help with the sleep thing. I am sure you know not to put him on his stomach or have toys or pillows in the crib with him, but when you do get up keep the lights low, don't play with him, rocking and singing are fine–I did hear you once last night and it made me go to sleep, thanks. Ryan does not know the difference between day and night yet so make daytime fun and night for sleep. Sooner or later he will figure out that if the lights are low it is just sleeping time. He should be doing better in a couple months."

"You are just a wealth of information dear Gretchen and thank you. So glad I could help you sleep grrrrr. The boys are coming how goes the French toast?"

"Hi sweet baby."

"Hi yourself Syd, ok I couldn't resist I know you were talking about Ryan."

"Are you positive, sorry I gave you a hard time?"

He sat down and put Ryan in his lap, "You are forgiven don't you dare throw that towel at me you might hit the sweet baby. So where is breakfast?"

Mom came in then and asked how things went last night.

I looked at Daniel, "Do you want to tell her?" I asked sweetly. "Nope."

Mom laughed, "Let me guess you were up all night and Daniel slept."

I threw my arms over my head, "Bingo."

"My dear daughter your father and I went through the same thing. Sorry there is not much you can do except accidently poke him whenever Ryan wakes up. That worked for me about two pokes then I got this big long lecture about how important it was for him to sleep. To be honest I don't think it is worth even trying."

Daniel turned to her, "Mom, bless you."

We finished breakfast and I told him I was going to go up and give our little feller a bath, "Want to help?" Up we went.

"Are you going to put him in the sink or something?"

"No Dr. Winters said we have to keep the umbilical cord stump dry and clean until it falls off by itself. If it does get brittle or dry we are just supposed to clean it with plain water. So I think the smartest thing to do is to just sponge him off. We can break out the rubber ducky's after the stump is gone. Oh and Dr. Winters recommends putting a wash cloth over his little personal areas unless we want to get sprayed."

"Can that really happen?" asked Daniel.

I looked at him and smiled, "Are you willing to take the chance?"

"Nope."

Really it was fun and little Ryan didn't seem to mind. He was such a good boy, didn't even cry. Daniel dried him off as I held him, then he got out a clean one piece sleeper and he was ready for the day. Dr. Winters came shortly after and asked how things were going. "I can tell by the dark circles that Mom didn't get much sleep, hang in there Sydney it doesn't last forever. Are you still sore?"

Only a little but it is better, and you are right this mom didn't sleep too well, but we are doing fine. Ryan just got his first sponge bath."

"So this perfect little one is Ryan, good name he looks like a Ryan. I have to get going and open my office. If you need anything just call, I will see you tomorrow at about this time. Bye for now."

After he left I sat down, "Daniel, there is something I have wanted to talk to you about, could we do it now?"

"Give me a sec I want to grab some coffee. Ok so what's up?"

"Well, it is about money," I said biting my lip, "I am not very good about this kind of talk but you are paying for everything in this house, our honeymoon, the whole thing. That's not fair you are supporting me and my whole family on what you have been making fixing up things around town for quite a while. Can't I help?"

Daniel turned serious, "Syd, I have worked for many years and saved a lot of money for just this, my family. I will be working again when things settle down, besides you haven't worked in a while and paid for all the renovations, so unless you won the lottery or something I don't want you to give up what you have."

I was so hesitant to tell him but I had to, "Daniel, I am a very rich woman. I inherited more money than I could possibly use in my lifetime from my father's estate. We could all live on that forever and probably have some left. Now please let me help out, after all we are a team now my money is your money, we share everything."

"Good heavens girl, I had no idea I don't know what to say, though if I had been smart enough I would have figured that out. So you married a dummy," he said and got up and left the room.

I jump up and ran after him, "Daniel stop, please stop, it is not my fault that my father had no one else to give his money to, and so what if he did. Are we going to let stupid money ruin something so perfect as what we have. Good God this kind of love does not happen to most people ever. And another thing you are not stupid, you have got more smarts than I ever will." He just kept going so I backed away.

I went into the living room and got Ryan and we went upstairs. He was asleep so I put him in his bed and laid down myself and just sobbed. Why did I tell him, but he would have found out sooner or later, why does this seem to make such a difference? I guess it is his pride, oh my, that must be it. I need to do something. Gretchen heard me and knocked on the door, "Honey it is me can I come in?"

I told her yes. "I just saw Daniel go out the front door and he looked strange, did you have a fight?"

"No but I thought I had better tell him about all the money Father left to me, he said he was stupid not to have figured it out and left the room. All I wanted to do was help out money wise, it just doesn't seem fair that he is providing for all of us. What do I do now?"

Gretchen sat down on the side of the bed, "My girl give him some space, after all he just witnessed the birth of his baby, I am sure he is emotionally drained, this is not the end of the world, he will see that you were only offering to help, though I do think maybe his pride is hurt a little."

"I too think his pride is hurt, maybe he doesn't think he is doing enough and that is why I offered, but that has nothing to do with it. For goodness sakes, if it is that big of a problem I will just give it all to you and Mom or some charity."

"Give him some time to think, now get up and top this blubbering. Someone named Ryan wants to be fed I will leave you two alone."

She was right as always, I picked up my sweet baby and put him to my breast, "Have a good snack little one Mommy loves you." Those beautiful eyes never left my face the whole time. Then there was another knock on the door, "Gretchen its ok I am feeding Ryan and can't get up, I'll be down later."

"It's me Sydney, can I come in?" Daniel opened the door a crack.

"Of course." He just stood there staring at the two of us.

He sat down next to me and rubbed his sons little leg, "You were wrong when you said I am not stupid, I am but for a different reason. Your words just hit me wrong, I thought you were saying that I was not doing a good job and that hurt and that is why I am stupid. All I have ever wanted is to be a good husband, son, and father and for some reason I felt like I had failed. No don't say anything let me finish. My love it is not your fault that you inherited money from your father, it is really a good thing, it showed he loved you and knew you would be responsible with what you did with it. Remember we are going to have twenty kids and I want them all to go to college so maybe we could use it for that, or if something else comes along," he said then smiled. "What I am trying to say, and not doing a very good job, is that I am sorry, I love you and Ryan more than life and I always will. Can you forgive me?"

I got up and changed Ryan then laid him back down in his little bed. When I turned around and saw pain in my wonderful husbands face. "Of course, but there is nothing to forgive, I shouldn't have brought it up, we have had so much in the last two days, but some day you would have found out anyway. You are my husband and I literally have to pinch myself every morning to be sure this is not a dream when I wake up with you beside me. Daniel I have said it a million times, I am the luckiest girl in the world to have you. If it would help any I could give all the money away, when I was by myself I was glad to have it but I don't need it now. You are a wonderful provider; I guess I just thought maybe I could help out a little and take some of the burden off of you. Pals again?" I asked as I held out my hand.

"Pals, though this would be a great time to get under these sheets and make up but we have about six weeks to go on that."

He grabbed me and we fell onto the bed holding each other like never before. "You are an amazing woman."

I think our little confrontation has made us even closer than we were, if that is possible, and the weeks that followed were wonderful, Ryan was becoming a little person and smiled almost all the time. I love hearing his little squeals and mumblings. He truly lights up my life in so many ways.

One night I wanted everything to be extra special as we could finally be together again. So when we went to bed I told Daniel, that I have a little surprise, "Ryan is sleeping better and I bought a breast pump so Mom or Gretchen can feed him with a bottle when he wakes up during the night at least for tonight."

He looked at me a little strangely, "So what's up?"

"Sweetie our six weeks is up, and I went for my last visit to Dr. Winters today, and he said all was well, so guess what we get to do tonight besides sleep?"

"Ah read a good book by the fireplace, get over here woman, we are wasting time." It was a wonderful night and when we finally slept it was all night.

When we woke up I immediately got out of bed to check on Ryan and screamed, "Daniel he's gone, Ryan is gone!"

He smiled and said, "Syd relax remember he is in his own room for the night with Gretchen on guard." Boy you ARE a mom aren't you. Now come back to bed and be a wife too. We finally went down to breakfast about eight.

"Good you guys slept in," Gretchen said then smiled in her all-knowing way. "You needed some time together. Your little one only woke up twice and went right back to sleep. He is such a joy, we are going to have to do this more often."

A few weeks later Daniel said he had some work to do on a neighbor's roof today so he would probably not be home until the afternoon. "Be careful up there," I yelled as he went out the door.

"So little man what are we going to do today? Well look at you, you raised your head and chest up down there on your blanket, wait til I tell Daddy. How about a quick game of tennis or we could go over and bother Grandma Edith. Let's take a vote, Grandma it is."

I decided to surprise Edith and not tell her we were coming, and she sure was. "Well look who's coming," she said as she got out of her lawn chair. "Please sit down, hello little one, another beautiful day huh?"

"Hope you don't mind us just popping in but Ryan insisted. Daniel is going to be fixing someone's roof and won't be home until later so by unanimous vote we came here."

"Daniel is right, you are a nut Sydney," then she smiled big. "You know you can come over any time you want. So how is my favorite little person, he is getting so big? I can tell he is a happy boy, all he does is smile."

I put Ryan in my lap so he could see what was going on, "Ryan do you want to tell Grandma or should I about your big event just before we came over? Ok I will tell her, Edith he raised his head and chest up while playing on the floor."

"Oh my goodness what a good boy you are."

"You know he does smile most of the time unless he is wet or hungry and stays awake longer. I think he will be sleeping through the night very soon. Thank goodness" and we both laughed. "How in the world did you live through five children with so little sleep?"

I could see that she was going back to that time, "I think I was on automatic pilot and found it best not to think about what I had to do, I just did it. But motherhood is worth every minute of it, don't you think?"

"You are so right, I think I was born to be a mom, I love it and Daniel is so wonderful with him, oh Edith I love that man so much."

She smiled, "So do I. Out of all my boys Daniel is the most sensitive and considerate, he loves you both so very much. Thank you my dear for taking such good care of him, I have never seen him so happy."

"That makes two of us. I see you are knitting again, what are you making this time?"

She held it up, "It is a sweater for your little man for the fall. I love the colors, so many and so bright. I hope he will be the best dressed boy in the neighborhood."

"There is no doubt in my mind, how sweet of you."

Ryan was getting a little fussy, "Edith it is lunch time, do you mind if I feed him now?"

She smiled, "Of course not dear."

I put him to my breast and shielded him a little with my sweater. "My dear do not worry about hiding all this from me, this is the most natural thing a mom can do and I want him to breathe," another smile.

After Ryan had just finished Gretchen came running across the yard, "SYDNEY, SYDNEY!" she yelled.

I grabbed Ryan and jumped up, "What is it what's wrong?"

She was so out of breath she could hardly speak. "You forgot your cell phone and I heard it ringing so I got it. It was Dr. Winters. There has been an accident, Daniel fell off the roof and is in the hospital he said you had better get right over there he is pretty banged up. Here give me Ryan, now go."

Edith and I went into panic mode. "Come on Sydney I will drive us over," she said as we ran across the yard to the garage. Eli saw us coming and ran over.

"What's wrong, has something happened?" I was really crying and went over and hugged him as Edith told him and we all got into the car and headed for the hospital. Thank goodness it is only a ten minute drive, but Eli got us there in five.

"Oh Edith I am so scared, please God please let him be all right." I repeated over and over. Eli dropped us off at the door and parked the car, though we waited for him as we had no idea where Daniel was. I went up to the front desk and explained as best I could why we were there.

"Mrs. McGregor he is on the fourth floor the nurses will direct you when you get up there."

When we got off the elevator I went right up to the desk. A nice nurse said Dr. Winters was in with him now but he will be out soon, "Sit down and try to relax." Relax you have got to be kidding.

I jumped up and almost fell when I saw Dr. Winters. "What happened is he all right, please tell me?" Edith and Eli were right there too.

He told us to sit down and did the same," As best as we can figure he must have lost his footing and fell two stories. He has a broken leg and wrist, dislocated shoulder, and is bruised from head to toe. He is on heavy duty pain killers right now and is pretty out of it."

"Can we see him?"

"Yes but don't stay long, he might not even be awake. He is going to go into surgery very soon for that leg."

There lay my husband looking like he had been in a war, Edith must have felt the same way as she gripped my arm. I felt like I was going to be sick but went over and put my hand in his. He opened his eyes and tried valiantly to smile but didn't quite make it. "Hi love, boy what some people will do just to get a little attention. It is your turn to do all the diaper changing tonight so I expect you to be all better by then. I was desperately trying to hold back my tears, but they came anyway. "I'm so sorry baby try to be brave we are all right here."

With that Edith came over and gently touched his beat up face. "Get better soon Son, we all need you home."

Eli was next, "Don't ya worry we will take care of Ryan and Sydney you just get yerself put back together again." Then they left but I stayed.

"Oh love you scared me to death but I really know you are going to be fine. Dr. Winters said so too. You are going to have to have some surgery on your leg, what did you do land on a pile of rocks?" I said trying to smile. He nodded his head. "Really, oh how awful, well Mr. McGregor you have always been an overachiever, unfortunately this time too. Ryan told me to tell you that he loves you and as soon as you get back he wants you to teach him how to play football. Oh and guess what the slugger did this morning, he lifted his head and chest off the floor when he was playing on his tummy. Hot stuff huh! Sweetheart I will be here as long as you are here, so try to rest and I will be back soon."

He tried so hard to speak but his mouth was so bruised he could hardly open it, but I am sure he said I love you, "Well I love you more, and we can continue this argument in a day or so. Now be prepared I am going to kiss you, it is one of those things you are going to have to bear so here goes."

I was sobbing when I got back to the waiting room as were both of Daniel's parents. We clung together as the gurney went in to get him for surgery. "We are all here baby, be a good little boy and we will see you after they fix you up," I said through mounds of tears.

We sat there in silence after he left and Edith finally said, "Let's pray, Dear God protect our loved one, guide the surgeons hands and bring him back to us soon."

All of a sudden I remembered I had to feed Ryan so I called

Gretchen, "Gretch, he is in very bad shape, he fell off a two story roof and looks like he was beaten up by about a hundred men–he is down in surgery now for a bad broken leg I just can't go home. It is so odd but for some reason I have been pumping my breast milk regularly so there is quite a few bottles in the fridge. Can you please take care of Ryan? I am sorry but I HAVE to stay here. Big hugs to you and Mom, please call me if you need to." I was assured he would be fine.

Only an hour had passed and Dr. Winters came over to us, "I just talked to the surgical nurse and there was more damage than we thought to Daniel leg so the surgery is going to take longer. I am sorry but they don't know if they can save the leg or not it was mangled badly. We will keep you up to date. Sydney are you all right?"

"I don't think so," and I fell to the floor. The next thing I remember is a bunch of people standing around me and Dr. Winters was kneeling by my side.

"What happened?" I asked.

"You fainted Sydney, now try to get up. Oh my you must have hit your eye on the way down you are going to get a shiner. The nurse will clean it up for you." She did and I felt like such a dumb dumb.

Then I remembered what the doctor had said, "Oh God how can just a broken leg turn into something so serious?" I asked.

"When Daniel was falling he must had hit something along the way and then he landed in a pile of bricks, with the force of the landing it damaged veins and arteries. His surgeon is the best and I am sure he will do everything he can to save it."

Edith and Eli were in just as bad a state as I was; both were holding each other sobbing. I went over and hugged them both. "Remember Daniel is strong he will get through this." We sat there for what seemed like days when finally the surgeon came into the room. We all jumped up.

"Are you Daniel McGregor's family?" he asked. "Well he is out of surgery and is doing fine, we were able to save the leg but he is going to need a lot of rehabilitation after the cast comes off. His wrist did not need surgery but is in a cast. You can see him in about two hours or whenever he wakes up. Who is Sydney, he kept repeating the name over and over even with his oxygen mask on and was totally out of it?"

I smiled, "I am Sydney, Daniel is my husband." I went over and hugged him, "Sorry I am probably not supposed to do that but Daniel is my life and I can't thank you enough for what you did."

"What the heck," said Eli, and he too went over and gave him a hug, Edith joined him.

"Well this is a little unusual but thank you all, Daniel is a lucky man," said the smiling surgeon. "I will keep a good eye on him."

Then I told him that I was not leaving that night. "If I promise not to say a word can I sit in his room?"

"Yes but try not to make him talk, he needs to rest. I will tell Dr. Winters you will be there."

When Daniel was brought back he was still pretty out of it. I held his hand and said I was here and would be staying all night, "Now go to sleep, that's an order."

That is exactly what I did. The nurses popped in every once in a while and told me to walk around a little, they would stay with him. One even brought me a sandwich and some milk. "You need to keep your strength up dear." In the morning Edith and Eli were back, I told them the night before that I was staying so go home and rest. I called Gretchen and she said Ryan was perfect last night, he slept six hours straight.

"Did ya sleep at all Sydney?" Eli asked "you look awful, sorry but ya do. Your eye looks very pretty so many colors. Here let me give you a hug, you is doing so well I am so proud of you." I could tell that Eli was still very upset because his speech was back to being not quite right and he has been doing so well lately.

"I do remember laying my head against his good arm and I think I slept for a couple hours. The nurse came in to do vitals and of course I had to move. I haven't even looked at my eye glad I am colorful."

Daniel was awake when we all went back in, still groggy but

I could tell he was doing a little better. He asked what kind of makeup I changed to, "Not very becoming switch back," then attempted a smile. "Did Mom hit you?"

Edith jumped up from her chair and went over to the side of the bed, "Young man if were not in a hospital bed I would spank you. Sydney had a fight with a chair in the waiting room, the chair won." We all laughed and it felt so good. Poor Daniel tried but stopped right away, with a moan of pain. "I am sorry dear, just rest for now, come on Eli let's go back out and reread those awful magazines in the waiting room. First though I do need to call the boys and tell them what has been going on."

"I laid my head on the side of my husband's head and said, "I love you you big klutz, there will be no more climbing on anyone's roof that's a new law. Guess what Ryan slept for six straight hours last night. Gretchen and Mom are taking good care of him. I left some breast milk so he is fine." Just then there was a knock on the door and in walked Mom and Gretchen with Ryan.

Mom went over and kissed him on the cheek then stated to cry. Gretchen just stood there shaking her head, "Daniel McGregor you scared the life out of me, and at my age that is serious business. There is a little man here that insisted on coming over to see his daddy." Daniel smiled so big! Ryan took one look and started cooing and smiling like I have never seen. Gretchen put him close to his good hand so Daniel could touch him. Ryan grabbed his finger and I swear giggled. It was so wonderful! Of course I had to hold my baby too and decided as long as he was here I would breast feed him. Gretchen and Mom left the three of us alone. When I was done, Daniel asked if I had anything left over he was thirsty.

"So you are thinking frisky thoughts you stinker, good that means you are starting to feel better but control yourself it is going to be awhile.

I asked Gretchen later how she managed to get Ryan in, "I threatened Dr. Winters."

I couldn't stop laughing, "You did what?"

"I just told him that if I couldn't bring Ryan in I would stalk him until the day he died. Don't look so concerned he laughed like a crazy person."

The days went slowly by and Daniel was improving with each one. He had daily physical therapy just to keep his arms and one leg from getting stiff and grumbled through the whole thing. One day he looked a little sad and I asked him if he was all right. "Physically I am doing ok but...I miss you Syd, I want to touch you to make love to you so badly."

"Oh baby I miss you too, I have an idea, do you suppose I could put a chair in front of the door so no one could come in?"

"Good heavens woman I don't think this is the place to do an all-out attack, but it does sound like fun."

I started giggling, "Well maybe we could make it a partial ravage, you game?"

"Do you need to ask, get over here?"

I sat at the edge of his bed and unhooked my bra, then I took his good hand and put it under my sweater, "ravage away my mad attacker but make it quick," and I bent down and kissed him the whole time.

Thank goodness the nurse didn't come in for about ten minutes and I got put together just a second before.

"So how is my patient doing?" she asked.

"Terrific thanks to my wonderful wife, she seems to know just what to do to lift my spirits, she also thought of an exercise to keep my good hand from getting stiff." I turned away quickly sure I was a hundred shades of red.

Every day my mad attacker asked if I wanted to tempt fate again, we were lucky and never got caught though a couple times when he decided to do a little more exploring it was really close.

After another week Dr. Winters said that he could go home soon. He gave me some pain medications and warned that he might be very uncomfortable. The therapy would be daily after the cast comes off and he was not to climb and stairs. It will be quite a few weeks before he will be able to put weight on the leg. I had been staying at the hospital day and night but once I felt sure that Daniel was all right I decided to go home at night, plus he told me to. After the talk with the doctor I spoke to Mom, "I hate to ask you this but can we sleep in your room until Daniel is better; the doctor says he can't climb stairs? There is another unused room upstairs, are you up to climbing?"

She patted herself on the back, "Yes dear I have been doing it all the time now, and of course you can stay there. MY therapist said it is good for me. Boy we are going to be a house full of therapists aren't we? What about Ryan, do you want Gretchen and me to do the nighttime feedings?"

"I think we will just keep him down here with us, at least try it, because he is sleeping about eight solid hours now. Let's just see how it works. I will talk to Daniel and see what he thinks." As it turned out we all decided it was best if Ryan stayed upstairs. With such full days ahead Daniel and I were going to need our rest.

The day I brought Daniel home did not turn out like I had expected, I picked him up about ten in the morning and when we got to the house there were four men standing outside. "Good heavens your brothers are all here!" I said surprised. They were waving like crazy and when I got out of the van I got a bunch of big hugs from them all.

They stood there staring at their brother, John was the first one to speak, "So little brother you tried to play superman huh. Well we are going to be around for a week to make sure you don't try to put your cloak back on. With a house full of girls you need manly men to help you out." The smile on Daniels face was amazing.

"You big lugs, it is so good to see you. My God you haven't even met my son. Help me get out of here and we can talk." With that they all went over and gently lifted him out and into the house. I introduced them all to Mom and Gretchen.

Of course Gretchen had to make a comment, "Lordy I think I am going to faint, all these handsome men in one room, it is too much. Really thank you for coming." She was then attacked with hugs and a couple lifted her off the floor. "Now I AM going to faint, you scoundrels."

Then went in and got Ryan, "Gentlemen, I would like you to meet Ryan Daniel McGregor, the new substitute lord of the manor while his daddy is recovering." He got passed all over the place and seemed to love every minute of it. That beautiful smile never left his face. Daniel finally got to hold his son, with a little help from me. He didn't say a word just held him close.

"Thank goodness he looks like Sydney Danny boy," said Scott. Daniel's good arm gave him a whack. We all had such a good time.

I called Edith to tell her we were home and that all her boys were here. "Yes," she said, "they came in last night. How wonderful to have them all here for a week. How is my youngest son doing? We will come over later this afternoon."

"The boys really did the trick, Daniel seems so happy to be back and then to have them around really has lifted his spirits. You should have seen the big guys melt when they met Ryan and got to hold him, it was great!"

I sent Daniel in the bedroom for a rest, with the help again of his brothers, for a couple hours and we all sat around and talked. I got to hear all the latest news about their families and was told if I ever need to talk all my sisters-in-law are ready and willing. That made me feel so good.

They guys left after dinner and the three of us were finally alone. "You know I think Ryan has grown, he is such a dear thing. I missed him so much. And you my girl, you stayed with me though it all and I am so grateful, thank you."

"And where else would I have been?" I told him how wonderful his parents were through the whole thing, "We literally held each other up. They are so strong and truly love you so much. My love I still have nightmares of you falling. It will be so good to sleep next to you tonight. Oh my I just realized I am going to have to sleep on your good side so I don't hurt you. Yikes I didn't think about I might bump into you or something. Do you think I should sleep upstairs?"

He grabbed for my hand and kissed it, "You're kidding right? There is no way. In fact how about we go now I am really tired? I helped him into his wheelchair and called for Gretchen who helped me get him changed and into bed.

"Sorry Gretchen," he said.

She gave him her best disgusted look, "Sorry for what, you are my family and families help each other, look what you have done for me. I get to live forever with a stinker like you, Sydney, Rose, and Ryan all the people I love the most. Now let's get you arranged and comfortable. Is this going to work, I am sure we can get a hospital bed?"

"Do they have them for two?"

"Oh God watch out for this one Syd, casts or no casts he is going to be trouble." Then she started to laugh so hard she doubled over. "Ok ok I will leave please call if you two need anything."

I told her I would be up in a minute to feed Ryan one last time, which I did. He went right to sleep with a smile still on his face.

When I got back to our room Daniel was asleep so I gently slipped in next to him and kissed his head. Then, I heard it, "How about a few hundred kisses to make up for lost time?" So I kissed him all over his face and chest. "Not quite what I expected but will have to do for now I guess."

"Enough with the kisses you need to get some sleep. Oh baby you really scared me big time. Did you know the surgeon didn't know if he could save your leg or not, you really did a number on it?"

He really look surprised, "Good heavens I didn't know, which honestly was good I guess. Oh Syd how awful this whole thing must have been for you all. I love you so much."

The next morning I got up early, fed Ryan then went in to wake up his dad. First I put my hair up into a sexy style and got out a mini shirt I had worn a million years ago along with a tank top that was cut way too low to wear outside the house–this is going to be fun. "Good morning handsome let me introduce myself I am your new nurse, my name is Babette and I am here to get you up and give you a quick sponge bath." I set the bucket of water on the floor and started pulling back his covers.

"Babette huh, does my wife know about you?"

I started unbuttoning his pajama top, "Yes she hired a Miss Snobgrass but she came down with a cold so I am taking over. I hope you don't mind?"

"Nah, this should be very interesting." I took off his top and exclaimed, "My sir you have such big muscles, you must be strong. Now let me wash you up." He never took his eyes off me and had the funniest little quirky smile on his face.

Next I started to remove his pajama bottoms. "Sorry sir this is a little hard with the cast but I am a trained professional. Don't be embarrassed I have given many men a bath before."

"Oh really Babette then I will relax, you have such a gentle touch, not like my wife she can get rough at times but then she is not a professional. Ouch watch it with the rubbing."

When I was done I smiled in my best professional way, "There now you are clean I will dress you for the day." I made sure I leaned over way too much and brushed against his chest as I was putting on his shirt.

He was really enjoying all this, "Babette are you sure you cleaned everything well, maybe you should do it again."

"I assure you sir that you have been cleaned enough, now you are ready for the day, is there anything else I can do for you?"

The evil eye was back, "Yes but I don't think my wife would like it, shut the door first."

I turned around and started laughing, "You really are a rotten man my husband, but lucky for you I will forgive your infatuation with Babette. Maybe when you start feeling better we should have Babette come back and give you another bath hummmm?"

"Well only if you don't mind," and he too started laughing. His brothers arrived just then and must have heard us laughing.

"Hey anybody home some hungry guys just walked in and are heading for the bedroom door get dressed you two. Just then I realized I looked like a call girl and changed quickly, all while Daniel was laughing.

I went out in the foyer and said they arrived just in time Daniel could use a lift to the kitchen, I will bring the wheelchair. Poor Gretchen made a face when we all showed up. "Ha I am prepared for a bunch of lumberjacks, sit down and dig in."

My girls have been very good through all this but I don't think they knew what to make of all the loud talking and laughter and Daniel zooming around in his chair, so they spend most of the time outside.

The next week was really great, all but when Daniel had to have his therapy. His brothers were so much fun always laughing and kidding around, just what was needed. Dr. Winters stopped by daily and was pleased with his progress. He took me aside and asked, "Sydney you are doing a great job, his spirits are high and he looks happy. Has he been in much pain?"

"No not too bad I guess but I do give him the medicine when he asks for it. Really I think his good mood is mostly due to his brothers all being here but thank you. Really thank you for everything. By the way I hope you take care of children as well as adults Ryan may need you someday."

"Of course, you know while I am here I will give him a little check- up." We went upstairs. Ryan was again a good little boy and the doctor said he is doing fine, sleeping better, good." I picked up Ryan and we went downstairs.

We all hated to see the brothers go but they promised to come back soon. There were hugs all around and Daniel got some good back pats. Steve thanked me and said I was to call if I needed anything, and they were off.

It seemed so quiet after they left, back to real life I guess. "Honey, do you realize how lucky you are to have brothers who care so much about you? They are really something else. It is fun for me too to have brothers!"

"I sure do but it is you Syd that makes my life complete and that beautiful son you gave me. I wonder how long it will be before we can start working on another one."

I gave him a little whack on the arm, "Yish man, give my body a little rest besides with you all casted up I think it may be quite a while. Hey how about we go sit on the porch it is a lovely day?"

I pushed him out and went back in to get Ryan; we just sat there staring at the lake. "This is so nice I had almost forgotten how beautiful it is."

"Look at the pretty boats sweetie, you and I are going to have to go swimming one of these days now that your umbilical cord stump is gone. Would you like that?"

He was getting a little fussy, "Is it lunch time, ok dive in?" How peaceful it was to just sit and relax with my little family.

"You know it still really gets me when I see you feeding him. You are truly bonding, I wish I had a special way of bonding with him," said Daniel almost sadly.

"My dear every time you pick him up you bond. Here, we are done," and I brought Ryan over to him. He held him tightly and seemed so happy.

I am glad that the wrist cast didn't seem to be that awkward for him anymore. The wind was picking up so I said we had better get back in there may be a storm coming. Just then the girls came flying into the house. "Yes there is a storm coming."

We sat and watched the rain and the lightning. Poor Ryan would jump whenever the thunder came. "Isn't that fun sweetie, go boom, this is your first storm it is just noises and pretty lights, right Daddy?"

"Yep."

The time finally came to remove Daniels leg cast. He had to have x rays first but Dr. Winters said he was healed. He took the wrist one off first and then the leg. His poor leg looked so strange, kinda shriveled. "Now you will begin therapy to get that leg working again, but remember no weight bearing, no walking for another few weeks at least. The therapist will let you know when. He will come daily."

Daniel said it felt so strange like it was kind of out there with no place to go and very stiff. We had a pillow on the foot rest so the leg would get some support and he said that felt much better. A male nurse helped us into the van and we left. When we got home I asked Gretchen to help me get him out and into his chair again. Between us we lifted him and the chair up the steps.

"Ladies I thank you but am worried that you are going to hurt yourselves."

She gave him her best Gretchen is out of patience look, "That is kind of you mister, but are we supposed to leave you down there in the muck and the guck and the beer? Or we could just bump you up, it's up to you."

"Ok I get it, but thanks. I love you Gretchen."

Even Gretchen turned a hundred shades of red before she waved her arms around and headed for the kitchen.

"Oh Gretchen, could you come back just once more, I would like to lay down for a little while after our busy morning at the hospital could you help me please?" asked Daniel. We got him settled and he went right to sleep, I told him to yell if he needs anything.

I went into the living room and grabbed a book to read, both of my boys were sleeping so this is finally my time. Mom came in, "Hi Sweetie can we talk?"

"Sure Mom sit down, is everything all right, good, so what's up?"

She sat down across from me, "Sydney I don't feel like I am doing anything to help out around here, Gretchen has pretty much taken over the kitchen and helping you with Daniel and gets up with Ryan at night. What can I do? I almost feel left out."

"Oh Mom just having you with me is really all I need but I have seen you with Ryan and how wonderful you are with him, how happily he responds to you. So, how would you like to be his official nanny when I am not around and at night? That would help me so much now that we are downstairs for a while. I am sorry you have been feeling this way, I just wanted to be sure you could walk comfortably before I asked you for too much help."

She finally smiled, "Oh I would love to take care of Ryan, I missed all that with you and really feel a need to be an almost mom. Thank you dear. What about Gretchen will she be upset?"

I went over to her and put my arm around her, "Let's both go tell her now."

Gretchen was making cookies as we entered, "Gretch I have a favor to ask of you, would you mind if Mom takes charge of Ryan's care from now on? Now that she is able to get around better I think it would help you, you do so much around here.

Of course if she needs your help I am sure you would. I would like Mom to be able to make up for the time she lost when I was a baby and she says she would really like to do it. So what do you say?"

"Of course Rose, you should have said something sooner. But warning I still want to cuddle and hold him. You are his true grandmother and this would be a great time for you both. So it is set, you can start tonight."

Mom hugged me and her and thanked us over and over. "Yes tonight, thank you."

Later I saw Gretchen and said, "Gretch I hope you understand why I did this with Mom, she told me she didn't think she was helping anyone around here. You are so capable of doing everything and she didn't want to butt in I guess. I have relied on you practically since birth and trusted you completely. You too are my mother but I want her to feel a part of us all and I think this will do it. Are you sure you are all right?"

"Yes my dear girl I am, I too wished that I had seen this coming earlier, but I don't think I was even looking. I was just glad that she was back. Now don't worry it will all work out just fine."

When Daniel woke up I told him what had happened. He was surprised but said he too was waiting for her to be able to move around better and just glad she was found. "We do need to pay more attention to her. I understand how close you are to Gretchen she has been your mother so naturally you feel the way you do. With all that has been going on here with Ryan we have been totally focused on him. We need to include her more in all we do she is a big part of this family."

"Thank you my love. How are you feeling? Does your leg hurt, how about your wrist? Can I get you anything?"

"No I am all right I just hate the strange feeling I have in my leg, it is like it doesn't belong to me someone just stuck it on. I know the PT will help and I am anxious to get more into it and tired of waiting for it to get back to normal, if it ever will. I know I know it will be fine but love, it might not be, I might have a limp or something and what if I can't go back to contracting?"

I sat down on the edge of the bed and took his hand, "So what if you have a limp does that make you a different person? No. If you can't be a contractor anymore then you will be something else and just as good at it. How about we just deal with whatever we have to if we have to. Right now I think I will lie down and cuddle with my man, if that's ok with him."

"What you said is true I am just so grateful that I am alive and CAN cuddle with you and be Ryan's dad. Nothing else matters."

All of a sudden he got very serious, "Syd I am going nuts, I lay down next to you every night and I can hardly touch you, I want you so badly and I can't do anything about it. We had such little time after Ryan was born that we could be together then my accident happened. God knows how long we still have to wait. I'm sorry I guess I am just feeling sorry for myself, you are here and I know you love me and have taken such good care of me."

"Oh baby, this has been just as hard on me, I want you too. Do you have any idea what it does to me to lay down by you and be afraid to touch you for fear I will hurt you? I don't want to get you too stimulated and then not be able to do anything about it."

Daniel smiled at me, "I have an idea, yea yea I know it is always the same let's make love but, come here I want to whisper it to you."

"But there is no one here but us you silly."

"Just do it you sexy thing," so down I went.

"Oh my, so what happens if you start moving around a little, and I can guarantee that you will, and hurt yourself and then I have to yell for Gretchen? Do you honestly expect me to tell her what I was doing?"

That did it we both laid back and laughed our heads off.

Just then there was a knock on the door, "You two had better not be doing anything naughty with all that laughter because I am coming in ready or not, I will count to five. One, two, three, four, five" and she opened the door. We were still laughing like crazy.

"Gretchen your timing is awful, I was just about to ravage

Syd," which led to even more laughter, even from Gretchen.

"Yea well back to real life, the ravage can wait it is time to feed us and Ryan. Can I help you up Daniel? Really you are going to have to stop laughing you idiot, I can't lift you." Then she too started laughing, "Ravage? Good heavens now that would be worth watching, the guy who can barely move a muscle suddenly jumps up and attacks his wife." She doubled over laughing and fell on the bed next to Daniel.

Daniel immediately grabbed her, "Want some too you sexy thing?" Gretchen screamed and ran out of the room, but was laughing hysterically as she flew down the hall.

Of course Mom heard all this and yelled at Gretchen, "What in the world is going on down there?"

"Ask the lunatic," yelled Gretchen.

Poor Mom she came down the stairs and to our door and peeked in, "Can I get in on the fun too?" I rolled over on my side and was laughing so hard I was crying poor Daniel was in bad shape too.

"Ok everyone pull yourselves together or I am going to wet my pants I'm not kidding," but I just couldn't stop laughing. "This house is full of crazy people," I screamed.

Later on Gretchen asked Daniel, "Did Syd tell you about our new arrangement?"

"Yes and I do think it is a good idea. There have been so much going on with us getting married and then right away having Ryan, Rose has been neglected I think and we didn't see it."

The summer was almost gone and I did want to take Ryan down to the beach to play in the sand and try out the water. I asked Mom if she wanted to come down with us, and she seemed more than willing.

Ryan loved the sand and was at first not too sure about the water but finally decided it was ok after all I guess because he yelled whenever I took him out. Daniel sat at the top of the hill watching and I felt so bad for him being stuck up there, but I just couldn't figure out how we would get him down and then back up. Mom had put her swim suit on under her clothes which I knew she was going to do but Daniel didn't. When she started taking off her clothes he yelled, "Woman put your clothes back on there is a horny man sitting up here." Then I couldn't believe what my demure sweet Mother did. She started doing a strip tease and was whipping her clothes off and flying them up in the air as she did a little dance. Oh my God I thought I was going to explode I was laughing so hard. Daniel just sat up there cheering as he laughed too. "Hey you sexy thing you really have the moves come up here I need a kiss." Which of course led to much more laughing and finally Mom had to sit down–really she fell down and roared with laughter.

"You dummy I have my bathing suit under here, thanks Daniel this has been so much fun."

"Mom you are a real character and I am so glad, bless you for making this afternoon so fun for us all."

The three of us did go into the water and Ryan squealed with delight when a little wave got him in the face. We sat on the beach for just a little while and I put Ryan in the sand too. "Daniel look, he's actually playing in the sand with his fingers." What a day this has been. "Now little person I think we had better go up and take a nap you have been a busy boy. Go collect your clothes you tawdry woman and we can get going," I said to Mom.

That afternoon seemed to change my mom, even Gretchen noticed. "What's happened to Rose she is so talkative and happy all of a sudden." I told her about the strip tease act and she threw her head back, "That's the Rose I used to know. Now you are going to see who your mom really is, be prepared she is a hoot."

Gretchen and Mom were sitting in the living room later in that evening. When I came in Mom asked, "Are you going to be able to do anything for our anniversary? It's only two weeks away."

"Oh my gosh I haven't even thought about it, time has passed so fast with all that has been going on I guess I forgot. No I am sure we won't be able to actually do anything. Maybe just invite his folks over for a good dinner. I can't believe it is almost a year, and what a year it has been huh! Wait I do have an idea, how about you two go over and spend the evening with Edith and Eli and take Ryan. Then I could make a candle light dinner for us. Sure wish we could get a little more romantic but I guess not."

Gretchen said, "Syd this is a little embarrassing, heck it is a lot embarrassing but Daniel has been bearing weight on his leg and the therapist said he is doing very well, has Dr. Winters said anything about you... ah... you getting together again?"

"Well no but there is no way I could ask him it's just too much. But he is doing so well, oh me Dr. Winters is coming tomorrow I will try to get up enough courage to ask." By this time poor Mom was as red as a beet.

"Knock it off Rose you aren't that old to have forgotten such things."

Dr. Winters did come and said Daniel was doing remarkably well, he has good mobility and he is hopeful for a complete recovery. As he was leaving I said I would walk him out to his car. "Dr. Winters I have a question for you, and believe me I am extremely embarrassed but, ah...how long do you think it will be before Daniel and I can... our first year anniversary is in two weeks and I was hoping..."

"Don't be embarrassed Sydney it is only natural to want to know and it has been a long time. When a couple is making love there are a few ways to position yourselves, I think the traditional way would be a little too much right now for Daniel but maybe there could be another way. I have had to give this information to so many of my patients, all I can do is advise you and I am sure Daniel will be all right. Happy Anniversary," he said and left.

Bless his heart I thought such a dear man. Ok now to the planning of our big night. I called Edith I see if everyone could go over for the evening and said I wanted to make a romantic dinner for the two of us–fine with her. Then I told Gretchen and Mom. Gretchen looked at me and said, "Is it going to be a memorable night my girl?"

"Yes it is."

I told Daniel what I had planned, well most of it anyway and he thought it would be so nice to be by ourselves for a little while.

Everything was set, the dinner was done, I set a fancy table with candles and got dressed up. Everyone had just left and Daniel and I sat down. "You look good enough to eat," he said.

"Do you mean to tell me that I slaved all afternoon to make a feast for us and all you want to do is eat me?"

"Yep."

"Well maybe later now you get food." Everything came out great and after dessert he pulled out a small package from his pocket.

"For you my dearest Sydney Happy Anniversary." I opened the box and there was a beautiful gold bracelet with one heart hanging from it with RYAN embossed in the center. "I am not sure if we can get twenty hearts on it but we can sure try. I love you! Syd would you please get me my guitar, thanks."

This song is for you my love, I truly mean every word, you truly are as beautiful inside as outside and have given me everything I have ever wanted in this life. I can't believe I have the woman I adore and a beautiful son. This has been a wonderful year. Thank you for loving me; you are my soul and my light. We are forever Sydney."

He began singing "You are so beautiful," very slowly and with such heart, and I was in heaven. I felt every word deep in my soul. This man does love me, how did I ever get so lucky?

"Oh Daniel, that was wonderful. I love that song and I love you with every inch of my being." Then I looked down at the bracelet, "This is so special, how in the world did you get it?"

He smiled and said he had connections. "Really your mom helped me. She got a catalog from a jewelry store in Port Shores when we went down to buy our Christmas presents. She wanted a watch for herself but didn't want to take the time to find one there. When I told her what I wanted to get for you she gave me the book and I picked it out and the store sent it. Aren't I the sneaky one?"

I hugged him and said, "You certainly are. My gift for you

did not come out of a store, though it is in the shape of a heart, mine. I want to give you ME on our first anniversary. I know this sounds strange but it took a lot for me to find out if what I wanted to give you would actually be all right for you. I know more confusion. The last time Dr. Winters was here I actually asked him if we could make love yet. Listen buster that took more courage than I thought I had. Daniel he said yes, with a little variation to our norm. Want to give it a try?"

I think at first he was a little stunned because he didn't say anything, then the evil little look came by for a visit, "Oh Syd how did you know that is just what I wanted your choice of gifts is perfect."

"Come on smarty lets go into the bedroom." After I got him into bed and undressed, "First we start out with a little music," and I found a sexy sounding tune. Slowly, very slowly I started taking off my clothes to the beat of the music, and flung them all over the room as I did a little dance.

"You know you are almost as good as your mom. Don't tell me, you took some classes and this is how you made some extra money in college."

"How'd you guess," and I made my way over to him, "would you like a massage first or perhaps just a bunch of kisses from head to toe? It's your choice."

"Surprise me."

It was a perfect night and once again Daniel whispered to me, "Better than the sandbox huh kid?"

"Daniel McGregor, are you going to tell me that at each anniversary? Hope so," and I kissed him. "I hope you aren't in pain."

"Nope. By the way, how did you learn how to ah do what you did?"

"I read a lot," then started laughing and he pulled me close. "Heavens, haven't you had enough for one night?"

"Never enough, we have weeks and weeks to catch up on, wonder if we could set a world's record for one night?"

I patted his head and said, "Probably but we would be dead."

We stayed in our room but heard everyone come back and

go up to bed. "Thank you for loving me baby," and we went to sleep.

About three weeks later Daniel was doing so well and we all decided to take one more boat ride before the season ended. I told him he had to sit down when driving, which of course led to the eye rolling thing. "But love I will look like a sissy."

"So what, if you can't be a good little boy I will have to do all the driving." That did it he promised. It was a beautiful day and we were having a wonderful time just cruising along, Ryan loved it and looked so cute in his life jacket. All of a sudden a boat was coming up fast behind us with a skier, as they passed we all waived but the skier suddenly shot out in front of our boat. Daniel swerved to miss him just as Eli stood up and the jolt threw him overboard. Edith and I screamed and I yelled at Daniel to stop. He looked horrified. Daniel said he was going in and I told him to stop, as I gave Ryan to Edith. "You are going to reinjure yourself stay put," and I dove into the water. It took a little time but I finally saw Eli and grabbed him, he was limp and I had a hard time bringing him back up. When we finally got to the surface I yelled at Daniel to help me get him in. Between us we did and I got myself up. Immediately I told him to call 911 or whatever you do in a boat, "Good God he is not breathing," so I started rescue breathing and checking on his pulse, he barely had one. "Come on Eli come on, breathe." I thumped him on the back and turned him on his side. Edith was hysterical and Daniel was holding her tightly looking just as scared as she was. "Please Eli breathe," all of a sudden he coughed up the water and took a breath. I just laid my head down on his chest and cried then started shaking. "Put the blanket on him and get us to shore NOW!" The paramedics were waiting for us and they took him to the hospital.

We left the boat in Thumb Harbor and took a cab to the hospital. The doctor in emergency said they are examining him now and would be out later. "Who got him out of the water?" he asked. I told him I did and he wanted to know if the water was cold and how long before I got to him. I told him the best I could and that it was probably only a few minutes. He said he would be back, "But first I want you to get out of those wet clothes you must be freezing." He called for a nurse who took me into a room and gave me some scrubs to put on then wrapped me in a warmed up blanket. Oh it felt so good!

We all just held on to each other and prayed. Poor Ryan all he did was cry in Daniels arms, he had no idea what was going on. I held on to Edith who had not spoken a word since this all happened. "Edith are you all right?" I asked. "Edith talk to me, please." Dr. Winters happened to walk by just then and looked surprised to see us all.

"What is going on, has something happened?"

I told him and said I was concerned about Edith, "I think she is in shock, do you have time to check her out?" Of course he did and I told Daniel to call Gretchen and ask her to come and get Ryan, then went into the room too with Edith. The doctor said he is going to examine her and maybe I should leave. Edith grabbed my hand. "I will stay now please try to relax."

The doctor said she has had a terrible shock but is thankfully not in shock just very traumatized. He put an oxygen mask on her and covered her with a blanket. "She just needs a little time to get out of this, stay with her and I will go check and see what is happening with Eli and will be right back."

"Edith I am going to go out into the hall for just a minute to talk to Daniel I promise I will be right back." And I kissed her cheek.

"Honey are you all right, Dr. Winters said your mom is very traumatized which isn't too surprising? Has there been any news yet? Daniel?" He just stood there holding Ryan tightly. "Sit down love, is Gretchen on her way?" He nodded but said nothing. "I have to get back to your mom she is in an awful state," I kissed him and left.

I sat there holding Edith's hand. She seemed to be resting more comfortably but suddenly looked up at me, "Where is Eli I need to be with him, get me up and out of here?" I brought her back to the waiting room just as Dr. Winters came back. I told him she wanted to be out here and he said it was best if she lay down but just keep her calm and in a warm blanket.

Just then the emergency doctor came in, Dr. Winters held Edith close, "Eli seems to be doing all right, YOU," and he pointed to me, "saved his life. He did get some water in his lungs and will have to stay here in the hospital for a while to be sure he doesn't get pneumonia but I think he is going to be fine." Edith fainted and Dr. Winters said he would take care of her. All of a sudden I started to shake. A nurse got me another warmed up blanket which helped a lot and I thanked her. Gretchen arrived and took Ryan.

I started to cry, what a horrible day this has been. Daniel seemed to see me for the first time and came over and put his arms around me. "Honey, I think we had better call one of your brothers and tell him what has happened." He dialed John's number and handed me the phone, "John this is Sydney I am sorry to have to tell you this but".... and I explained it all. "Your Mom and Daniel are here with me now, they are very shook up that is why I am calling you, and so am I, but at least your dad seems to be doing all right. I will call you as we learn anything more. He is going to have to stay in the hospital for a while and I am going to try to convince your mom to come and stay with us." He sounded awful but thanked me for calling.

We were told we could go in and see Eli now, but just for a short time. I took Edith's arm and we all went in. Eli was awake and Edith went over to him and hugged him for a very long time then kissed him. "Oh God I am so thankful you are all right, I love you my dear." Daniel was next.

"Hey Dad," then he too started to cry and hugged him.

I decided I would go and leave them alone then all of a sudden I heard, "Sydney, are you there?"

"Yes Eli I am here, please don't try to talk just rest. I am so thankful you are going to be all right," and I bent down and kissed his cheek.

"My daughter you saved my life, how am I ever going to repay you?" and the tears fell down his cheeks. He put his arms around me and pulled me down to him and just hugged me.

"My dear dear man, I lost one father and there was no way I was going to lose you too. I love you. Now get some rest please."

I went out of the room and Daniel and his mom stayed just a little longer with him. I guess all of a sudden what happened hit me because I started sobbing and shaking violently. A nurse saw me and came over and held me tightly, "My dear, I heard you jumped in and saved him, my goodness you are so brave. Sometimes it takes us a little while after a tragedy to feel the effects, just hold on to me for a little while. Sarah get me another warm blanket please," she said to another nurse, and she wrapped it around me. Just then Daniel and Edith came out of the room and saw us.

Daniel went over and told the nurse he was my husband and would take over, "Thank you very much for helping her."

"My wonderful wife, you literally did the impossible; you did it all, including what needed to be done here at the hospital. You took care of us all. I am so sorry I couldn't help I felt paralyzed. You are truly amazing and I love you even more than I did, if that is possible. I think it is time for us all to go home, Mom lets go home now we all need some food and some sleep."

Edith grabbed me and I was sure she was never going to let me go. "Someday in some way I am going to try to figure out how to thank you, you saved me too when you saved him, right now I have no words except that I love you with all my heart."

"Edith I want you to stay with us until Eli is well again, no arguments. I did want to tell you that I called John and told him what has been going on and he said he would tell the others. Now let's get out of here." We stopped by Eli's room and said we would see him in the morning and I told the emergency doctor that Edith would be with us and gave him our phone number if he needed to call. We would be back in the morning.

We all ate some hot soup and went right up to bed. Mom helped Edith get into bed then came to our room. "Sydney I am so proud of you and love you so much, we will talk more tomorrow" and she gave me a kiss, Daniel too.

I took a hot shower then got into bed and held on to Daniel and we both went right to sleep. I woke up to a mound of kisses, "Good morning my love, did you sleep well?" he asked.

"Yes but I sure had nightmares, how about you?"

"Me too but hopefully all is well now and Dad will recover quickly. I am going to take a quick shower."

I peeked my head into Edith's room and she was still asleep. Good I thought she sure needs it, and I went downstairs.

My little man was eating his breakfast and I went over and gave him a big hug. "Hi baby how is my favorite cowboy this morning?" He smiled so big as I hugged him.

I looked up at Gretchen, "Oh Gretch it was all so awful, when I got into the water I couldn't find him, I was frantic. Poor Eli I grabbed him by the hair and hauled him up. Good heavens I was scared."

She came over and hugged me tight. "You saved his life my girl, and from what I hear took complete charge at the hospital. I think you should get a metal or something."

"So do I" said Daniel as he came into the kitchen. "Gretchen she was amazing. I just couldn't do anything it was like my brain and body shut down–Mom was hysterical, Ryan was crying, and Syd was doing it all." He came over and kissed me, "I wish I could thank you enough my dearest girl."

Edith finally came down and thanked us all, she said she was surprised that she had slept so soundly. "After breakfast can we go back to the hospital Daniel?"

We all went and the doctor said Eli is doing very well but he will have to stay for a few more days. "His brain function seems to be normal and his lungs are improving. He is a very lucky man to have survived. I hear Sydney saved him, Eli told me about six times already this morning. So who is Sydney?" I smiled and said I was. "A little thing like you, well we all do things we don't realize we can when there is an emergency."

Eli was in pretty good spirits, "I am so glad Edith is staying with you, so how is my hero this morning? You look tired."

"Well if you had just dragged a big strong handsome man out of the depths of Lake Huron while fighting off the sharks and sting rays you would be tired too," and I started to laugh.

He was laughing too, as were Edith and Daniel. "Thanks Sydney I needed that." I told him I did too and went over and kissed his cheek.

Eli came home in three days and while he needed to rest he was doing fine. Thank you God! His boys were all waiting for him and stayed for the rest of the week. Before they left they all came over. "Sydney, I speak for all of us when I say thank you, we love you very much, what you did was more than amazing. We are all so proud to have a sister like you," said Michael. Then I got hugs from them all.

–9–

HERE WE GO AGAIN

Fall is in full swing and our trees are really showing off. I will never tire of the beautiful reds and gold's. Ryan only needs a little support to sit up now and we have spent hours out in the yard playing with the leaves. I piled them up and plunked him in the center, he would laugh and then the whole thing would start again.

Halloween was so much fun, no party this year but Ryan got all dressed up, he was a lion, and we went trick or treating to Grandma's next door. They went nuts when they saw him and of course took lots of pictures. He was really into the whole thing and got so angry when we had to take off the costume before bed.

A couple days later while Edith and Eli were here we were all talking and playing with Ryan and bingo he rolled over. "Daniel did I see what I thought I saw, did Ryan really just turn over?"

"He sure did, good boy, wow" and we were all clapping. Then the smiles started and an actual laugh.

Well it has happened again, right before Thanksgiving I started getting a queasy stomach for no particular reason and made a beeline for Dr. Winters. He confirmed it, I was pregnant. He congratulated me then asked, "Sydney how is Eli doing, I know I have been checking on him regularly and he seems all right but is he really, he had quite a shock and that must have scared him big time? Good heavens it just occurred to me, you did that whole thing and you were pregnant, thankfully you didn't miscarry."

"Oh my I didn't think of that either, am I all right, could there be a delayed reaction I'm scared?"

"No my dear you are fine something would have happened

by now."

"Thank goodness, and yes Eli he is doing well, seems to still be a little tired but his spirits are up."

That night I told Daniel, "I think we had better not celebrate any more anniversaries at least not do what we did after dinner last time because my love you are going to be a daddy again in seven months." He started dancing around, "Whoa there you have only been out of that wheelchair for a little over a month. Careful!"

"Oh God I love you Syd, this is so exciting!"

"Before you ask yes, I have seen Dr. Winters. It was so funny, he smiled and asked if we had a happy anniversary and I gave him my yea yea yea look. You should have seen him laugh. He is very happy for us. Oh baby, I was pregnant when I saved your dad. I asked the doctor if I was all right and he said yes. Thank God! Now let's go in and break the news to the nanny's, who do you think is going to run screaming out of the house first?"

"Oh Syd how scary, I am so thankful all is well."

Both of my moms were in the kitchen drinking coffee. "Ok," Daniel said, "I have an announcement, we didn't think it was fair that one of you gets to take care of Ryan and the other has no one so guess what we are giving you another baby in seven months." I thought they were going to knock us down as they ran over and grabbed us.

"Are you sure, how do you feel?" that was Mom.

Gretchen just stood there with her mouth open, "How did you do it, yea yea I know how to make babies but, wait a minute two months ago, anniversary, let's get everyone out of the house to make a fancy dinner. Now I get it, must have been tough on you Daniel."

"You can't imagine Gretchen, you just can't imagine," the goof said with a huge smile.

I sat down in the chair and put my hands on top of my head. "I think now is the time to divorce you both, Mom is the only one who can stay. Really Gretch you are awful," Then I leaned over and hugged her. "What a bunch of crazy people I have to live with."

"Warning Daniel, this time you had better have given me a girl, Ryan has been asking for a baby sister and we don't want to disappoint him do we?"

He pretended to look surprised, "Oh so Ryan can talk now huh, all I can do is put in the order, the rest is up to my little girl or boy little swimmer buddies, whoever got there first."

"That's it I am going to bed," I said as I got up to leave.

Daniel jumped up and went after me, "Wait for me you sexy witch."

Gretchen was laughing again and I just heard, "It must be wonderful to be so much in love Rose."

"Not all the time," I yelled as I shut the door in Daniel's face.

He knocked and knocked, much to the amusement of my mother's I am sure. "Come on Syd you know you can't sleep without me, I promise I will be good. Syd?"

Of course I opened the door, "I am so mad at you, stop it, I said stop it…in about an hour."

The next morning we went over to his parent's house to give them the good news and took Ryan.

He was being his usual cute little self and Daniel said, "You know Syd maybe we should have a bunch more soon. How do you think Mom and Dad would react if we told them you are pregnant again?"

"Gee I don't know why don't we see?"

Complete silence, then "Is it true Sydney, are you going to have another baby?" Edith was already up from her chair ready to attack.

"Yes and I am so excited." Then the hugging began and so did the tears. We are a family of hugs, kisses and tears.

You would have thought this was the first grandchild for Eli, he jumped and cheered. "When, when?"

"Probably about Ryan's birthday, this time Syd wants a girl." Daniel said.

Eli suddenly looked alarmed, "Sydney were you pregnant when you saved me? Oh my God!"

"Yes but I didn't know it, Dr. Winters said I am fine and the baby is too so please don't worry."

A few days later I left Ryan on his blanket on the floor when I went in to get him some juice. When I came back he was off the blanket. "Hey little thing how did you do that? Daniel come here your son is showing off."

"What's up?"

"Watch, ok Ryan show Mommy and Daddy what you have been up to." As if right on cue he started to scoot, then brought his little legs and arms up and crawled about two feet. I yelled for Mom and Gretchen, "Look." We all cheered and he started to laugh and fell over. Then he rolled on his back and clapped too. It was so fun and he got so many hugs. My baby is growing up. "From now on everyone he has to be watched."

Thanksgiving was wonderful as usual, Edith make a feast for us all. Ryan of course did his scooty crawling thing and kept us well entertained. He is such a sweet boy I sure hope his sister is just as good.

That night I rubbed my belly and wished my new baby a Happy Thanksgiving and was very surprised to feel a bump. "Daniel feel this, put your hand on my tummy."

"Syd you have a bump, isn't it a little early, maybe it is just gas."

"I'm sure you are right but it doesn't go away."

When I went in to see Dr. Winters in December I asked him about it, "Aren't I getting bigger faster this time?"

He said. "Sometimes with a second child this happens but you are starting to show. Maybe it would be a good idea if we get an ultra sound to check you out. In fact today is the day they do them at the hospital, want me to check and see if I can get you in? Yes they can do it in two hours."

"One more thing, I am much more nauseated than with Ryan and my breasts hurt more."

"Let's do the test and see what is what." Then he smiled and patted me on the shoulder.

When I got home and walked in the door Daniel was on the floor with Ryan playing. I get such a kick out of seeing my little boy sitting up by himself now. "Honey, I just saw Dr. Winters and he wants me to have an ultra sound to be sure all is well as I am getting bigger earlier than last year. It is scheduled for one o'clock will you come with me?"

Of course he came. The nurse got me all set up and I was getting excited I was going to see my little peanut though it is probably too early to tell if it is a boy or a girl and I don't want to know anyway. Daniel held onto my hand as the tech started.

She did a little bit then turned the screen to us. "I think this picture speaks for itself," she said and smiled big.

"Oh my God Daniel, look there are two of them, we have twins. Look, they actually look like little people you can see their faces and arms and legs, they look a little fuzzy though, and look at them squirm around. Daniel?" I looked over and my big strong husband was wiping back the tears.

"My love I can't think of a thing to say, I am so overwhelmed," and he kissed me. "You always said you were an overachiever."

The tech congratulated us and gave me a picture, "Oh thank you I had no idea we would be getting one. No one is going to believe this without a picture I am sure."

"Dr. Winters will get the results and I am sure he will call you, but when he made your appointment he said he was pretty sure what the results would be."

"That stinker," I said then laughed. "I am so excited this is going to be so wonderful! Oh could you tell if they are boys or girls yet, no don't tell me I was just curious."

The tech smiled then said, "I think I know but it is a little early yet."

When she left and I got dressed Daniel put his arms around me and held me so tight, "Oh Syd this is truly a miracle, twins I just can't get over it. I am the happiest person alive."

"Second happiest," I said as I looked at the picture again.

When we got in the door Mom was standing there, "Honey I don't know if something is wrong but Dr. Winters called and said he wants one of you to call him right back. I know you saw him this morning Sydney, is there something I should know?"

"Yes Mom but it is good news, I will call the doctor now to be sure."

Daniel took Mom into the living room, "You look cold Mom here," and he wrapped her in an afghan. "Don't' worry nothing is ever going to go wrong around here again, not if I can help it. There that is the smile I have been waiting for."

I put the phone down, "No worries he wasn't sure if the hospital had told me the news or not."

"Hospital? Did you go to the hospital?" and she jumped up.

"Yes but it was just for an ultra sound to be sure the baby is fine, about this time most women have one. Ok now, good, but we did find out something quite amazing."

I looked at Daniel. "Do you want to be the one to tell her, or should I?"

"You do it Syd."

I sat down next to her, "Mom we are going to have twins."

She let out a very loud scream and hugged me a little too tight. "My baby is going to have babies this is just too much we haven't had multiple births since your aunt's."

I looked at her strangely, "My aunt, your sister?"

"Yes, Ophelia had identical twin boys but they died a month later, they were born too soon."

Right then Gretchen came thundering down the stairs, "Can't I even take a shower without someone screaming. What's going on?" she asked as she tried to dry her wet hair.

"Gretch, we may need even one more nanny for our baby we…"

"So is it going to have three heads or something?"

I leaned back on the couch, "Gretchen stop it the poor thing is not going to have three heads, but it isn't one thing it is two. We are having twins."

Never in all the time I have known Gretchen have I seen a reaction like the one I got. She fainted right on top of Daniel.

Daniel being his silly self of course had to make light of it all once we got her conscious again, "I have had girls fall for me but never like this."

She immediately got up and sat next to him. "Don't get your hopes up boy, you are too old for me, I like um young. But you do get a kiss for saving me. Twins, really twins? Good heavens are you trying to set a world's record for having your twenty in about three years? Seriously I am so very happy for you two crazy kids and for Rose and me too. What fun it is going to be."

Eli and Edith popped in right then, "Hi all what's up?"

Daniel went over and hugged them both then told them to sit down. "Well let's see, Syd and I went to the hospital, Dr. Winters called and scared everyone half to death, Rose screamed, and Gretchen fainted and landed right on top of me. I think that covers it."

They sat there looking stunned, "Back up Son start from the beginning," said Eli. All Edith did was nod.

"Dr. Winters thought it would be a good idea for Syd to get an ultra sound to be sure all was well so we went to the hospital, everything is fine. Then he called the house to be sure we knew everything was fine. We told Rose what we found out and she screamed, Gretchen came running down the stairs with wet hair, fainted and landed on top of me after we told her what we found out. So, grab your tissues and smelling salts folks, we are having twins."

Screams from both as they came over and hugged us. "You aren't kidding are you Son?"

"No Dad and I have the proof. Show them Syd."

I made a big production of it, "Family here are our babies, compliments of the ultra sound." There were a lot of oh my God's and a few tears.

Mom just sat there saying, "What a miracle, what a miracle. I have never seen one of these before; they look almost ready to go. Do you know if they are boys or girls or a mix?"

"No but aren't they adorable?" said Daniel, "all curled up in there."

It was getting close to Christmas and I told Daniel I just can't get out and shop for presents.

He came over and patted my tummy, "How about I take care of it all, you just give me a list and I will do the rest, of course if Gretchen and your mom would care to come along I sure won't object."

At dinner that night I told my mom's that they were going to have the pleasure of accompanying a very handsome man down to Port Shores tomorrow to do some Christmas shopping if they wished.

"Who?" said Gretchen and got hit in the arm by the very handsome man.

"Me you wretched woman, just think what we could do without Syd there, oh my, the possibilities are endless. Are you game? Good ok then it is set."

Mom was excited and said, "I sure am too, maybe we could ditch Gretchen and head for the bar."

I was the one rolling my eyes this time, "Mom you are just as awful as Gretchen you guys have had too much free time around here."

So off they went and Ryan and I had the day to ourselves. I decided this would be a good time to call Edith, with everything that has been going on we haven't had much time together. "Hi Edith, it's Sydney the whole gang has gone down to Port Shores to do some Christmas shopping so Ryan and I are on our own would you like to come over for a while? I miss you. I would come there but Dr. Winters said I can't go anywhere without someone being with me in case I lose my balance. Somehow I don't think Ryan counts with that," and I laughed.

"You bet I would it sounds like fun. Let me get bundled up and I will be right over."

I quickly made some hot chocolate and got out some cookies. "Oh it is getting cold come on in and get warmed up," I said when she got here.

We sat by the fireplace and I brought in the goodies. "Now that hits the spot, thank you dear," she said as she sipped the chocolate. "I have missed you too Sydney, things sure have been busy around your place huh? I still can't believe you are having twins. What fun that is going to be, and a lot of work too, remember I went through it too."

"Can you give me any advice?"

"Just love them, and sleep when you can though I must warn you that is not going to happen much," and she started laughing. "Really at times it can be overwhelming but the rewards are wonderful. I am sure Daniel will help, he really seems to love being a daddy."

I grabbed for another cookie, "Oh Edith he has been so wonderful with Ryan and is very excited about the new babies. I feel so blessed in so many ways, I have a beautiful son and a husband that I adore, my mother has come back in my life, and Gretchen is still with me. I pray you and Eli have not felt left out with all the craziness that has been going on around here. You are and always will be my family too; you are just as much my mother as Rose is. The love and support you have given me means more than I could ever say. I do love you both so much and thank you again for loving me." Well that opened the flood gates and we both just sat there hugging each other and crying happy tears.

"My dear girl I have never heard anything so beautiful, of course we love you too and have from the start. It is so much fun to have a daughter after a houseful of men. We really do need to find more time to get together. Oh there is something I have been meaning to ask you about, late last summer one evening Eli came over here to ask Daniel something about the dock and when he came home he was laughing like a crazy man and couldn't stop. I asked him what was so funny and he just couldn't stop long enough to tell me. Do you remember what happened?"

I started laughing and said I did remember, "But there is no way to tell you without both of us getting very embarrassed. Oh, we were not doing anything wrong but Eli just showed up at an awkward moment. It really was funny if you want any more ask Eli again, I am sure he would remember. By the way, how is he doing, any more dementia problems?"

"Well he does get confused at times but it doesn't seem to last too long thank goodness. Dr. Winters gave him some medicine and it seems to be helping a lot. I read all the print outs you gave us and know this is never going to go away so I guess the best we can do is be thankful for every good day. He is still doing a lot of reading about how to improve his speech and I am so proud of him, I think he is doing so well."

"Yes he is and I truly believe that is making him feel better about himself. He is really so special! Hey how about some lunch I am getting hungry, Gretchen made some vegetable soup and there is a loaf of French bread." We chatted away as we ate and it was so much fun. Just as we finished I heard Ryan and got up. "Guess nap time is over, give me a minute and I will go get him he is probably hungry too."

"Hi big fella come on downstairs I have a surprise for you."

Ryan started giggling like crazy when he saw Edith and put out his arms to her. Of course she got up and held him tight. "Hi big boy I am so glad to see you, come sit down with Grandma. He just seemed so happy to see her and smiled and smiled. "Oh Sydney he is such a treasure, such a happy boy and I love him so much. None of my grandchildren have ever lived nearby so this is so special for me to have this little one close. You two have done such a good job with him."

I got Ryan some lunch then we sat back down in the living room again. I went over and put another log on the fire, it seemed to get chilly all of a sudden and I looked out the window. "Edith it's snowing and looks like it has been for a while, I guess I didn't pay attention. It is so beautiful."

"Oh me maybe I will have to stay for a while until it lets up, I don't like to go out when the snow is too deep."

Just then I heard Daniel pull up. "Oh the gang is back."

Everyone piled in with their goodies and were so happy to see Edith. Daniel went over and gave her a kiss, "So you ladies have been spending your day together how nice. Whatever Syd told you about me Mom is not true," and he gave me a kiss too. Ryan put up his arms for his daddy and of course got a big hug. "It is getting pretty nasty out there so when you are ready Mom I will drive you home but please stay for a while."

"So Gretchen did you and Daniel have fun without me, and what about you Mom?"

My husband looked at both of them and said, "My dear you have no idea but for the sake of our marriage I don't think I had better tell you, it might embarrass the ladies."

Gretchen got up and smacked him on the head, "You are an

awful man, sorry Edith but he is." And we all started laughing. It really was a fun afternoon.

A couple hours later Edith said she should probably go home and make Eli some dinner. "Thank you all, especially Sydney, it has been a long time since I have had such a nice day." I got up and gave her a hug and kiss.

"We are definitely going to have to do this more often," she said and they left.

The next day Dr. Winters came by for a visit, and brought us a huge basket of fruit for Christmas. "You all have been so fun and I just wanted to say thank you and wish you a Merry Christmas."

Daniel jumped up and shook his hand, "We are the ones that need to thank YOU, and here we have a little something for you too." It was a picture of all of us. "Now when you are telling everyone about that crazy family that drives you nuts you can show them this. Doctor what are your plans for Christmas day? Do you have family here?"

"No I don't, my wife died about seven years ago and we had no children so I just celebrate by myself that is unless I have to go to the hospital."

"I have a great idea, how about you come here and have Christmas with us? We always have a fun time and would love to have you," I said and really meant it.

He seemed to think about it for just a minute then said, "That would be so nice if you are sure you don't mind." Everyone assured him it would be great. "What time do you want me?'

"Whenever you can but I think it might be a good idea to tell all your patients not to get sick until the next day," said Daniel and we all laughed.

"I will do my best, goodbye all, see you soon." And he left.

Christmas morning I decided to make it a little extra fun for Daniel. I slipped out of bed undressed and put a huge red bow over my tummy then got back in bed. When he woke up he looked over at me, "Can I unwrap my present early or do I have to wait for the whole family to get here?" I started laughing as he gently removed the bow. "Ok the bow is gone so where is my present?"

"You are so naughty. I hope Santa is watching."

"I don't," and he started hugging me.

Our little cowboy decided right then to wake up. "Perfect timing," I said, and grabbed for my nightgown, "go get him and bring him in here before he wakes up everyone."

We played for just a little while then decided it was time to go downstairs, "Want to see what Santa brought you little one? Let Daddy get dressed quick and we can go peek." They left and I got dressed too and the day began.

We had a very fun Christmas and as always with the whole family there. Dr. Winters came about eleven, and fit is perfectly, it was nice to really get to know him. Mom is our official picture taker and made up albums for all of us with pictures of Ryan from day one until now. We were all so touched and thanked her over and over. Daniel had told me that morning that he had gotten something special for Gretchen but he wanted it to be a surprise so I had to wait to see what it was. So when he took a small box and handed it to Gretchen, I was very curious. He bowed to her and said, "From me to you dear woman." She looked surprised but opened it up, then just held it up and didn't say a word as she was crying so hard. It was a metal shaped in a heart that said, *For Gretchen Blanchard, a true hero, who single handedly delivered my baby son during the battle of SYD under extreme flood conditions and because of her skills and bravery kept me from fainting. She has a permanent place in my heart for all time. With love from, Daniel McGregor, Lord of Rose Manor.*

My Daniel has done some wonderful things for all of us but this one really takes the cake. No one seemed to know what to say, except Gretchen finally, "Daniel you are a nut for sure, but this present means more to me than you will ever know. I do love you and thank you so much," and she went over and kissed his cheek.

I asked him where he got this made and he said, "There is a new little shop in town that makes sheriff badges for kids with their names on them so I decided to see if they could do this too.

And the rest, as they say is history."

We were all so touched, even Dr. Winters had tears in his eyes.

Eli stood up and pulled a little package out of his pocket and handed it to me. "Since this seems to be awards day, for you my daughter from your dad." There was another metal and what it said about did me in, I read it out loud. *To my incredible daughter Sydney, who bravely risked her own life to save mine, I will be grateful for every moment in my life because it is a gift from her. I love you and always will. Eli.*

I was so shaken, "Oh you dear man, you didn't have to do this but it truly means the world to me, you mean the world to me. I am just so thankful that God gave me the strength to help you. I love you so much," and I got up and hugged him big time.

Well that really did it the whole gang was sobbing. Daniel asked if he had gone to the same place as he did to get it made. "Yes, I am sure the owner must think we are a very unusual family huh?" and he started to smile.

Edith finally stopped crying long enough to say, "My boys you are really something, I am so proud of you both and very thankful too." We sat in silence then Daniel started quietly singing Silent Night and we all joined in.

Just as we finished the phone rang; it was Brother John wishing us a Merry Christmas. We got calls from all the brothers throughout the day who were literally shocked when we told them our big news. Daniel told me later that Scott remarked how talented we must be to have produced twins when I could barely move, nice work.

Ryan was in heaven, until Daddy Santa appeared and he screamed like crazy. Not the greatest first introduction to Santa. "But Ryan, Santa has brought you presents because you have been such a good little boy." My baby could have cared less, just burrowing into my chest was all he wanted. So Daddy Santa became Daddy again and all was well with the world. We took a pile of pictures of him playing with his new toys and all the wrapping paper he could get a hold of. And of course my new babies got their picture taken too, just like their brother they were hiding with Mom.

We all sang Christmas songs as Daniel played his guitar and had a wonderful dinner that Mom prepared this year. She said Gretchen needs to build up her strength so she could be ready for my babies.

"You are getting older my dear friend."

"I am only two years older than you and neither of us is THAT old yet, this is prime time, now shut up and sit down."

"How are you feeling Sydney," asked Dr. Winters. "That's good, now as long as I am here I think we had better talk about the special care you will need during this pregnancy. You are eating for really three now and are going to be very hungry so try to eat good food not treats, some women eat about five small meals a day. We don't want you to gain a lot but the babies do need extra nutrition. Twins seem to want to get into this world a little faster than single babies do so the last two or three months you are going to have to be very careful–if there is any trouble at all, even swollen feet I will put you on bed rest for the rest of your pregnancy. The longer you keep them where they are the better. Be sure to take your vitamins and get a lot of rest. Toward the end I want to see you weekly. Now do you think you can do all that?"

"Yes sir, I promise."

"Oh and one more thing, this time you are going to be in the hospital when those little ones decide to come, even if you have to stay a month beforehand."

I pretended to cry, "Dr. Winters doesn't love me anymore," then smiled big.

"Sydney Sydney what am I going to do with you?"

Daniel raised his hand, "If you figure it out tell me please, I have had no luck on my own."

When the doctor left he said, "This is the nicest Christmas I have had in many years thank you all." I was so glad he didn't have to run off to the hospital.

That night I thanked Daniel for doing such a nice thing for Gretchen. "Well I told her when Ryan was born that she deserved one and I meant it. I am still so thankful she was here.

And you my wonderful wife certainly deserved the metal you got too. If you hadn't done what you did I...I just don't know what...I love you so much."

I spent quite a bit of time resting in the afternoons. I just lied down when Ryan did and he really thought that was great.

On New Year's Eve the whole gang came back over and again we had a fun time. I didn't make it to the midnight hour but everyone else did. When Daniel finally got into bed he wished me a Happy New Year. I asked him, "Should we move back upstairs after the babies are born, we can't be running back and forth all night and I sure don't expect my mom's to do it, though they might want to do it anyway?"

"Yea I think we should, this is really going to get confusing you know."

"Yep."

Daniel started kissing me, "Honey can we still make love, is it safe?"

"Do I need to ask why you are asking me this? Didn't think so. The doctor said as long as everything is going fine and I feel good there is no reason why we can't do it pretty much until just before I deliver, though I think that might be a little much. But...maybe we had better do it soon before I get as big as a condo and you can't even see my face during the whole thing."

"Gee I guess we had better though I am not really in the mood tonight," and he flipped over.

I jabbed him in the back, "Since when have you EVER not been in the mood, ok for you I am extra frisky tonight, your loss." That lasted two seconds.

Winter has set in with a vengeance and there is no way I am going to go out of this house until spring. Even my girls go out only when necessary. We are all getting a little nutsy being cooped up and seeing nothing but white outside. My Ryan is scooting all over the place and it is so much fun to watch. The girls follow him everywhere. One day they started barking like crazy and Daniel went over to see what was going on. "Syd come here your son is trying out for the Olympics."

When I got there he was about one fourth of the way up the

stairs. I sat down on the step next to him, "So you little bugger you are thinking about entering the stair climbing event huh, well I do think you have a good chance at it but how about we give it a rest for now? Mommy and Daddy don't want you to go boom." He started laughing and grabbed for my shirt. I picked him up and started tickling him, more laughter. "Here Daddy take this silly little thing. Do you realize before too long we are going to have three little ones scampering all over the place? Really though, Ryan has been the center of attention for so long how do you think he is going to handle it all when the twins come?"

"Oh man I hadn't even thought about that. I guess he is going to have to be a part of everything, be included and made to feel very important every step of the way. He is so well adjusted and happy I want to keep him that way."

I got myself up from the steps and blew on Ryan's little belly, "You my darling child will never feel neglected I promise."

"Daniel I think maybe we had better start getting a room ready for our 'girls. It just hit me, they are both going to have to sleep in with us and I do think they are going to have to be in the same little bed. I think I heard something about you don't separate them for a long time, as they are so used to being together. I had better look that up. At least Ryan is in his own room now. Another thing, we only have four bedrooms upstairs, one of the mom's is going to have to either go up to the third floor or go downstairs, that might lead to a war."

"Why don't we go find them and see what they think?"

They were talking by the fire in the living room when we went in. Daniel set Ryan down between them and we took the chairs across from them. He said we need to have a family conference and then explained our little problem and asked if they had any brilliant ideas.

"Well, this is a problem," said Mom. "By the way, are you going to breast feed both of them Sydney?"

"Goodness one more thing I hadn't even thought about, what do I do put one on each side, and what about Ryan I am still nursing him? The only thing to do is grow another breast, don't say a thing husband."

"But Syd, don't I at least get one for me too, it's only fair as the other three will be busy all the time?" By this time poor Mom was hiding under a pillow, and Gretchen was holding her sides and laughing so hard the tears were literally flowing down her cheeks.

I gave him a not so great look, "You are really awful. With possibly five, I'll look like a cow." Everybody burst into even more laughter. "I want to feed them though, it is so much better for them. Ryan is going to be weaned at a year anyway thank goodness. And you my husband need at least two though I know you would be ecstatic if there were more. And what if everyone wants theirs at the same time; it will look like a mob scene. Can you imagine the look on Dr. Winters face if I ask him how to grow three more breasts, he will faint but do a lot of laughing beforehand when I tell him who gets what. I will feel like a milking machine, breasts all over the place, they will finally shrivel up to nothing and just lay there like pancakes, plus I will never sleep again."

Daniel was beet red and laughing like a lunatic, "I... I can just picture this whole thing," then he grabbed Gretchen and the two held onto each other and roared. "Well, this time I am going to get up with you and at least change them after they are done, my cute little bovine."

"You do know that I hate you don't you," but I too couldn't help but laugh. "Is it too late to cancel this whole thing?"

"Yep to both."

It took quite a while for everyone to settle down but finally I told him I think it is a good idea to put this whole bedroom thing on hold for now and when the time comes we will decide who gets banished to the first or third floor, everyone agreed.

Gretchen said as she picked up Ryan and sat him in her lap. "You little mister are so special and can be our helper when your new sisters are born."

Daniel leaned over and put his face right up to Gretchen's, "So you too are sure they are going to be girls huh, well for the past fifty years or so the little boy swimmers in our family seem to be winning so the chances are very slim, so there."

I buried my face in my hands, "You and your little swimmers, let it go man, just let it go."

"Ladies be prepared, I am going to go over to my wife and give her a big smackie kiss, or at least try, wish me luck I am going to need it." He leaned over my chair and sorta got his wish as I was laughing so hard. "Well that was better than nothing I guess," he said and went back to his chair.

Mom just sat there shaking her head, "You two are completely insane."

Daniel told them about finding Ryan climbing up the stairs. "We are all going to have to keep a good eye on him. Oh man he should be trying to walk before too long too. Boy am I even more glad that you are both here."

January slipped quietly into February and I was more than uncomfortable. Dr. Winters said I was doing very well and everything was progressing normally but from now on I have to be extra careful, if the twins are identical then they seem to come earlier than fraternal. It is way too early for them to be born. I did seem to need more rest and everyone was so good about helping me.

Our love making was cut way down but we both agreed it was for the best. One morning though I was lying in bed and all of a sudden started to cry, Daniel flipped over and asked what was wrong. "I am truly as big as a condo and still have maybe two months to go. I want to make love but who would want to ravage a condo?"

He started laughing and raised his hand, "I would."

"But baby there is so much of me I bet you couldn't even find your way to the front door."

He was laughing even harder, "My dear every condo has a way of getting in from the front and back." I must have looked a little confused. "How about we try something different for a change? .... Are you all right?"

"Oh yes, my aren't you the clever one," and I started to giggle. "I have an idea, do you mind if we do this on a regular basis?" Now I was really laughing.

"Ah I don't mind at all but I thought we agreed to cut things back not speed things up?"

"All your fault."

Toward the end of the month Daniel and I were sitting in the living room and all of a sudden I poked him and whispered, "Daniel look at Ryan." He was trying to pull himself up to a chair. We both held our breaths; he landed a couple times then finally made it. I looked over at the door and Gretchen and Mom were both watching too.

A huge YEA came out of all of us and Ryan looked back then held out one hand and said, "Dada."

"Daniel ran to him, "Oh my big boy you are standing up and you said your first word, Daddy is so proud of you." At that moment we were all in tears and let them have their moment together. It was so special. Then we all went over and hugged him.

I was still overcome and couldn't think of one word to say. Of course my smarty husband could, "Don't be jealous Syd that your little boy said Dada as his first word, I am sure he loves you too." With that he got a conk on the head.

From then on my little athlete pulled himself up on everything and about a week later started cruising along the furniture. "Syd he is actually walking sorta holding on. Before long he will be flying all over the place. Wow how wonderful!" That night at dinner Daniel said he had a mushy announcement to make, "Ladies and little gentleman, I am so proud and thankful that you are all in my life, even you Gretchen," as a piece of bread went flying across the table at him." He blew her a kiss, "Sorry couldn't resist. This is the family I have dreamed of my whole life and I want you all to know that I love you very much. So there, mushy stuff over."

Then I took over, "More mushy stuff from me now. The past almost two years have been the most exciting and happy time I have ever had. I moved, renovated a house, found my soul mate and my mother, found another mother and father and was welcomed into the McGregor family, my Gretchen came, I got married, had a beautiful baby boy, and now twins are on the way. That is a lot of happiness in such a short time. Thank you my family, thank you"

This seemed to be the night for being thankful. "We are not done yet, I would like to add to the mush," said my mom then gave us an amazing smile. "I have done some very stupid things in my life, but God gave me back my wonderful daughter in such an amazing way. Now she has opened her heart and her home to me and I have never been happier. As to that crazy person she married, he is the spark that makes my heart sing and I thank you Daniel for loving my daughter so completely and for letting me invade your life. I will love you all forever, even Gretchen, as someone just said, sorry I couldn't resist."

"Ok all you mushy people who seem to get great joy out of beating me up I have just one thing to say, thank you, if you didn't love me you wouldn't pick on me," said my Gretchen. "I have loved my girl Sydney forever and thought my heart was so full there was no space left but there was and you all filled in the empty spaces, even Daniel got in there, sorry couldn't resist. My life is so full and I have never been happier. All right you all let's finish eating I am sure it is ice cold by this time."

Ryan started clapping, "Well I guess he needed to say something too," said Daniel.

March marched in with a big ice storm but thankfully it only lasted a day. It left behind a magical glistening wonderland. Daniel and I took Ryan out on the porch so he could touch the icicles hanging from the roof. He licked one and I guess thought it was too cold so he handed it to Daniel. That afternoon Daniel brought Ryan in when he came to wake me up from my nap. As I opened my eyes Ryan reached for me and said "Mama" I jumped a mile.

"Oh my baby boy, yes I am your mama and I love you very much." Then Daniel laid him down with me and we cuddled. "Now I know how you felt my love when he said Dada. It is beyond words."

April fourteenth turned out to be a momentous day. The sun was shining and spring was in the air. I stepped out on the porch to get some fresh air. The babies have been quite lazy lately so I gave them a little pat," It won't be too long now my girls." Then I got my first real pain, "Daniel come here NOW."

"Are you all right, what is it?"

"I think your daughters are getting ready to make the great escape, I just had a pain call Dr. Winters."

He went flying into the house, I could hear him yelling. "Mom call Dr. Winters, then Mom and Dad Syd thinks the babies are coming."

"Dr. Winters said to go to the hospital right away, it may be false labor but he wants to be sure." Gretchen said she would stay with Ryan and Daniel asked Mom to come with us.

They admitted me right away and said Dr. Winters was on his way. We all went into a room and the nurse said she needed to get me into a gown so Daniel and Mom left. Dr. Winters met them in the hall and opened my door. "Stay out here while I examine Sydney."

I could hear the nurse as she went out the door and told the doctor that my water had just broken. "Well it looks like it is show time," he said.

"Thanks for waiting for me this time Sydney," he said and smiled. "I am going to examine you now to see how far along you are." When he was done he sat down next to me, "You are dilating to almost three cm. but have a ways to go. How are you doing?"

"Not too good I really hurt, here comes another one, ahhhhhh."

"I know you want to do this naturally but remember you have two births which means you will go through this whole thing twice in a row, though the second baby should come out faster, as the path is clear. Labor is usually slow. We are going to do an ultra sound so see what positions the babies are in. I hope at least the first one is head down. When we are done with that your mom and Daniel can come in."

After the test the doctor came back in, "We are lucky baby number one is head first but right now baby two is breech. Now don't panic it might turn. We will deal with that if and when the time comes. I will get your family now."

"Hi going to be mom how's my girl?"

"Awful, how is my soon to be ex-husband, unless he can get these kids out of me in two minutes." Mom was the only one laughing.

"Here comes another one, Owwwwwwwwww." They must be boys girls wouldn't hurt me so much. You might as well put your evil eye away for good sir you are never touching me again."

He looked so concerned, "Syd I love you can I help, I really want to baby?"

I reached up to him, "Yes give me your hand, now hold on here comes another one ahhhhhhhhhhh."

"Good God woman remind me never to tackle with you, you have the strength of a tiger. I didn't know cows were so strong. Come on I was only kidding, if you kill me with your looks who is going to father the rest of our seventeen kids?"

"This is it buster like it or not. Did Dr. Winters tell you that one baby is breech, well he is and if he doesn't turn around they may have to do a C section. I don't want to do that."

"So now they are he's huh. I don't care what they are I just want you done with this and back home. Rose can you do anything to help her?"

Mom came over and took my other hand, "My daughter you are strong and I know you are in a lot of pain but don't get nasty with Daniel he is only trying to help. Now grab my hand. Breath Sydney, breathe deeply in and out."

"I am sorry love, it's just that I hurt so much, would you mind doing the rest of this for me we are supposed to share everything?"

"That's my girl, ok but how are we going to get the little ones in me. Think about it and let me know what you come up with. Also how are we going to get them out once they get in?"

I couldn't help but laugh. Right then Dr. Winters came in, "A laugh I sure didn't expect that," and I told him as soon as we figure out how to get the babies in Daniel and then out again he is going to take over. He laughed too.

"Have you told him you hate him yet? That is usually the

first thing Mothers in labor tell their husbands."

"No but I am sure it will come up."

The doctor ordered everyone out, "I need to see how things are going. We still have a ways to go Sydney you are about half way there."

"Only half way oh man, ahhhh that hurts how many Mothers do you lose Doctor, the way I figure it I should be dead in about fifteen minutes?"

He put his hand on my arm, "You girl are going to get through this just fine, and think when it is over you will have two beautiful little people. Have you picked out names yet?"

Again we had totally forgotten all about it, "No I guess we should do that in the fifteen minutes I have left."

He headed for the door, "Daniel you and Rose better get in here I can't deal with her anymore," He smiled at me and gave me a thumb's up.

Daniel stood there with his arms crossed trying to look stern, "So you are being your usual Sydney self huh. Well shape up he is the only one who is going to get those little buggers out of you, want to make love?"

"Daniel!" This time it was Mom.

"Hush Mom that sounds very good to me right now, I need to get my mind off what is going on."

Mom looked disgusted at us both, "You two belong together could we please concentrate on getting my granddaughters born?"

I looked her straight in the eye, "Sorry Mom but they are both boys, girls would not hurt their mother like this, I have decided."

"Oh God, something is going on all of a sudden I feel like I need to push, call the nurse." She came running in and I told her how I felt. She said she would call Dr. Winters.

He came in quickly, "Sydney, you are just getting stronger contractions but let me check. I don't understand but you are more dilated than you were just a few minutes ago at about seven cm. I have never seen this. I will be back in about half an hour to check again but do not push no matter what."

"Doctor the contractions are really getting strong and last about minute with maybe a few minutes in between. I am getting a little scared, is this the way it is supposed to be?"

"Yes Sydney, when they are out two minutes apart and last about ninety seconds we will be ready to go. Don't be scared you are doing fine."

About two hours later Dr. Winters told us it was time. "Rose you had better go to the waiting room and Daniel I want you to put on scrubs we are going to take Sydney to the operating room so we will be prepared in case something goes wrong. You will be with her during the whole thing, can you handle that?"

He looked a little green to me but he said if he could be there for Ryan he can do this too.

Off we went, I hate operating rooms and I told anyone who would listen to me all about it. The doctor said, "This is just a precautionary measure, I am sure everything will be fine. Now Sydney it is time to push, HARD let's see if you have a boy or girl." Daniel held my hand and the nurses held my legs as I gave a huge push. I lied back panting but the doctor said I did great. "Now push again even harder, yes you can do it." I held on to Daniel with all I had and pushed.

"I see the crown Sydney, one more time PUSH."

The next thing I knew I saw a little person and heard that wonderful first cry. The doctor announced, "Daniel, Sydney you have a little girl and she looks perfect, a little small but perfect, as he put her on my chest." My daughter, so tiny and so beautiful.

"Hi my darling I am your mommy, I love you," I said as I kissed her little head.

"Oh God I can't believe it is a girl, I am so proud of you love," then Daniel kissed me and the baby.

"Sydney we have to do a quick ultra sound to see how the second baby is positioned. Relax for a minute." When he came back he looked a little concerned, "The baby is breech so I am going to try to move it around and see if we can get it head first. If not we will have to do a C section right away. This may be a little uncomfortable but has to be done." Daniel and I waited please God turn my baby please I prayed silently.

"We did it, now Sydney we have to start all over but this time it will go quicker. PUSH girl." I gave it my all and the doctor again said he saw the crown. "One more time should do it now PUSH."

My baby cried and so did Daniel and I. "What is it Doctor?"

"It is another girl Sydney you have twin girls," and he put her on my chest. She was so beautiful I just couldn't get over it.

"Hi my sweet baby girl, I am your mommy and I love you."

Daniel again kissed me and baby, "Hi little one I am your daddy. Syd you did so great I just can't believe we have girls, how absolutely wonderful!"

The nurse told us that baby number one weighs five pound 2 ounces, and baby number two weighs five pounds 3 ounces. "They look so small as compared to my son who was born about a year ago. Are they all right?"

"We will have them checked out now, just relax I am sure they are fine. Good lungs."

Dr. Winters wanted me to stay in another room for about an hour or two. "Are you going to breast feed? Ok then we will start as soon as I have examined them. I would like you to stay in the hospital for a few days just to recoup. I am going now to give your girls their first check- up, I will be back soon with two little bundles."

"Oh Doctor, are they identical?"

"If you like I can have a DNA test done to see."

I looked at Daniel and he nodded, "Will it hurt them?"

"No it is just a swab in the mouth, we should know for sure tomorrow."

"Ok then please do, and thank you sooo much."

Two nurses brought in my babies to be fed. I asked them how to tell who is who and was surprised that they put a dot of fingernail polish on the big toe of the first born. I sat in a chair and they put a pillow on each side of me then they put my girls on the pillows. "Have you ever breast fed?" they asked. I told them I was still doing it with my son, but he will soon turn one year so I will wean him off then. I opened the little flap in my gown and put the first one to my breast. She seemed a little confused but took to it quickly and began sucking. The other one followed. It was the most wonderful experience.

"Syd I just don't know what to say this is so beautiful. I just can't believe I am a father of three wonderful little ones. It is too much, too much."

I got to finally really look at my darling little girls. "Daniel, they have my eyes I didn't notice it before, and they are blond just like their daddy." The nurses said they will need to be fed eight to twelve times in twenty-four hours. "Yikes am I going to do anything else all day?"

They smiled then said, "Probably not, but you can pump the breasts after each feeding or so and then Daddy can help with a bottle. Your daughters are doing very well do you want them in your room tonight or shall we bring them in when it is time to eat?"

"I want them here if I can, what do you think honey?"

"Yes definitely, I want to stare at them all night, can I hold them now?"

The nurse put baby number one in Daniels arms and the look on his face even made the nurses tear up. "Hi sweet girl, I am your daddy and I promise to love and take care of you forever. First rule, no dating til you are thirty." We all laughed.

He seemed reluctant gave her back to the nurse so the other nurse just picked up baby number two and he held them both. "Hi little one, I am your daddy and I love you very much. I am not used to little girls but if you are anything like your mommy I know we are going to have so much fun." The tears were rolling down his cheeks as he turned and looked at me.

Finally the nurses took them from his arms and looked at us both, "We are all so happy for you, these little girls are truly going to have a wonderful life. Goodbye for now."

When I got back to my room Mom, Edith and Eli, and Gretchen were there. "Where is Ryan?" I asked immediately.

Gretchen said he was not allowed up here so the nurses are playing with him downstairs. "Don't worry he is fine. So tell us what did you get?"

I said with tears, "We have two girls at a little over five

pounds each. We are going to stay for a few days and if the girls pass their check-up they can come home then too."

"Was Daniel in the delivery room with you?" asked good ole Gretchen.

"Yep."

"Did he faint?"

"No Gretchen he did not, though he did look a little green," I said and smiled.

Daniel made a face, "I did not, how would you know you were a little busy?"

Everyone was so thrilled, and couldn't believe we broke the boy trend, especially Eli. "Well Son this is a big day, how fun it is going to be to have girls."

Edith couldn't stop crying, "I am so thankful you and your girls are all right."

Dr. Winters came in then and said the girls ARE fine, "They seem to have a little time keeping their body temperature up there so we have them all wrapped up in blankets. Don't worry this happens a lot. They are very healthy and you should all be going home before long. I think it would be a good idea for Sydney to get some rest now, you can all come back later and see the babies, or better yet first thing tomorrow."

Everyone agreed that they would come back tomorrow. I got a lot of hugs and they left.

The nurses brought in my babies in one little bed. The looked so sweet all snuggled up next to each other. I told Daniel that he should go home and get some rest but he refused, "I am not going anywhere, if I do get tired I will take a nap here in this chair. How are you feeling, are you in pain?"

"No, but very tired, if I move over a little could you sleep up here with me, I really need to hold you?"

He got up and carefully landed by my side and held me close, "Much better, but what are the nurses going to say if they come in?"

"Who cares, now let's try to sleep our little ones will probably be awake soon."

We probably slept for about an hour and then my daughters

decided it was time to eat. Daniel got up and helped me into the chair and arranged the pillows. Then he got our girls and gently laid them down next to me. "Oh honey I just can't get over this, I am so tired I can hardly see straight but I just don't care, all I want to do is look at them and at you. I didn't know I could love anyone as much as I love you all. Our lives are going to be busy but wonderful. I can't wait for Ryan to meet them."

We did get up all night and I was tired but very happy. The next morning the whole gang was back but Gretchen, she stayed home with Ryan, and so thrilled that the girls were in our room and they could hold them. Good ole Mom was taking pictures like crazy. I asked how Ryan is doing and she said, "He is fine but says 'Mama and Dada' all the time, he misses you."

"Please tell him we love him and will be home soon, hey I have an idea, how about we ask Gretchen to bring him to the hospital lobby this afternoon and we can come down and visit with him for a little while. Would that help?"

Mom lit up and said she was sure it would, "Can you do that?"

"I am sure going to ask."

The nurse said it was fine she would stay with the girls so when Gretchen called and said they were there Daniel pushed me down in a wheelchair. My big boy was standing up next to her holding on to her legs, and when he saw us he started reaching for us, so Gretchen took his hands and walked him over. Daddy went right to him and picked him up, "Hi pal how ya doing and hugged him big time." He laughed and laughed, then looked down at me, "Mama" and Daniel put him in my lap.

"Oh baby I have missed you, guess what you have two new little sisters to play with. We will bring them home in a couple days. Now I want you to be a good boy and always remember Mommy and Daddy love you very much."

We stayed for almost an hour then went back up. Poor Ryan was crying so hard and trying to get out of Gretchen's arms and back to us. It just ripped me apart. "Oh Daniel this hurts so much I feel so awful, my poor little guy has no idea what is going on, maybe this wasn't such a good idea to see him."

"Sweetie we will be back soon but we are going to have to be sure he doesn't feel left out, the girls are going to need a lot of attention. Please don't worry I am sure it will all work out fine."

When we got back to the room I told Daniel we are going to pick out our babies names right now, baby one and baby two are just not doing it. "Why didn't we do this sooner? I have always loved Emily, what do you think, Emily Rose? I feel strongly that I have to add the Rose."

"I think it is perfect, Emily Rose McGregor, has a good ring. So is she baby one or two?"

"Baby one. I picked number one so you can pick number two."

"How about Winifred?" And he started to laugh.

I was shaking my head, "How could you do that to such a sweet little thing, get serious?"

"You know I have always liked Sarah or Abigail-Abby, either one is fine what do you think?"

"I want this to be your choice love, think how proud she will be when we tell her."

He really thought hard about it I could tell, "Then it is Abigail, Syd that was my grandmother's name and she was a remarkable woman. Now to a middle name, isn't Gretchen's middle name Jane, how about Abigail Jane McGregor–Abby Jane I like it?"

I was so touched all I could do was bring him down to my level and give him a kiss, "I think the whole name is perfect, your grandma would be so happy and wait until Gretchen hears this, she should be by tonight and I want you to tell her."

That night the whole gang came again, except Mom who stayed home with Ryan. They all went crazy again when they saw our babies. Edith asked if we had picked out any names yet and I said yes. So with this big event we called Mom and told her to listen carefully. "Daniel will you do the honors?"

He picked up baby number one after checking to be sure we had the right one. Yep the polish was on her little toe. "Family this is Emily Rose McGregor, her mommy picked out her name."

Mom didn't say anything for a minute. "Oh Sydney I feel so honored and I am so happy, I love you so much. Thank you it means the world to me."

Daniel put Emily down and picked up her sister. "One more family, I would like to introduce you to Abigail Jane McGregor." Both Edith and Gretchen gasped. "Syd named baby number one and I proudly named baby two."

Edith was the first to speak, "Daniel my mother was named Abigail oh my I think I need to sit down."

"Mom Grandma Abigail was a wonderful woman and I loved her very much, now her name will live on." He went over and hugged her.

Next was Gretchen, "Daniel McGregor what I am going to do with you, I know," and she went over and gave him a huge hug and kissed his cheek. "As you know I have never had any children and this, this is almost too much. There are just no words... thank you. I feel so blessed to be a part of this family. I think I had better sit down too. Now give me that precious baby."

There was so much emotion in the room everyone was so happy and obviously loved our choices. Mom was still crying when I told her I would talk to her later. "I love you dear. Come home soon."

Dr. Winters came in right then. He looked around at all of us and asked if things were all right. "They couldn't be better," then I introduced the babies to him and explained the significance of their names.

"Wow no wonder everyone has tears, you picked out perfect names. How are you feeling Sydney, any pain?'

"No just a little sore and tired, the girls had a sleepover here last night and Daniel and I were up a lot."

The doctor looked directly at Daniel, "I did hear about that and also that you didn't spend the night in the chair like most father's do," and he gave us a wink. "To be honest all the nurses on the floor came in for a quick peek."

"Good heavens Daniel what did you do?" asked Gretchen.

"I hopped into bed with my wife; want to make something out of it?" Then he started laughing. "Look at poor Syd she is red as a beet. Good heavens we weren't doing anything but hugging and sleeping. It was all HER idea," and he pointed to me, "I was totally against it but...."

"Stop it you idiot I didn't drag you up there."

Dr. Winters threw back his head and laughed along with everyone else. "When are you going to have another one Sydney?"

"Probably never so all you are going to have to do is take care of colds or whatever, though we did plan on twenty kids," which I did tell him was our running almost gag.

"Good heavens I don't think I heard about that, well you do have a good start, I guess I can never retire huh? I am going to have the nurses take Emily and Abigail for a little outing, I want to check them out. We will be back soon."

It only took about half an hour and everyone was still there. "They are doing fine, the temperature thing is much better now. Any trouble nursing Sydney? No, good then I will see you all tomorrow. Oh the DNA tests came back and you have identical twins–good luck. Goodbye."

Daniel let out a big "YES, identical how exciting! Better buy a lot of nail polish Syd so we don't get them mixed up."

I guess with all that was going on the girls finally woke up, Gretchen said this is the first time she has seen them awake and went over, "Syd they have your eyes," and everyone went over. "Call your mom later and tell her, she will be thrilled. Oh they are so beautiful; even have their daddy's light colored hair–a true blending."

"I planned it that way," said Daniel. "After all Ryan got Syd's hair color and my eyes so it is only fair. Before they were conceived I put in an order to the little swimming guys..."

"Daniel don't you dare tell them any more about your silly little swimming guys," I yelled.

More laughter from the gang. "Stop before I wet my pants," Gretchen was pleading, "you should be put away."

I couldn't stand it, I had to call my mom and tell her about the girl's eyes, "Hi Mom it's me, no everything is great, I just had to tell you that my daughters have your and my eye color. Yes it is wonderful I am so thrilled too. Oh and they are identical, neat huh!" I will talk to you later bye."

"It is feeding time so how about you all come back later this evening I think Daddy and I are going to try to sleep a little more too."

Daniel just couldn't take his eyes off us, "I can't get over this, so natural. Want me to change one of them now?"

As he tossed the diaper in the container he smiled and said, "I am getting pretty good at this but I have a feeling it is going to be a few more years before we are done. Honey before we go to bed I want to hold them both for a few minutes," he picked up Abby and went over to the rocking chair, "could you please give me Emily?" They looked so cute, and this was too good to pass up so I grabbed the camera that Mom had forgotten and took their picture.

"Now that is going to make a great picture for our Christmas card this year," I said. Then he started singing a lullaby to them and I almost lost it. "My love you are too much, what did I ever do to deserve a man like you?" Right then a nurse opened the door.

"I just wanted to be sure all was well and it sure is," she said and stood there smiling, then I guess another nurse passed by and she motioned for her to come in. They both were as overcome as I was I guess because they had tears running down their cheeks. "I have been here for twenty years and never seen anything so beautiful, call if you need anything," and they left.

"Well you can add two more people to your fan club list, time for bed my husband," and I went over and took Abby from his arms and kissed his head. "Good heavens I love you."

Then we got into bed and he started kissing me and ran his hand gently over my breasts, "They were large to begin with but now yikes, want me to make up a sling?"

"No but thanks" and I giggled. "Really baby you shouldn't do this the nurses could come back at any moment, so how about I give you sixteen hours to get your hand out of there, I think that's fair?" We both laughed and went to sleep.

–10–

SIMON

A couple hours later a nurse came in and woke us up and said we have a visitor. Daniel looked only slightly embarrassed as he said, "Uh sorry about this," meaning us curled up.

"No problem we are all used it now," and she smiled. "I think it is wonderful but don't tell anyone."

A visitor, who in the world? I almost fell over when Mr. Edgeworth walked in. "My goodness what a wonderful surprise, it is so good to see you. Mr. Edgeworth this is my husband Daniel McGregor, Daniel this is Mr. Simon Edgeworth my lawyer and my father's old law partner."

They shook hands, "Sydney we have known each other forever do you think you could call me Simon now?"

You could have blown me over, "Well honestly I will try but this is going to take some getting used to, thank you though."

"I had to call Gretchen about a legal matter and she told me you were expecting twins, I decided this would be a good time to come and see you, it has been such a long time. Sydney I have never seen you so happy. When I arrived yesterday I heard that you had baby girls. My goodness, look at those beautiful babies," and he went over. "What are their names?" I told him and he seemed touched. "I brought you a little gift for your girls," and he reached into his pocket and took out two small boxes. Inside were two tiny heart necklaces.

"Oh Mr....Simon, they are beautiful, that is so kind of you, their first gifts. Have you ever been an uncle before? No, well how would you like to start now? You have been with our family so long I think it is only right. Do you agree Daniel?"

"You bet I do."

Simon seemed a little surprised but said, "How very kind of

you I would be honored. May I sit down I would love to hear about your son too." Like a typical daddy Daniel whipped out a picture. "He is a very handsome little man and look at that smile. Sorry Sydney he looks just like his father, except for the hair color. The girls have Daniel's hair."

"Yes but guess what they have my eyes, Simon."

"I was hoping to see your mother while I was here it has been so many years."

I told him that if he can stick around for about another half hour she will be back.

"How about I go down and get some coffee and maybe the girls will be up and Rose will be here."

"That is a great idea I have to feed my girls now anyway. Daniel why don't you go down with him, if Simon doesn't mind, then you two can get to know each other better, you have barely been out of this room since we got here. But first could you get me set up?"

Daniel looked at Simon, "I'm game, give me one minute while I get the girls set up to be fed." Simon gave him one of his rare smiles and nodded and stepped outside, soon they left. As I was finishing feeding I started thinking about Uncle Simon, I do wonder what Father would have said about all this. Simon has always been so prim and proper I am wondering if he is just shy and doesn't actually know how to have fun. It is really a shame that he lives so far away, as this family could sure show him a good time.

Mom and the rest of the family did come and were no more in the door when I saw Daniel and Simon come up behind. "Hello Rose."

She turned around quickly, "Why hello Simon it has been a long time, please come in. Sydney look who is here." I told her that he had come up earlier.

"Rose, Sydney told me your story and I can't tell you how sorry I am that you had to go through so much, but again am thankful that she found you. You look exactly the same and very happy."

"You look good too, there is a softness to your face and it

becomes you. Simon did you ever marry?"

He smiled, "Charles took away the only woman I ever cared about, you Rose."

Mom was taken back I could tell but said, "You never said a word, I had no idea."

"You were so much in love with Charles I knew I would never have a chance."

I just sat there with my mouth open, Simon was in love with my mother and I guess no one knew. Good heavens. "Simon it is too bad you live so far away, it would be so nice to see you more often," I said.

He seemed to squirm a little but said, "That is another reason I am here to tell you I have retired. Ronald Peterson is taking over. To be honest I think it is time for me to live, I have been doing my profession long enough and I have forgotten HOW to live. I am actually considering moving here, I have been here many times and now I think the time has come to stay. I hope none of you mind?"

"Why that is wonderful, you are very welcome, and now that you are an uncle it is important." Then I told everyone that we have made him the girl's uncle, and they seemed pleased. Simon had the most wonderful smile on his face. I kept thinking what in the world is Gretchen going to say about all this? "So is it settled?"

"Yes and thank you so much."

"I do have to warn you though, we are a bunch of nuts but we sure have a good time." I said and put my hand on his arm and smiled, "You might go screaming into the night when you get to know us better."

He actually laughed. "Your father is so proud of you I just know it, you are a remarkable person Sydney. Now can I take you all out to dinner tonight to celebrate?"

I pointed to the girls, "I will have to take a rain check as I am stuck here for another day but if the rest of the gang wants to go that is fine."

All agreed but Daniel said he wants to stay with us, "Nothing personal I just can't take my eyes off my babies for more than about ten minutes."

"Hi all," said Dr. Winters as he walked in. "I am leaving now but just wanted to be sure all is well. How are you doing Sydney?"

"I'm good thanks," then I introduced him to Simon and they shook hands.

"Daniel," he said with a huge smile, "I hear you are making quite a name for yourself here at the hospital, besides the cuddling thing."

Edith looked at him and asked what was going on.

"Well from what I hear a couple nurses found him holding his two daughters in the rocking chair and singing to them, they were really touched, wish I had been there." He went over and patted Daniel on the back, "In my next life I am going to come back as one of your children." He smiled and left.

Edith said almost in a whisper, "I do love you my son, you are so special and I am so proud of you." We were all smiling, there were no more words left to say.

It took a couple more minutes to get us back where we were but we did and had a nice chat. I couldn't believe I was happily talking to Ichabod Crane but he wasn't really him, I feel so bad that I didn't give him a chance.

When everyone left for dinner I called Gretchen, "Guess who is in town, Mr. Edgeworth or as he wants me call him Simon."

"You are kidding, I know he called and I told him about your twins but I never expected him to show up. So what happened?"

"First and foremost I do not want you to tell Mom any of this, she was right there but it might embarrass her. Are you willing, truly Gretch? Ok then here goes, he brought the girls some beautiful gold heart necklaces and Mom asked him if he had ever married and he said, quote 'No Charles took away the only woman I have ever cared about, you Rose'. To say the least I was shocked. He is not the stuffy man I thought he was, he really seems to have a heart and I told him since he has no children that he can be the girls Uncle Simon, even Daniel agreed. He said he is retiring and wants to live here, as he has been here many times and likes it then he asked if it was all right with us. Can you believe? What really got me was that he said he wants to finally live and have fun; his job has kept him so busy he has forgotten how to do both. Tonight he is treating everyone but Daniel and I to dinner. You know Gretch I actually like him." Then I told her about Daniel singing to the girls.

"Wow that was a mouthful I just don't know what to make of all this. Of course he is welcome but I do wonder if he is hoping to win Rose? It does sound like he needs a family but ours is crazy did you warn him?"

I started to giggle, "Oh yes and he actually laughed. I too wonder about him with Mom but she is a grown up person and can do what she wants. You know it might be nice for her. We will see."

"Well thanks for telling me I will think about all this more. That man of yours is really something do you think we could clone him and add a few years for me? Hey did you get the DNA results back?"

I made a little drum roll, "Yes and they are identical. YEA!"

"Wow how are you going to tell them apart?"

"Didn't I tell you about the nail polish, they put a dot on Emily's big toe, the first born- clever huh?"

While I was feeding Daniel and I talked about what happened that afternoon, "You know I feel very sorry for Simon, he has no family, hope you didn't mind me asking him to be one of their uncles? He needs us I think, I hope we can help. He has known me since birth and honestly I thought of him as a pain in the neck, so stuffy and proper but he has kept in touch with me since I moved and me with him for lawyer stuff plus you and Mom. Hey how did your coffee thing go with him?"

"He seemed a little on edge but we had just met, he went on and on about how nice you have been to him, and how tired he is of just working. It did throw me though when he said what he did about your mom, and I do wonder if he might try again with her. But he is going to have to be very careful because I am going to watch him like a hawk. Your mom means a lot to me and I don't want her to get hurt."

I smiled and gave him a sideways kiss, "You my darling are

wonderful, thank you for taking such good care of us all, even Gretchen." We both laughed so hard that the girls got a little shook up. "Oops I guess laughing is not allowed at snack time. We are done and so am I let's try to sleep for a while."

We were all cuddled up and my husband decided to start with the kisses again. "My love I want you as much as you want me but we have to wait," I said.

"Why?"

I told him I was sure it is because I have to heal, "There was a lot going on down there," and I smiled. "Maybe I should ask the doctor. Somehow all I picture is a ton of laughing on his part, especially after the night the girls were conceived."

"Sure you want to risk it?" Daniel laughed and pulled me closer.

"Not really but you know YOU could do it."

He looked at me like I had just turned purple, "You have got to be kidding, kiss me you fool."

Of course we would wait, but this time I think we had better talk about some birth control and I told him.

"So what do you think, honey we have three little ones to take care of now and I definitely want more but not right away. Let's enjoy the ones we have."

"You are right as usual but do you know anything about birth control? All I know is what I can do."

I didn't and I told him so but, "When Dr. Winters comes in tomorrow maybe he can give us some advice." He told us all the different ways and said I could start taking the pill right away if I wanted to. I really didn't want to do that, too many problems and risks. So I guess we are going to discuss it more when the time comes.

Today is the day, we are going home. My babies got all bundled up and Daniel brought in the car seats for them, thanks to Eli who went out and bought them and is picking us up. We all got hooked up and headed for home. Of course the whole family was there waiting. My baby boy screamed and held out his arms when he saw us, "Mama," and then "Dada."

We got the girls in and Daniel went right to him and picked

him up, "I missed you little man, give your daddy a big hug."

Then I got to hold him and kissed him all over his sweet little face. "Mama missed you too baby. Now come here and meet your sisters."

He looked at them as if trying to figure out what they were. Then he gently reached his little finger out and touched each one of their faces and started to laugh. Thank goodness. The dog girls got to see them too but not that close up. "You girls need to be very gentle with your new sister's ok?"

Then the mom's took over, all three. They had a little bed set up in the living room all ready for them and after getting each one settled together just sat there and stared at them. "They are so beautiful I can't stand it," said Edith, "so tiny but so perfect."

Ryan sat there on my lap, very quiet and watched them. Oh oh I thought "Listen up all Grandmas' there is a little person," and I pointed to the top of Ryan's head, "who may get his nose out of joint, we are all going to have to give him a little extra attention, ok?"

Edith came over to where we were sitting, "Ryan, you are such a good boy do you want me to get you a cookie, come on Grandma will take you into the kitchen." He lifted his arms up to her and off they went. I guess it was fate or something but when he came back he wanted to play with Daddy on the floor, Daniel got up on his knees holding onto his hands and Ryan let go and just stood there. No one said a word, and then my big boy took his first step toward Daniel.

Daniel just smiled and said, "Come on Son just one more, and he did but started laughing so hard he fell into Daniels arms. We were all down there in a shot telling him what a big boy he is.

I grabbed him and held him so close, "Oh baby you walked you really walked, Mama is so proud of you." Of course he loved all the attention. "Did Grandma give you a magic cookie that made you walk?" He was really enjoying all this, and nodded and nodded, though I doubt he understood. Who cares it sure was fun.

That night when all the kids were asleep I called Mom into my room. "It has been some day huh? I have wanted to ask you about how you felt when Simon basically said he loved you? I must admit it was a shock to me."

She sat down on the edge of the bed, "Sydney I was as shocked as you were, I had no idea he had any feeling for me at all, oh he had always been nice but..."

"How did the dinner go?"

"Very well he was nice and polite and seemed to be enjoying talking to everyone. You know he is a nice man, I guess I didn't pay attention before. He seemed genuinely concerned about all I had gone through. He said he is going to be moving as soon as he can. I wonder where he will stay, maybe in a hotel until he can find a little house or something. Simon said he would like to come over and see the house before he leaves and I told him that would be nice. Sydney, no man will ever replace your father in my heart and truthfully I never thought of anyone else in my life."

I went over and put my arm around her shoulder, "Mom you will never have to replace your feelings for Father, but sometimes people make way for new feelings, open their hearts and see what happens. Be willing to at least give something a chance, you never know how things will turn out. Perhaps Simon just wants you as a friend."

"You are so wise I should be me telling you about these things. I am so sorry I missed such a big part of your life."

My heart ached for my mother, it must have been so hard for her, "Mom there are so many years left for both of us, I think we are doing great and I thank God every day for bringing us back together. My life is so full and I am so happy. I love you so much."

"Back at ya, as the kids say."

Simon came over for dinner a couple nights later. Mom did the cooking and we had a very nice evening. Simon was so impressed with the house and told Daniel over and over what a good job he had done. He also liked what I had done inside. "My Sydney you completely transformed the whole inside, it is like it has been reborn." I noticed that every chance he got he looked at Mom.

"So when do you plan on moving?" Gretchen asked him as she refilled his coffee cup.

"I found a nice hotel in Thumb Harbor and will stay there until I find a small house, hopefully on the water, it is so beautiful."

Daniel immediately spoke up, "If you need any help just let me know, or we could ask Syd to do the whole thing, she is very strong, never let her touch your hand when she is in labor."

Simon looked at me and I just shrugged my shoulders. "Thank you that is very nice. I hope to be settled in within the month."

When he left he took my hand and thanked me, then Rose's. "It has been so nice to see you again," and he left.

Today is May Day my little man's first birthday. It really was an all-day affair, we woke him up and he got a birthday hug, then a birthday breakfast. Then Daddy took him outside and they rolled a ball back and forth on the grass. After lunch we took him down on the beach to play in the sand, the water was still a little cool so he just got his feet wet. Then it was birthday nap time and of course later in the day we had a big party and the whole family was there. He opened a mound of presents but his favorite was the cowboy hat the Eli gave him. He put it on and grabbed the new horsey Mom gave him. She showed him how to ride with the stick between his legs, and he started running, well as running as he could. It was a covered stick that had the head of a horse and when you pressed his ear it would neee like a horse, it even had reins. It was so funny to watch, "Ride um Ryan," yelled Mom. We had a big dinner and then birthday cake and ice cream. He really thought he was hot stuff when he blew out the candle and clapped and clapped. It was a truly wonderful day.

That night as we tucked him into bed he looked up at us both and said, "Fun." Then he went right to sleep.

We stayed there just a little while longer, "Daniel I am so full of love for this little person I can hardly stand it. He is US, you and me, could anything be more wonderful?"

Several weeks have passed and I am still very tired but very happy too. We are getting into a schedule and I am finally getting a little more sleep. The Mom's do every other night when it is feeding time and I take the third. The girls are doing so well, they have a strong grip and seem to like to stare at their fingers a lot, and best of all they smile. Oh how they smile, especially when their big brother is around. He seems to feel so important and wants to be with them all the time. It is hard to believe they are just shy of one month old.

Finally I had my last check up with Dr. Winters. I told him we were going to try to prevent another pregnancy for a while at least, and he thought that was a good idea. "I am still going to come and check on the girls but only about once a week. You be sure to call if you need me."

"I wish I could figure out a way to thank you for being so kind to us all. Get ready I am going to hug you," which I did. "You are so special and we all are so grateful."

"Go home little Mother and love your babies, now scoot."

That night was our off night so we could actually sleep. "Daniel I want to do something special for Mom and Gretchen they have gone above and beyond to help us. How about we get them each a nice T.V. for their rooms?"

"Great idea, I will go out tomorrow and find some. Let's make it a surprise."

I leaned over and gave him a big kiss, "Speaking of surprises, do you happen to remember the one I gave you on our anniversary? Probably not," and I giggled, "but guess who just had her last appointment with the doctor after six very long weeks?"

He just stared at me, "Has it really been that long? You know I do recall something about our anniversary night. Do you think you could refresh my memory and show me what happened?"

"Come here you and I will demonstrate. Are you starting to remember clearly yet?"

"Oh now I remember, you read some book and shared what you learned with me.

"Was it this?"

"Whoa... yea, that was it."

"I love you husband," and I started giggling.

"Yes I know."

The ladies were thrilled with their new T.V's and of course said it wasn't necessary but I know they were glad to get them.

Simon has been moved in for almost a month now. The night of his arrival we had him over for dinner. It was such a nice warm night we decided to have a big picnic on the beach. Eli and Daniel took care of the BBQ meat and the girls brought the rest. Simon seemed so happy that night. It did take me a little time to get used to him in a short sleeve casual shirt he looked so different from the man I had known for so many years who never wore anything on but a suit and tie. I did notice too that he had let him hair grow and that seemed to make him look younger to me. He was also starting to get a tan and had put on some weight. Ichabod is officially gone.

Simon just couldn't seem to get enough of the kids; he was always talking to one of them and smiling. Ryan especially seems to like him a lot and crawled up in his lap. I went over and told Ryan maybe he had better not do that but Simon said, "It is fine with me, he is such a dear little guy." He actually played a little finger game with him and they both wound up laughing. Later in the evening he asked if he could hold the girls. It was so cute, I doubt if he had ever held a baby before but he sure turned to mush when they smiled up at him.

He and Mom talked a great deal and seemed to be developing a nice relationship.

Even Daniel noticed and pulled me aside, "They look cute together, he really is a nice man if something is meant to be between them then I do hope it happens."

All in all we had a wonderful night. Daniel told everyone that on the fourth of July the whole family will be coming to his folk's house again and Simon is welcome too. "I do hope ya will come," said Eli, "we would like that very much, but be prepared we got four other sons and their families and things can get a little crazy." Simon thanked him and said he would love to come.

Simon was truly beginning to be a part of our family, a welcome part as far as I was concerned and I am sure the others felt the same. At least once a week he came over and took Mom out for dinner. One night it was a little warm and humid outside and I had the windows in our room open to let in a little breeze. Since they are right over the front porch I heard Mom and Simon come home. I probably should have given them some privacy because I could hear every word they said. Daniel was with me and I whispered if we should shut the windows, "No, ok but I feel like a spy."

They started out reminiscing about old times then it sounded like Simon was getting serious. "Rose it has been so nice to be here with you and your family, I just want to thank you I have had a lot of fun. I know I told you that you were the only woman I have ever cared about and I hope I did not offend you, it just came out. But it is true, as the poets say, 'I have loved you from afar'. I do not expect you to feel the same but I am hoping that we can be good friends. That would make me very happy."

Mom didn't respond right away so I guess she was thinking about what he had said. "Simon I am very flattered with your words, you HAVE been a friend and even a little more perhaps, I am just a little confused right now. My life is so full with my family and I am the happiest I have ever been. Sydney told me to open my heart and let new things in and I think I am ready to do that but very slowly this is all new to me. I do value our friendship and have enjoyed our time together let's give time some time, all right?"

"Of course Rose and thank you for your honesty, may I take your hand in friendship?" We heard nothing more until he left."

"Yikes Syd I am really impressed with both of them. He even asked to hold her hand that is so sweet."

"Yea not like someone else I know who wanted to attack me after only a week. Stop looking at me like that you did, didn't you?"

"Yep."

"So what happened to the mad attacker, he got married and had kids and then nothing, lose your steam big fella?"

He started to come at me, and I played the innocent little thing and backed away. "So you think I am burned out huh well little lady hold on to your hat you are in for a big surprise."

"Oh Sir, you are frightening me, I think I shall faint," then I started laughing my head off. "You, you man," and I jumped into his arms.

The next morning Mom asked if we could talk in the parlor. "Sure what's up?"

She looked a little embarrassed but said, "I know you heard what Simon and I were talking about last night only because after he left I could plainly hear you and Daniel." I must have turned a hundred shades of red but she just smiled. "Don't get alarmed I left after the Southern Belle said, 'I think I shall faint'. Oh God, I just about lost it, I was laughing so hard. Sweetheart I know how it is, you two have something so very special and I am glad you have some fun with it. I know you know already but Daniel is really one of a kind and I love him very much too. It is so rare to find the kind of love you two share please never take it for granted."

"Oh Mom I love you so much, what you just said is beautiful thank you. Believe me I know how special our love is and am more than thankful that I have him, he is my life. He is a nut!"

"Yep," and we both burst out laughing, Daniel's favorite comment on everything.

I got up to leave but Mom put her hand on my arm, "Honey I did want to ask you something else. Like I said when Simon left I heard you two, but it was Simon I really wanted to talk to you about, we just got way-laid by what happened afterwards. You did hear everything right?"

"I am so sorry I really didn't mean to and yet I did want to hear, and one more sorry Daniel did too. He cares very much about what happens to you and wanted to be sure Simon wasn't trying to force you into anything. Forgive us?"

She took the pillow from behind her back and held it to her chest, "I am glad you heard I need to try to make sense of what we both said. Please tell me what you think."

"Well, it is obvious that he loves you but is not going to push you, which is good I guess. You two have been getting to know each other again in a different way. I think you have a good friendship but now I think it is going to be up to you if you want to move on from here. He is a perfect gentleman and has a sense of humor that is finally coming out. I like him very much and so does the rest of the family. We are behind you no matter what you decide to do."

"Sydney what scares me is that I do want to move ahead with him, but I can't get over the guilt I feel with your father. Truly I know that he would want me to be happy but this, I am not so sure, and with Simon. Beside I don't have any idea how to move on with Simon, it has been a very long time since I have played this game."

She looked so confused and sad I went down on my knees in front of her and took her hands. "Mom it has been thirty years since you and Father have been together and I know you loved each other completely but you are still young and there is so much more in life to discover. Tell ya what if you are serious about 'catching a man' then I will help you though I really don't know the first thing about it." We laughed and laughed. "My best advice is to just be yourself, warts, if you have any, and all. Let him see Rose, the beautiful witting warm Rose. Touch his hand occasionally, smile. Get your feelings from your heart and go with them and remember no matter what happens you will always have us, all of us."

Mom started sobbing, "Oh thank you dear, my how I love you."

Daniel popped in right then and saw us crying, "What happened you two can I help?"

I looked him straight in the eye, "Yep." Of course that dried up the tears and Mom and I were holding each other and rolling with laughter.

"I am leaving, you two have finally gone over the edge," Daniel said and of course made the whole thing more dramatic with the rolling eyes thing.

My baby girls are growing so fast, they can hold their heads up briefly while they are on the tummies and then just smile at each other. They truly are connected. Ryan is still their constant companion and is walking pretty good on his own now. I just melt when he says 'Mama' and walks slowly over to me with that wonderful smile. Life is truly good. We are all spending more time on the beach and one day Daniel sat on the hill and yelled to Mom who was holding Abby below. "Hey sexy lady, have you given up dancing, how about one last one for old time's sake?"

She put Abby in her car seat and jumped up. "You got it man." My nutty mother did a little dance then grabbed a long stick and swished around the "pole". The whole time he was cheering her on and singing. What we didn't see was Simon, who came at us from an angle. He just stood there staring at Mom. Daniel saw him first and stopped the singing then we all saw him.

I truly almost lost it when he yelled, "Go Rose, go for it." Then sat down next to Daniel and they both roared with laughter.

Mom looked at me like, what do I do now. "Go for it Mom," and she did until she finally fell over laughing.

"I'm sorry everyone, well sort of it sure was fun."

Simon went down and lifted her up then looked back at Daniel. "Daniel I would very much like to kiss Rose right now, all right with you?"

Daniel bowed, "Go for it Simon, go for it."

"Sydney turn around, girls hide under your blankets, Ryan cover your eyes, Grandma is going to get kissed." Once the laughter settled down he did kiss her, I peeked, and it was a warm wonderful kiss which Mom responded to.

"Poor Simon our crazy ways have rubbed off on him, he is one of us now. Poor Simon, welcome to the looney bind." Of course that was my husband.

"Thank you I am glad to be here. Daniel you are going to have to help me with this I have no practice," said Simon smiling at Mom.

Mom gave Daniel a look, "Good God don't teach him too good, one Daniel is more than enough." She took Simons hand and they went for a walk.

I just sat there stunned, "Did all this really happen wow! I feel left out. Poor Sydney, her mother gets all the kisses."

Daniel went over to the girls and Ryan, "My little man and

ladies, your daddy is going to kiss your mommy so hide, don't look."

Of course they all did and I got my kiss, then Ryan came up to Daniel and said, "Me Dada," and puckered up. Of course he got a big kiss from both of us.

"My little one do you realize you said two words together. Wow what a guy," and he swung him round and round.

I was so proud this has been a momentous day. That evening the whole family was sitting on the porch, we were quietly talking and all of a sudden I had an idea and went into the house. I found Daniels guitar and brought it back out. "Sweetheart it has been so long since you played could you sing us something now?"

He looked a little embarrassed but said, "Sure, the first snicker and I am done, got it?" Of course we all smiled and encouraged him. "So what's it to be?"

"How about "Country Roads" I love to hear John Denver sing it, soft and yummy." I said.

He started and once again I just couldn't get over what a beautiful voice he has.

When he finished no one spoke for a moment then, "Oh my Daniel that was wonderful," said Mom. "You have a beautiful voice," even Ryan clapped his hands. Abby and Emily had fallen asleep and we all just sat there contently staring into the night lost in past memories I guess.

It is July 4th and we are all getting ready to go over to the McGregor's. Simon got here a little earlier and seemed nervous. I went over to him, "Simon you look a little uneasy, I was in your boat a while ago but these people are so real, they are fun and I know we're all going to have a good time, now smile, that's an order."

Of course he did, "Thanks Sydney."

We had a ball, everyone was so happy to see us all, especially the kids. Oh my they got so much attention. Daniels brothers just couldn't get over how well he looked, "Last time we saw you you didn't look so hot my brother," said Steven. "Have you completely recovered?"

"Yes, thank goodness so much has happened and I am really happy with my life and family, it is what I have always wanted," and he took my hand.

Steven looked down at me and said, "You are a fortune man, this woman seems to love you very much, though I have no idea why." Daniel jumped up and grabbed for him, which of course started the rough housing. The other guys got into the act too.

All of a sudden Edith yelled, "Children stop your fighting, we have company." Then she laughed like crazy as did everyone else. She looked over at me, "Sydney they never grow up, not completely anyway, I am so glad."

I smiled at her, "Yes I know exactly what you mean and I love it too."

Everyone made a point of making Simon feel welcome. I saw him many times smiling and laughing. I am so glad he came. Again when it got dark we all sat around a bonfire on the beach singing silly songs and just relaxing. Daniel and I each held one of our girls and Ryan was asleep in Gretchen's lap. Abby was very fascinated with the fire and kept pointing to it. It is getting easier to tell the girls apart finally, they are developing their own personalities and if you look carefully there is a very slight difference in their faces. Emily seems to be the one in charge and Abby follows but once in a while they change jobs and Abby starts things. I love watching them try to figure out what is what. They are so beautiful and I love them with all my heart.

When it was finally time to go Simon told us how much fun he had and thanked us for including him. "They are a remarkable family."

A month later Simon and Mom were engaged. We had a party and all the family was there. "When are you getting married," Edith asked.

Simon smiled and said, "As soon as we can I hope," then looked at Mom.

"Don't ask me I am still in happy land and am trying to figure out what my name is." Daniel and I looked at each other in total disbelief.

"Rose, this is exactly the same thing Syd said when my mom asked US when we were going to get married," said Daniel. "Wow, are you sure you two aren't really twins?"

Then Simon said there is only one small problem, "I have been trying to find a house and there just are not any available."

All of a sudden it hit me, "Yes there is and I know it would be perfect for you two and it's right on the lake." They both looked confused. "Ok this might be a little much but please think about it. Why don't you move into the cottage right here? As a wedding gift I will have it totally redecorated for you. It would be so wonderful to have you both so close and I know it would be so hard on the kids and really all of us if you moved farther away."

"Hey what about how Gretchen feels, don't you think she has a say in all this, Rose is my dearest friend and Simon if you took her away I would lose her again, not going to happen."

They looked at each other then made a beeline for me and I got squished from both sides. "Hey don't kill the landlord? Does this mean you will do it, how wonderful?"

Daniel was grinning from ear to ear. "Perfect! Then it is all set, Gretchen won, as always."

I was truly amazed that everything worked out so well. "I am so excited I can't stand it, you guys set up a date and if you want to we can have the wedding right here at the house. But do give me a little time to redecorate, I have to check with my contractor to see if he is busy or not, what ya say contractor?" as I looked at my husband.

"I just happen to be free now so how about we get this thing going, Rose you tell me what you want and I am sure my assistant, the pretty woman sitting over there smiling, and I can work it out. Now I think some champagne and apple juice for the pretty lady over there would be good right about now, we have a lot of celebrating to do."

The next day Mom and Simon and Daniel and I went down to the cottage to check it out. Daniel asked them if they wanted any structural changes. "The main room is quite large with the living area and fireplace at one end, kitchen in the middle, and then an open area where the bed is. The bedroom and bath are off of that." Mom and Simon looked a little confused. Daniel said he thought we could make better use of the space by moving the kitchen to the far right which makes the living room quite large. "But that would make this only a one bedroom house. We could also just put up a wall with a door and make the bedroom area an actual room so you would have two bedrooms. So what do you think?"

They looked at each other for answers I guess and Mom said, "Well since my whole family is just a short distance away I don't think we will have any overnight visitors, and we could always get a pull out couch just in case Daniel gets into trouble and Sydney kicks him out of the house. He could sleep there. So I think just the one bedroom is enough."

Before Simon could say a word Daniel went over to her, "Mom you can get a regular couch, if Syd gets mad at me she will probably just beat me up and I will sleep on the floor." We all started laughing like crazy.

Simon finally got to speak, "I have no family except you all so the one bedroom is fine with me."

Then Daniel said he would draw up some plans and if they approve we can start right away. They were both so excited. Simon asked how long it would take. "Well with my crew and some help from you if you are willing we should be able to get it done in about a month or less. How's that? It will be good to get back into things again. Oh do you want the bedroom made bigger or the bathroom?"

Mom said she thought they were fine, Simon agreed. "I don't want to change the look of the place it is so charming just like it is," said Mom.

"We will give it a new coat of paint though and spiff up the outside," Daniel said, "it needs a little work."

"Mom we are all going to have to go down to Port Shores when things start to progress and pick out some new furniture, do you want to just paint or have some wallpaper too?"

She looked at me in a very motherly way, "First things first my girl, we haven't even started yet."

A few days later Daniel showed them the plans. They really liked them, me too. So Daniel said his crew is ready and they will start in a couple days.

Once again we were in a construction zone, but it was all inside so it wasn't near as hectic as with the big house. Every day I would bring Ryan down to watch his daddy being busy. He was so cute and kept yelling "Daddy work." The guys seemed to love to have him around and paid extra attention to him. One of them said he just can't believe in such a short time we have three kids. They really wanted to see the girls too, so the contractor brought both girls down the next day. Oh my how they fussed over them.

Mom and I always brought them coffee and snacks and fixed them lunch. Ron asked if we had any other projects coming up, "You are spoiling us rotten, thanks."

Daniel seemed so alive again doing what he loved to do. He came home messy but happy. "You know Syd I was so scared I wasn't going to be able to work again, this is wonderful. I am getting as much out of this as your mom and Simon are."

"You know what so am I" I said, "only in a little different way. I get to see my handsome husband all duded up in his tool belt and sweaty grungy clothes again, sexy."

"I hope you don't expect me to jump into bed like this cause it is not going to happen woman."

I put my arms around his neck, "Too bad it would make for an interesting change," and smacked him on the butt.

"You sexy witch," and he picked me up and headed for the stairs.

The stinker asked me later if I remembered Babette who gave him a sponge bath after his injury. "You know maybe we should introduce her to the contractor I bet they would get along great," he said then ducked the pillow I threw at him.

Things were progressing quickly and I asked Simon if they had set a date for the wedding yet. "Not quite yet but there is something I want to talk to you about, do you have time now?"

"Sure what's up?"

"Sydney you and Daniel are doing so much for us I want to

pay for any expenses for the wedding. No, don't say a word, I insist."

I gave him a hug, "Simon that is so nice of you, of course if that is what you want. Do you really truly want to have the wedding here or someplace a little more romantic, I will totally understand?"

He asked if he could sit down then said, "You have all made me feel so welcome and I am still flying high that Rose actually loves me and agrees to marry me, I want to start out our lives around the people we both love in a place we both love. We would be very happy to accept your generous offer. One more thing, because I am marrying your mother I will be in a sense your father, please know if you feel uncomfortable about this we can just leave it as I am your mothers husband. I know you loved Charles very much but he being the man he was didn't demonstrate his love for you very often. If I were given the privilege of being even a stepfather I can assure you I would take it very seriously. You have been so special to me since you were born and since I never had children I think I silently adopted you in my heart. I will let you think about this, my dear." Then he left.

My emotions were running wild, what an amazing man this was. I will never forget the words he said to me and how they made me feel. Later I told Daniel and he too was very touched, "Oh Syd how lucky you are to have such a man be so open and honest with you. He is really special. What are you going to do?"

"You know I really do need to think about this and talk to Mom," which I did and told her all that Simon had said. "Mom he really got to me, he offered to be my father even a stepfather you are such a lucky girl to have him. What do I say, am I betraying Father, yet I am truly drawn to this man's kindness?"

Mom seemed to be overwhelmed too but said, "Sydney, as you told me not too long ago, you will never forget your father, he has a permanent place in your heart but you need to be willing to fill in the empty spaces with new things and people. I am sure your father would understand whatever you choose to do. Look at me, I did that and I am very happy."

Later that night Simon was out on the porch playing with Ryan, as Mom and Gretchen finished doing the dishes. "Hi you two, Ryan are you having fun playing with Grandpa Simon?"

He looked up at me with such warmth, 'Sydney are you trying to say something?"

I sat down beside him, "Yes, first there will be no step, it's all or nothing, but I have decided that I will call you Dad not Father so both you and my father can be separate yet the same, if that makes any since. I have always wanted a dad. I am honored that you want me as your daughter I really am, so welcome Dad."

He leaned over and hugged me tightly, "Now all my dreams have really come true I have a daughter and the woman I adore. Thank you, I will always be here for you no matter what."

I started to cry and saw Mom and Daniel at the end of the porch, he was holding her too, I am sure they heard the whole thing then they turned and went into the house. We followed soon and Ryan put his arms up to Simon and said, "Pick up", which he did and hugged him. What a day this has been.

The next morning Mom was waiting for me in the kitchen when I came down. "Hi Mom Hi Gretch, well the girls are fed and back to sleep and after breakfast Ryan and I are going down to watch his daddy. Life is good!

"Speaking of Daddy's, rumor has it that you have a new one."

Gretchen immediately sat down next to us, "Ok what did I miss, tell all?"

"Mind your own business Gretchen," Mom said, "oh well you will hear soon anyway. I heard you Sydney and Simon last night on the porch. What you did was so special, thank you. Simon is flying high."

"Get to the point woman what happened?"

"Gretchen Simon told Sydney that she didn't have to accept him as her father once we are married, he even offered to be her stepfather or just the man I married, but she did a remarkable thing. She told him that she would always have Charles as her father, but she needed a dad too. I can't tell you what that did to me."

Gretchen got up and came over to me and took my hand, "Sydney Rose McGregor you never cease to amaze me, what a wonderful gesture you made. I am so proud of you, you do need a dad, and he sure needs a daughter." Both Moms hugged me at the same time.

I couldn't speak right away I was just savoring another beautiful moment with my mom's. "Mom your words are what did it, though I know they were mine originally, you were so right I did need to fill in the empty space in my heart with something new. Can things get any better for us all? I don't see how."

Ryan started pulling on my leg, he looked so cute in his cowboy hat that he got for his birthday, "Daddy Daddy" and he waived his arms around.

"Ok hot shot off we go," I scooped him up and ran all the way down to the cottage. Ryan was squealing the whole way, and of course Daddy heard him.

"Did your horsey gallop to fast little cowboy, Daddy brought your little chair down so you can watch but you have to sit still ok? Mommy how about you come and see what we have done."

Just as I started to turn away a plank from the roof fell and hit Ryan in the head. I screamed and ran for him, "Oh my God, oh my God he is bleeding so much oh my God." Daniel told me to go get Gretchen. I screamed for her the whole way back.

She came running "What happened?" I was so out of breath I couldn't speak just grabbed her and we ran. "Ryan oh no, tell me what happened." Daniel told her though I could hardly understand him he was shaking so badly. "Don't move him, has anyone got their cellphone on, good then call for an ambulance. How long has he been unconscious? We have to be sure he didn't injure his neck." I just fell on the ground sobbing and held his little limp hand.

"I can't stand this someone do something."

The ambulance came very quickly and Daniel and I got in. "Gretchen call Mom and Dad have them meet us there, Mom and Simon too," he yelled. It was a terrifying ride and I was so scared.

"Hang on baby we are here."

The emergency room doctor took him right in. We explained what happened and he started cleaning up the head wound then they took him off for x rays. "We will know more when they are done."

The doctor came out about thirty minutes later and said he is conscious and wants his mommy and daddy. "We had to put three stitches in his forehead. The x rays showed no damage but he does have a slight concussion. We are going to keep him here overnight to keep an eye on him he is a very lucky little boy."

I asked Daniel to please go out to the waiting room, "Something tells me there are four frantic Grandparents out there."

There lay my precious little boy looking so small in his big bed. "Ryan boom," said my baby.

"Yes sweetheart Ryan go boom but look at that pretty bandage you got on your head, you are such a brave boy. Guess what you get to stay here in that big boy bed tonight and Mommy and Daddy will be here too. Won't that be fun?" He kept shaking his head. "But honey all cowboys need to get out and see new things, just think I bet you will get some ice cream." Then he smiled, thank you God.

They put him in the children's section and got out two chairs for us. I asked the nurse if his grandparents could come in. "Yes but just for a little while we don't want him to get too excited. I will get them for you."

Daniel had been so quite I asked him if he was all right. "No, this is all my fault, if I had just held him he would have been fine, I will never forgive myself."

"But baby he is all right, you know that, look at his smile." The Grandparents came in then and I told them to be calm he is fine.

Eli went up to him and gave him his cowboy hat back, "Here little buckaroo one of the ambulance men gave it to us," he said as he put it on his head, "that looks better. Grandpa is going to give you a kiss for being such a brave little one." He turned his head just as the tears started rolling down his face. "I will wait outside."

Simon said he looks so special with his hat on and his pretty bandage, "Maybe they would give me one too." The sweet nurse went over and found one for Simon, "There now I match you."

I put my hand on Simons arm and kissed his cheek, "Thanks Dad and you are just that."

Mom and Edith were not as composed but gave Ryan a kiss and said they would see him tomorrow and have a special treat for him; "We bought it for you and have been waiting for just the right time to give it to you."

Ryan smiled and said for the first time, "Gamma," then reached out to both of them. Then we really knew he WAS all right. Good thing they were holding on to each other's arms or they might have done a Sydney and fainted. But still Daniel said nothing, and I was getting worried.

Edith noticed it too and said, "What is wrong with Daniel?" I told her what he had said and she went over to him, "My dear boy, all little guys get bumps and bruises, this is just the first one for Ryan. You and your brothers kept me in panic mode for many years. I am sure you don't remember when you tried to climb up a ladder for the first time at about three and the ladder tipped over. You had a good gash on your forehead but with all your brothers around they snapped you out of your tears in a hurry. It is tough being a parent but there are so many rewards too. Now go over there and tell your little boy how much you love him and for heaven's sake give Sydney a kiss."

"Yes Mom, thank you, can I start by giving you a hug?" I heard what she said and mouthed thank you and blew her a kiss.

Naturally Dr. Winters came in just as Daniel gave me my little kiss. "Don't you two ever take a break?" Then smiled down at Ryan, "So little man you got a boo–boo huh?" Ryan nodded and pointed to his bandage. "Well that is very special, just like you. I am sure Mommy and Daddy will stay with you tonight and tomorrow you can go home, I know your sisters will be happy to see you. He is going to be fine," he said to all of us then left.

Ryan slept all night and in the morning he started poking me,

"Mommy home."

"Good morning little buckaroo, shall we wake up Daddy? You call him."

"DADDY!" he yelled. Poor Daniel jumped a mile.

"Good morning champ, want to go home? Ok let's see what we can do about that."

The nurse brought in his discharge papers and told us to keep him as quiet as we could for the next couple days. "Yea I know well try anyway."

Of course everyone was there waiting for us. We ate ice cream at nine o'clock in the morning and the grandma's brought out Ryan's surprise, a little wooden pony on rockers for our cowboy to ride on. He loved it and played for a little while, but finally I said, "The horsey is getting tired so how about we let him have a nap and then you can too. Daddy will take you up to your room." Surprisingly he didn't object.

In three more days he was Ryan again and Dr. Winters said after his last visit that he can do whatever he wants. Daniel was still a little funny but I think that helped a lot to hear. He went back to work which helped too. One night I decided to really try to get his mind off his guilt and planned a big seduction, roses on the bed candles everywhere, the whole nine yards. He opened the door and said how nice things looked, "Even your wife with something as small as a hankie on?" I asked.

"I need to take a shower." Right then I knew we were in trouble, now what am I going to do I thought. I need to get him to talk to me.

He got into bed and just flipped over. "Sweetheart talk to me please, you are scaring me. You need to get this all out."

He turned over and looked so sad, "Syd, when I went down to the site all I saw was Ryan's blood I couldn't work. I felt paralyzed, I just stared at it. He could have died all because of me."

"Daniel please, remember what your mother said, all kids get hurt at some time. Ryan is fine you have to let it go."

"I can't," and he held me close, "I just can't." He finally fell asleep in my arms. Tomorrow I am going over to see Dr.

Winters if I can maybe he can help.

He did get me in, "So how is Ryan doing, good are you sick Sydney, what's up?" I explained the whole thing and asked him to please not tell Daniel that I was here and that I am very worried.

"He loves his son so much and I think he feels like he is not a good father because he did not protect him. I have seen this before. I think the best thing you can do for him is just be supportive, have him spend as much time as possible with Ryan. I know how much he loves you too and I think that will help. Give him some space to work through this though." I thanked him and left.

When I got home Mom and Gretch were in the kitchen talking. "Is something wrong Syd?" asked Gretchen. "You don't look very happy."

I decided not to tell them what was happening, "Nothing major just something I need to work out. I think I will go up and see the girls." Mom told me they are in the living room with Daniel. Daniel, I thought he was working. I paused at the door and listened. He was telling them that he loves them and promising that he will never let anything hurt them. I went in and put my arms around him.

"My love, you can't promise them that, all you can do is promise to be there if they do get hurt. Life isn't all things good as we both know. I am just as scared as you are about all this. We just have to trust that nothing serious is going to happen. All we can do is love them."

He turned around and stared at me, "What in heaven's name would I do without you, of course you are right, but I love him and the girls so much it hurt me more than Ryan when he got injured. I'm sorry if I worried you I guess I just lost it for a while. Do you still have that hankie thing you wore last night?"

"That's my mad attacker, yes I do and I will model it for you tonight. Welcome back my husband."

We clung to each other and then Gretch popped in. "Don't you two ever stop?"

"Nope. You want some Gretchen," and he headed over to

her.

She sailed out of the room with Daniel in pursuit, "Get away from me you lunatic." Then they both stopped and started laughing. "Ok I give up one kiss and that is it," and she puckered up.

He planted one on her cheek then smacked her on the butt, "You are a wench woman, tempting me like that, what would my wife say?"

"Sir you never told me you were married get out of my kitchen before I forget I am a lady. Syd you really need to put this man on a leash."

Things were back to normal and I was so glad. That night when I came into the room he was lying on the bed with just a sheet on. "You promised me a full body message way back remember, well how about now?"

"Give me a minute to change into my messaging outfit," and I went into the bathroom.

He yelled, "You have a special outfit you have to wear?"

"Usually I just wear my jeans but you can choose between them and this," and I came out in a very short sheer black nightie.

"Like your choice."

"Flip on your stomach and I will begin. Feel good?"

He started moaning, "Oh yea, can I flip over yet?"

"Yep, now I will start at your neck and shoulders then work my way down how's that?"

He got a goofy smile on his face, "You do realize where this is going to wind up don't you?"

"Yes, and I really don't think it is going to take much longer," and I giggled. It didn't. "Sorry sweetie you didn't quite get your full massage. Maybe next time but I have big doubts." Then we just held on to each other and laughed.

"I do love you my wife."

"I love you more."

A couple days later Mom and I were talking about the wedding, "Do you have a dress Mom?"

"No I didn't even think about it, what am I going to do?"

All of a sudden I remembered the dress in the attic I had seen while exploring, "Come with me. Let's see it was close to the door I think. Yes here. I think this is a wedding dress let's take it down to your room and check. Obviously someone in our family wore it."

"Oh my I think this was my mother's, let's see if we can find some pictures." It took most of the morning but we finally found the one we were after.

I lifted one up, "Is this it? Good, now let's see what kind of shape the thing is in after all these years." We carefully looked at the whole thing, there were a few little tears but that was about it. "Now strip down Mom let's see if it fits. Goodness it fits you perfectly, do you like it?"

It was all lace with tiny little pearls scattered all over it, several bows, and a satin sash. The style was very old fashioned but charming, "Yes I love the high neckline and long sleeves that have a point at the end. So what do you think?" she asked.

"I love it too maybe Gretchen could help fix it up. This really needs washing though I don't know if it would ruin it. Edith is really good with old things let's ask her." I said getting very excited.

Edith said we could give it a little test to see if it would hold up to soap and water before we try anything else. It came out fine so she dunked the whole thing in a mild detergent and let it soak. Then she swished it around and again let it soak. Finally she rinsed it gently and pushed some of the water out of it and wrapped it in a towel. "Just let it dry naturally, I think it is going to be fine." It took a couple days but it looked so much better. Gretchen mended the small tears then Mom ironed it and we were set.

"I forgot I need a veil too," she said, "any ideas?"

I went into our room and found the box that held my wedding dress. "Here, how about mine?"

She put it on her head, "I love it but it is so long and do I actually need one? Maybe I could just put a flower in my hair."

I took the veil off the circle of roses that held it. "Bingo, how about just the roses?"

"Perfect roses for Rose, thank you honey. Can I borrow your

shoes too we are the same size?"

"Done is done!" I said as we both smiled. "How about we go down and see how your house is coming. Let's get Emily and Abby it is such a nice day, they need to get outside."

When we got there Daniel was so excited to see his girls, "Well my little ones Daddy is all dirty and can't hug you but come on in and see what is going on. It shouldn't be more than a week Rose and the place will be ready, do you like it?"

She just stood there staring, "You have really done a good job it looks like a totally different place, so much larger. Sydney I think we had better do some furniture shopping."

The guys decided to leave the shopping to us so the next day we were off to Port Shores. Mom picked out two big chairs for either side of the fireplace, a smaller couch and a couple tables. She said she likes the old kitchen table but the chairs were a little beat up so we found some new ones. "What about curtains?" she asked.

"Gretchen said she would make some for you but I think while we are here we had better get some fabric to match the furniture. She gave me the dimensions so let's find a fabric store."

It was such a fun day and Mom was so excited about everything, just like a bride should be.

The wedding is just a week away and we are all flying around trying to get the last minute things finished. The cottage is done but I told Simon and Mom they couldn't see it until after the wedding, I wanted them to be surprised. Gretchen made up a truly gigantic bow that she is going to put on the front door. The other day while we were all eating dinner Mom asked if Ryan could be their ring bearer. "Well why don't you ask him?" Daniel said.

So Mom leaned over to him and said, "Ryan Grandpa Simon and I want you to be in our wedding, if Grandma gives you the pretty rings that we are going to wear could you bring them up to us?"

He looked a little confused and I doubted he understood but said, "Yes Gamma." I think if we practice a little he will do fine.

This is going to be fun.

Today is the day. Simon is downstairs in the music room getting dressed and Mom is upstairs in our room with me. She is a very typical bride, a nervous wreck. We decided since it is just the family that we are going to have the wedding down on the beach. Daniel and Simon set the chairs up yesterday and thank goodness the weather is perfect. Daniel is Simon's best man and I am the Maid of Honor. Gretchen and Edith are her bridesmaids. Eli is going to give the bride away bless his heart. When Mom asked him he got all choked up, "My goodness I get to give all you girls away I am honored."

Mom looked so beautiful, I did her hair and the dress was spectacular. At the last minute I gave her the gold rose necklace that was Elizabeth's, though I know it was hers originally. She was so shocked to see it she said she thought it was lost. "My father gave me this when I graduated from high school." Of course there were many tears that morning but all were happy.

Mom and Simon are going to spend their first night in the cottage and then tomorrow are going to Hawaii for a two week honeymoon. How romantic, they are going to have such a good time I am sure.

It was time. Eli came up to get Mom and the men were waiting down at the beach with our twins. "Oh Rose you look like a princess, you are just as beautiful as you were thirty years ago," and we left.

The procession began at the top of the hill, first Edith and Gretchen then me and my little man, then Eli and Mom. Daniel had arranged for a small group of musicians to play off to the side as we descended. I could not get over how beautiful the whole scene was. There were flowers everywhere and the minister stood between the two men. The photographer started taking pictures as soon as he saw us come down. My beautiful daughters were just to the side of Daniel in their car seats. They were both in pretty little pink dresses and Daniel was down on his knees playing with them. Then he looked up and saw us, stood up and smiled.

Simon looked so grand and very handsome as he waited for

his bride. As soon as he saw her the smile on his face almost made me cry. He loves her so much and it shows. Once we were all together, Eli gave Mom's hand to Simon and kissed her cheek. Then he made a quick speech, "Rose we are so happy to have you as part of our family and now Simon too. We all wish you much happiness." I was so proud of him and I could tell Edith was too. When he stepped back I gave him a quick kiss on the cheek.

The ceremony went well and then it was time for Ryan to do his thing, my little man stood up there so straight as he lifted the pillow up to Simon, "Here Gampa." We all melted. Then, "Up Gampa," and he held up his arms. Gampa picked him up and finished the ceremony with Ryan still in his arms, even when he kissed his bride. Ryan got a kiss too from both of them. It was the most wonderful thing I have ever seen. Finally Daniel took Ryan from Simon.

"Ok Simon now really give her a kiss," which of course he did and we all cheered. We stayed on the beach for quite a while longer then went up to the house for lunch. Gretchen really outdid herself. She even baked a little wedding cake.

"My family," said Rose, as she clung to her new husband, "there are no words to say to thank you for this beautiful day, I am so proud to be a part of this nutty family. I love you all so much. I think Simon wants to say something too."

"Yes I do, I have loved this woman forever and am the luckiest man alive to have her as my bride. I promise you all that I WILL love and cherish her all the days of our lives. Never would I have ever thought that I could be a part of such a wonderful family and that you accepted me so quickly. All these lost years were just that, lost, but now I have found something remarkable and thank you all."

Again we all cheered. "Hey lets go down and see your honeymoon cottage," said my husband. We all trooped down, Daniel and I carried our daughters and Ryan got a ride on Eli's shoulders.

"Giddy Gampa," he yelled.

Gretchen's bow looked so grand and Mom was really tickled

when she saw it. "Thank you dear friend, I love you for making this so special." Gretchen just kissed her and for once said nothing.

I almost lost it when Daniel opened the door and Simon picked up Mom and carried her in. They just stood there trying to absorb it all. "Oh Daniel," Mom said as she grabbed him, "you really are a miracle worker, it is so beautiful, you have made this a true home and I feel so touched that you did this all for us. Thank you so much, and you too Daughter, you really have a decorating talent." Poor Simon just stood there with his mouth open.

"Wow I can't believe this is all for us," he hugged us both. "Thank you will never be enough, and to think we are so close to you all too. It is just so wonderful," he finally said.

"Well family, I think it is time for us to leave these love birds alone. The fridge. is stocked but if you want to come up later and have dinner with us then please do," I said as we left.

Everyone stayed for the rest of the afternoon and we all ate dinner. Mom and Simon stayed where they were. That night while Daniel and I lay in bed I snuggled up close to him, "I am so full of happiness right now what a perfect day."

"Syd I couldn't get my eyes off of you when the ceremony was going on, you were my beautiful bride again, you're the mother of three children and you still look as beautiful as the day I married you, even more so. We sure have had some challenges since then but an awful lot of fun too. Just think we have at least a hundred years left of all this," then he kissed me. "Can we pretend we are on our honeymoon too?"

"No need to pretend we will always be."

The next morning Simon and Mom were at our door early for breakfast. They looked so cute always holding hands. "So, today is the day huh, you are off for your honeymoon, Syd and I started ours last night."

"Daniel you are awful." I yelled at him.

"Sorry Simon this goes on all the time around here," said Mom.

"Sorry nothing, I love it my dear," said Simon and then

smiled.

"Hey man you are getting that evil eye thing down pretty good, keep practicing," said Daniel. "Now get going you two and have a wonderful trip. We do expect tanned faces when you get back but if that is impossible we will understand," and he gave them his best snicker.

"Daniel stop it," I yelled again.

We all hugged each other and after many goodbyes they left.

I can't believe a year has passed. Mom and Simon are so very happy, we all are. Daniel keeps asking them when they are going to start having kids. Mom just shakes her head, "I think we have more than enough around here right now." Daniel is still my nutty Daniel thank goodness and I do love him more every single day. Emily and Abby are walking now and are so adorable with their curly blond hair. They are totally girly girls, always in dresses with bows in their hair. I can't wait to take them upstairs to the attic when they get bigger and we can play dress up. I love them so much sometimes it literally hurts. There is no one like their daddy, and they fight to see who can climb up in his lap first. He loves it, and so do I. They walk and my little Ryan runs, everywhere, and gets into everything. He talks constantly especially to his sisters. He is still my wonderful little man and I feel so blessed every day that we have him. I love to watch Gretchen charge after them all. She is my savior and I know loves every minute of it–I don't think either of us sits down all day. Edith and Eli have been spending more time with us and really enjoying their grandchildren. Once in a while Edith and I will go out shopping or hide in her yard to escape for a few minutes. They are so special to me. Wait until I tell Daniel what I found out today from Dr. Winters.

"Guess what my love, I guess the fates have decided we need another little boy, to balance things out, or even another girl to really mess you up, baby number four is on its way. You and your Happy Anniversary celebrating."

AUTHOR'S NOTE

Hello again. Out of all the books I have written this one was the most fun. All I had to do was put my fingers on the keys, and the characters seemed to take over. There is so much more I would like to tell you about this crazy fun family and I would love to write a sequel. If you like it too please write a review on Amazon or wherever you bought this book or tell me. I need your input. Thank you for your encouragement and support.

JoAnn

CPSIA information can be obtained at www.ICGtesting.com
Printed in the USA
BVOW01s2038070814

361875BV00002B/141/P

DOUBLE PLEASURE, DOUBLE PAIN

DOUBLE PLEASURE, DOUBLE PAIN

NIKKI RASHAN

www.urbanbooks.net

URBAN BOOKS
1199 Straight Path
West Babylon, NY 11704

ISBN-13: 978-1-60162-052-1
ISBN-10: 1-60162-052-7

First Printing: May 2008
Printed in the United States of America

10   9   8   7   6   5   4   3   2

Submit Wholesale Orders to:
Kensington Publishing Corp.
C/O Penguin Group (USA) Inc.
Attention: Order Processing
405 Murray Hill Parkway
East Rutherford, NJ 07073-2316
Phone: 1-800-526-0275
Fax: 1-800-227-9604

Acknowledgments

There are so many people I have to thank for helping me reach this much anticipated point in my life. It would take pages upon pages to name everyone, so, it is here that I will list just a few and trust that those of you not named will still know how very much you mean to me and know in your hearts how grateful I am for your support.

Joylynn: Without you I would not be writing these words. I'm so thankful that the Spirit whispered my name to you . . .

Dawn: It's not the same without you here. Thanks for your encouragement from so many miles away.

Bo: As always, your support means the world.

Bernell: Your belief in me is immeasurable. It's happening!

Apple: For opening my eyes and heart in ways I couldn't have imagined.

For JJ and CooCoo
My two brightest stars . . .

January 1, 2001

It's 7:30 in the morning and for the second time in two days, I'm suffering from a major hangover. I'm hoping this isn't a preview of what the rest of my year will be like.

Last night's festivities were exhilarating, yet exhausting at the same time. But hey, it was well worth the pain I'm going through today. I partied hard with my family and friends and toasted a few more times than necessary. But with each toast to health and happiness, I silently prayed for more clarity in my life this upcoming year than what the second half of last year brought me.

I don't even know where to begin. The big question is, *how did I get here?* I thought for sure I'd wake up today and realize that it had all been a dream. You know, one of those really real dreams you have that when you wake up, it takes a minute to realize that all you had just seen and all you had just felt was only your imagination. But that would have been the easy way out for me.

So here I am—about to start the most important year of my life thus far; where one decision will make life-altering changes for many and have lifelong consequences for myself. Let's see . . . I guess I'll begin with when the straight and narrow path I had been walking on my whole life suddenly curved, and I stumbled upon a fence protecting this field of thick, beautiful green grass. And as the saying goes, if the grass is greener, you'd better believe the water bill is a lot higher. And right now, I'm paying the price.

PART 1

PLEASURE

1

"**M**mmm, that was nice," I said as I stretched my arms up to touch my brass headboard. I closed my eyes and exhaled, my body calm, satisfied, and tension-free.

"It was all my pleasure," Jeff said, smiling as he lifted his head from its resting position on my damp thigh. He kissed the wetness on my skin. "And yours too," he teased.

Then he winked at me. So I winked my sexiest bedroom eye back at him and quickly stuck my tongue out. He laughed a deep baritone chuckle, rolled out of my queen-size bed and walked into the attached bathroom.

I rolled over, stuffed my face in the silk pillowcase, and laughed with him. I gently shook my head at myself. I have never been good with words, so sticking my tongue out has a variety of meanings depending upon what Jeff provokes in me at any particular moment. Sometimes it means *you're cute* as I watch him coach the boys' basketball team of his high school alma mater on to victory. Or it means *let's have some fun* when I slowly and seductively lick my tongue across my lips while we slow dance to our favorite song. And it even means *I love you* those times he caresses my thigh under the table while we sit at dinner with our friends. And then of course there are the times it means *kiss my ass* after Jeff has tweaked my last nerve by leaving the damn toilet seat up again. I've tried improving the art of transmitting my feelings and thoughts from my mind to my mouth, but I haven't mastered the process yet. Somewhere between my brain cells and larynx, there is a lost connection.

Because of this default in my system, I shower my love on Jeff in ways that don't actually force me to use my quivering vocal cords: spur-of-the moment weekend getaways, surprise gifts, and deep-tissue massages are my specialty. Unfortunately, I can count the number of times I've *told* Jeff I love him on two hands—eight fingers, to be exact. The last time was about two months ago when Jeff amazed me with a pair of Manolo Blahnik heels after he caught me salivating over Carrie's closet while watching an episode of *Sex and the City*.

I know how good it feels to hear those cherished three words, so why don't I tell him more? I don't know. It's no question Jeff was the one to utter the *L* word first. Of course, I remember it like it was yesterday. No girl ever forgets the first time her man professes his love to her. At least she better not; we always have to be able to throw that shit back at them when they start acting like an ass.

Anyway, we had been dating about four months when the moment arrived. Jeff had just secured a job with the city as a civil engineer, so I took him out to dinner to celebrate. Because Chinese is his favorite food, I had taken him to China Port restaurant, whose decor shamed the place and would send any out-of-towner running if unfamiliar with the newspaper-worthy reviews often received. We devoured his meal of choice, egg foo yong and fried rice, when out of nowhere he reached for my hand and squeezed, looking at me like he could see right through me and could feel my heart racing with anticipation.

"Kyla," he said, clearing his throat and looking directly into my bucked, nervous eyes, "you know I've had more than a few relationships in the past. More than I care to admit, actually. But there's never been anyone who makes me feel like you do. I feel like I've known you for so much longer than I have and I knew you had stolen my heart the first time I laid eyes on you. I want you to know that you mean the world to me." He shifted in his seat. "What I'm trying to say is that I love you, Ky. I really love you." His skin blushed as he stuttered over the last words.

Oh, I just thought I would melt right there in my cushioned seat. I paused a moment, a little uneasy and unsure if there was a proposal to follow. But even with my hesitation and the extra moment of thought, all I could muster up was a barely audible, "I love you too." Although I was a little disappointed with my response, you would have thought he had just hit the million-dollar jackpot in Vegas. I swear I saw a tear in his eye.

But that's the kind of man I have: sensitive, smart, and a good catch, according to everyone I know. First of all, he's real easy on the eye. So fine even Helen Keller couldn't help but take notice (I know, that was wrong). My guy is in the six-foot-one-inch range, not too short, not too tall, just right for my five-eight frame. His skin is a caramel complexion that cleared up silky smooth after a bout with acne in middle school. When he showed me pictures from his younger years, I was certain he was playing a joke on me, claiming to be one of the young men from the basketball team in the awkward boyhood to manhood stage. But it wasn't a joke. Still, I'm sure every young girl that wouldn't give him any play back in the day would be kicking herself if she were to see his fine ass now.

His eyes are a deep chocolate brown with thick, dark eyelashes and eyebrows you would swear were crafted by celebrity makeup artist Sam Fine. Jeff has a perfect set of soft lips that always feel like lip balm was freshly applied. And he has thick, naturally curly hair that he chooses to wear cropped close to his scalp. A firm and sculpted body completes the package with a perfect six-pack resulting from the hundred and fifty sit-ups he does every night before climbing into bed.

I can't stop with just his appearance, though. Not only does the man deserve to be on *People*'s fifty most beautiful list, he's also educated, thoughtful, charming, and he cracks jokes so corny that you have to laugh out of embarrassment for him. His heart is genuine and he has a strong sense of family.

His parents, Mr. and Mrs. Oldham, have been married for over twenty-eight years and Jeff takes great pride in the longevity of their relationship. For their silver wedding anniversary, he and his brother Kent, a younger but two-inch taller version of Jeff, gave them a marvelous, black-tie celebration. Guests were treated to a slide-show presentation and a program guide filled with pictures of everything from their parents' individual childhoods to pictures of them caring for their own two boys.

Jeff's toast to his parents was so touching and heartfelt that there was not a dry eye in the place. I could see every unattached woman in the place panting and licking her lips, ready to devour this sensitive man as her prey. Mind you, we had been dating for only five weeks, and from that moment on, I knew I had found my needle in the haystack. Not to say that a good man is hard to find, but just as Jeff said he had his share of relationships, I had more despite our two-year age gap.

My mother taught me at an early age that boys will be boys and to break their hearts before they could shatter mine. "Better them than you, honey," she advised. Words I have never forgotten and have lived by ever since. Well, I slipped once and let a cocky, lip-licking, LL Cool J wannabe senior break my heart back in high school. I know it sounds like it may have been puppy love, considering I was just the tender age of fifteen, but it sure didn't feel like it then. You know how you can admire someone from afar for so long, and when that person finally shows a little attention, you already feel like you're in love? So was this case. My nose was wide open. He jumped in, took advantage of that fact, and left as quickly as he had come (no pun intended). Those around me may not have known how devastated I was since I didn't shed a tear. I couldn't even express my feelings back then. So I sucked it up, never forgot that crushed feeling, and vowed never to let heartache venture in my direction again. For seven years, I wandered in and out of relationships with my eyes half shut and my heart half closed.

This brings me back to Jeff and the four years we've spent together. Sometimes I doubt that I deserve the kind of love he gives me: totally unconditional. Especially because I'm not willing to give him that same love in return. I definitely love Jeff more than I have any other man in my previous relationships, but I know that Jeff loves me more than I love him. For some inexplicable reason, I have been unable to fully surrender my heart to him. There has always been something, somewhere, that prohibits me from loving him completely. So, my guard is up, firm and in place, and even Jeff hasn't broken down the walls to release all the love I have inside.

I'm sure my parents' divorce has made me leery of commitment and doubtful that love conquers all, like every love song proclaims. For so long my parents seemed to live the perfect life. We had a four-bedroom home in a decent neighborhood, always had two shiny late-model cars in the driveway, never worried about a meal, or whether or not my parents could afford to buy me the latest fashions I craved every fall when school began. Each summer our family would load up the van with our tent, grill, and sleeping bags and take a weekend trip to one of Wisconsin's favorite family getaways, the dells, where we would hike and bike ride through the wilderness, spend hours at the water parks, and sing made-up songs around the campfire at night. We felt and looked like the ideal, successful family.

My dad made his way from the mailroom to the corporate offices of one of the major health insurance providers in America. My mother worked as an executive secretary for one of the officers in the same company. Neither of them has ever volunteered the cause of their breakup, but I often wondered if the constant closeness got the best of them. You know, breakfast together in the morning, seeing each other as my father darted in and out of meetings, sharing the after-school chore of transporting their children from cheerleading practice to basketball games, and finally retiring to bed only to wake up and do the shit all over again. Or, maybe it was the fact that my sister had just graduated from high school and since I had finished two years earlier, they felt their job was done. After twenty years of marriage, my parents parted ways.

My sister Yvonne, who picks up the slack for my lack of emotion, took it the hardest. She was fearful of what was going to happen to her future since she was due to attend college out of state the following fall. She fussed and cried and literally threw a temper tantrum when we received the news that our family was no longer going to be "one." Luckily, our parents decided to tell us over dinner at home and not the restaurant we had faithfully visited every other Friday for as long as I could remember. Trust me, Yvonne would have thrown her hissy fit either way. I, on the other hand, tried to calm their youngest daughter down.

It was a rough summer for all of us. I continued my sales clerk position at the department store that I started working at after I graduated high school. Yvonne completely put her studies on hold and began working as a checkout girl at a grocery store. Six years later, she's the store manager and hasn't picked up one college book to date.

I know my parents carry a tremendous amount of guilt for their divorce and continue to try to make unnecessary amends with us. The both of them shower Yvonne and me with gifts and spoil us like little kids at Christmastime. My best friends, Tori and Vanessa, tease me about my lavishly furnished apartment, compliments of my parents, along with the brand-new Toyota Camry they gave me for my twenty-sixth birthday. All while I continue to work part-time (yep, at the same department store) and attend school part-time. I'm still trying to figure out what I want to be when I grow up and I'm taking my slow, sweet time doing so.

Although I had little experience caring for babies beyond playing mom with my dolls as a kid, I initially considered a career in neonatal nursing. But after watching a *Nova* tape in class and seeing an actual delivery, I quickly cast that thought aside. Being the natural-born klutz I am, I visualized myself taking hold of this innocent newborn creature and just as he or she takes its first breath of life, the slippery little fucker slides out of my gloved hands onto the floor. The doctors, nurses, and parents demand my immediate beheading.

Then I considered majoring in fine arts, focusing on

fashion design. But while I could easily put together a DKNY outfit for the mannequin on the floor display of the store, turns out my actual fashion *creativity* was minimal. So I decided that wasn't my niche. Then there was mass media communications. "You'd be great in front of the camera," everyone would always say. Simply not my thing, either. I won't even go into what happened the first time I had to do an impromptu report on the 2000 presidential election in front of my class last spring. I could tell by the what-in-the-hell-is-she-taking-about look on everyone's faces, they were trying to figure out if I was following the same Gore-Bush election as they were.

So this fall I'm taking my first course in social welfare. Long ago I settled my prerequisites, so if my ass can decide on a major, I'll be well on my way to graduating.

Fortunately, I have a patient family, friends who support me, and a guy who loves loving me, degree or no degree. As of right now, I'm content with life. I'm twenty-six years old, in great shape, and have no addictions, except for the occasional face-to-face meeting with my toilet bowl after one too many apple martinis. Overall, most days I feel like nothing could go wrong. Knock on wood.

2

Tori, Vanessa, and I started our Monday morning off as usual at the Bally gym on the northeast side of downtown Milwaukee. I don't do the workout thing any other day, but we meet Monday mornings to energize ourselves for what work, school, and life have in store for us over the next seven days. For some reason we believe getting all hot and sweaty and wearing ourselves out on the worst workday of the week is a beneficial thing to do. But it's more like self-torture; well, at least the shit is for me. Most people know to sleep until the last possible second on this dreaded day, while we choose to get up a whole hour and a half early.

Like so many gyms, the place is a hot spot for those with or without significant others looking for a little bit of body watching. I, myself, am able to tune out the six-four, bench-pressing, tight-short, bulge-protruding men in the place. Takes a little concentration, you know, but I handle it. On the other hand, it's a perfect place for Tori, whose lusting eye is always on alert.

I had just finished thirty minutes on the treadmill when

Tori walked over to me dressed in an outfit more suited for the beach than the gym. Her tattoo of a chocolate-dipped strawberry glistened as sweat rolled down her not-quite-Janet six-pack. She leaned on the treadmill, ass in the air, and struck a pose for the hottie behind her, who tried not to gawk as he worked his biceps.

"Ky, it's a good thing you didn't come out with us on Saturday," Tori said. "Girl, the men in Liquid were scary as hell and I about wanted to die when one of my daddy's frat brothers tried to talk to me."

I dried the sweat on my forehead with the back of my hand and looked at her in shock.

"What? Your dad's friend?" That was sick.

"Well, no," she explained as she switched her weight from one leg to the other, intentionally creating a subtle ass-wiggle, almost causing her admirer to drop his weight and break his toe. "But he was old enough to be my daddy. You know what I'm saying, girl."

That's Tori for you. I often have to repeat what she says in the form of a question to clarify what she means. She's good for exaggerating the truth or implying something was a certain way when it really wasn't. Then when you confront her, she laughs and says, "Well, that's not what I *really* meant." Yes, she's one of those embellishing people but you have to love her. Tori has more personality and charisma than anyone I know.

"Okay, so what happened?" I asked, feeling better that it wasn't really her daddy's friend that was eyeballing her.

"Well, I'm out on the floor shakin' my ass all by myself because you know I got it like that. Plus, it lets all the men know that I'm available. Right? So here comes Joe Cool steppin' in my direction with his curly gray hair and flashing his yellow dentures and shit. Girl, he must have been at least fifty! He comes up rubbing his hands together and licking his lips like he's about to eat a damn piece of fried chicken. I turned around and started dancing with the wall, hoping his ass would get a clue. Next thing you know, I felt his hands on my hips and felt his hot-ass breath on my neck. He leaned into my ear and told me I looked like a fudge popsicle and he couldn't wait to lick me up and down."

I couldn't help but laugh. Especially with the wide-eyed expression of disbelief on her face as she told me the story.

"So I turned around and looked him dead in his blood-shot eyes. I told him that my chocolate was indeed good, but a brotha like him would get lost in the creamy filling." She rolled her eyes and snapped her fingers. "Girl, he looked even more excited! That's when I knew it was time to exit. What's a man that old doing in the club anyway? Shit, I'm damn near too old myself, but at least I'm still in my twenties. I'm probably as old as his damn daughter."

"So what did you do afterward?" I asked, half afraid to hear the answer. My girl had a new after-the-club story every other weekend.

"I was hungry so I stopped at the diner a few doors over to grab a cheeseburger. Marla's ass went home because she and Mom had to be at church at the crack of dawn. Now for *her* to be the club-hopping age, she sure doesn't act like it. I got a boring-ass sister," she sighed. "Anyway, there was a group of fellas who had left another club early so I struck up a conversation with the finest one of them. His boys finally left because he was taking too long with me. We exchanged numbers and, girl, he called me when he got home, talking about he wanted to see me again. So I let him come over at two in the morning. Need I say more?" she asked as a sly smile graced her lips.

That was also Tori for you. My girl has had more men than me, Vanessa, our cousins, and our cousin's cousins put together. I used to worry about her and her endless sexcapades, but once I realized that it's her life, and if she's content with her rendezvous, then I shouldn't worry about her. She's a strong, independent woman who enjoys the company of men and a "good session of hot, butt-naked fuckin' " as she puts it.

Fortunately, she protects herself in more than one way. The girl keeps condoms in her nightstand, the kitchen drawer, bathroom cabinet, wallet, car, and in her desk at work. She never lets a man near her precious goodies unless he's wrapped up nice and tight. Thank the Lord for that.

Second, she has a dog that has fooled plenty of men. His name is Sparky but the little horror is more like Cujo. She intentionally gave the dog a soft, gentle name because most people will assume Sparky is a Chihuahua or some little harmless dog with no bite. He's just the opposite. Sparky is a ferocious pit bull that obeys Tori's every command. If she says, "Sit," he sits. If she says, "Go," he leaves with his head down. And with the simple command, "Get him," Sparky will latch on to the leg of any victim Tori requests.

The dog only got Tori into trouble once. When she has company, she leaves Sparky in his bedroom (yes, a whole bedroom to himself). Tori brought Mr. Michael Jones home with her after an evening of clubbing and booty-grinding on the dance floor. After Michael confessed that he had to hurry up because his pregnant girlfriend was waiting at home for him, Tori wasn't feeling his company any more and asked him to leave. Well, Michael didn't want to hear it and told her he wasn't going anywhere after she had gotten him all pumped up and ready for some loving. She gave him one more chance and kindly asked him to leave again. That's when he picked up a picture of Tori's grandmother off her coffee table, threw it against the wall, and told her he couldn't stand cock-teasing bitches.

Unfortunately for Mr. Jones, that was a mistake. Before he could blink once, Tori had opened Sparky's door, and call it instinct or what, Sparky headed straight for Michael's nuts. Now my girl isn't completely heartless, so she made Sparky release him, but Michael cried and crawled his way out the door and straight to the emergency room.

Tori rewarded Sparky with leftover steak for a job well done, made herself some coffee, and waited for the arrival of the men in blue. Mr. Jones dropped the charges when he realized he didn't have a case. Tori had left the broken picture frame and glass just as it had fallen after it crashed against her wall. For added effect, she disheveled her hair, poked a hole in her stockings, and sniffed an onion until her eyes were bloodshot red from crying. We still laugh about Michael Jones to this day.

"Where is Vanessa?" I asked, looking around. "I'm ready to go."

"Girl, she's probably over there interviewing the alderman. You know her ass is always working."

Sure enough, there she was, over by the StairMasters, deep in conversation with our first district alderman. Vanessa is a workaholic. That woman can fit thirty hours into a twenty-four-hour day. I admire her energy and determination. Wish I could bottle it up and save a little bit for myself.

Vanessa is a journalist-slash-reporter for our local newspaper. And she is more than good; she's great. She's an excellent communicator and spends weeks researching and investigating before reporting a flawless story. She hopes to work her way to television and I'm one hundred percent sure she will. I encourage her to move south to Chicago, since it's a bigger city with more exposure, but Vanessa's waiting for her fiancé Roger, to finish his master's degree in finance and then she might consider a move. Both Tori and I are so proud of her because we believe she's going to follow in the footsteps of her icon, the one and only Oprah.

Vanessa will stop just about anything to rush home to watch Oprah's daily talk show. And if she knows she can't be home on any day, you better believe her VCR is set for the 4:00 PM time slot. She analyzes Oprah's interviewing skills, her interaction with the audience and Oprah's reactions to some of the crazy things people say or do when they get on national TV. Sometimes the girl even takes notes, so I know she's serious about her job.

Tori and I headed to the locker room, leaving Vanessa to follow when she was ready. I halfway listened to Tori chatter on about the size of her one-night stand's dick and the magical things it did to her body. The girl talks about sex like she has penis on the brain 24-7.

As I walked toward the shower, soap in hand and towel wrapped around my body, I envied the confidence of the women who walked around naked as if they were in their own private bathroom at home. Breasts of all sizes bounced around me and I kept my eyes lowered, trying not to acknowledge any of them. Some were small, some large, and some were hanging a little low from extra skin after childbirth. I've always been fascinated with women's bodies and what we are capable of doing. To be able to reproduce and bring life into this world is awesome! And men have the audacity to feel dominant when we're the ones who brought their asses into this world? What in the hell kind of sense does that make?

"So what class are you headed to, Kyla?" Tori asked me.

"This class is Introduction to Social Work."

"Social work?" she practically screeched. "Girl, do you know how broke your ass will be? And how stressful that kind of work is? You sure you want to do that kind of shit? Girl, you better pick another major," she instructed.

By the way, Tori curses like her dad was a navy sea captain and she was raised on the ship. She's making an effort to tone it down, but not successfully.

I had to break it down to her, the reasons behind my choice of study.

"I thought I would give it a try," I explained. "There are so many underprivileged children in the world that experience things in their childhood that we can't even imagine. Those are the kids I want to protect. It's not their fault that they were born into certain unfortunate situations; and they didn't even ask to be here in the first place. It's not fair to them, and those kids deserve the same chance kids like us had.

"A woman at work told me about a nine-year-old girl who committed suicide. Her dad was molesting her as long as she could remember and her mother did nothing but get annoyed when the girl came to her for comfort. She got her dad's gun one night before he came to her and she shot herself in the head. Now tell me there's not something wrong with that picture. It's just not right!"

"Well, damn, Kyla, okay. I hear you. Good luck, girl. You sound pretty passionate about it." She picked up her bag and headed for the door. "Call me later and tell me how the class went. I'll be at the restaurant until nine."

"All right, Nictoria," I said, teasing her, calling her by her given name.

She rolled large doe eyes at me.

"Don't call me that damn name! I don't know what in the hell my mother was thinking."

Me, either.

Tori was the manager of Eden's, one of the hottest, most popular restaurants in the city. The place is well known for its martinis and burgers, an unusual combination. But she knew how to keep the crowd coming. She hired only the best waiters, most skilled bartenders, and attractive hostesses. She once told me that her hostesses are instructed to sit attractive people up front, since the front of the restaurant is all windows. I told her that was discrimination and her reply was a quick, "So." Jeff and I spend most Friday nights at the restaurant with Tori, Vanessa, and Roger.

After getting dressed I waved at Vanessa on my way out of the gym. She held up a fake phone to her ear, pointing at me, telling me she would call me later. Then she turned her attention back to the alderman.

I was so used to the drive from the gym to the campus of the University of Wisconsin-Milwaukee, that I could drive the route blindfolded. I arrived to the first class right on time. The professor, Mr. Jelenchick, had just introduced himself and asked us to go around the small room and introduce ourselves, like we were in third grade. I let out a low groan and tried not to feel negative about his request. But, damn, I was in college, right?

A nervous girl, who looked like this was her very first class in college, spoke first. "Hi, my name is Trisha and I'm a freshman and I took this class because I want to help people and I think this might be a start to that . . . somehow . . . I think," she said.

"Okay, Trisha, welcome. Hopefully, you'll find some of the answers you're unsure about in this class," Mr. Jelenchick responded. "Next," he continued, looking at the young man seated next to Trisha.

"Hi, I'm Harold. I'm also a freshman. I'm here because I needed another class to get into for financial aid and this one was open so I figured, why not?"

We all laughed at Harold's honesty. Even Mr. Jelenchick laughed before speaking. "Thanks, Harold. Welcome and I appreciate your honesty. And I hope that as we venture into the true definition of social work that you might see the benefits of this class for your life and the world around you."

This continued on with three others before it was my turn.

"Hi, I'm Kyla Thomas," I began. "I'm twenty-six and in my junior year. I've been with the university on a part-time basis since I was eighteen and I'm taking this class because I want to assist others with having the chance to live their lives to the fullest without any hindrance of poverty, lack of self-esteem, or lack of awareness of the opportunities available to them."

"Thank you, Kyla. That was quite a bit, but good," he said, smiling. "Hopefully, you'll get the inspiration you need to complete your degree in social work."

The only other person around my age was Stephanie, an attractive African-American female who spoke after me. She spoke with intensity and earnestness in her voice.

"I decided to enroll in school and major in social work after my son's experience spending the night at a friend's house. He and his friend were so engrossed in PlayStation that his poor friend forgot to take the garbage out. His friend's mother beat him until his back and legs were welted. My son, Jaron, came home terrorized by what he saw, and his friend was so embarrassed that he avoided Jaron at school from that point on. So I took that opportunity to talk to Jaron about differences in households and that although he and I may not be rich, we should count our blessings for what we have in each other. And I reported the incident to the school counselor."

The entire class was touched by her story, Mr. Jelenchick particularly, pleased that someone in the class shared the passion he felt for the field. He said, "Welcome, Stephanie. You sound like someone destined to make a change. Well, let's get started."

We all pulled out folders, notebooks, and pens, and began listening to his lecture. He spoke for two hours, interrupted by numerous questions from the class, and dismissed us thirty minutes early with a reading assignment. The youngsters, and even Mr. Jelenchick, packed up and left the class in less than a minute. I slowly gathered my handouts together since I wasn't due at work until noon and it was only 10:15.

Stephanie lingered behind also. I could feel her staring at me while I jotted a few extra notes on my notepad. Should I look up at her and say hello, or ignore her and pretend like I didn't have peripheral vision? And if she wanted my attention, why didn't she just say something?

When I zipped up my backpack and stood to leave, I smiled at her.

"So what do you think of the class?" she quickly asked, making it obvious that she had been waiting for me to make eye contact.

"It seems like it will be informative, but pretty basic," I said, shrugging. "I think we'll dig into the nitty-gritty stuff with the later courses."

"Probably. This field is so much different than what I do now. I'm a little nervous," she confided.

"Oh, what do you do?" I asked, suddenly curious, removing my backpack from my shoulder and placing it back on the table.

"I'm a human resources specialist."

"Yeah, that's very different," I agreed. "Corporate America, huh?"

"Yes, and I'm beginning to realize that it's really not my thing. Too much politics and I don't want to play the game anymore, you know? I mean, I enjoy interviewing and helping people find suitable jobs, but I see and meet a lot of people and it's quite disturbing to watch some of my coworkers interview people they're not familiar with and then those people don't get jobs they're well qualified for. You know what I'm saying?"

"I hear you. Well, we'll be going through this together. Anyone can tell by my résumé that I'm still working on finding my calling. But I feel this really may be it. The money doesn't bother me," I said, recalling Tori's statement from the gym. "As long as I feel good about what I'm doing and I'm actually helping someone, that's all that matters to me."

"I agree," she said. "I think you have to have a strong personality for this type of work and need to be able to deal with all kinds of people."

"Definitely," I said and looked at my watch. "I better get going. I have to be at work at noon and I want to grab a bite to eat before I go."

"Oh, I'm hungry too," she said and started to pack her papers like she was in a race and the gun had just been fired. "Do you mind if I join you?"

I was going to call Tori and hit her up for pancakes, but I could pass. Stephanie seemed like a nice enough person.

"Sure, but please, not in the student union. I save that for near-starvation emergencies only! How about the Nook? You know that little restaurant over by Clooney Park? They serve the best breakfast casserole."

"I'll meet you there in fifteen minutes," she answered happily.

"Okay."

We headed different directions to our cars, and since I didn't want to dwell on my reading assignment already, I thought about her on my walk. She sure was an outgoing person, wanting to come to breakfast and not knowing me from Adam. I, unlike her it seemed, have never been good with new friendships and opening up to people. I've been best friends with Tori and Vanessa since third grade and none of us ever felt the need to form another sisterhood with anyone else.

All these years, the three of us have practically been attached at the hips. In grade school, we had our own private club, appropriately called "OSC" (our secret club) that allowed no members but us. Even with the eager requests from our classmates to join, we vowed that it was, and would always be, just us three.

In junior high, after Vanessa moved and transferred to a different school, she quickly transformed from close friend to cousin. You know how all of a sudden your best friend turns into your cousin and you start dressing alike? Well, that was us from ages twelve to fourteen, coordinating our pinstripe jeans and T-shirts with iron-on letters displaying our names on the back. Those were the days.

I drove behind Stephanie to the restaurant, reading and trying to figure out what the black letters on her license plate meant: *YES I AM*. Yes I am what? Happy? Crazy? Married?

Once we arrived at the Nook, we found a table for two and she ordered coffee while I sipped on water with a lemon wedge. I watched her add at least five creams and six packs of sugar to her coffee. She saw me looking and laughed.

"Bad habit. If you haven't started, I don't recommend it. I have two cups a day, and trust me, I'm feeling it if I miss one. It's truly addictive." She took a sip and licked her lips. "But so worth it!"

I laughed this time. "So how old is your son?" I asked.

"My Jaron is nine. He starts fourth grade today and he's a little angel." She paused a moment and replayed what she just said in her head. "Every parent says that, right?"

"Probably so, but that's okay. All parents should think their kids are fantastic. My little cousin is a doll, but her mom will tell you in a heartbeat that she's the devil in disguise. She says Brianna puts on a good front when other people come around."

"I believe it. Jaron likes to play into my emotions and he acts more spoiled with me than with anyone else. Kids are smart and they know how to get over on parents if you let them. I have to remind him, and myself sometimes, that I'm running the show."

The waitress came and took our food order. I was hungry and had a long day ahead of me at work so I ordered a bacon, sausage, and cheese casserole with hash browns and toast on the side. Then Stephanie ordered a blueberry muffin. I looked at her in disbelief.

"I thought you said you were hungry? No, you didn't just follow up with a muffin?"

She smiled and said, "To make up for the coffee."

"Whatever, girl. Don't be looking at my food all hungry-eyed when it comes."

"I can't have a little bite of bacon even if I ask nicely?" She winked at me and smiled, a cute smile with the right corner of her mouth turned upward.

"We'll see, but I'm pretty greedy. Luckily I worked out this morning."

"Really? Do you go to the gym?"

"Yes, only once a week with my two girls."

"Well, once a week is better than nothing. I started working out every other morning at home. The older I get, the harder it is to maintain my weight. I'm twenty-seven and my metabolism is already starting to slow down," she said, sounding a bit frustrated.

I was so glad she told me her age because I was dying to know. And since I'm not too fond of telling my life story to strangers like some people I know, I decided to ask her more questions to divert the conversation away from me.

"So how did you get into HR?" I asked her.

Stephanie's voice was raspy, reminding me as she spoke of Demi Moore. "I started working half days my senior year of high school as a file clerk, handling miscellaneous clerical duties, making copies, ordering supplies, that kind of stuff. I took on a full-time position after graduating, with the intention of attending college at night. Only, I got pregnant shortly after graduation and college was put on hold. Since then, I've worked my way from a file clerk to office assistant to performing interviews for entry-level positions. Now I handle interviews for some of the highest positions in the company."

Her story reminded me of my dad.

"It's funny," she added, "because here I am, a young black woman without a degree, hiring Bill and Tom into management positions. Some of my coworkers aren't happy that they spent four years at a university and yet we have the same position. But I've been there ten years and earned my position. I put a lot of work into that place for myself and for Jaron."

Her eyes seemed to twinkle every time she said her son's name. I examined every inch of her face as she continued to talk. She was a very pretty woman with honey-colored skin that sprinkled a handful of toasted freckles around her nose. Her almond-shaped eyes were a piercing light brown that sparkled in the sunlight and widened when she spoke intensely. She had long, dark eyelashes that even Twiggy, the most famous supermodel of the 1960s, would envy. Beneath her red lip-lined pouty lips was a set of straight white teeth that I assumed only braces could have perfected. Her hair was a wavy texture that she wore pulled back in a ponytail that hung down her back. Being slightly taller than me and with a body you'd think she paid for, she easily could have graced the cover of *Vogue*.

She must have asked me a question because her silence and stare brought me out of my trance.

"I'm sorry, Stephanie, what did you say?" I blinked.

She didn't answer, only smiled and continued to stare at me. I didn't know what to say and her stare made my stomach flip like I had just gone down the steepest roller coaster in the world. I was grateful when the waitress arrived and interrupted the unusual exchange. I dug into my casserole, a little embarrassed, and kept my eyes lowered for at least a minute. She eventually broke the silence.

"So, what do you do, Kyla?" she asked.

"Well, nothing like you, that's for sure," I answered. "I work in the women's department at Newtons. I've been doing that since high school and I think I've been there longer than most everyone. I don't know how many people make careers as a department store clerk."

"You're doing what you have to do to make a change, so don't even worry about how long you've been there," she encouraged me. "It won't be forever. But, in the meantime, can a girl use that discount of yours?" she teased.

I smiled. "Do you know how many times I've been asked that question?" I thought for a moment while looking into her warm eyes. "But for you, I think I'll make an exception."

"Why, thank you," she said, grinning. "So can I get that piece of bacon now?"

"How much do you want from me?" I laughed. "Here," I said, breaking off a piece of casserole with a chunk of bacon and placing it on her plate. "Is that good?"

Stephanie quickly ate the bite. "Tasty," she said with a light, playful smack of her lips. "Much better than the muffin."

"Next time order some real food then, okay?"

"Oh, so you'll have me for breakfast again?" she said, smirking.

What? "Um, yeah, I mean, sure," I stammered. "We can go out to eat again," I said, smiling inside, unsure why.

"Wonderful," she responded. She finished her muffin, and I devoured the rest of my casserole

"Thanks for letting me join you," she said after the bill arrived and we each placed our money on the table. "I'm off on Mondays so I have to get back to school for my afternoon class. How many other classes do you have?"

"One more on Wednesday mornings."

"Okay, well, I'll see you next week."

"I'll be there," I said.

"Bye, Kyla."

"Have a good week, Steph. Can I call you *Steph?*"

"Girl, that's fine."

"Take care," I said as we walked to our separate cars, mine parked along the side of the restaurant, hers directly opposite mine with our rears facing each other.

I sat in my car and began to touch up my makeup. I stopped, though, to watch Steph through my rearview mirror. She picked up her cell phone, listened intently for a moment, and then ended the call. Suddenly, she looked in her rearview mirror right back at me. I looked away quickly, then felt silly, so I looked back and waved. She waved back, put her car in reverse and pulled up next to my Camry. I lowered my power window.

"Hey, if you ever want to talk about class, give me a call," Steph said and then handed me her business card with her home number written on the back.

"I'll do that," I replied, placing the card in my purse.

She flashed those brilliant pearlies again and drove off. I smiled as well as I finished applying my lipstick. She seemed like cool people. I thought it would be nice to have someone close to my age in class. Usually the women were young, eighteen to twenty, or much older than me, fresh out of a divorce or returning to school after the kids moved out of the house. Steph was a definite welcome relief.

3

Jeff and I were sitting in Tori's restaurant with Vanessa and Roger. We usually spend Friday nights with our friends, winding down from the workweek and getting pepped up for the weekend. It's kind of routine, like Tori's, Vanessa's, and my Monday morning workout sessions, but the difference is that I truly enjoy this time together. The only workout I get here is raising my right arm to lift my glass and bring it to my thirsty lips.

The place was packed as usual, filled with everybody, from colleagues still socializing after work to those getting ready to hit the clubs. But our girl had reserved a table just for us, up front, of course. She planned to join us with her booty-call friend from the club after she finished up behind the scenes in the office. I couldn't wait to see this dude, even though I figured he'd be just another smooth-talking, mack daddy fella that we'd become accustomed to as her date.

"So, Ky, how was your first week of classes?" Roger asked me.

"Not too bad," I answered. "I have quite a bit of homework already, but I'm handling it. I think I may be on to something in this career."

"Glad to hear it," Roger replied. "My first week was busy as hell too. I need to be at home reading, but I wasn't about to miss out on the Friday night festivities," he said, taking a sip of his gin and tonic. "And definitely not miss out on spending time with my baby," he added, with a kiss to Vanessa's cheek.

Roger was a sweetheart, an intelligent black man, whose main focus in life was to please his women. And when I say *women,* of course I mean Vanessa, but I'm talking about his mama too. Yes, Roger still lived at home, bending over backward to cater to his mother's every need in between school, work, and Vanessa.

I've received many late-night phone calls from Vanessa, holding back her tears as she told me how Roger canceled their evening plans because his mama needed him to stay home to write her bills out because her wrist was hurting (carpal tunnel, she claimed). Or to unclog the basement sink so she could wash her favorite skirt to wear to her church meeting the next day (favorite doesn't mean *only* skirt, does it?).

But even though Roger's mother had hidden the scissors to cut the apron strings and he was tucked neatly inside the pocket, Vanessa loved him dearly and agreed to marry him, mama and all.

"Hey, *V,* I met a girl in class that's also majoring in social welfare," I said. "We're about the same age so I think we'll be good leaning partners."

"Good girl," she said, patting my hand. "We need someone else to keep you headed in the right direction."

"I am," I said defensively. "I feel like something good is going to come out of this." I raised my martini glass. "Here's to my degree and Roger's success in grad school."

"Cheers," we all said in unison.

Tori joined us an hour later with Doug, the infamous one-night stand. What I learned so far is Doug is a twenty-five-year-old truck driver with a silent wish to become a porn star. Only Tori could get a man to admit that kind of shit. Unfortunately, knowing this about him and knowing Tori's own sexual prowess, I had a hard time engaging in conversation with him. I kept picturing them having sex and it was seriously disturbing me. I kept laughing to myself while Jeff looked at me like I had just escaped from the insane asylum.

Later, I mouthed to him numerous times throughout dinner.

We moved our party from the restaurant to Maxima, a hip-hop club on Water Street, a strip downtown known for barhopping. Tori and Doug headed straight to the dance floor for some foreplay, while Vanessa and Roger searched through the crowd for a table.

"Doug wants to be a porn star," I blurted out when Jeff and I were alone. I couldn't hold it in any longer.

He raised his eyebrows and smiled. "I'm sure Tori's got him working like he's a star already. From the stories you've told me and what Mac used to say, she wouldn't do so bad in the industry herself."

I punched him in the arm and stuck my tongue out to shut him up. Mac was one of Jeff's Kappa brothers that Tori just had to have, once she laid eyes on him; a short, tawny-colored man with flirtatious green eyes, a red 325i, and a fierce dedication to his fraternity, rarely seen without sporting his Greek letters. They used to hit the sheets pretty often until Mac moved to Indiana with a job transfer. Personally, I believe Tori was disappointed when he left, but she would never tell us that. Broken heart or not, Tori always had a man waiting in the wings for her. With her smooth chocolate skin, never unkempt short haircut and gorgeous face, it was never hard for Tori to find a man.

Jeff headed toward the dancing crowd, with me in tow, moving his head to the beat before his feet even hit the shiny black floor. We flirted with each other while we danced, and I let him get a couple of free feels by grinding my backside against him. He responded with subtle thrusts against my dress, heating my body and thrilling my senses.

We finally headed back to his apartment around one in the morning. Jeff lived in newly remodeled apartments on the southeast side of the city, where the early stages of new development of condominiums and restored warehouses were beginning.

Once inside Jeff's bedroom it didn't take long for me to slip out of my dress and Jeff to come out of his pants. He laid me on the bed and knelt at my feet. Jeff's tongue made its way from my toes all the way up to my ear. Slowly but intently, he was determined to please me. His breath was hot as his tongue dug deep into my ear, forcing an immediate tremble of my shoulders that sent a flutter straight down to the spot between my legs. I reached for his penis and guided him there. He entered me with ease, and tickled both my insides and outsides with each thrust. I twisted my hips in the way that pleased us both the most, and his face strained with pleasure as his momentum increased. He buried his face in my neck and his body shook as I felt him come inside of me before I did. He rested just a moment, then resumed his penetrations, still determined to please me. My body responded with a hard climax. Exhausted, we must have fallen asleep in that position because I felt him slip out of me and roll over about an hour later. I snuggled up close behind him and went back to sleep.

*   *   *

On Monday morning I was sweating bullets after running five laps around the indoor track at the gym, but Vanessa, fully energized like Popeye after a can of spinach, was chattering on about an upcoming interview with a prison inmate. We were now sitting side by side on the exercise bikes alongside the gym mirrors, which provided a full view of the gym and all of the crazy early-morning risers like ourselves.

"He's being released after his conviction was overturned for being wrongly accused of abducting and murdering a five-year-old girl," Vanessa explained. "He's spent the last twelve years in prison and was let go because the actual killer came forward after getting life on another murder. Can you believe that?"

"That's crazy as fuck," Tori said. I agreed with a nod of my head.

"You don't know how exciting this is," Vanessa continued. "I'm getting the exclusive. My boss is working on getting the interview televised and who knows what will happen after that? Girls, my career might be going to the next level!"

I slapped her a high-five. "You go, girl! I knew you could do it."

"Thanks, Ky. Maybe I can get you two on the set. Would you like to be there when your best friend makes her claim to fame?"

"Girl, yes," Tori squealed.

A prison? A place full of horny men? That might not be a wise place for Tori to go. I grabbed my towel and left the exercise bike I had rested on. I was just sitting there pretending like I was about to do something on it anyway.

"All right, ladies, I have to hit the showers and get to class. I want to catch up to Steph before class starts," I said as I began to walk off.

"Steph? Who's that?" Tori questioned with a quick jerk of her head.

"She's another girl in my class. I thought I told you about her?"

"That was me," Vanessa corrected.

"Oh, right," I remembered. "She's real cool and I think we can help each other out this semester. You all keep reminding me that someone needs to keep an eye on me, right?"

"You got that right," Tori said, laughing. "All right, girl, I'll call you later."

"Bye, Ky," Vanessa said.

"See ya, ladies," I said, heading to the locker room, wondering why I was leaving a whole half an hour early to see Steph. I mean, we'd get together after class for breakfast so I could talk to her then, right? Still, I couldn't wait to see her to find out how her week had been. We seemed to click and I liked the way it felt.

The second week I was the first to arrive in class. I put my backpack in the seat next to mine and saved it for Steph. She arrived about ten minutes later and flashed that celebrity smile as soon as she saw me. Again, I felt myself teetering at the hilltop of a roller coaster with a flustered and excited stomach.

"Hey, lady, how are you this morning?" Steph asked brightly.

"I'm great. Just came from my usual workout," I answered. "And you? Had your morning boost of energy yet?" I asked, referring to her coffee.

"You know I have. I'll save the second for breakfast. We're still on, right?"

"Of course. Where to this week?"

"I enjoyed the Nook. Why don't we make that our spot?" she suggested.

"Sounds good to me."

Mr. Jelenchick arrived and started class and it seemed like he talked for hours. I couldn't wait to get out of there and get to breakfast, though I still couldn't figure out why I was so anxious to be alone with Steph. He finally dismissed us at 11:15 with a new reading assignment and our first paper due the following week. Steph and I couldn't get out of there fast enough as we met up at the Nook.

Steph and I found the same table in the restaurant. To start off, she ordered her coffee and water for me again. I looked at the menu trying to decide what I was going to have.

"I'm not pigging out today like I did last week. I'll gain a hundred pounds eating like that every week with you," I said.

"Girl, you look great! I can't imagine you worrying about your weight," Steph complimented.

"Thanks," I said. "My boyfriend actually once told me I could use an extra pound or two."

Steph put her menu down and leaned back into the cushion of the leather booth. I thought I saw her lips form a circle as if saying, "Oh." But as quickly as it happened, it was over, and she was smiling at me. She was always smiling. "That didn't bother you, did it?" she asked.

"No, not too much. I was surprised when he said it, though. But I appreciated his honesty. At least he didn't tell me to lose some weight. Now *that* probably would have hurt my feelings."

The same waitress from the previous week came to take our order. Stephanie ordered an onion bagel and I asked for a veggie casserole.

"Yeah, that would hurt anyone's feelings," she said, resuming the conversation. "What does your boyfriend do?" she asked.

I guess at this breakfast meeting it was my turn to open up.

"He's a civil engineer. He's been doing that for a little over three years now and he's very happy with it. He's one of those people that knew exactly what he wanted to do right out of high school. He went to college, got his degree, and the rest is history. I wish I had been that focused."

"Everybody moves at their own pace," she comforted me. "That's what makes people so interesting. We're all different. What if everyone looked the same, talked the same, lived the same lives? How boring would that be?"

"I never thought of it that way. It's just so easy to look at someone else's life and wish it was yours."

"The key is learning to be happy with what you have at the moment, and to be confident that you'll get yours when the time is right."

"Thanks. You're right," I said. Then I asked, "Do you have a boyfriend?"

She looked me directly in the eye and hesitated. Maybe I had gotten too personal or touched on a sensitive subject.

"I'm sorry. You don't have to answer that if you don't want to," I said in response to her reluctance.

"No, that's okay. No, I don't have a boyfriend."

"I know it can't be because no one is interested. Look at you," I said, admiring her perfect features. "You must have men lined up and banging at your door."

She laughed like I had just told a really funny joke. "If they are, I haven't been paying attention. I'm not trying to find a boyfriend."

"So my trying to play matchmaker is out of the question, huh?"

"Hell yeah! Don't even think about it," she warned quite seriously.

"Okay, just let me know if you change your mind. Jeff

has some pretty decent friends," I said, already trying to figure out who she would be a good match with.

"Jeff? Is that your boyfriend?"

I nodded, since I had a mouthful of food.

She took a bite of her bagel and didn't respond. She seemed to be contemplating something because she suddenly shook her head no.

"What's up?" I asked her after getting my food down.

"You just reminded me of a time when a friend of mine set me up on a blind double date with her boyfriend's cousin. I decided to meet them at the restaurant so I could make an escape if I needed to. And I barely made it through the appetizers before I pretended to use the phone and said I had to get home to Jaron."

"Was it that bad?"

"Girl, yes! He was such a typical man. Arrogant, everything was all about him, and he was so sure he was going to take me home that night." She paused, still thinking. "I don't know why my friend did that to me anyway. She knew I wouldn't be interested. I don't even know why I went."

"You don't date at all?" I asked her. Surely the girl had to have a little fun in her life.

"Sure, I date." And she left it at that. And I figured I wouldn't pry anymore.

"So what do you do when you're not working, at school or with Jeff?" she wanted to know.

"I usually hang with my best friends, Tori and Vanessa. Both of them are pretty busy with work, which is why we set our girl time for Monday mornings. We also get together on Friday nights. Other than that, next to homework, I spend time at home reading books or watching movies."

"Do you have any plans this weekend?"

"Friday night we'll be doing our group thing, and Saturday Jeff is headed up north for a conference. Tori is working, and Vanessa will most likely be preparing for her big news interview."

Her eyebrows raised in excitement. "Are you talking about Vanessa White?"

"Yes."

"For real?" she asked as her sparkling eyes widened. "We went to Eisenhower Middle School together. I love her work! I'm always searching the paper for her latest report. That girl does some serious investigative reporting. She's not afraid to ask the questions we all want answers to."

"I know, she's fantastic!" I thought for a moment. "It's a small world, isn't it?"

She nodded in agreement. "Girl, you know this city is small. Too small at times."

"I already told both of them about you. I'll have to let her know that you're one of her former classmates and admirers."

"You told them about me? What did you say?" She looked flattered.

"That I met this really cool person at school that I think can help me find my way," I said.

"Find your way . . ." she said with a smirk.

"Yes," I answered.

"Hmmm . . . oh, back to this weekend. On Saturday my department is having a picnic, and I was wondering if you were free to go."

Damn, this was only the second time I met the woman and she already wanted to hang out outside of class? Funny thing was, so did I.

"That sounds like fun," I said. "Do I get to meet the little man?"

"Yes, my baby is coming. Call me Saturday morning. We can meet at my place and I'll drive to the park."

"Here, take my number," I said grabbing a pen and writing my number on a napkin. "Department store clerks don't have cards."

"That's temporary," she responded. "Social workers do."

I held up my water in a toast (as you see, I toast to everything). It was time to go so I started gathering my things and so did she.

After we paid our bill, she surprised me with a quick hug when we stood up.

"See you Saturday," she said.

"Okay," I responded, smiling, my eyes glued to the floor.

Steph grinned at me as I passed her while she held the glass door open when we walked out. She seemed delighted by my unprecedented onset of bashfulness. I was thrown off by it too. I returned her smile with all the confidence I could gather at that moment and headed to my car.

Turns out that Saturday was going to hit a record high temperature of 95 degrees in September. And not a hint of a breeze, just hot-ass humid air.

I spent the first couple hours of the morning tidying up my place as best I could. My apartment was so small, I couldn't squeeze a new floor plant anywhere even if I wanted to. But it was worth the luxury of living within walking distance of the lakefront.

During my years of school, I also found that interior design wasn't a specialty of mine either; therefore, one of the members of the design team from Eden's helped me out, thanks to my parents footing his bill. Alvin was a fine gay white man who flirted endlessly and harmlessly with women about their boyfriends. He often threatened Tori that he could snag any of her men right out of her hands, and teased Vanessa that all he needed was five minutes alone with Roger in the men's bathroom and she'd find Roger desiring to marry him instead of her. He took special amusement in badgering me about Jeff, asking if he lived up to the notorious stereotype about black men. I had informed him that he could never turn my man out, that Jeff was dedicated to me and only me. I mean, who gets turned out at his age?

Because there wasn't enough room for a full couch, Alvin decorated the living room with a cream-colored leather love seat and chair, covering them both with large red and mustard pillows. A red and mustard–striped rectangular rug covered the hardwood floors, which held a glass coffee table covered with my favorite magazines, *Ebony* and *Essence*. I used to keep books on my table, but too many guests who borrowed the books and never returned them forced me to switch to magazines instead.

In the corners of the wall with the balcony doors stood two ceiling-high tree plants in orange baskets. Large black-and-white pictures ranging from Miles Davis to Martin Luther King, Jr. graced my walls between the black African masks I started collecting as a teenager. The room was definitely busy, and almost didn't match, but Alvin styled it based upon my favorite colors and the personality chart he had me complete.

Oh, last but not least, a wall-mounted, flat-screen TV hung on the wall in front of the love seat (um, I forgot, that was part of my birthday gift too). Jeff drooled over that TV for weeks after I first got it. He found any and every reason to come watch a basketball game during the play-offs, and would hop his ass out of bed to watch *Good Morning America* as soon as his eyes cracked open.

I had seen him off to his conference in Appleton early this morning, and since he would be gone until late Monday morning, I was glad I had someone to spend my Saturday with.

Considering it was going to be as hot as the Fourth of July and I was spending most of my day outside, I decided on a lightweight, knee-high khaki skirt with a white, scoop-neck cotton shirt with a low dip in the back. I hoped it wasn't going to be too revealing for a business picnic, but hey, emphasis on the word *picnic*. Silver earrings and white slip-on sandals completed the ensemble. I pulled my shoulder-length hair back into a ponytail, hoping it wouldn't be too hot on my neck.

I decided against the toast foundation I normally wore and opted for loose powder to control the shine. I accented my dark brown eyes with black eyeliner and mascara and finished up with copper lipstick. I packed my makeup bag for afternoon touch-ups and grabbed my car keys.

Steph lived on the northwest side of town in an apartment complex that used to have a waiting list to get a unit. Now they're lucky if they can get anyone in who isn't on rent assistance. The neighborhood had slowly become a more challenging place to live, and Steph expressed her desire to move when I called her this morning for the address.

I pulled into the complex and parked next to her Chevy Malibu. I saw an adorable young boy standing on a patio bouncing a basketball. I knew it was Jaron because he had the same striking light brown eyes as Steph. I got out of the car and walked over to him.

"You must be Jaron," I said, extending my hand to shake his.

"Yes, I am. Hi," he said politely.

"I'm Kyla. I'm coming to the picnic with you today. Is your mom inside?"

"Yes. I'll tell her you're here." He dropped his ball an inch away from my big toe and ran inside. He came back holding his mother's hand, guiding her in my direction. She approached me and gave me a gentle hug.

"You look nice today," Steph said, giving me the once-over. "I'm glad you could join us."

"Me too," I replied. "Can you believe this heat?"

"I know, it's crazy," she replied. "Let's go get this over with," she said as we walked to her car.

On the way to the park I talked to Jaron about fourth grade. He told me that fractions were new to him and that he hoped to understand them better soon.

I said, "Guess what? Math just happens to be my favorite subject, so if your mom doesn't mind, I can come and help you sometime."

"Can she, Mommy, can she?" he asked excitedly.

Steph grinned at him through the rearview mirror. "Of course she can."

During the drive I caught her sending affectionate smiles at Jaron through the mirror or while we waited at a stoplight. The love she felt for her son was evident.

Once we arrived, Steph parked in the lot at Brown Park, and we all walked to a crowd of employees and their families. I suddenly wondered what happened with the relationship between Steph and Jaron's father. She hadn't mentioned him yet. I figured he must have done her wrong, since she seemed so turned off to dating.

Steph introduced me to her boss, a tall, slim man with a strangely shaped head. He told me I could call him Dick. Go figure. There was only one other African-American there, a slender older man with a handsome face and salt-and-pepper curly hair. I got an odd vibe from him when he shook my hand. He looked at me as if he knew something I didn't know. It bothered me, so as we were preparing our plates of bratwursts and chips, I asked Steph about him.

"What's up with Mr. Man over there?" I said, pointing. "Is it me or did he look at me funny?"

"Jerome? Girl, he looks at everyone I bring around funny. He's been with us five years and he asked me on a date shortly after he started. I turned him down, and ever since, he's real shady with me. It's too bad, considering it's just the two of us. But when it comes to equal opportunity and affirmative action in the workplace, we know how to stick together."

"I'm glad to hear that. I'm always amazed when I meet an African American who doesn't believe in affirmative action. Can you imagine where we would be without it?"

"Back in the cotton fields," she said.

"You know? Sad, but true," I agreed.

Steph and I mingled for what felt like eternity in the heat. *So this must be what hell is like* was all I kept thinking while I was trying not to melt into the ground.

Most of her coworkers seemed overly friendly when Steph would introduce me. Some of them nodded their heads saying, "Oh, okay," as I shook their hands. And then I could feel their eyes burning a hole in my back when I'd turn around and walk away. I wondered what that was all about.

We finally found shade under an oak tree and sat while we watched Jaron play with the blond-haired children of Stephanie's coworkers. Of course he brought his basketball with him and I watched in amazement as he played other games without ever putting his treasured ball down.

"Looks like you have a future ballplayer over there," I said, admiring his skill.

"That child of mine hardly ever stops bouncing that ball," Steph said, smiling. "A basketball hoop will be a must when we buy a house, which will be very soon, hopefully."

I wiped my sweaty neck with my hand. "Girl, I'm about to fry!"

"Here," she said, taking a piece of ice and carefully wiping it across my open back. "How's that feel?"

I closed my eyes and let the dripping water cool my skin. When I opened them, Jerome was staring at me with a repulsed look on his face. What was his fucking problem? I turned toward Steph, and she answered my question before I could ask.

"Don't sweat him. He's just jealous it's not his back." Steph threw the ice into the grass and dried my back with a clean napkin. "I'll see these folks bright and early Tuesday morning, so I'm ready to go. Will you get Jaron for me?"

I went and played cans with Jaron while Stephanie said her good-byes. It sure had been an interesting afternoon, to say the least.

Getting into the air-conditioned car felt like stepping into a movie theater on a hot summer day. I laid my head back and closed my eyes. I didn't even realize I had fallen asleep until Stephanie turned the car engine off outside of her apartment.

"Welcome back, sleepyhead," she said when my eyes opened.

I stretched my arms and shook a kink out of my neck. "I didn't know I was so tired." I yawned. "Must be the heat."

"I feel it too, but if I take a nap now, I'll be up all night. And I don't want to be up all night unless I'm doing other things," she said deviously. "Do you want to come in for a while?"

I checked my watch. It was 5:30 PM and I didn't have shit else to do that night. "Sure, I can stay a while," I said as I

stepped outside of the car and walked toward her complex.

The atmosphere of Steph's apartment was warm and
inviting. Her living room was decorated in neutral, earth
tones with a soft brown leather couch and love seat. There
was a big-screen TV with PlayStation games sprawled in
front of it. Pictures of elegant African women hung on
her beige walls with a nude black marble statue of a
woman with upward outstretched arms next to the fireplace.

"This is beautiful," I said, touching the woman's face.

"That's one of my favorites. I have two more in my
room. A close friend of mine gave that one to me a long
time ago."

I sat on the plush couch. "Where did Jaron go?"

"Girl, he hopped out of the car before you opened your
eyes. He's over at the ball court, where else? Would you
like something to drink?" Steph asked.

"Do you have any cranberry juice?"

"With a twist of vodka?" she asked, grinning.

"I'll save that for later." I laughed.

She brought me a glass of cranberry juice and sat it on
the table.

"I hope you don't mind, Kyla, but I have to take a quick
shower. I don't like feeling this sweaty. I'll be out in five
minutes."

"Go ahead," I said.

Her shower gave me the opportunity to give myself a
tour of the rest of her apartment. The kitchen was small
but clean, with Jaron's schoolwork hanging on the refrigerator with magnets. A picture he drew of him and Stephanie
titled *My Family* hung in a magnetic frame. His bedroom was
every little boy's dream, decorated in dark blues and
greens with a racecar bed. I noticed there was no picture

of him and a father figure on his nightstand, though there were two of him and Steph.

I didn't venture into Steph's room, since that would have been way too bold on my part for this first visit. I went back to the living room to drink my juice. I looked at several pictures on the end table. A picture of Stephanie as a child, another young girl, and adults that must have been Stephanie's parents were in a silver heart-shaped frame. A picture of Jaron sat in a frame that read THIRD GRADE across the bottom. The picture that caught my eye was of Stephanie a few years younger. She had her arm around what I assumed was her mother's waist, and her other arm was around a beautiful woman about our age. Next to that woman was an older woman with similar features. Each woman was dressed in evening attire, smiling brightly at the camera as if a celebration were taking place. Steph came into the room just as I put the picture down.

"Beautiful picture. That's your mom?" I asked, pointing to the woman who looked like an older version of her.

"Yes. And that's Michelle on the right with her mom next to her. We had just come from an annual church dinner where her mom had been selected mother of the year. Not only had she raised fantastic children, but she led the youth group at church. She was a fabulous woman," she said, reminiscing.

"Why do you say *was?*"

"She died shortly after that picture was taken. Breast cancer. She didn't tell anyone until it was too late. She said she didn't want to worry everyone and that God was taking her when she was ready. She said it was her time."

"How sad. How did Michelle take it?"

She let out a loud exhale. "They were very close so she took it really hard. I tried to be there for her, but she wanted to deal with it alone." Steph studied the floor and then looked back at me with a faraway look in her eyes. "She eventually moved back to North Carolina to be with her father."

"Do you still talk to her?"

"Umm . . . not really. But I think of her often and pray that she's all right." She stared at the picture from across the room. It was obvious that she was close to these people.

We sat and talked about everything, school, music, and current events. I learned that she went to my rival high school and was a star athlete in track, though she never attended any other sporting events. This would explain why I didn't see her at the overcrowded basketball games between the two schools, even though I spent my last two years doing cheerleading routines at halftime. Her music interests ranged from R&B to rock to classical. She pulled out a Janis Joplin album and introduced me to one of the rocker's most famous songs, "Me and Bobby McGee." Steph also shared that one of her uncles was a well-known state senator who successfully implemented a health-care bill for the benefit of the unemployed. She was so easy to talk with and it felt like I had known her for years, not two short weeks.

Before we knew it, Jaron came in and announced he was ready for bed. I raised my eyebrows in astonishment because I had never met any child that willingly went to bed at a decent time, especially on a Saturday. Steph had him in check.

I looked at my watch and realized it was 8:30 PM and dark outside. The time had gone so fast. As Jaron went to get himself ready for bed, I took my glass to the kitchen and prepared to leave.

"Do you have to go?" Stephanie asked.

I wasn't really tired, but I figured I had taken up enough of her time already. I didn't want to wear out my welcome. "I just thought you might want some quiet time."

"I'd rather spend it with you. Please stay." She made an expression like a kid asking for a piece of candy. I just couldn't turn down that sweet face of hers.

"Of course I'll stay," I said, taking a seat back on the couch.

Shortly after Jaron was tucked in bed, Steph asked if I wanted to take her up on that shot of vodka in my cranberry juice. You know I just had to oblige. I was already feeling pretty mellow by the time we had downed our first round. I felt comfortable enough to ask her about Jaron's father.

"I was looking for a picture of Jaron's dad. Is he in Jaron's life?" I asked.

Without answering, Steph picked up my glass from the table along with hers and went for refills. Dammit. I guess I was prying again. She had already taken several sips from her glass before she returned. She sat down next to me with her head resting on the side of her hand.

"His father is in prison. And Jaron doesn't know who his father is, but I'll tell him someday. He's not ready for it yet," she finally answered.

"What did he do to end up in prison?"

She stared at me long and hard. For a moment it looked as if she were in another place, reliving a moment in her past. When she came back there was a mixture of sadness and fear in her eyes.

"He went to jail for rape. He was a rapist."

"Oh, Steph, I'm sorry."

Instinctively I reached and grabbed her hand. She held on tightly. I couldn't imagine how she must have felt when she realized the man she was dating was a rapist.

"What did you do when you found out? That must have hurt you so bad."

Suddenly, the look in her eyes went from sadness, to confusion, to pure amusement. First she smirked, and then smiled . . . a little chuckle escaped, and then she erupted into uncontrollable laughter.

"What?" I asked. I was confused now. How in the hell was that shit funny?

"It must be the vodka, Kyla, because it's really not funny," she said, holding the sides of her stomach. She wiped her eyes and went to grab a Kleenex from the bathroom. She stood at the entrance to the living room.

"He raped *me*, Kyla. I got pregnant from the rape."

I let out a loud gasp and covered my mouth. *Damn, Kyla!* I felt so embarrassed and completely ridiculous.

"I'm really sorry, Steph. I didn't put it together. I feel so silly," I said, looking down at my hands. I felt like someone had given me a two-piece puzzle that I wasn't able to put together.

"Don't worry about it. Eventually, I end up telling some people. There are times when I lie and tell people that he's dead. Usually that's when I know I'm not going to have a lasting relationship with someone." She sat back down next to me. "But when I feel close enough to tell someone, I do."

I was scared to open my mouth with the fear of something stupid coming out. She tugged at my ponytail.

"Don't feel bad, Ky. Really. How would you have known?"

"I know. I just don't like to invade people's privacy and you didn't have to tell me if you didn't want to. I was being nosy."

"You asked and I didn't want to lie to you."

I was glad she wasn't mad at me. But then I went ahead and let the vodka do more talking for me anyway.

"Is that why you don't date? You don't trust men anymore?" I asked.

"Right now I'm going to concentrate on Jaron, school, and work. But, remember, I didn't say I don't date. I just haven't had a relationship in a while. I haven't found too many people I'm interested in spending that kind of time with."

"You don't have anyone in mind?" I asked. She just smiled and sucked on an ice cube. I guess she was done opening up for the evening.

Still feeling bad about the misunderstanding, I decided to invite Steph over for dinner.

"Hey, Steph, how about you and Jaron coming by my mom's house for dinner tomorrow? We try to get together at least one Sunday a month to hang out and catch up. Usually it's just my parents, my sister, and me. But I'd love for you to join us."

"We don't have any plans tomorrow so we'd love to. What should I bring?"

"Don't worry about that. My mother has it all taken care of. I'll pick you up around three?"

"We'll be ready," she said.

By this time it was nearing midnight and definitely time that I get home.

"Let me get out of here, Steph, it's been a long day," I said.

Steph checked the clock on the end table. "You're right, it's late. And I told you I don't like to be up late unless I'm doing other things," she said with the corner of her mouth tilted upward.

"Yeah, okay," was all I came up with in response. We hugged good-bye and I could smell a hint of a soft, musky perfume behind her ears. It was a sensual, delicate scent against her skin.

I went to bed that night thinking about the warmth of Stephanie's personality, smile, and her tender embrace. I hugged my pillow tight in remembrance and fell into a peaceful sleep.

4

The next morning I phoned my mother to let her know that I was bringing guests. She asked if Steph was fat or skinny to make sure she had more than enough food prepared. Sometimes my mother can be a tad blunt—even tacky—with her questions and comments about people. Yvonne and I were used to it, but sometimes she'd catch unsuspecting folks off guard.

Dinner at Gladyce's was an event I always looked forward to. Partly because we were all so busy living our own lives that we didn't get to see each other very often. But mostly because I got to see my parents together. I guess no matter how old I got or how long a divorce had been in place, it still felt good to have a family gathering, even if it's only pretend.

Although both my parents seemed happy with their lives, I think they enjoyed the monthly gatherings just as much as Yvonne and I did. Only once did my dad make the mistake of asking my mother if he could bring a friend of his along. My mother said she didn't mind because her home was welcome to everyone. Well, almost everyone.

When my dad showed up with a female friend, my mother lost all her Christianity. That was one of the moments she caught an unsuspecting person off guard and it took several months of groveling for my dad to be invited to dinner again. So, despite the divorce, I guess my mother wasn't interested in seeing my father fancy another woman.

After I picked up Jaron and Steph, we rode to my mom's house and arrived to a spotless home that smelled of baked barbecue chicken, collard greens, macaroni and cheese, corn on the cob, and sweet potato pie. Sometimes I got overwhelmed with childhood memories when I entered Gladyce's house, the home I grew up in. Even with the new leather furniture and redecorated walls, I easily slipped back into a childlike mode.

My dad arrived shortly after we did and after introductions and a peck on Gladyce's rosy cheek, he took Jaron out for a game of horse. Stephanie and I were setting the dining room table when the interrogation began.

"How old are you, Stephanie?" my mother asked from the kitchen.

"Twenty-seven, ma'am," Steph replied.

My mother waved off Steph's attempt at politeness with a hand in the air. "Oh, don't *ma'am* me, honey. Gladyce, please. How old is Jaron?"

"He's nine."

I could hear Gladyce doing the math in her head and I anticipated the next question.

"So you're marr—"

I cut her off. "Looks like we're all set here. Steph, do you mind getting the men?"

Her expression was a look of relief and her eyes whispered, "Thank you." When she went outside to get Jaron and my dad, I cornered Gladyce in the kitchen.

"Ma, I know you'd like to get to know my friend, but let's hold off on the twenty questions with Steph, especially about Jaron's father. That's a sensitive subject and I just learned about it myself. Now isn't the time, okay?"

Gladyce almost looked hurt. My mom was such a sweet person and took delight in getting to know people. Her forwardness was a result of a true desire to be close to others.

"All right, honey. I wasn't trying to be nosy," she reasoned.

"I know, Ma. But we'll talk about it another time."

Yvonne arrived as Steph was coming inside with the men.

"Yvonne, this is my friend, Stephanie. Steph, this is my sister, Yvonne," I said as they shook hands. "And this young man is Jaron."

Jaron took hold of Yvonne's hand to shake it. "Hi," he said brightly.

"Hey, cutie," she replied. She turned her attention back to Steph. "You look so familiar to me," she said, thinking about where she may know her.

Steph thought for a moment with no recollection of Yvonne. "I'm sorry, I'm not sure. From where?"

Yvonne continued to stare at Steph. "I'm not sure either, but it'll come to me," she said confidently.

I finally gave my sister a hug before we finished setting the dining room table. Yvonne and I weren't what you'd call close sisters, although we loved each other tremendously and talked as often as our schedules allowed. But we just didn't have that much in common. When she wasn't busy making sure shelves we stocked and checking on the cleanup in aisle six, the girl spent all her time doing crossword puzzles and bowling with her league. I swear they bowled at least three nights a week.

Once, she convinced me to join the league because all her fat, beer-belly friends hadn't met the sister she talked about and wondered if I truly existed. I lasted two games.

I had enough squinting my eyes through the smoke to see the pins and slapping five every time someone got a spare or a strike. And when I busted my ass on a well-oiled lane, I was done. I quickly realized that one had to have a true love for the sport to participate in the game as often as she wanted me to. And I clearly was not the one. Give me a remote in one hand and a glass of wine in the other and I'm good to go.

When we sat for dinner, Jaron, far from a shy child, led us in a cute prayer, thanking God for the food on the table and for the new friend his mom found. We all wolfed down Gladyce's cooking until we were good and full. There's nothing like home cooking.

As we were cleaning the table and preparing to wash dishes, Yvonne blurted out, "Chickpeas." We all looked at her wondering what in the hell she was talking about. Her eyes were planted on Stephanie.

"You came into my store looking for chickpeas."

Steph thought for a moment until her mouth dropped open. "You've got a serious memory on you," she responded. "Yes, that sure was you that helped us find them. Wow, that was at least two years ago. I haven't made hummus in so long."

Yvonne looked proud. "That's my job. I never forget a customer."

"I'll have to make sure I shop at your store more often," Steph said.

Yvonne blushed. My sister took a lot of pride in running her store. Her goal is to be district manager within two years. At times, my parents urged her to go to school at least part-time, but it went in one ear and out the other.

After we polished off the sweet potato pie it was 7:30 and time to get Jaron home and ready for bed. I thanked my mother for a great dinner as usual. I told my dad I would talk to him soon, and Yvonne and I made lunch plans for Wednesday that week.

"You have a really nice family," Stephanie said as I pulled onto Interstate 43. "Thanks for saving me back there. You can guess I get that 'married' question a lot."

"I can imagine," I replied.

"It's easy to say, No, I'm not married. But then there are those people that won't let it end there. They want to know if I'm divorced or widowed, *anything* but never married."

Steph turned in her seat to find Jaron bobbing his head up and down and mouthing lyrics to whatever song was playing through the headphone of his CD player. "One time," she continued, whispering, "I actually told the truth to a woman I barely knew just to see her reaction. Told her I was raped coming home one night and got pregnant as a result. She laughed and slapped me on the shoulder and said, 'You're such a kidder.' I just walked away. I think some people really don't want to know about some of the things that go on around them. People are so good at saying such-and-such is a shame and how it's so sad that something bad happened. But rarely do these people step up to the plate and take a stand to prevent those things from happening again. I'm not going to be one of those people oohing and aahing a cause but doing nothing about it."

"I agree with you."

"That's why I want to concentrate on human rights," she said. "We all deserve the chance to live the best possible lives without society and politicians telling us what we can or cannot do with ourselves, our bodies, and our lives."

"Amen."

Steph seemed deep in thought as she looked out of the

window. I was glad to have someone like her to talk about these issues with. She helped me to feel more secure with the major I decided on.

"Do you think you'll ever get married, Steph? Don't you want to find a father for Jaron?"

She smiled to herself, a habit I noticed she had. Not a bad habit, though.

"I doubt it," she said, shrugging. "Every so often he seems a little sad when he talks about the camping trips his friends took with their dads. I'm trying very hard to fill any void he may have and I'm doing the best I can."

She paused and turned and looked directly at me. I tried to meet her stare but I didn't want to crash into the SUV in front of us.

"Plus, the chances of me finding a man I'd actually marry are slim to none. More like zero."

"Whatever, Stephanie. As pretty and smart as you are, any man would be lucky to have you."

She looked down and started picking her cuticles.

"Kyla, I know we've only known each other a couple of weeks, but I feel like we're headed toward a great friendship. So I don't want to feel like I'm keeping anything from you." She took a deep breath and stared at the sky through my open sunroof. "I don't *want* to marry a man. I'm gay."

I looked straight ahead at the freeway, then out of my side window and then back at her. It probably looked like I was shaking my head but I wasn't. I think I was in mild shock and I just couldn't believe it. Very quickly I replayed several of our conversations in my head and remembered how vague she was when we talked about her dating. She shared no stories of guys she dated or when her heart had been broken. Or her seeing a fine man in the elevator that she'd wished she had said hello to. Nothing. And that's when it really set in that her child was not the result of a union of two people in love, but rather an invasion of not only her body, but also a violation of her sexuality. Gay? How could she be gay? She was too pretty. It wasn't like I didn't know any gay people, but most of the gay women I had seen dressed like men. Here was a girl who could have any guy she wanted. Why would she want a woman?

All of these thoughts ran though my mind in about fifteen seconds, but I'm sure the silence felt like hours to Steph. I couldn't think of anything clever or funny to say to ease the tension, so for once I said exactly what I was thinking.

"That's fine with me, Steph. I like you for who you are, not who you like."

She looked so relieved. I was proud of myself.

"I should have known I didn't have to be nervous about telling you. I wanted to bring it up a while ago, but then again, I don't know why I feel like I have to announce it to people. I mean, straight people don't shake hands and say, 'Hi, I'm heterosexual.' You know what I'm saying? I shouldn't have to tell someone I'm gay to make sure they're okay with it. But if I don't, then they feel like I hid something from them when they find out. It's a silly game I have to play on a daily basis."

When we arrived at Steph's place, she picked up her black Coach purse, and the take-home plate Gladyce insisted she have.

"Are you sure you're okay, Kyla?" she asked cautiously.

"Oh, yeah, I'm fine," I said, hoping I didn't sound like I was trying too hard to be polite. "You're not the only gay person I know. You know, everybody has a gay cousin or uncle in the family!"

She laughed and winked at me. I winked back.

"See you in the morning," she said, smiling.

"Jaron, I'll see you soon for some one-on-one?" I asked as he got out of the car and took his headphones off. He looked at his mom for approval. She nodded.

"Okay!" he exclaimed.

I waited until they were safely inside her place before driving home, my head spinning. Stephanie's announcement came as a shock, but the biggest surprise was in *me*. The fact that she was gay made her even more intriguing. I wondered what it was like for her growing up gay. Did she always know she was like that? What did her parents say when they found out? Did Jaron know? I had a million and one questions.

Then I wondered if I somehow knew it subconsciously, but didn't want to acknowledge it for one reason or another. I liked talking with her, being close to her and looking into her eyes. And I felt butterflies whenever she winked at me. I felt different when I was with her, compared to when I was with Tori or Vanessa. Her naturally loving and nurturing personality made me feel comfortable in a way that made me want to be close to her. *Physically* near her.

I quickly stopped myself from analyzing the situation. What was I doing? In the last hour I had gone from having a good friend to questioning myself on whether or not I *liked* her, simply because she told me that she was gay. I needed to get a grip.

And I meant what I said about the gay cousin or uncle thing. In my family, it was my cousin David. David was my mother's nephew, the son of my Aunt Shari. David was the stereotypical gay male, "flaming" as he put it. He spent a lot of time with Yvonne and me when we were kids, and although he was four years my senior, we never had a hard time bonding. That's probably because he enjoyed playing "dress up" more than we did. I don't think any adults in the family ever questioned David's sexuality, so he never officially had to come out. Everyone just knew.

By the time I reached high school and was old enough to understand, David had graduated with the legacy of having been the first male to bring a same-sex date to the prom. Needless to say, he and his date were immediately ejected after trying to dance to Atlantic Starr's "Always." And if you were wondering, David and his date both wore tuxedoes, but David admitted he would have preferred a sequined spaghetti-strapped number.

Once home and preparing for bed, I remembered Steph's coworkers and their reactions when they met me, and now it all made sense. I realized they must have thought I was her new girlfriend. For a brief second, I was irritated with her for putting me in that position. I mean, I didn't want anybody thinking I was gay. But I guess that's what you have to put up with once you decide to have a gay friend. And not being her friend didn't even appeal to me.

Still, I hoped breakfast wouldn't be awkward the next morning. But why should it be? She was still the same person. Now I just knew that she preferred to sleep with women.

"So what's up with Dwayne? Or Dan? Or is it Damien?" I asked Tori Monday morning while we sat in the sauna.

"*Doug's* ass had to go bye-bye," Tori replied. "Girl, let me tell you. We all know I'm not one to say no to a little adventure, right? So, since his fantasy is to become a porn star, we pulled out the camcorder over the weekend for some rehearsing while we were at his house, okay? We stood the tripod real high so the camera pointed directly at the bed to get everything. Girl, so we were going at it really good . . . I'm on top, he's on top, can't tell whose leg is whose, that's how good the shit was! Afterward, I hopped in the shower and I thought he was out like a light. You know I wear 'em out like that, so I didn't doubt that his fool ass was really asleep. But then I hear his nasty ass talking while I'm in the shower. So I leave the water running and crack the door open a little bit to listen. I saw that mothafucka on the phone grabbing his dick, talking about, 'Yeah, I got another one for the collection, man.'"

She stood up and grabbed her crotch and mimicked his ghetto voice.

"I watched him take the tape out of the camera and put it in a box in his closet," Tori continued. "When he got in the shower, girl, I grabbed that tape and left. Do you know he had even written my name on it? There were at least twenty other tapes. I was so pissed! I picked up his treasured camcorder and threw it out the window before I left. You know I would have had Sparky all up in his ass had I been at home!"

Vanessa and I looked at one another, not knowing whether to laugh or sympathize with the girl.

"He started hittin' my cell phone up back-to-back when I was about two blocks away. I ignored it but I should have cussed his ass out! Girl, these men are a trip." Tori sucked her teeth. "I don't know how much longer I can take this shit!"

I felt bad for her. Sometimes I didn't know if Tori was happy with her one-night stands and meaningless relationships, or if it was all a front. I never knew her to admit that she wanted a boyfriend or even utter the word *marriage*. But I knew all that bed-hopping had to get tiring at times.

"Hang in there, *T,*" Vanessa offered. "I'm sure Mr. Right will come along soon."

Tori looked at Vanessa like she was insulted. "Mr. Right? Girl, fuck Mr. Right! I don't believe in that shit! I'll settle for a Mr. Right Now who isn't going to try to fuck me over! That's all I'm asking for. I don't believe in that *forever* shit. I'm not knocking your thing with Roger or Ky's relationship with Jeff, but I don't believe marriage is all it's cracked up to be. First of all, over half of all marriages end up in divorce, so obviously that says something about the shit. Second, most relationships get boring as hell after a couple of years, anyway. I can't imagine fifty years with the same man. That's like eating the same shit for dinner every night. Eventually you get sick just by the smell of it."

I looked around to see if the new arrivals into the sauna had tuned into the delightful conversation we were having.

Vanessa got defensive. "But what about the simple idea of being in love? Finding your soul mate? There's a certain comfort in knowing there's someone who thinks the world of you and would do anything to be next to you. For myself, there's comfort knowing I'll have someone to come home to every day. I can share all my feelings and experiences with one person only. I have someone to lean on when I need support and I have someone to hold me when I'm scared, or to encourage me in a new endeavor. And what about making a family and sharing the joys of parenting with someone? I find a lot of comfort knowing I'm going to spend the rest of my life with one person. It's something I look forward to."

Tori rolled her eyes, a real bad habit of hers. "Girl, did you hear how many times you just said *comfort?* That's my point. The shit gets *too* comfortable. Routine. Eventually it will be the same shit, just a different day."

Vanessa just shook her head at Tori. "Well, just make sure you're in a bridesmaid dress at *my* wedding, celebrating *my* joy at beginning a new part of *my* life."

Tori calmed down. "You know I wish you and Roger all the happiness in the world, *V.* Maybe you'll be one of those rare success stories. Knowing you and your determination, you and Roger will grow old together with about ten kids and fifty grandkids. You go ahead and do your thing, girl!"

We all laughed. We were proof that the saying "birds of a feather flock together" doesn't always apply. It was possible that Vanessa would stay married for the rest of her life, while Tori continued to freak all the men she could until her coochie got too old and wrinkled to handle it. But nothing would stop us all from being friends. Unless Tori were to try to freak Roger or Jeff, and that wasn't a possibility.

Tori always maintained a safe distance from the men that Vanessa and I dated. And she never would cross that line, because we all know it's not hard to find a man. You can go to the mall and pick one out, just like picking out a new pair of shoes. But a true friend is harder to come by. And, anyway, who wants a man that's been all used up by your friend? You know everything he's doing to you, he's done to her. I don't understand women who ruin friendships over sexing the other one's man. Pointless.

"While we're on the subject, how are the wedding plans coming?" I asked Vanessa.

Vanessa closed her eyes and sucked in a deep breath of air. "Oh, girls, I don't even want to talk about it! You know how organized I am, so it's really hard for me to allow so many other hands and opinions all up in this thing." She started talking really fast. "Roger's mom wants the wedding at her church, but my grandmother wants it at hers. And my mother suggested an outside wedding, since the weather will have just changed and a warm day might sneak in. Now you know I can't go on a *might*, so outside is definitely not an option. I love my granny and all, but her church just isn't big enough. So we may end up at his mother's church, which will make her all too happy. We

BankofAmerica

For Customer Service call
1-800-432-1000

Find the right Home Loan for you at:
bankofamerica.com/yourhome

07/02/10 15:05 INYN4712

XXXXXXX9728
*1580 FLATBUSH   NY
BROOKLYN

Deposit to   Savings
To PRIMARY

Ser. No. 8627
Check Deposit Amount $96.00

Check No. 115747

THE BANK OF NEW YORK
OF NEW YORK

PAY

TO THE

Part of the check image has been
Obscured for security reasons

Total Deposit
Posts On
Sav Available Balance

still haven't decided on a place for the reception or whether or not to have a band or a DJ. We want to have the band "Underground," but we also know some people may want to have some serious dancing going on with some hip-hop and R & B. I know it's our day, but we want everyone to have fun at the same time. I just don't know, I'm about to lose my mind," she said, sounding completely distraught and out of breath.

Whoa, I thought she didn't want to talk about it? I didn't say that, though.

"You're right, Vanessa. You're going to go crazy if you try to please everybody. Do something that will be special for you and Roger for *your* wedding day. And if anyone doesn't like it, that's their problem."

"I know, Ky. But it's hard because I don't want to deal with the attitudes that may arise."

"From the sound of it, everyone isn't going to be satisfied anyway, so you may as well go ahead and start making your own decisions. And while you're at it, make sure my dress isn't too low in the back, because I don't want my birthmark to show."

She knew I was teasing her. "Whatever, Ky!"

"I have to get the hell up out of here," Tori said as she wiped sweat from between her breasts. "It's too goddamn hot." We got up and headed to our lockers.

"What did you do all weekend, with Jeff out of town?" Vanessa asked me.

"Oh, umm . . . I hung out with Stephanie." I grabbed my soap, washcloth, and towel and headed to the shower. I didn't know why I suddenly felt uneasy talking about her. I must have walked away too quickly and answered too vaguely because they both followed me. They knew me too well.

"So what did you do?" That was Tori.

"Let's see," I said, pretending I couldn't remember.

"Saturday I went to a picnic with her, and Sunday she came by Gladyce's for dinner. She brought her son along, and he and my dad had a great time playing basketball," I turned on the shower.

"You didn't tell me she had a kid," Tori said.

"I haven't said much about her at all," I confessed. "But, yes, she has a nine-year-old boy."

"That's cool. Is she trying to better herself by going to school?" Tori asked.

I didn't like her comment and I felt like I had to defend Steph.

"She actually has a well-paying job now in HR. She didn't get a chance to go to school when she was younger because of her son. Now he's a little older and she has the opportunity to get her degree. I think it's pretty admirable."

Vanessa agreed. "Hell yeah, it's hard enough going to school at eighteen with no kids, no worries, and parents paying the tuition."

Vanessa, Tori, Roger, and Jeff all went to college straight out of high school and graduated in four years. Sometimes I felt like the outcast and wondered if the day would come when I would walk across the stage and hold up my degree after my name was called. I hoped I wouldn't need a walking cane by the time that happened.

Thank goodness, Tori changed the subject. I didn't want to answer any questions about Steph just yet. "I thought we would do something a little different this Friday, girls. Instead of getting together at the restaurant, why don't we go on the midnight moonlight cruise? The new radio station is sponsoring it, and I can get passes from a guy I know that does PR for the station." Tori has all the connections from her restaurant patrons.

"I'm up to it," Vanessa said. "Roger will enjoy that."

"Sure, Jeff will like it too." I realized I hadn't thought

about Jeff very much over the weekend. I missed his phone calls on Saturday, and he finally caught up with me last night on my way to sleep. I looked at my watch. Eight-ten AM. He should be back in a couple of hours. I finished my speed shower and prepared to leave.

"Hey, Ky, why don't you ask your friend to come along? That is, if she can find a babysitter," Tori said.

I thought about it and couldn't think of a valid reason not to ask her. I needed to get over the paranoia I suddenly felt.

"Okay, I'll ask her when I see her in class later," I replied. "I'll give you a call tonight. Bye, ladies."

I blew them a kiss, left the shower and dressed quickly. In the car I applied a bit of my makeup while listening to the radio. The DJ asked the question of the morning and the first caller with the right answer would win a prize. The DJ asked what Gladys Knight song was the title-track song of a James Bond film. Because Gladyce (my Gladyce) was an avid Gladys Knight fan, I knew the answer. I didn't usually call into radio stations for contests or to win tickets to the latest concert, out of fear of sounding silly on the radio, but hey, I was feeling pretty good this morning. I put my mascara away, turned my radio down and dialed the station number on my cell phone. The line was busy the first couple of times, but I got a ring on the third try.

"Hot one-oh-four," the DJ answered in a voice too sultry for this early in the morning.

"Hi, I know the answer to your question," I said nervously, not knowing if we were live on the air or not.

"What's your name, hon?"

"Kyla."

"Okay, Kyla, what's the song and movie of the same name that Gladys did for a James Bond flick?"

"*License to Kill*," I said loudly. I was excited now.

"You got it, girl!"

I surprised myself and let out an impulsive scream, stunned that I had any energy left after the draining sauna.

The DJ laughed. "Here's what we got for you, Kyla. Two movie theater gift certificates, a twelve-pack of cola and a Hot one-oh-four T-shirt! And we'll enter your name and qualify you for an all-expense-paid trip for two to the Bahamas! The drawing will be held in two weeks. What do you think about that?"

"Sounds great!"

"Hang on the line, Kyla, and tell all of our listeners, who turns the most listeners into winners?"

"Hot one-oh-four," I said.

I gave the DJ my name, address, and phone number and made arrangements to pick up my prizes later that day. I finished my makeup and drove to school with a smile on my face.

In class, I was sitting at the table catching up on some reading I had failed to finish, when someone tapped me on the shoulder.

"Excuse me, ma'am," I heard a voice say. "Can I have your autograph, please?"

I turned around to find a grinning Stephanie holding an open notebook and a pen for me. I took them both from her and wrote, *To my new friend. Looking forward to getting to know you better.* She read what I wrote and I saw a hint of rose color her cheeks.

She sat down next to me. "Hey, lucky winner. Congratulations."

"Please tell me I didn't sound ridiculous. I don't normally do that kind of stuff," I said, somewhat embarrassed.

"Whatever it takes, girl. There's nothing wrong with free! Just let me know when you're taking me to the movies," she kidded.

In class we talked about foster care and adoption.

Mr. Jelenchick discussed several situations about the personality development of children who grow up in foster care. He also talked about the differences in children who were adopted as babies versus children adopted after the age of four. I wondered if Stephanie had considered giving Jaron up for adoption. I asked her at breakfast.

"Oh, hell no! You heard what Mr. Jelenchick said, didn't you?" she said with authority. "I didn't have to take this class to know that my baby would be better off with me, his real mother, than with anyone else. Even though I was a teenager and got pregnant under horrible circumstances, I had to look at it from a different perspective. Everything, good or bad, happens for a reason. At the time we may not understand why it happened; maybe never. But Jaron didn't ask to come here, and I know God brought him to me for a reason. I always knew he was my responsibility."

"That was a brave decision, Steph. I bet a lot of people in your situation would have been quick to go to the clinic," I said before taking a bite of my spinach casserole.

"I was in a rape counseling group while I was pregnant and that's what so many of the women said to me. I didn't meet one woman who said she would have kept the baby. Not one. They said it would have been a constant reminder of what happened to them. Even though I was young and about to start college, I saw the pregnancy as a blessing. I knew then that I probably wouldn't get married, so I was happy to have a child."

I sat there and stared at her in pure admiration. I had my share of counseling friends and a few acquaintances through unexpected pregnancies and abortions. Of my two best friends, it was Vanessa that got pregnant our senior year of high school. She had begun dating a young man who'd just moved to town from Mississippi. We'd all heard how chivalrous Southern men were, and this guy was no exception. He was polite, well-spoken, and always called Vanessa's parents *sir* and *ma'am*. He opened our car doors when we went on joy rides and treated all of us to the movies.

Since Vanessa's first sexual experience at fifteen was anything but pleasant, she kept her legs closed tight for two years. But this man was super-smooth, so she gave up the goods after two months. And two months after that she was pregnant. Even though we all were concerned about Vanessa's future, we were confident Mr. Nice Guy would marry her and support the child they conceived together. He turned out to be Mr. Too Good to Be True because you would have thought Vanessa had the plague after she told him about the pregnancy. He avoided her at school, dodged her phone calls, and acted like she simply didn't exist anymore. Vanessa's parents didn't know about the pregnancy, and we weren't wise enough to tell his parents and hope they would make the man be a man. Instead, we hustled our fast-food paychecks together and went to the clinic. That was one of the most traumatic experiences we've been through together.

I suddenly remembered Tori's invitation to Steph on Friday.

"Remember I told you that my friends and I all get together on Friday nights?" I asked. "Well, this week we're going on the midnight cruise, and I was wondering if you want to come along. Actually, Tori suggested it this morning."

"Sure, that sounds like a good time," she said.

"Good. You can meet everybody." I hesitated before asking my next question. "Do you, uh, have someone you'd like to bring?"

"Uh, no," she said, mimicking me. "For the hundredth time, I'm not seeing anyone right now. I have a couple of friends, but no one I consider dating material. Will Jeff be there?"

"Oh yes, he'll be there. You won't feel left out, will you?"

"I'm a big girl. I think I can handle socializing among the heterosexuals. I've been doing it forever."

My cell phone rang right in the middle of my mouthful of grits. I checked the caller ID and it was Jeff. For some reason, I debated on whether or not to answer the phone. Steph looked at me with an are-you-going-to-answer-it look. I swallowed my food and pressed the green talk button.

"Hello," I answered.

"Hey, darling, I'm back!" Jeff exclaimed.

"Welcome home. You had a safe drive?"

"Yes, there was hardly any traffic so I hit the gas all the way," Jeff said.

"Be careful doing that. I don't want you hurting yourself or anyone else."

He got cocky. "I know. What would you do without me?"

"Anyway," I said sarcastically.

"What are you doing?"

"Stephanie and I are at breakfast."

"Okay, I'll let you get back to her. I'll see you later, right?"

"Of course," I said.

"I missed you, Ky."

I looked up at Steph. She was staring right at me, amusement dancing through her pretty eyes.

"I know, Jeff. I'll call you when I'm on my way."

"I can't wait."

I hung up and tucked the phone back in my purse. Stephanie was still looking at me with a grin on her face.

"What?" I asked.

"You didn't miss him?"

I laughed. "You don't miss a thing, huh?"

"Never. Don't forget that," she said with a nod of her head.

After we made arrangements to hook up Friday, I

headed to the radio station to claim my prizes. I spent the rest of the day at work studying every woman I encountered. I looked at their hairstyles, checked their makeup, analyzed their clothing, their walk, their talk, and anything I thought would clue me in on their sexuality. I wondered if every single woman I saw was a lesbian.

Compliments to my ignorance, I assumed every woman with short hair and even the mildest hint of tomboy was gay. Then I realized I shouldn't make that assumption, considering all feminine women weren't straight. Look at Stephanie. She was a prime example. Most women would feel intimidated if they caught their man in a conversation with Steph, not knowing Steph couldn't care less about having the man for herself.

Later that afternoon I watched one particular woman who reminded me of Vivica Fox. She was tall and nicely shaped, with curves in all the right places. Her hair and makeup were done to perfection. She was shopping alone for about ten minutes before I asked if I could help her find anything, since I didn't like to attack people as soon as they come into my department. I didn't work on commission anyway. She said she was just looking but would let me know. Her cell phone rang several minutes later.

"Hey, baby," she said in a sexy tone.

I put my ears on a bionic dial and tuned in. She was listening to a story the person was telling on the other end. Finally she said, "Girl, I would have told him to go to hell!"

Girl? Up until then I had been doing so well pretending like I was concentrating on folding sweaters. But my head darted in her direction. She didn't appear to notice and kept on with her conversation. Could this beautiful black woman be a lesbian? I studied her every move for the next five minutes looking for a sign. What kind of sign, I'm not sure. I moved to the counter and stood behind the register, anxiously waiting for her to check out. She decided on a brown pair of nylon and spandex slacks with a matching sheer shirt.

"How do you think this will look on me?" she asked when she laid her clothes on the counter.

I looked at the fitted pants with a flared leg and pictured her in them. It was a nice visual.

"I think the outfit will look great on you," I told her. "You should check out the lingerie department for a teddy or bralette tank."

"I was thinking the same thing," she said, studying the shirt.

"It's on the next level up." I felt like being nosy, something I was getting good at lately. "Going somewhere special?"

"Yes. My girl and I are celebrating her birthday. I want a new outfit to look extra special."

Okay, no big deal. I would buy a new outfit if I were going out to celebrate a birthday with Tori or Vanessa, so that was no help. And I always call them *my girls* too.

"Sounds like fun!" I couldn't think of anything else to ask so I hoped she would volunteer. And she did.

"Yeah, we've been through four birthdays together, but this is the big three-oh, so I want to make sure she has a great time. Wednesday is her birthday, but we're going on that radio station boat cruise this Friday night and this is what I'm going to wear."

"You're kidding? I'm going this Friday too."

She smiled and checked my wedding finger. "Wonderful. And who might you be going with?" she inquired, trying to get into my business the same way I had hoped to get into hers.

"Um, some friends." Why did I leave Jeff out?

"Mmm, okay. I guess we'll see you there," she cooed. She took her receipt and plastic bag and sashayed up the escalator.

I beamed the rest of the day and couldn't wait for Friday to come. And then I wondered if I was going to spend the rest of my life examining every woman I met to determine if she was gay. What was I doing to myself? I had a fun afternoon watching everyone, but why were gay women suddenly so fascinating to me?

Women are naturally intimate with one another, so it doesn't seem so odd to hug a woman, lay next to a woman or even kiss a friend. But I've always been uncomfortable in the presence of another naked woman, always avoiding looking at her body. Suddenly I wondered why.

5

Jeff greeted me at his apartment door, wearing nothing but boxer shorts, holding a rose in one hand and a bowl of ice cream in the other. I could see what he had on his mind. I dropped my book bag and purse and put my arms around his neck. No homework was going to get done.

He smelled of Irish Spring soap and Tuscany cologne. He kissed my neck and licked my collarbone up to my ear. His breath smelled of Colgate toothpaste. I let his tongue flicker around my ear before reaching for his mouth with mine. We kissed a deep kiss to let one another know how much we missed each other.

He gently released himself and scooped a spoonful of French vanilla ice cream and fed it to me. I opened my mouth for another helping and he gave me more. This time I let the spoon linger in my mouth and licked it clean, looking at him, to let him know what was to come if he was a good boy. He studied my tongue until I thought he was about to start drooling. He took my hand and led me to his couch. I stood in front of him while he sat down and unzipped my jean skirt, tugging it until it fell to the floor. He brought his mouth to my stomach and kissed my belly button, sending shivers up my spine from his cold tongue. He moved lower, down to my underwear. He kissed, licked, and rubbed his mouth all over my silk thongs until I thought I was going to scream. He reached and pulled down one side of my panties and I lifted my left leg out, positioning it on the couch. I stood with a pair of wet panties around my ankle, with Jeff's head between my legs. It didn't take long for me to come. I could feel my juices rush down to greet his waiting tongue. He loved the taste and continued as if he were licking a plate clean.

One thing I learned about Jeff early in our relationship was that he had no hang-ups venturing down south. At first I was uneasy about that, unsure just how many places his lips had been. But I let go of that worry and let my man please me as often as he wanted to. And luckily, he didn't automatically assume he was getting the same in return.

I reached down, cupped his face in my hands and kissed him to taste the sweetness in his mouth when, suddenly, Steph's face unexpectedly popped into my head. I let out a quick gasp and stopped kissing. We finally spoke.

"You all right?" he wanted to know, with a concerned look on his face.

"Umm . . . yes, I'm fine. I'm sorry. I must have bit my tongue." I lied, something I tried not to do very often.

"Let me see," he said, trying to inspect my mouth.

"No, no, I'm okay," I said, covering my mouth with my hand.

He ran his fingers down my spine and rubbed my ass, his way of telling me he wasn't finished. I lay on the couch and he got on top of me. My head was racing and I hardly noticed when he entered me and when he came. My mind was elsewhere. Why was I thinking about Steph? I've always enjoyed kissing Jeff and tasting myself on his lips, because I find it so erotic. But I had never imagined tasting another woman until that moment. I could only assume that other women tasted the way I did. Hmm . . . I was suddenly curious.

"Hmmm, what?" Jeff asked.

"What?" I asked, afraid I had been thinking out loud.

"You said 'hmmm,' like you just had a revelation or something."

"No, I wasn't thinking anything." Another lie. I was on a roll.

He positioned himself next to me and started telling me about his weekend. Robert, a colleague of his, had gone to the conference with him. On the trip he found out that Robert had been having an affair with one of the female bosses. Apparently, this woman finagled a reason to attend this conference and the two had shared a few too many glasses of wine and lost all inhibitions in public.

Saturday night Jeff had gone down to the gift shop looking for pain relievers and found them cozily seated in the lobby waiting for a cab. He said the look on Robert's face went from the shock of being caught to embarrassment of the same thing. The two of them talked about Robert's affair the next day. Robert had been married twelve years and I'd met his wife on several occasions at company events. She seemed like a sweet woman, wore a bit too much makeup like Tammy Faye, but I assumed they were happy. Apparently, looks can be quite deceiving.

Robert said that their marriage was just a picture, an image of what family life is supposed to be. They had two children together, an older son and younger daughter. He worked, she stayed home. The kids attended private school and exceled in academics and extracurricular activities. However, he and his wife lived in a joyless household. Since the birth of their daughter, he said he and his wife's sex life had been nonexistent. She told him that the demands of motherhood took first priority and having sex with her husband was last on her list of chores. It had become another task that didn't get completed at the end of the day. Robert said that while they were great partners at parenting their children, they were strangers in all other aspects.

Jeff turned and looked at me. "Do you think that will happen to us?"

I shook my head. "No, not at all. You know how I feel about marriage as it is, and I have no intention of doing it unless I'm sure it will last forever."

"How do you feel about it right now?"

My heart rate picked up the pace. Was he about to pop the question? I chose my words carefully.

"I know right now I'm very happy and I can't imagine us not continuing to get along as well as we do."

Was that satisfactory? I hoped so.

"I feel the same way," Jeff said, pulling me close to him so I could smell his freshly applied deodorant.

Whew, good. I guess the answer was all right. I'm not saying I didn't love Jeff or that our relationship wasn't the best I'd had so far. But even though we'd been together over four years, I wasn't sure how I'd feel if he wanted to get married. Marriage scared the hell out of me. I had no role models except for Jeff's parents. Of course, I admired my own parents, but they're divorced, so I didn't know how much of their marital advice I was willing to take.

"So can you tell me that you missed me now?" Jeff asked, reaching for a hug.

"You know I did, Jeff. I always miss you when you're away. But Steph and I spent time together, so I stayed busy."

"You're becoming good friends, I see," he observed.

"Yeah, she's pretty cool. Oh, she'll be coming out with us on Friday. Tori planned for us to go on the midnight cruise instead of meeting at the restaurant. It's not really at midnight. I think we board at ten and get back at midnight, something like that."

"That's cool. Something different will be nice," he said.

I replayed that statement in my head. *Something different will be nice.* That simple statement right there can easily be taken out of context. That statement says that routine becomes uninteresting and boring. A job becomes routine, the same Friday-night plans become uneventful, and people in relationships become predictable. I guess that's how my parents felt and that's why so many relationships end in divorce.

What makes relationships get to that point? In the beginning, it's so exciting and thrilling to receive a phone call, a kiss, a touch . . . Why does that wear off? Do we dislike the person the more we get to know them? Do people change? I don't know if I believe that people change. I think we eventually learn things about that person that they didn't clue us in on before. And maybe they weren't even aware of it themselves.

After my Wednesday-morning class I met Yvonne for lunch. We decided to meet at Percy's, a little joint frequented by everyone from NBA players and public officials, to drug dealers and retirees. For once, she wasn't geared up in her polyester blue slacks and starched white oxford, her standard work uniform. Instead, she wore black pants and a long-sleeved, scoop-neck olive sweater. She wore her hair pulled back in a bun, emphasizing her prominent cheekbones and high forehead. Her eyes were coated with soft brown eyeliner and mascara with a light golden gloss covering her lips. I knew she had to be off today because that girl wore her uniform as proudly as if she were in the armed forces.

I greeted her with a hug and a kiss on the cheek. I could

smell the scent of jasmine perfume on her skin. She was smiling and seemed extra perky today.

"What are you grinning about, young lady?" I asked her.

"I have a lunch date," she said excitedly.

"Well, I know you're glad to see me, but damn," I said, playing with her.

She rolled her eyes while still smiling. "This man who shops in the store asked me to have lunch with him today and I agreed. He's so handsome, Ky!"

"He must be something because I can count the number of dates you've had in the last year on one hand," I said, holding up a fist, indicating none. "What's his name?"

"His name is Byron and his business card says he's a financial advisor."

I looked over my menu. "I take it you won't be eating then, huh?"

"No, sorry, sis. I didn't want to cancel on you, though, since we rarely get together. But maybe I should eat something so I don't go pigging out in front of him. What do you think?"

"I think if your ass is hungry, then you need to eat. Don't pretend you don't like food when you really do. Then when he finds out you can throw down just as well as he can, he'll wonder what else you're hiding. You know what I'm saying?"

"Yeah, you're right. I'll hold off and eat with him. Especially because we're going for steaks, and you know I love some steak," she said hungrily.

A waitress who looked like she was skipping school came and took our order. I decided on fried chicken, mashed potatoes, and lemonade.

"I thought your friend, Stephanie, was really nice," Yvonne said. "She seems to have a good relationship with her little boy too. He was well behaved. You don't see that too much these days."

"They take good care of each other. That's what she says."

"You know, the more I thought about it, I remembered she used to come into the store pretty often."

"Yeah?"

"Um-hm. She was usually shopping with this really pretty woman," she went on.

"Yeah?" *Just get to the point, Yvonne.*

"Yep, they grocery-shopped together a lot, so they must have been roommates."

Yvonne was looking at me as she took a sip of her water. I realized she was feeling me out. *She must know.*

"Maybe. She doesn't have a roommate now, but she may have at some time." I toyed with the straw in my glass, then asked as casually as I could, "What did the woman look like?"

"Wow, she was a beautiful brown-skinned woman with one of those sharp short haircuts. She didn't wear a lot of makeup, but it was always done right. She looked about your age with large, gorgeous brown eyes."

She'd just described Michelle, the woman in the picture on Steph's table. *That must have been her ex-girlfriend's mom that died. No wonder the death affected her the way it did. And then she lost Michelle because she couldn't cope with her mother's death.*

"You know, I thought I saw them holding hands once," she said.

"Yeah?" That was my word for the day. Why didn't she just come out with it?

"Um-hm."

Now she waited for me to respond, but I wasn't biting the bait. I hated to play these games with my sister, but I wasn't interested in gossiping about Steph's business. I was sure she had to deal with that all the time.

"Mom's birthday is coming up," I said, changing the subject.

Yvonne gave up. "It sure is. What do you want to do for her this year?"

"I thought we could take her out for a nice dinner. She always likes that."

"That sounds good to me. Just let me know when, so I can take that night off."

"I was thinking, next week Saturday."

Yvonne thought out loud. "That should work because Mark, the other manager, is returning from vacation next week. I'm sure he won't need Saturday off already. I'll check with him and then go ahead and make the plans."

We talked about Gladyce a while longer until Yvonne checked her watch. "Oh, I gotta get going. I need to get downtown and I don't want to be late."

I finished my potatoes and guzzled the last of my lemonade. As I paid the bill, I realized that I spent a lot of time in restaurants. That's one thing I would have had to change if and when I settled down. I know eating at home saves lots of money. Then I wondered who cooked the home meals, Stephanie or Michelle? Who was the "woman"? I also wondered if that stereotype even existed.

Friday night I decided on a figure-fitting black mini–rayon-and-polyester shirt dress with black pumps. I pinned my hair up and curled a few ringlets around my forehead and neck. I chose silver-and-black earrings with a matching necklace and bracelet. I bathed in a warm vanilla bath so I was smelling candy sweet and feeling extra sexy. Stephanie was meeting me at my apartment, and Jeff was picking us up from there.

I was putting on a shiny clear coat of polish over my

copper-colored nails when my doorbell rang. I waved my hands in the air as I walked to the door and managed to turn the knob with the palm of my hand. There was Stephanie, looking absolutely stunning in a lavender silk pantsuit. She wore open-toe matching lavender heels. Her hair was blown straight and was silky smooth with a part down the center, and hanging well beneath the middle of her back. Her eyes were rimmed in black eyeliner with a hint of lavender eye shadow, and her lips were a shiny color of jazzy plum.

"You look beautiful," I said, meaning every word. It was out before I could even catch it.

"Thanks, Kyla," she said as she walked in. "You're not looking too bad yourself."

I think I actually blushed. What in the hell was wrong with me?

I suddenly felt inadequate next to her. Generally, I was confident with my appearance and felt secure about myself; not saying I felt like I was in competition with other women, because I've always been one to appreciate another woman's beauty. But tonight Steph will have everyone twisting their heads, saying, "Who is that?"

I finished polishing my last two fingers and scrunched my fingers under the shade of my floor lamp.

"Girl, what are you doing?" Stephanie asked.

"Drying my nails. You've never done this?"

"I can't say I have," she said, watching me.

"It works because of the heat. You'll see."

A few minutes later I let her touch my smooth, dry polish. I could smell her lavender-scented lotion when I leaned close to her. "You smell wonderful," I told her. "I can smell lavender on your skin."

"And I can smell your vanilla. I like it. Got something planned for tonight?"

She did her half-mouth smirk. Was she flirting with me?

Oh hell, of course not. If Tori or Vanessa had asked me that same question I would know they meant some hot sex with Jeff. So why should Steph be different? *Lord, I can't go taking everything this girl says to me out of context. I have to be careful.*

Still, I said, "I'll let the night take its natural course and see what happens." She had to figure out what I meant by that, although I wasn't completely sure what I meant myself.

Jeff interrupted the moment with the ring of the doorbell, before he opened my front door with his key. Stephanie looked at the door and then at me, slightly startled. His entrance caught her off guard.

"It's Jeff," I assured her.

He came in looking dapper in khaki-colored slacks and a white, lightweight oxford shirt. He had on camel-colored dress sandals that only masculine men can get away with. He smiled at me as he walked toward me. He suddenly stopped midway when he noticed Stephanie on the couch. His eyes flickered with surprise by her beauty. Normally I commented on other women's physical beauty, but I hadn't mentioned Steph's.

"You must be Stephanie," he said, extending his hand.

She stood up to greet him. "That's me," she said as they shook hands.

"I've heard a lot about you. I'm glad Kyla has someone she enjoys taking classes with. You're not going to go and change your major on us, are you?"

"No, I'm dedicated to this one," she responded.

"Good, Kyla needs some direction." He was teasing, but I wasn't sure if Steph realized it.

The three of us exited my apartment and rode in Jeff's Chevy Blazer, heading downtown toward Third Street.

"How was Jaron tonight?" I asked Steph.

"Oh, he was fine," Steph replied. "He enjoys going by

my mom's. She spoils him rotten, so you know he's not complaining."

"He knows you need some Mommy time?" I asked.

"Girl, yes. And he needs his Jaron time. It's always been us, so he doesn't mind a healthy break too. I know some women who will never do anything apart from their children. While I think it's an admirable quality with good intentions, you can lose yourself in motherhood. I mean, you do give up a lot of time and make sacrifices, but every so often you have to treat yourself."

"I hear you," I said, even though I had no idea what parenting was like.

Jeff joined the conversation. "You're right. I think that's why my parents have managed to stay together so long. While my brother and I were growing up, we always had a babysitter every third Friday. Faithfully. One of those Fridays they would go to dinner or a movie together and the next they would do their own thing."

"That's what I mean. You have to keep a healthy balance between yourself, your children, and your mate," Steph said.

I feared her comment opened the door for Jeff to ask personal questions, but he didn't. I knew he was saving them for me later.

Roger, Vanessa, Tori, and her latest boy toy were waiting for us when we arrived to the dock. Tori introduced us to Juan, a super-fine Hispanic man who reminded me of Benjamin Bratt from his *Law & Order* acting days, with silky jet-black layered hair against clear, olive skin.

I introduced Steph to Tori and Juan first.

"Hey, girl, nice to meet you," Tori said, eyeing Steph up and down and nodding her approval. "Your suit is nice," she complimented Steph.

"What up, girl?" Juan said to Steph upon introduction. He spoke with enthusiasm.

Both Tori and I looked at one another, acknowledging the exchange.

"Hi, nice to meet you," Steph answered before immediately turning her attention back to me.

A slight disappointment swept through Juan's eyes, but dissolved when Tori grabbed hold of his hand and diverted his concentration back to her.

I brought Steph to Vanessa last.

"Hey, Vanessa White. You don't remember me, do you?" Steph asked her.

Vanessa stared at her, trying to place her face. Her eyes suddenly widened and she said, "Stephanie Coleman?"

"Yes."

"Oh my goodness!" Vanessa hugged her. She looked at me and said, "Did she tell you she was first in academics in our eighth grade class?" Vanessa twisted her arm through Stephanie's, like best friends reunited.

"No, she kept that a secret," I said.

"Everybody wanted to copy off of Stephanie Coleman's homework, but she held on to it tight. I didn't know this is who you were talking about, Ky. Ky said you work in HR?"

"Yes, I do," Stephanie said. She looked pleased that I had been talking about her.

"Small world, isn't it? We'll have to catch up later. We better get on the boat before it leaves without us," Vanessa said, noticing the other guests had disappeared.

Tori and Juan walked ahead of us, hand in hand, and deep in conversation. Vanessa let go of Steph's arm for Roger's hand, so naturally Jeff grabbed hold of mine. He was on my left with Steph walking close at my right. I liked having her there.

We found a large table for eight in the dining area, and with an empty chair next to Stephanie, it was obvious that she was dateless. But she didn't seem to mind.

Most of the cruisers were couples or people on dates. There were a few groups of women only, but no groups of single men. But, hey, what was I looking at men for anyway? Stephanie surely wasn't interested, and I had my own man. *Maybe I could find a gay woman for her.* I thought my gay radar was tuning in.

Juan, who turned out to be quite the talker, was in the middle of telling us about his little sister's *quinceañera* when I noticed the Vivica Fox lookalike walking toward a table behind ours. Following her was a woman several inches shorter than her. The woman wore a short curly 'fro with no makeup and small diamond studs in each ear. She was dressed in a black pinstripe suit and even had a black tie to top it off. This woman wasn't particularly eye-catching, but she had a cute face with big, brown inno-cent-looking eyes. Unfortunately, at times, eyes tell the truth. I knew she wasn't all that innocent, because after she caught my stare, she raised her eyebrows in a do-you-like-what-you-see expression. I almost choked on my water.

Vivica followed her friend's stare and saw me. She walked directly to me and stood next to my chair. I couldn't figure out if she was going to say hello or charge me up about looking at her woman. She put her hands on her hips and did a full circle turn like she was on a Paris runway.

"You like?" she asked when she finally struck a pose.

Now everyone about choked on their water.

"Umm . . . yes, the pants fit really nice," I said.

"I know that. I'm talking about the bra," she said, point-ing two acrylic fingernails at her chest.

Vivica had settled on a brown lace bra to go under her sheer blouse and that's it. Underneath her blouse I could see smooth brown skin, a sparkling belly button ring and perky brown nipples through the bra. She was seriously wearing that outfit, with no shame.

I tried not to stare at her nipples, but for the first time,

I couldn't take my eyes off of them. When my eyes finally made their way back to hers, she was grinning hard as hell. I was so embarrassed.

I noticed my dinner party was patiently waiting for an explanation.

"Everyone, this is—" I cut myself off because I didn't know her real name.

"Trina, and this is Mya," she said, placing her hand on Mya's shoulder.

"I helped Trina at the store the other day," I said. "By the way, happy birthday, Mya."

Help me, Lord, but when Mya opened her mouth to thank me, I saw a flash of gold and nearly fell out of my chair. Trina and Mya said their hellos, their eyes lingering on Stephanie for a moment, and then took their seats.

Now you know my mind was flipping, right? Mya was the kind of gay woman I was used to encountering. Occasionally, I'd wondered why a woman would want a woman that looks and dresses like a man. Then what's the point of being with a woman? I made a mental note to ask Steph that question when the time was right.

Tori and Vanessa silently gave me a look that said, *Girl, did you see her in that suit?* I shrugged my shoulders and looked back saying, *Hey, you got me.*

I turned to Steph, who observed the exchange. She didn't seem bothered by Tori and Vanessa's amusement, and I assumed she was used to this reaction. I leaned in to her ear and wondered if she heard me sniff before I spoke. She smelled so good.

"Do you know them?" I asked.

"Um-hm. They've been together for a while, and I'm surprised that it's lasted as long as it has." She spoke in a low voice, since they were right behind us. "I'll fill you in later," she promised as she patted my thigh.

I silently wished she could tell me the story right away. I

also wished I didn't like the way it felt when she touched me. I was sitting next to my boyfriend but longing to be somewhere alone with Steph. This wasn't supposed to be happening. Did I feel this way just because she was gay? And just because she was gay surely didn't mean she wants to be alone with me.

My thoughts were interrupted by Jeff asking me if I wanted appetizers. I looked over at the buffet spread and spotted a platter of buffalo wings that were calling my name.

"A few wings, please." I turned to Steph. "You want something?"

"Sure, I'll take some wings too," Steph answered.

"You better watch that pretty suit of yours. You'll regret it if you get some greasy red sauce on it," I said to Steph after the men went to make the plates of food.

She was about to reply before Tori butted in. "Kyla says you have a son."

It wasn't a question but just a statement. I had the feeling Tori was feeling neglected. One thing about my girl, she loved to be the center of attention. Isn't that what they say about Leos?

"Yes, I do. He's my heart," Steph said lovingly.

"None of us have ventured into motherhood yet," Tori said, looking at Vanessa and me. "Must be hard, huh?"

I sensed a little tension from Tori and wondered why. Steph was either oblivious to it or simply ignored it.

Steph leaned forward. "I think parenting is a challenge for most parents, no matter when they have a child. You learn most things along the way, whether you're fifteen or thirty-five. Of course, it's an added benefit to be financially prepared when you have a child. So, yes, that can be difficult. But if you're questioning single-parenting, then for me, I'll have to say no, it's not that hard. I made the choice to have Jaron and have made sacrifices in order to keep my son happy and make sure he has a promising future. I have no complaints and no regrets."

Okay, maybe she wasn't oblivious to it; she put Tori in her place. Tori took a sip of her martini and waited in silence for Juan to return. I wasn't about to allow Tori's problem to upset our Friday night out. So I turned my attention to Vanessa, the gentlest of our threesome.

"How's your inmate interview coming along, Vanessa?" I asked her.

"I'm almost ready," she answered. "The plans have changed, though. He's scheduled for release in two weeks and I'm supposed to interview him the day after. I can't see what the delay is for his release, so I'm looking into that also. I mean, if he's innocent, let him out! But I guess the DA is verifying the killer's story to make sure everything is on the up-and-up. And to make sure there's no connection between the two, like he was paid to confess."

"That is crazy," I agreed. "Are we still coming with you?"

"I wish you were, but that plan has changed, and now that I'm interviewing him in his home, I don't think so," she explained. "He's going home to his wife somewhere on Twenty-seventh Street. But even though he's not a convicted murderer, I still want someone to come with me. He might have some pent-up anger or have a flashback or something, and I don't want to be the victim of temporary insanity."

We all laughed but knew she was serious.

"You'll have a cameraman, right?" I asked her.

"Girl, this guy Jerry is assigned to work with me that day. He weighs about a buck and a quarter, so I don't know how much good he'll be."

"Let us know," I said. "I'll be glad to watch you become a superstar and make television history." Vanessa smiled at my support of her.

Once the men returned, the table temporarily quieted

down as we devoured our wings. You know, there's just something about us and chicken. After the DJ finished playing "You Dropped a Bomb on Me" by the Gap Band, he announced that the raffle was going to begin and asked us to take out the tickets given to us when we boarded. We wiped (and some of us licked) our fingers clean and reached for our tickets.

The first winner was a tall, basketball player-type with a shaven, bald head. He took long strides up front to claim his prize of dinner for two at a restaurant I had never heard of. He thought he gave Steph an undercover wink, but I caught it, so surely his date must have seen it as well. Steph just stared back at him with a blank expression.

Ironically, Trina was the next winner of movie passes to the premiere of the latest Vivica Fox movie. She bounced to the DJ, with brown nipples saying, "Hello" to everyone as she passed. Some of the women were annoyed when the tongues of their boyfriends wagged as she walked by.

Stephanie clapped her hands as the next numbers were read. Our table cheered with her when we realized she was the next winner. She was pure eye candy as she gracefully walked up front. We all screamed with excitement as she won tickets to the upcoming comedy show featuring Martin Lawrence at the Riverside Theater. As far as I knew, none of us had tickets to the $80 show.

I put my arm around her and hugged her when she returned. Her long hair tickled my face and shoulders as I leaned my chest into hers.

"Can I go?" said a voice I wasn't used to.

We turned around to find Juan leaning forward, looking at Stephanie and licking his lips. The look on Tori's face was a mixture of disgust and embarrassment. *Ah-ha, that's* her problem.

Steph's face scrunched up just like Tori's, pissed off by his question.

"I don't think so. Actually, wait, no, you can't go. How about purchasing two tickets and taking your lovely date with you?" Steph said, nodding and pointing her finger at Tori, whose chocolate face burned with anger.

Tori looked at Juan and waited for him to reply. Someone must have told Juan he was fine a few too many times because he seemed amused by Steph's answer.

"You know you'd look good on my arm, girl, stop trippin'," Juan came back.

Where did Tori find these assholes?

Tori slammed her glass against the table, sprinkling Juan's shirt with pink dots from her cosmopolitan. At least his attention was finally diverted back to her. I know she would have taken him outside and cussed him out if we hadn't been out on a boat on Lake Michigan. Instead, she leaned forward and whispered in his ear.

The lecture lasted a good two minutes. The rest of us pretended to be eating, while glancing at each other in disbelief. Juan's toasty skin turned rosy in the cheeks as he clenched his napkin in his hand.

I looked at Steph who rolled her eyes and mouthed, "Men." I just shook my head.

We spent the rest of the cruise quietly listening to songs ranging from Cameo to Jill Scott, and engaging in casual conversation.

Juan had spoiled the festive mood. We were all relieved when we docked on schedule at midnight and headed back to our cars. Tori asked Vanessa and Roger for a ride home. Juan quietly excused himself without saying goodbye. I gave everyone a hug and Vanessa told Stephanie not to let this be the last time she hung with us. Tori tried to nod in agreement but failed.

"That was interesting," Jeff said when we got inside his car. He was referring to Juan.

"You okay, Steph?" I asked. "I'm sorry about Juan."

"No need for you to be sorry. I just hope Tori has sense enough to leave him alone, regardless of how nice-looking he is," Steph said.

"I wouldn't worry about that. Tori has no problem loving them and leaving them."

Steph raised her perfectly arched eyebrows at me but didn't question. Maybe that didn't come out as I meant it. Jeff knew the remark could mean a couple of things also, but he kept his comments to himself.

We drove most of the way to my apartment in silence. It was 12:30 AM and I had a lot of research to do at the library the next day. I needed at least seven hours of sleep if I was going to try to have a productive day. And then it clicked. *Why should I work alone when I could have the pleasure of Steph's company?*

"Say, Steph, are you going to be working on your research paper this weekend? I'm going to the school library tomorrow to get started. You want to come along?"

I discreetly crossed my fingers behind my back.

"I have to take Jaron to winter basketball camp tryouts in the morning," Steph replied. "And after that I was taking him back to my mom's because I had the same thing in mind. I can meet you later if you'll still be there around two."

"I should be there all day long, trust me, girl."

We pulled up to my apartment and I hugged Steph good-bye before she got in her car. She had hardly closed the car door when Jeff said, "Wow, you didn't tell me she was fine! You can't tell me she couldn't find a date. Any of my boys would fall to their knees for a date with her."

"I know. Any man would be crazy not to be attracted to her. But she's not interested in hooking up with a guy right now." Was I setting myself up for another question?

"No?" Jeff asked like he couldn't believe it. "What, is she one of those women waiting for a pro athlete or something?"

"No, she's not like that, Jeff," I said defensively. "She wants to concentrate on school and taking care of Jaron, you know, without the hassles of a relationship."

A look of surprise came over Jeff's face. "Since when are relationships a hassle?"

Shit. He was reading too much into what I was saying.

"I didn't mean relationships are a hassle. It's just harder to maintain a relationship in a situation like Steph's when she works full-time, goes to school, and is a single parent. She has to find a person that can handle filling a caretaker role with Jaron and can handle the responsibility of a ready-made family. Just any old Joe Shmo won't do in her eyes."

I laughed to myself. Anyone named Joe, literally. I wasn't sure where I was getting this information from, but I had to think of something. I wasn't ready to tell Jeff about Steph's sexuality.

"I see what you're saying. A girl like her has her selection anyway."

"Yes, she's beautiful," I said.

We were both tired. Too tired for showers, so we stripped down to our undies and slipped under the covers. I laid my head on his shoulder and inhaled the musky, pine smell of his cologne as I twisted the swirly hairs on his chest.

I closed my eyes and pretended I smelled lavender body lotion and the chest hairs disappeared. I stroked one of his nipples until it became hard and aroused and I drifted off to sleep listening to Steph moan at my touch.

6

The ring of my telephone woke me up at 7:00 on a breezy Saturday morning. I unwound myself from Jeff's embrace and reached for the receiver.

"Hello," I said with a groggy voice.

"Hey, Ky, I'm so sorry to wake you. I'm having a crisis."

I sat upright. "What's going on, Vanessa?"

"Roger's mom says she won't have anything to do with the wedding if we don't get married at her church."

I laid back down. It was too early for this shit. "Girl, why not? What's up with her?"

She groaned. "His mom is such a control freak, and she just wants to get her way and impress her family and friends. This is her manipulative way of getting what she wants."

"What are you going to do?" I asked her.

"I don't know. I need to talk to Roger. But I know he's not about to defy his mother. God forbid he actually disagree with her."

"And Roger is how old?" I asked sarcastically. "He's a grown man, Vanessa."

I could almost hear Vanessa's eyes roll in the back of her head.

"To answer your question, he's twenty-nine. But sit him next to his mama and take away twenty years. I love Roger to death, Ky, but his mama is going to drive me crazy. I know it already."

I started picking the clumps of mascara out of my eyelashes and turned over so I could quit blowing my morning breath in Jeff's face.

"Remember what I said before, *V.* It's your wedding day, so do what feels right for you. Even if it pisses some people off."

Vanessa sighed and was silent for a while. I almost fell back asleep.

"You're right," she finally said. "I don't know why I'm tripping, anyway. Roger and I don't have a church home of our own. Maybe it shouldn't even matter where we get married. But what happened to it being the bride's day? Shit, my family and I are paying for most of this wedding anyway."

Vanessa rarely said a cuss word and it was almost funny when she did. This wasn't the time for me to laugh, though. Plus, she had a point there.

"Just talk to Roger and see what the two of you come up with," I suggested.

"Thanks, Ky. I'm sorry, you can go back to sleep now. I just needed someone to vent to."

"Don't worry about it, *V.* I want your day to be special, so I'm by your side no matter what you decide. I have to get up anyway and head to the library. I have to do some research on teenage pregnancy. Particularly, statistics on age groups, ethnic backgrounds, broken homes, whether the girls were sexually molested as children, and on and on. I think I'm going to be there all day."

"Okay, well, I'll let you go. I'll see you Monday morning."

"Bye, *V.*"

I hung up the phone and put my face back in my pillow. I usually tried to sleep in on Saturdays, but this paper wasn't about to write itself. I looked over at Jeff and watched his chest rise and fall with each inhale and exhale. He could sleep through a tornado as long as his bed didn't move. Even with his mouth hanging open and drool peeking out of the corners, he was still so handsome.

He'd told me a number of times that he couldn't wait for us to have babies. *We'll have such pretty kids, Ky,* he says. All I know is, I've seen some of the cutest couples with some funny-ass looking kids. And then some people uglier than boogers make some of the cutest little babies. You know, in the back of your head you're looking at the mother and the supposed daddy, thinking, *Now she knows her ass is lying . . .* But no babies for me yet. I wondered how Steph does it.

I kissed Jeff on the ear and rolled out of bed. I ran a hot bath and poured sesame oil under the running water before searching my closet for something comfortable, but cute, to wear. I settled on light blue, boot-cut jeans, and a red ribbed-fitted turtleneck I'd ordered from the Victoria's Secret catalog. I decided on my black shoe boots, since I would be sitting most of the day.

While bathing, I shaved and trimmed every unwanted hair off of my body. I scented my skin with exotic bouquet bath gel, another favorite from Victoria's Secret. After my bath, I put on my makeup and unwrapped my hair, smoothing it with a flatiron. I was packing my backpack when a sleepy voice startled me.

"You sure are looking pretty good to be going to the library," Jeff said, wiping that crusty drool from his mouth.

I teased him. "Is that jealousy or insecurity I hear, mister?"

"A little bit of both, I guess," he admitted.

I walked to him and pinched his nose.

"Now you know where I'll be, who I'll be with, and what I'll be doing. Should I keep my pager and cell phone on so you can hit me up every hour on the hour?"

He laughed. "I don't know, Ky. The two of you will be like male magnets. The fellas won't be able to stay away. Even if you are just in the library."

"There's only one fella for me, and I hope he's here when I get back," I said.

Jeff tapped his fingers against the headboard. "I thought I told you that Kent and I are having dinner with Mom and Dad tonight. Then Kent wants to go have some drinks afterward. He said he's got something to talk to me about."

That meant more time with Steph.

"Oh, that's okay. I'll probably be tired and brain-dead by this evening, anyway."

I picked up my bag, kissed his dry lips and headed out the door.

The university library was already pretty crowded when I arrived. I found a table in the corner near the social sciences section. I marked my territory with my backpack and jacket and began searching for books and periodicals on teen pregnancy.

It took a while before I found material that would help me with my paper. But it probably took so long because I was looking at the clock every minute and a half to see how close it was to 2:00.

I finally immersed myself in reading, taking notes and making copies when I realized it was 1:45 PM. I hopped up and went to the bathroom to freshen up. I combed my hair, which was tousled from playing in it while I was thinking and studying. I touched up my makeup, adding fresh powder and M•A•C lip gloss. When I stepped back to look at myself in the mirror, I had to laugh. I was getting all dolled up for a girl. Now that was a first. And why was I doing it? She was going to know that I just added makeup, considering I've been here since 9:30 AM. But I didn't mind. I wanted her to know.

I was back at my table reading a journal when I felt a gentle tap on my shoulder.

"Hey, lady," Steph said as she sat her backpack next to mine.

I looked up and almost thought I looked in the mirror. She looked great in blue jeans, a red turtleneck, and a black leather jacket and boots. The only difference was her hair still hung straight, but the part had been moved to the right side. To top it off, her lips glistened with a fresh coat of lip gloss. That made me smile.

"Were we on the same wavelength this morning or what?" I asked as I stood up to model my outfit and give her a hug. She smelled delicious as usual.

"Are you getting a lot done?" she asked while taking out a pen and notebook.

"I am. I've gathered enough information that I can start the rough draft of the paper. There's a couple of web sites that may be beneficial, but I'll see what I can do with what I have so far."

"We can stay here for a while and then go back to my place to use my computer if you want." She looked around. "It's so crowded in here, and I bet all the computers are full."

"Yes, they are. I checked, and they're all logged out for the rest of the day."

"Okay, I only need a couple of hours here looking for material on gender discrimination, wherever that may be. I'm sure I'll have to check a few areas to find what I want."

I had been in school so long and visited this library so many times that I knew where everything was. I pointed her in the right direction.

"Thanks. Off I go," she said, standing up.

"Good luck!"

I watched her walk off and wondered how a baby ever came through those hips. She had a flat tummy, curves in the waist, and hips that led to strong, muscular thighs underneath those jeans. She walked confidently, speaking to those she made eye contact with and smiling at those awed by her beauty.

I was poorly humming an oldie by Earth, Wind & Fire, "Love's Holiday," when she returned thirty minutes later.

"*Would you mind . . .*" she sang, joining in with me. I could hear the talent in her voice with just those few notes.

"You sound good, Steph!" I said, surprised. But why was I suprised? A beautiful voice from a beautiful woman.

"Thank you," she said, smiling. "I usually only sing to Jaron. I've been singing to him since the day I found out I was pregnant."

"Where did you get your voice from?"

"My daddy used to sing," she said, speaking softly. "He would sing a song to my sister and me almost every night. We would take our baths and put on our pajamas and wait for him to sing us to sleep. My parents never had to fight to get us in the bed. He had a soulful Teddy Pendergrass type of voice, and sometimes I would hear him sing to my mom after he left our room."

She smiled as she reminisced. "He missed his calling."

"What does he do for a living?"

"He was a mailman. He died when I was ten. My mom said he would sing through his whole route."

"I'm sorry. It sounds like you were close."

"Yes, we were. I loved him so much. My mom still says

she can't believe I'm gay, considering how close I was to my father. She was so sure I would be all up under some man looking for a replacement. So I told her that was more proof that we're born this way. I didn't choose it." As an afterthought she added, "Who would choose it?"

I didn't know what to say, so I went back to writing, while she started flipping the pages of one of her books.

We worked in silence for a couple of hours, though periodically I would look up and catch her nibbling on the cap to her pen or biting her bottom lip while she read and considered which notes to jot down. Only once she looked up and caught my gaze. This time I managed to hold my stare, her eyes receptive to my silent survey of her demeanor. We remained fixated on one another, until a tremor so sudden and so intense swept through my body that I was forced to look away. What was happening to me?

By the time we decided to leave, it was 5:30. My paper was almost complete, and her outline was ready. Though we each accomplished much and could call it a day, I wasn't ready to leave her.

"I haven't eaten, Steph. You hungry?" I asked her, hopeful we could get a bite to eat together.

"Yes, I'm glad you asked. You're still coming over, right?"

Yes!

"You want to pick up something on the way to my place? That'll give me a minute to straighten up, okay?"

"What would you like? Barbecue is sounding pretty good to me right now."

"Works for me. Speed King," she suggested.

Speed King was a restaurant on the edge of the central city that had some of the best 'cue in town. Just don't go after a night of club-hopping because you'll be stuck in drive-through 'til dawn.

"You go ahead home. I'll pick up the food and meet you there," I said.

"Okay. Should I make some red Kool-Aid to go with that or more Absolut?" she joked.

I laughed. "After today, I'll go with the Absolut," I said with a smile.

"You got it." She laughed.

I waited a good twenty-five minutes for our pork shoulder dinners. The smell had my stomach growling all the way across town to Steph's place.

When I got inside, I immediately took off my boots and relieved my squished toes. Steph had lit candles and placed them on her kitchen table, and two small shot glasses filled to the rim waiting. We toasted to A+ papers and seven more weeks of class. My food went down as smoothly as the shot (and just as quickly). Steph must have been just as hungry because she was right behind me scraping up the last drips of barbecue sauce with her white bread.

After we tossed our containers she asked if I was ready for the computer.

"I don't even want to think about teens and pregnancy the rest of the day. No thanks!" I said.

"I didn't think so." She paused. "You know I fit into that category."

"What?"

"I'm a statistic, being a teen parent."

"But your case is different, Steph."

"I was eighteen with a child. The age says I'm a stat, regardless of the circumstances. You may want to look into teenage pregnancies that result from rape, for your paper. Especially date rape."

I felt insensitive, considering I hadn't even thought of that. "You're right. I'll see what information I can find."

Steph poured us another shot, and I was glad that she did. Not that I was nervous around her and needed to relax. But there were some things I wanted to ask her that I was hoping we both would be comfortable talking about.

Alcohol always helped inch those thoughts of mine from my brain to my vocal cords.

"I'm not feeling the study thing anymore either," she said as she nestled with a pillow on the couch.

I sat on the opposite end, close to the picture of her ex-girlfriend.

"You know, Steph, I think Yvonne knows about you and a previous relationship you had."

"What makes you think that?"

"We had lunch a few days ago and she hinted around to seeing you and a woman holding hands while grocery-shopping."

She raised her eyebrows.

I continued. "And based on her description of the woman, I'm thinking it must have been the pretty lady in this picture," I said, pointing at Michelle.

"Ah, very perceptive you two are," she said, grinning. "Yes, Michelle and I were a couple. I don't remember paying much attention to Yvonne when I went in the store, but Michelle and I used to grocery-shop together all the time. We lived together, so it only made sense."

"She lived here in this apartment with you?"

"No, we lived on the east side for a year before she moved back home. We were together almost three years, and it's been two years since she moved. It took a while for me to get over her leaving. She was my first true love."

I took this moment as an opportunity to ask my questions. *Here we go.* "Have you had many relationships with women?"

"I've *only* had relationships with women and I've had several. I first started dating undercover back in high school with a member of the girls' basketball team. She was a jock, and most people assumed we were a couple but no one had proof. We broke up after graduation when she went to Iowa State on a scholarship. She plays in the WNBA now."

I waited for her to volunteer a name, but she didn't. *Damn.*

"As you know, shortly after that, I got pregnant, and dating was at a halt for a while. I still had the opportunity to date because there are so many lesbian women who want to parent a child, even at that age. But I had to emotionally work though the rape, and I wanted to keep my focus on my baby and my future. Loneliness got the best of me, and I went on a dating rampage shortly after Jaron turned one. My mom was so helpful and understanding and she allowed me lots of free time. I dated many women over the next two years until I met Michelle. I dropped everybody like a bad habit right afterward."

Question two. "How did you meet?"

Her face turned tender. "I was at a housewarming for an older acquaintance of mine. She was a woman I had just met and she was interested in me, but I just thought she was cool to hang around with. She was a social butterfly, so once the party got started, she mingled about with all of her friends, often leaving me alone. Michelle was there with a friend of hers, and we ended up in the same room together. We started a conversation about a piece of art, and it took off from there. We exchanged numbers and talked every day, beginning that night."

"Sounds like it was meant to be."

"I think so. Even though we're not a couple anymore, I still believe we came together at the right time, when we were supposed to."

"You're saying you believe in fate?" I asked her.

"Definitely. I don't believe in chance meetings. I try to gain something from everyone I meet, whether I talk to them for only a minute or make a lifelong friend." She winked a hazel brown eye at me.

Question three.

"You've said that people are born gay. You've always known you were gay?"

"Oh, yes," she said, getting up to bring the bottle of vodka into the room with us. "As a child I had a crush on my female teachers, a couple of my mom's friends, and the girl next door. Her name was Stephanie too, and in sixth and seventh grade you couldn't tear us apart. We were so close and shared such an intimate bond. Not sexually, of course, but our emotional energy for one another was deep. She had my back and I had hers."

"I had a friend like that," I said, remembering Stacey, my best friend in kindergarten and first grade (pre–Tori and Vanessa days, of course). Then, it was Stacey and I that were joined at the hip, until her mom and dad divorced. Neither wanted the responsibility of caring for her, so she was sent to live with her grandmother in another state. I was devastated when she left. But that didn't mean I was gay. Right? I was just a little girl.

"We moved across town a year after my dad died, and we weren't able to keep in close contact anymore. I just knew I would see her in the clubs as I got older, but I haven't."

"And I haven't run into her either. She must be straight or she's moved away," Steph said, laughing. "More?" she asked me after pouring herself another shot.

"Yes," I replied, downing the drink right after she handed it to me. "Um, what are the clubs like?" I asked.

She ran a hand through the glossy strands of her hair. "That depends on the club and where you are. There's only a handful of female clubs in the city, so I go down to Chicago, but not as often as I used to. And the clubs for *us* are even more slim. They come and go just like the straight clubs. I love mixed clubs. And when I say *mixed*, I mean gender and race. I love watching the drag shows, because some of those men put a lot of work into their bodies, and the results are amazing! There are a few that you would never know were really men."

"I have to see that one day," I said, remembering the few times I'd seen David dressed like a woman.

"Yeah, it's crazy," Steph said.

"So, at the club, men dance with men and women dance with women?"

"*Yesssssss,*" she answered, like that was a stupid question.

I guess it was. "Do you still go out?"

"Not like I used to," she said.

"Would you take me?" I asked.

Steph frowned. "Why?"

I didn't want to say anything stupid again. "I'm still learning about diversity, even at my age, and I want to experience as much as I can about all groups of people. And I want to be able to share as much as I can with you, since we're friends."

She gave me a look that said, *Come on,* and I had to laugh at my politically correct answer.

"Uh-huh. You're not going looking for some freak show, are you?"

"I do want to see what it's like, but I promise to be cool. I won't embarrass you."

"When do you want to go?" she asked.

I looked at my watch. It was 8:30. "There's no time like the present. Let's go now," I said, standing up..

"Not yet, girl, calm down," she said as she stood up next to me. "There's nothing jumping until at least eleven. Let me think, it's Saturday so the Dollhouse is a nice place to go." She looked at me a little concerned. "Are you sure, Ky? What if you see someone you know? There are more of us than you think."

"I'm not worried about that. And if I do see someone,

then we *both* saw each other in the club, so there's not much they can say, is there?"

"I see your point. What about Jeff? Are you going to tell him?"

"I haven't even told Jeff that you're gay, and I don't think it's necessary to fill him in on this little outing either. He's hanging with his brother tonight anyway, and I doubt that they'll be there."

She corrected me. "Don't be so sure. Lots of straight men hang out in the club. The Dollhouse is for females, but there are most definitely a few men in there looking for some freaky shit. It's so annoying. Just be careful. I've known a couple of girls that have gotten busted at the club with their 'friend' and it's not pretty. Some men love it, others get pissed. I don't know what kind of person Jeff is, but I don't want to get you caught up in something ugly. *Especially* with me in the middle."

"Thanks, Steph, but Jeff is open-minded. He's always been cool with my cousin David."

Steph's eyes quickly rolled to the back of her head and then back at me. "Girl, don't you know there is a major difference between being cordial to a gay person and taking it to a personal level? Some men find it intimidating when their woman has a gay female friend."

"Why?" I asked, like I really didn't know the answer.

Steph crossed her arms across her chest and struck a pose leaning on one hip. She cleared her throat in a listen-to-what-I'm-about-to-say manner.

"What's the reason you haven't told Jeff about me?" she asked.

My eyes immediately widened, and I tried to cover them with a blink. And another blink. And another. I finally answered.

"I don't think it's an issue. Just like you said, I don't introduce my other friends by their sexual preference. That's your private life. I thought I should respect that."

She waited, but I was finished.

"Mmm, all right. Whatever you say." She paused. "That's the only reason?" she asked, searching for a deeper explanation for my hesitancy to talk about her with Jeff.

Even with her standing right in front of me, I pretended like I didn't hear her and changed the subject.

"Can I wear what I have on?" I asked.

"Of course, but I'm going to change. Otherwise, people will think we're trying to dress alike and that is so played!"

"I heard that. So what are you going to wear?"

"Let's go check my closet," she said, leading me to the bedroom opposite Jaron's.

I felt like I had stepped into Cleopatra's lair when I walked through the door. She had a king-size canopy bed covered in black-satin sheets with a gold bed skirt and gold silk fabric draped around the canopy posts. There were at least six large pillows across the top of the bed. Some in black-and-gold satin pillowcases, others in leopard print. At the foot of the bed sat a black chest with gold trim. A beautiful statue, at least four feet tall of a nude woman, stood in one corner, and in the other was a similar statue. Only, this statue had another woman embracing her from behind. The statue wasn't tasteless, but gentle and intimate.

There was a gold mirror hanging above her bed with matching black-trimmed mirrors on each of the walls at the sides of the bed. Also gracing the walls were two pictures of beautiful African women in gold wrap dresses keeping a watchful eye over Stephanie.

My feet warmed up as I stepped onto the plush black carpeting toward her walk-in closet. Inside the closet to the left hung business suits in gray, navy, and black. On the opposite side were jeans, khakis, jogging suits, sweaters, and casual tops. Her variety of shoes ranged from Nine West pumps to Nike running shoes to Old Navy flip-flops.

"I might get lost in here," I said jokingly. "Where do I start?"

"Since you're wearing jeans, I'll wear jeans too."

She pulled a pair of black fitted jeans from a hanger and a brightly colored sweater with a plunging neckline.

"Hey, this jacket is cute," I said, picking up a black, button-down leather jacket.

"You were reading my mind," she said.

"Are you going to shower first?" I asked her.

"Of course." She laughed. "You can shower after me. Do you want to wear something of mine?" she asked.

"Maybe I'll change tops," I said, picking up and admiring a fuchsia blouse.

"That will look pretty on you," she commented. "Please wear it."

I blushed a color nearly as bright as the top. "Okay, let me run and grab my overnight bag," I said.

"You brought one with you?" she asked, curious.

"I keep one in the trunk just in case," I explained.

"Of what?" she wanted to know.

"In case of emergency or car breakdown. You never know when you'll get stranded somewhere," I said. "Or who you may end up spending the night with," I added.

She smiled at my flirtatious remark. "My, my."

I left the closet and picked up my keys before going outside. It was a clear night with a crisp fall breeze. Autumn had definitely arrived, a reminder of the chilly, snowy winter that lay ahead.

I felt like a kid on my way to the circus. I was so excited to go to the club with Steph and to get a taste of what her lifestyle was like. I wondered if the scene was similar to the straight clubs. Were there groups of friends who came to relax, have a drink and converse with one another? And yet another crowd that came strictly to get sweaty on the dance floor? And were there the aggressors on the prowl approaching every woman for a phone number or an invitation home that evening? I couldn't wait to find out.

When I got back inside, Stephanie had put on a 112 CD and "Peaches & Cream" was playing. I sang the words and thought about the song in an entirely new perspective.

The shower was running, so I sat on the couch and waited for her to finish. I stared at the picture of her and Michelle and imagined their relationship: waking up in the same bed, getting ready for work, preparing Jaron for school, having dinner together, talking about each other's day in the evening, and falling asleep in each other's arms, the same activities that my parents did on a daily basis, but in this case, with two members of the same sex. There didn't seem to be a big difference. So what was all the hoopla about?

I heard the water turn off, and in came Steph, wrapped in a black towel, water dripping down her glistening legs. I watched one drop roll down her inner thigh and over her calf until it rested on the floor.

"All yours. I put a towel and washcloth in there for you already," she informed me.

I unglued my eyes from her thighs and thanked her. I believe it came out just above a whisper. I picked up my bag and went into her bathroom, avoiding eye contact with her. After I brushed my teeth and put on my shower cap, I took a cold shower.

When I returned, Stephanie was sitting on her floor in a black bra and panties while polishing her nails. Shit, was she doing this on purpose? *Of course not. Tori, Vanessa, and I see each other this way every week.* So why did my knees get weak at the sight of her bare skin?

"Umm . . . where is your iron? I need to re-iron my jeans," I asked, concentrating on just her eyes.

She pointed toward the kitchen.

"The laundry room is through the kitchen to the left. It's in there. I already turned it on for you."

I whispered thanks again and walked away wrapped in a towel that I wore *over* my bra and panties.

Okay, no offense to my male species out there, but no man had ever laid out my towel and washcloth for me. They just pointed me toward the linen closet. And I'd had the iron left on for me, but never turned on in advance. Was Steph more thoughtful, or had I just dated some trifling-ass men? Before Jeff, of course.

I dressed in the laundry room before going back to Steph's room. She was ending a phone call.

"I'll see you in a little bit," she said to the person on the other end. She looked at me and laughed as the other person responded.

"Off-limits, girl. Bye!" She was still chuckling when she hung up. "That was my crazy friend, Karen. She'll be at the Dollhouse tonight, so you can meet her. She's funny as hell. It's been so long since I've been out, she couldn't believe I was going."

"Well, I'm glad I could get you out."

I applied makeup to my freshly washed face, using black eyeliner and shadow for a nighttime dramatic effect, and emphasized my lips with a hot pink gloss. Steph and I both used her flatiron to smooth our ends. Once dressed, and as usual, she was beautiful.

We took her Malibu to the club, which surprisingly turned out to be no more than a corner bar just five minutes from my own apartment. I felt nervous excitement like I was going on my very first date. My heart was racing when she opened the door to the dimly lit, smoky bar. Janet's "You Want This" was playing as Stephanie paid our covers and we were in.

My eyes darted right to left, and all around. Women,

mostly African-American, of every shade, height, size, feminine and tomboy, surrounded me. I felt like a baby first opening my eyes to a new world. There were women with nearly bald haircuts, in baggy jeans, sweatshirts, and Timberlands. Others casually dressed like Steph and me. And a handful wearing sexy outfits with ass and titties hanging out.

Steph nudged me toward the bar and ordered vodka and cranberry for both of us. I drank it like water as we made our way to the back by the pool table and dance floor, which was about the size of my bedroom. Steph greeted a few women but introduced me to none. I made eye contact with several, who looked at me and tapped the person next to them, like I was the new girl in school.

We were watching a group of women shoot pool in teams when someone shouted Stephanie's name. Just about everyone looked. Approaching us was a cute, petite brown-skinned thing with short, wavy hair. She wore dark blue jeans with a matching jacket and Ralph Lauren Polo sweatshirt underneath. They embraced.

"What's up, Karen?" Steph asked.

"Nuttin', nuttin', just chillin', you know what I'm sayin'. Keepin' it real," Karen replied.

For such a little person, her voice boomed over the music.

"Karen, this is Kyla. Kyla, this is Karen. Keep her at a safe distance, Ky," Steph said teasingly.

"*Heeeeeeyyyyyy,*" Karen said, licking her bottom lip as she shook my hand. A little too much spit lingered and shined when she spoke.

"Nice to meet you," I said, probably sounding too professional.

"You came alone?" Steph asked Karen.

"Yeah, I thought I would, you know, since you was steppin' out tonight and shit. But I see why you been stayin' in these days," Karen said, eyeing me up and down.

"Anyway, mind your business," Steph responded, taking a step closer to me. "How's Sharice?"

"*Maaaaaannnnn,* you been on the low-low for real, girl! Sharice moved to Texas a munt ago. Her moms needed some help wit' her younger brotha, you know. He fell in wit' the wrong crowd and started doin' stupid shit. She say it's temporary, only 'til he graduate, but I told her I can't be sittin' around twiddlin' my thumbs while she gone, you know what I'm sayin'," she said, glancing around the room, looking at everybody's ass. "I'm goin' to the bar. You ladies need somethin'?" she asked after seeing a piece she wanted to bite.

I looked at my cup of melted ice. "Vodka and cranberry," I said.

"I'm good," Steph said. She had only taken a few sips of her drink.

Karen walked to the bar, slapping five and slapping asses all the way.

"I told you she was crazy," Steph said when Karen walked away. "Can you believe she owns and runs three day-care centers?"

For real?

Steph continued. "I hope I didn't make you feel uncomfortable by letting her assume whatever she wants about us. I have to let her think what she needs to. Otherwise, she's going to be up in your ass all night."

"That's okay. Thanks for looking out. She's kind of cute, but loud as hell!"

"I know. Don't go to a restaurant or the movies with her. She'll embarrass the shit out of you. We used to hang a lot when Michelle lived here. Michelle was really close to her girlfriend at the time."

"I see." I waited a moment and then asked, "Do you still miss her?"

"Michelle?" Steph asked.

I nodded.

"Not like I used to," she answered. "My heart ached for her when she first left and for quite some time after that. Now I miss her the way you miss an old friend you haven't talked to in a long time. But she'll always have a special place in my heart. Definitely. You miss your old loves?"

I thought for a brief moment. "Honestly, no. I've done a good job holding on to my heart since the first time it got broken. Since then I haven't cared enough about anyone to miss them now."

"But you love Jeff, right?" she asked.

"Sure, he's the best man that ever happened to me."

She played with my words. "Why do you say it like that? The best *man?*"

"Because there were quite a few men before him that treated me nothing like he does."

"Do you think there's a difference between loving a man and loving a woman?" she asked.

"Here you go, baby," Karen interrupted, handing me my drink.

I took a swig immediately, grateful for the save. The two of them reminisced for a while, so I studied the crowd. Yep, the cliques were the same. I saw a group of feminine women sitting at the bar engaged in conversation, acting like they were too cute to talk to anybody. There was a crowd of couples bumping and grinding on the dance floor. And yet another group of women, with a few men, holding up the wall, staring at every ass that walked by.

Suddenly, a sparkle caught my eye. I focused my eyes toward the twinkle and found Mya's gold tooth flashing across the room. She walked straight up to me. I expected to see Trina as well, but there was no sight of her.

"It's a pleasure seeing you again," she said, extending her hand. I shook her hand, but she didn't let go. Instead, she stroked my palm with her thumb. "I knew it," she said.

"Knew what?" I asked, silently praying she would let my hand go.

"I knew you had it in you. I couldn't even tell who you were with last night."

She finally noticed Steph and let my hand rest.

"I don't know what you mean," I said.

"I watched you all evening, talking to your guy but leaning on your girl over here. You better watch it. Girl, body language is a killa! It tells the truth."

She turned to walk away but added, "Don't deny what you can't hide."

I finished the rest of my drink listening to those words over and over in my head. Was it that obvious? Could Steph tell? Or worse, could Jeff see it? I couldn't conceal it any further, my attraction to Steph was undeniable. She was the prettiest woman I ever laid my eyes on. She was smart and independent and she stirred feelings in me that I didn't know existed. I got excited spending time with her and my body tingled by her touch.

Jay-Z's "Give It to Me" came on, and Karen yelled, "Das my jam! Le's go!" She grabbed Steph's hand, Steph took hold of mine, and we headed to the cubicle-sized dance floor.

Karen danced super-cool, bopping from side to side, trying to look like a mack dancing with two women. And Stephanie completely took me off guard. The girl moved like she had just stepped *into* Jay-Z's video, hips grinding the air with her arms stretched over her head, fingers snapping. She never missed a beat. She closed her eyes and let the music guide her.

We danced two more songs before heading back to the bar. Steph ordered another drink for me while I went to the bathroom. I felt like I needed to splash cold water on my face, partially because I was sweating, but mostly because of Stephanie's seductive dancing. The girl turned me on.

When I returned, Karen was cornered up with a delicate, thin girl with thick, long braids that looked too heavy for her head. I just knew she'd fall over if she turned her head sideways. Steph was sitting at the bar, saving a stool for me with her hand. She was talking to a beautiful, older woman behind the bar.

"I've been busy lately," she was saying. "But I'll stop in more often. Promise."

She introduced me when I sat down.

"This is my friend Kyla."

I put my hand out, but instead of taking it, the beautiful woman leaned forward and kissed me on the lips. I wasn't expecting a kiss and I tried not to show my surprise.

"Having fun?" she asked.

I looked into her darkly rimmed charcoal eyes. "Yes, I am." I almost said *ma'am* but I caught myself. She looked like she tried hard not to look her age.

She nodded at Steph and went back to making drinks.

"That's the owner," Steph explained.

"Okay," I said, "but what's up with the kiss?"

"She kisses everybody. And I mean *everybody*. Most of us know to turn our cheek to her. Girl, can you imagine everywhere those lips have been?"

I sipped on my drink and noticed Steph eyeing it.

"Thirsty?" I asked, and handed it to her.

She put her mouth on my straw and took two quick swallows. "Enough. I'm driving tonight. It's on you next time!"

"Next time? So you'll bring me back?"

"I think so. I thought maybe you'd be all stiff and scared, but you're not. I like that," she said.

"I like it here," I said, looking around at all the women

enjoying each other's company. "It's nice to hang out without a bunch of men breathing down my neck."

"Tell me about it. I don't mind going out with my straight friends, but sometimes I'd rather stay home and avoid the whole game."

"Mmm-hmm," I agreed as I sucked on an ice cube.

I stared at her and admired how her honey-colored eyes glowed in the dim light. How they had grown slightly heavy and twinkled when she looked at me. I reached up and touched her hair, stroking it from the part at her scalp, down to her ends, where it hung just beneath her breast. The tips of my fingers grazed the fabric of her sweater over her breast.

"Your hair is so pretty like that," I commented.

"Thanks," she said, looking back at me. Her eyes were now filled with questions.

"Did you hear what Mya said to me?" I asked her.

"Yes, I did."

"Why do you think she said that?"

"You have to answer that question for yourself, Kyla."

We sat for a moment in silence, looking at two women across the bar that needed to leave and get a hotel room.

"What do you think?" I asked her.

"About what, exactly?" she asked, not making it easy for me.

"What she said. I mean, do you think I'm hiding something?"

She twisted her stool to face me and rested a hand on my thigh.

"I don't know if you're hiding something, unless you come out and tell me. I don't like to speculate. I prefer the truth."

I sat and let the vodka relax me. Dammit. Why do we lose all inhibitions at this point? I twisted so I could face her as well and rested my hand on top of hers.

"I don't know what I'm feeling," I admitted. "All I know is, I like spending time with you way more than I should. And I have these visions about you and what a relationship with you would be like. And I don't know why I get butter-flies whenever you're close to me. And I don't know why I'm telling you this, because you're going to think I'm crazy."

Without a second of hesitation she reached in her purse and got her keys out. "You ready?" she asked.

"Sure," I said. I felt tears of embarrassment burn my eyes but I forced them back.

Karen yelled, "Lata" to us on our way out, but Stephanie barely acknowledged her.

We rode in silence, no radio and no conversation. Did I piss her off? I wanted to ask but I was filled with too much fear to look at her, let alone ask a question. Her hands gripped the steering wheel tightly and her face held a stern look. She barely slowed the car as she took turns and sat impatiently at each stoplight that held us up.

"I want you to stay," she said when she parked her car next to mine outside her apartment. "Don't drive home tonight," she instructed.

"Okay," I said quietly, opening the door and walking so slowly you would have thought I was on death row.

Inside, I changed into the pajamas I also kept in my overnight bag and asked Steph for a blanket so I could make a bed on the couch.

"No, you can sleep with me." Her voice was flat, show-ing no emotion.

I was so tired and hurt that I went straight to bed and pulled the covers over my head. I made sure to lie close to the edge and turn my back to her side of the bed. Still, I wouldn't let the tears of shame fall.

She shuffled about the room for several minutes before

getting into bed. She faced my back and touched the skin peeking just above my tank top. My body warmed.

"I'm not mad at you, Ky," she said, her fingernail tracing a circle around the small mole on my shoulder blade. "I know that's what you're thinking. But I want to talk in the morning, okay?"

"Okay," I said, slightly relieved. She turned over, but remained close enough that the smalls of our backs were touching. I stayed awake until her breathing became heavy and slow. Eventually, I fell asleep also. If it weren't for the vodka, I probably wouldn't have slept a wink.

I was sprawled across Steph's bed like I owned it when I woke up. The bedroom door was closed but it didn't block the smell of frying bacon, and my stomach grumbled with delight. I sat up and looked in the black mirror to my right. It was a scary sight, with my hair stuck to the right side of my face and mascara smeared under my eyes like a linebacker.

I washed my face and brushed my teeth before entering the kitchen. Stephanie was at the stove making scrambled eggs.

"She's arisen," she said cheerfully, her mood obviously brightened since last night.

"Good morning," I said, surprised by the gleefulness in her voice.

"Barely. It's almost noon."

I looked at the clock. It was 11:53. I must have needed that sleep bad. She fixed our plates, and we sat at the table. We both ate like we were in an eating contest. I felt the need to explain my actions at the Dollhouse.

"I'm sorry if I made you uncomfortable last night. I shouldn't have said the things I said," I apologized.

"Yes, you should have. I'm glad you did. And I'm sorry

for the silent treatment. I just didn't think you were in the right frame of mind to talk about it at the time."

I agreed.

"I like you, Ky," she continued. "I think you're one of the nicest and sweetest people I've met in a long time. But I don't know if crossing the friendship line is a good idea for us. I've been in this situation before where my straight friends think they're attracted to me. But that's where it ended. It never went any further."

For the first time, she lowered her eyes when she spoke. "It's different with you, though. I feel close to you in a way that I shouldn't either. I mean, I admit I've been flirting with you a little bit. I can't help it," she said, smiling. "I look forward to seeing you every Monday in class. It's one of the highlights of my week. But you're in a situation that I stay away from. You're involved with a man and that's dangerous. I feel like I could really get into you and I'm not prepared to deal with that, considering your circumstances. And most importantly, I need a woman who's secure in herself and her sexuality, not someone testing the waters."

I let her words digest before responding. How could I know if I was testing the waters if I hadn't even dipped my toe in yet?

"I understand what you're saying, Steph. I know I'm in a relationship and this isn't supposed to be happening. But this is the first time I've ever felt this way about anyone since I've been with Jeff. And it's definitely not something I planned. I don't know how to comment on the curiosity issue. I've also never felt this way about a woman, so I honestly can't say how I would feel if I ever experience what it's like to actually be with one. But whatever happens, I don't want to risk our friendship."

"It's hard now, Ky. The door is open. Do we walk through or close it?"

I heard my cell phone ring from the living room. I knew it was Jeff wondering where in the hell I was.

Selfishly I asked Stephanie, "Can we leave it open for now and maybe walk through when and if the time is right?"

She wiggled in her seat. "That's fine. I'm okay with that. But think about this, would you even ask to leave the door open if you truly felt you were with the right person?"

I had no answer.

7

Monday morning I overslept by forty-five minutes after a night of restless sleep. Tori and Vanessa were already on their StairMasters when I arrived at the gym. I had spent the previous afternoon shopping for Gladyce's birthday gift and hanging out with Jeff, the whole time lying about my whereabouts Saturday night.

I told him Steph and I stayed at the library until 8:00, which was why I missed his first phone call at 5:00. My cell phone was turned off at the library, you know, to avoid those irritated stares if my phone were to disturb others' studies. We were starving when we left, so we went back to Steph's place and ordered pizza. Oh, why didn't I call him back? Because he was out to dinner with Kent and I didn't want to interrupt. See, Steph and I fell asleep shortly after eating and slept the rest of the night. So why didn't I answer my phone when he checked in after getting home from the bar (I guess the fact that I was supposed to be sleeping wasn't enough)? Well, my phone was in my purse, which Steph had put in the closet with my jacket. I guess I didn't hear it ring.

I was mentally exhausted from telling those lies, and the guilt was eating me alive. I figured that's why I wasn't able to sleep. That is, until about 3:00 in the morning when my body finally gave in. So I slept until 7:15, even though I'm normally at the gym by 7:30.

Vanessa was full of enthusiasm when I arrived. Tori seemed a bit annoyed. I had enough on my mind, so I'd worry about her moody ass later.

"What are you all smiles about?" I asked Vanessa. Her smile made me smile and perked me up a bit.

"Roger and I moved the date up," she screamed, excitement belting through her veins like electricity. "We found the perfect place for the wedding and reception together. This way, no one else is getting *their* way but us!"

"What's the new date?" I asked.

"Take a guess. You'll never guess!" she exclaimed.

"All right, just tell me then," I said, sharing her excitement.

"New Year's eve," she almost screamed.

"Really? As in only two and half months from now?"

"Yep," she squealed.

"You'd better start hustling. That day will be here before you know it."

"I know, girl, I know. But I got so much done this past weekend already. After I talked with you Saturday morning—by the way, thank you," she sang to me. "I called Roger and he came over right away. We sat and talked for hours and agreed that our wedding should be just that, *ours*. So we put our heads together and decided to combine the wedding and reception into one neutral place. Guess where?"

She was really into the guessing game this morning. I looked over at Tori who was eyeing a cutie lifting weights across the room. Obviously, she had heard this story already.

"Tell me, Vanessa," I said.

"The museum," she said, actually clapping her hands.

"Really? I never would have guessed that. That will be beautiful. And different. You won't be by the dinosaurs, will you?" I asked, joking with her.

"Yes, I thought that would be unique," she said, a little disappointed.

"What?" I was only kidding with her.

"I'm just playing," she said, slapping me a little too hard on the shoulder. "But that really was an option. Anyway, we decided on the African Serengeti. They even provide the catering!" The girl was too thrilled.

"It sounds great, *V,* I'm so happy for you both," I said, hugging her.

She continued smiling and went back to working her thighs on the StairMaster, energy bursting through her body. I decided to find out what was wrong with Tori.

"What's up, Tori? You're quiet over here," I said.

She stared at me. No, she *glared* at me. I was a little startled.

"Where were you this weekend?" she demanded, like she was Gladyce and had given birth to me.

"Saturday I worked on a paper at the library, and I was with Jeff yesterday," I explained, like I really was her kid.

"That's it?" she asked like she knew I left something out.

I was too tired to tell another lie. "I spent Saturday night with Steph," I told her.

She continued to stare at me. She couldn't possibly know about the club, so I wasn't even about to volunteer that information.

"What happened with Juan?" I asked, changing the subject.

"Dismissed."

"Good. That was wrong of him to flirt with Stephanie."

"You know," she said with an irritated edge in her tone, "you two spend a lot of time together."

"And?" I challenged.

"I'm just saying. She sees you more than we do."

Please tell me this isn't about jealousy over friendship. We're seriously too old for this. I understood the bond that the three of us shared, but with it being so strong, why did she feel so threatened?

"Our schedule hasn't changed. I'm still here every Monday and we're still on every Friday," I said.

"And every other day you're with her. You're not going to start bringing her every Friday, are you?" Tori asked like I better not consider it.

"Why? Would there be a problem if I did?"

"I'm just used to our little group, that's all. It's our own club."

Did she say *club?* I guess we *were* retreating back to third grade and OSC days. She was pissing me off now and forced me to resort to her level.

"That doesn't stop you from bringing a new member every week, now, does it?"

I dared her to respond. Vanessa kept quiet, continuing to smile to herself. I finished my workout alone while trying to figure out why Tori was acting so childish. We'd been friends since we were kids, and I wasn't interested in fighting over petty issues.

I tried to put myself in her shoes to see how I would feel if she or *V* gained a new friend. Would I resent that person for spending so much time with my lifelong friend? I seriously doubted it. Or was I not being a true friend by not being honest about my whereabouts with Stephanie? I wasn't sure if she and Vanessa were always 100 percent honest with me. We were still entitled to private lives. Still, I couldn't go all week with an attitude, so I approached Tori in the shower.

"What's going on, Tori? Is there something you want to talk to me about?"

She stopped lathering herself in deodorant soap and turned to face me. Although I was three inches taller than Tori, her stare dominated the moment.

"You tell me," she demanded.

"What do you mean?" I asked, feeling slightly uneasy.

She shook her head. "Never mind, Ky. I'll just wait. Meanwhile, we're still cool."

I felt like I was having a conversation with someone I had only known a short time, not twenty years. And what was I supposed to tell her? Was my attraction to Steph as obvious as Mya said and as lucid as I feared?

"Are we still meeting at the restaurant Friday night?" I asked.

"Yes, I'll be ready around nine," she answered and stepped out of the shower. Then she turned around. "You *are* bringing Jeff, right?"

"Of course I am."

She gave me one last stare, shook her head and walked away. I stayed in the shower long enough to make sure she would be gone by the time I got to my locker. Vanessa was hanging up from a call on her cell phone when I returned.

"Okay, I need you and Tori at Tie the Knot Saturday morning at ten. Does that work for you?"

"Yes, I'll be there."

I hated to open the door for an answer I wasn't prepared to hear, but I needed to know if Vanessa knew what was up with Tori. Truly, I needed to know if either of them knew about Steph.

"Do you know what's going on with our girl?" I asked her.

"Girl, no, but I wish she would tell us so we can move past it. She came in this morning all agitated, and I have no idea why. Maybe she's still mad about Juan."

"Maybe. But it's not like she hasn't dealt with assholes in the past. I think it's something else."

"Well, whatever it is, I know she better get over it quickly because I don't want attitudes messing with my wedding day."

That's the first time I'd ever heard Vanessa say anything remotely selfish, and I still knew she was halfway kidding.

On my way to class Yvonne called my cell to touch base about Gladyce's birthday this Saturday. She had made the reservations to Luca's, an upbeat Italian restaurant located downtown.

"Are you bringing anyone?" Yvonne asked.

Was I bringing *anyone*? What happened to "Is Jeff coming?" I suddenly felt like everyone could see something coming and I was blind to it. Or maybe I was just pretending like I didn't see it either.

"Jeff is coming," I said, somewhat irritated that she would ask. "Are you bringing Byron?"

"Yes. We've seen each other several times since our lunch date, and now he's presentable," she informed me.

"I can't wait to meet him," I said.

"I hope you like him. Dinner is at eight, so we can meet there. Dad is picking Mom up, so don't worry about her."

"Okay. I'll see you then."

"Bye, Kyla."

Steph and I were eating cheese omelets in our usual spot when I vented about Tori. She had me feeling like I had done something to upset her, and I knew I hadn't. At least not intentionally.

"I hope she doesn't have a problem with me," Steph said.

"You know, she almost made it seem like she knows

something about you and me. I don't know how. I could just be paranoid."

"What makes you think she knows anything?"

"Well, she kept staring at me like she was waiting for me to tell her about you. I asked her what was up, and she told me to tell *her*. I don't know what she meant by that."

"Hmph. Yeah, it sounds like she thinks she knows something. I told you, Ky, it only takes one person at the club who knows somebody, who knows somebody that knows you. And then the word is out. Especially because you were a new face."

"I guess I didn't think of it that way."

"Tori will come around and tell you what's bothering her eventually. She doesn't seem like the type to hold her tongue."

"I hope so, because I don't like this tension," I said.

"I guess you'll think twice about coming again," she stated.

"Please, I'll go back to the club if I want to," I said defiantly. "I can't let people dictate what I do."

Steph smiled. "Good for you, Kyla. But be careful, all right?"

I knew she wasn't referring to Tori, but rather Jeff. "I will."

We didn't approach the topic of "us." I don't think either one of us had anything new to bring to the table. But I grew fonder of her with every minute I spent with her. Still, that didn't change the fact that I was involved in a relationship already. So what could I do about it? We didn't make any plans to get together this week, but I was hoping we would talk.

Our hug good-bye was different today. It was soft, but meaningful, lingering and sensual. Her arms rested around my waist, pressing my body into hers so we were touching from head to toe. The sensation that ran through my body was overwhelming.

"I'll talk to you soon," she said in my ear.

Never in my life had I wanted so badly to hold and kiss someone and never let go. I smiled before releasing her, and we went our separate ways.

I had three voice mail messages when I got home from work that evening. One was from Gladyce, thanking Yvonne and me in advance for her birthday dinner that week. Another from Jeff telling me he would be over around 9:00 tonight. And Katie from Hot 104 called to tell me the station tried contacting me this morning live on the air but there was no answer. Turned out I was the grand-prize winner of the all-expense-paid trip to Nassau, Bahamas. I couldn't believe it! I played the message three times to make sure I'd heard it correctly. I was so excited that I started jumping up and down on my love seat. I damn near fell and broke the glass table. I took all the information down to call Katie back in the morning.

While I took a shower I fantasized about lounging on the beach sipping a mai tai and watching a breathtaking sunrise from my balcony. And taking a romantic walk along the shore with waves splashing my thighs with each step . . . but whose hand would I be holding on these walks?

Confusion overcame me. Why was my mind tormenting me with thoughts of another woman? Why was my body yearning for a touch I'd never felt before? I tried to dig deep in my heart to figure out why these feelings were emerging. Had something happened to me to turn my attention toward women? No. I'd been in a happy, loving relationship with Jeff for over four years. I'd had my heart broken once and never since then, so I can't say that a bad experience with a man had done this to me. David, and now Stephanie, said that people are born gay. But, hell, I was twenty-six years old; you'd think I would have had an inkling of it by now.

According to David and the therapist Aunt Shari sent him to, a person can be gay or straight, with many people falling somewhere in-between. There are women that never have and never would consider sleeping with a man, and vice versa. Then there are those that experiment with same-sex relationships but don't consider themselves gay. And then there are bisexuals, who swim somewhere around the midpoint, loving both same- and opposite-sex relationships. David thought bisexuals should make up their minds and make a choice, and then in the next breath he'd say he won't judge them because he didn't want anyone judging him.

So where did I fit it? I'd always believed I was heterosexual, considering I'd only had boyfriends in the past. Sure, I'd admired the beauty of Nia Long and Vanessa Williams, but did I want to get with them? Hell no. Had I ever been comfortable in the nudity of other women? No, I hadn't. Did that mean something? I have no idea. All I know was that after all these years, I couldn't figure out why I was torn between the love of a man and the desire for a woman.

I was still deep in thought when my apartment buzzer rang and Jeff let himself in. I was lying on my bed, rubbing lotion on my skin, when he stood in my bedroom doorway. His presence seemed so masculine as he watched me without saying a word. I continued to bathe my skin in Victoria's Secret Turquoise Paradise as I studied him. He stood tall and handsome in a navy blue business suit with a blue and yellow tie. His shoulders were strong and broad with long arms at his sides. The shadow on his face needed shaving, giving him a slightly rugged appearance.

His eyes twinkled with delight as I put lotion on the inside of my thighs slowly, seductively . . . inviting him in.

I needed him to make love to me. I needed him to lay me down, look down at me and rock my body as only a man could. Could he wash away these thoughts and urges I was feeling for someone else? Could each stroke touch a part of me that a woman could not? Could I feel his heart pound against mine and feel a bond and unity that couldn't be replaced? I hoped so. I *wanted* it to be so. I needed comfort and security in his embrace. Jeff obliged me.

Afterward, I lay in his arms, feeling his breath on my neck, trying to force back the tears of confusion that bled through my eyes.

8

Saturday morning I stood in front of the three-way mirror in a satin, floor-length bridesmaid dress in fire-engine red. It flared from the waist down and had a ruffled trim at the bottom and around the puffy-ass sleeves. I turned around and stared at the big bow sitting on top of my butt. I looked at Tori, who looked back at me in disbelief. I silently prayed that Vanessa would choose another dress.

"What do you think?" I asked Vanessa, fearing her answer.

"It doesn't look how I thought it would," she said, studying every angle of my body.

"Yeah," Tori jumped in.

"I think the bow might bounce on our asses when we walk too," I said, hoping she would get a clue.

"Yeah, you're right. I'll be back," Vanessa said and she was off with the saleslady.

"Girl! What in the hell is this?" Tori asked as soon as Vanessa left the fitting room, which was more like a glamorous Hollywood dressing room, with velvet cushioned chairs and fresh flowers scenting the air.

"I wish I knew. Please go help her," I asked Tori.

"Oh, hell yeah. I can't be walking around looking like Little Red Riding Hood all day."

Tori left, and I took off that hideous dress, wondering why someone as intelligent as Vanessa had zero sense of style.

My relationship with Tori seemed somewhat back to normal. We had shared an enjoyable evening last night at the restaurant, sipping martinis and devouring appetizers of nachos and mozzarella sticks with marinara sauce.

Jeff and Roger talked sports all evening with Tori's new friend, Malik. He was a tall, chocolate, Morehouse graduate who worked as supervisor of the call center for the phone company. I could only imagine the pussy that was thrown at him on a daily basis.

The girls and I talked about the upcoming holidays as well as the wedding, of course. The chip on Tori's shoulders must have fallen off because she was her usual upbeat, sassy self. I was glad to have her back.

Vanessa returned with yet another dress straight from the 1980s. Who still made this out-of-date shit? Tori rushed in behind her carrying a deep red, sexy, spaghetti strapped dress with a high slit right up the front. There was a matching shawl that draped across the back and upper arms. The dress was sharp.

"Try this one!" Tori said, and practically threw the dress at me. She didn't have to tell me twice.

I moved carefully, trying not to feel self-conscious as they watched me dress. Neither of them seemed to be paying attention to me, only the way the dress eased onto my body.

It was fantastic! The dress curved to my waist and hips

and flashed a little thigh with each step. *Please let her choose this one, please let her choose this one*, I prayed again, asking God for this one favor.

"What about this one?" Vanessa asked, holding up her dress looking like something Queen Elizabeth would have worn.

"No!" Tori and I yelled together.

"I mean, this one looks good, don't you think?" I crossed my fingers.

"But it's expensive. I was trying not to have you spend too much money," Vanessa responded.

"Don't worry about that, *V.* This dress is more versatile because it can be worn more than once," I said, trying to convince her. "I can wear it to a dinner party or a Christmas party. Right, Tori?" I added with a nod of my head, encouraging her to agree.

"Oh yes! I'll go find my size and try it on." She skipped away before Vanessa could protest. The saleslady even looked relieved.

I snapped my fingers and did a little dance in the mirror just to make sure there was enough room in the dress to get my groove on the dance floor.

Vanessa conceded. "The dress looks great on you, Ky. You and Jeff will look so handsome walking down the aisle together. It'll be good practice."

"You don't see a ring on this finger, do you?" I wiggled my left hand.

"Don't speak too soon."

"What do you mean by that?" I asked.

"Oh, nothing." She grinned and turned to Tori as she walked back into the fitting room.

Did she know something I didn't know? Had Jeff talked about marriage with Roger? Inquiring minds wanted to know!

After we left the bridal salon, we went to Brookfield Mall to pick out shoes and have lunch in the food court. I was full and sleepy after eating my chicken sandwich and large fry, but I had one more stop to make. We said our good-byes, and I headed straight to Barnes & Noble, cautiously making my way to the gay and lesbian section.

I mimicked a shoplifter, looking all around to see if anyone was watching me. Anybody who *was* watching me must have thought I had some serious issues by the way I literally tiptoed across the carpeting. There was already a man in the area flipping through a book, so I made a shadow next to him.

There were books ranging from parenting gay children to gay parents with children. One cover of two women hugging a smiling little boy caught my attention. I saw Steph, Michelle, and Jaron in their faces.

Finally, I got up enough courage to pick up a lesbian magazine and took a look at some of the articles. I was amazed by the clothing advertisements of women hugged together, or women intertwined in a swimming pool advertising a lesbian resort. Who knew lesbian resorts existed? And gay cruises and conferences and movies and books?

I walked to the counter, purchased the magazine and immediately folded it into my purse like it was FBI top-secret material. When I got home, I read the magazine cover to cover before placing it between my mattresses and taking a nap. I dreamt I was sliding down a giant rainbow from the sky into a pool that glittered red, orange, yellow, green, blue, and purple. So that's what those car window stickers meant.

Jeff and I met our dinner party late because I overslept for the second time that week. I was slobbing on my pillow when Jeff started tickling my feet to wake me up. He had arrived dressed and ready to go, while I had to fit at least an hour of preparation into thirty minutes.

You know that feeling of paranoia you get when you're hiding something? I kept peeking my head out of my bathroom to make sure Jeff wasn't digging between my mattresses in the bedroom. As far I as know, Jeff had never lifted my mattress before, so I was feeling crazy for thinking he was going to this particular night. He wasn't even in my bedroom; he was in the living room watching TV.

When we finally arrived at Luca's, I searched the heads around the restaurant, and spotted Yvonne and her brownish-blond hair that I'd envied my entire life. The girl looked like she had been to the beauty salon for a complete makeover. She had taken her medium-length hair and set it in curls. She added sable eyeliner to accent her brown eyes and caramel lipstick over her full lips. She wore a midnight blue jumpsuit I wanted for myself out of the Spiegel catalog. That girl never showed any skin, but she looked fabulous.

Sitting next to her was a square-looking brother that reminded me of the new millennium version of Roger from *What's Happening!!*, big glasses and all. So that was handsome Byron? I vowed to myself not to talk about him because my sister was beaming next to him. She looked so happy.

"Look who finally made it," Gladyce said as I bent down to give her a kiss.

"Fashionably late," I replied, handing her a medium-size box wrapped in silver paper with a white bow.

"Thank you, sweetie." She smiled.

I looked at my mom and studied her movements. She turned forty-nine today but didn't look a day over forty. She covered her gray hair with dyes of her natural brown hair color. She lightened her makeup as she got older, but she kept her eyebrows defined, and mascara, blush, and lipstick natural looking. She was lovely in black slacks and a rose silk blouse, unbuttoned to show the gold necklace with diamond cross that my dad gave her for their tenth wedding anniversary.

Throughout dinner I watched my mom and dad's interaction, amazed by the love and friendship that remained between the two of them. Sometimes I wished one of them would share the reason why their marriage ended. A casual observer would think they were still a married couple in love. I was happy that the two of them maintained a healthy relationship, and even if it was strictly for the benefit of Yvonne and me, I didn't care.

Byron was leading a stimulating conversation about the potential wealth to be made in investments, and just when I thought my head would hit the table, the waiters gathered around us to deliver my mom's birthday cake. We sang "Happy Birthday" with several other tables joining in. She blew out the number four and number nine candles on the cake and everyone cheered. The cake was her favorite, marble with cherry filling in the middle. It wasn't high on my list of favorites, but I ate it because she loved it.

My dad presented her with a bottle of perfume. This was a tradition of theirs that didn't dare cease after the divorce. There is no doubt in my mind that my mother had splashed, spritzed, and sprayed every cologne, body splash, and scented lotion ever created. When Givenchy came out with a new perfume, Gladyce got it. When Calvin Klein came out with Obsession, she had one of the first bottles. And Bath & Body Works will never go out of business as long as Gladyce is around.

When we were children, Yvonne and I would sit at her vanity table in awe of the tens of dozens of bottles lined across the table. This year, Gladyce received Coco Mademoiselle, a new fragrance by Chanel. We passed it around the table for all to smell, inhaling the fragrance over the natural garlic scent floating through the restaurant.

Yvonne gave Mom a Tiffany bracelet. You know, it look like the chain link bracelet with a heart charm that every Claire's boutique was imitating, minus the official Tiffany engraving.

I presented her with a music box that opened playing Beethoven's "Largo." Inside were two small African American girls dressed in leotards and tights twirling together. Above them, inside the top cover was a scanned picture of me and Yvonne after our first dance recital. With our hair in buns and our arms wrapped around one another, we cheesed into the camera with missing teeth. Gladyce's eyes filled with tears and my heart was pleased.

When it was time to leave, I could tell that Yvonne preferred to be alone with Byron, so I didn't invite them to go out for drinks. Instead, Jeff and I headed to Blockbuster for a late-night movie.

We had driven my car because Jeff was getting a new ride on Monday and didn't want to risk any accidents; he was a firm believer in Murphy's Law. I parked outside his place and instinctively popped my trunk open to grab my overnight bag, which normally carried my extra toiletries and a sweatsuit. I stopped in my tracks when I realized that the clothes I wore to the library were still in my bag instead. I had changed into my sweatsuit before leaving Steph's place the morning after our visit to the Dollhouse. If Jeff saw the clothes, he might realize that I didn't "accidentally" fall asleep at her place and leave fully dressed the next day as I had said.

I quickly closed the trunk as he got out of the car.

"I forgot that I took the bag in my apartment when I cleaned out my car," I lied before he even asked a question.

When had I cleaned out my car? He didn't inquire, even though the leaves on my car floor made it obvious that my Camry hadn't been vacuumed in a while. He put his arm around my waist and escorted me to his place. My little white lies were adding up, and I knew they were only going to get bigger.

A couple of weeks later, I arrived to class fifteen minutes early, anxiously awaiting Steph's arrival. Besides sneaking to see a movie with the passes I'd won from the radio, I hadn't seen her outside of class and breakfast, although she had been on my mind constantly. When I was at work, or studying, and even hanging with Jeff, she was there; dancing around the back of my head, behind my neck, whispering in my ear, making her presence known.

We remained platonic, though our connection and attraction toward one another grew stronger with each encounter. How I yearned to hold her hand and lay my head against her shoulder while at the movies. With each good-bye hug my body ached for more; a stroke of my hair, a nuzzle in my neck, a kiss to my lips. I was ready to walk through the open door.

Steph finally entered the room looking professional in a black pantsuit with a heather blue blouse tucked in by a black leather belt. Her hair was pulled back with a simple, black scrunchie. Her face was flushed by the late October chill in the air.

"How was your week?" she asked after a quick hug.

The younger students stared at us curiously. I ignored them.

"Busy, but nice. And yours?" I replied.

"The same and still going. I have a business meeting I have to get to after breakfast and then I have to get back down here for my afternoon class." She pulled out her books and started telling me about Jaron. "Last week

Jaron was out of school a couple of days and tried his best to convince me that he's old enough to stay home alone. I know my baby is a good kid and he's fairly responsible, but he's only nine and in the fourth grade. Eight hours is too long for him to be alone to me. He loves his grandma's house, but I think he's struggling for a little independence. He heard the term *mama's boy* from a girl at school early last week, so now he fears he's going to be one. Too late!"

"If your mom ever has something to do and I'm not at the store, I don't mind hanging out with him. As a matter of fact, I'd love to," I told her.

"That's sweet, Ky. I'm sure he would love that. He actually asked about you."

"What did he ask?" I asked, feeling special.

"He wanted to know if you were coming by again. I think he might have a little crush on you. I guess I have even more competition!"

I was surprised by her subtle joke about Jeff being competition. Did that mean she wanted more than friendship from me? I sure as hell hoped so. I reached in my bag and handed her a vacation booklet titled *Nassau, Bahamas.*

She flipped through it and sighed dreamily. "This looks so good to me right now," she said.

I took a deep breath and dug deep inside to get up the courage to ask this woman I had known for only two months to go on a romantic vacation with me. I needed to ask her to keep it a secret from my family and friends because they wouldn't understand. I wanted her to be my date, my companion, and my lover for three nights, knowing someone else would be at home waiting for me when I returned. I needed her to feed the hunger in my body that craved her whenever we were apart.

"Will you go with me?" I asked.

"Kyla, are you sure?" she asked. But before I could respond she answered. "Yes, I'd love to."

I wanted so badly to kiss her right then and thank her for feeling the same way I did.

"I missed you last week," she confessed.

"Why didn't you call me?" I asked.

"I can't call and risk the chance of Jeff being there. I know I would be hurt even though I shouldn't be," she admitted.

I felt bad because I knew this situation was unfair to her. Still, because of the way she made me feel, I couldn't walk away. At the same time, I couldn't lose Jeff over an uncertain future with someone else. I was being selfish. A quality I hated in people, and especially in myself.

Over breakfast I told Steph I was the grand-prize winner of the radio contest and that we could take our trip anytime now through the end of February. I wanted to go now.

"How are we going to do this?" she asked, downing her second cup of coffee as we sat in the restaurant. We had only been there fifteen minutes.

"I want to plan the trip for the day after Thanksgiving. I plan to tell Jeff that I'm going with David. He'll think David won the trip."

She shook her head. "Why would David take you instead of some hot, manly body? Won't Jeff ask?"

"I thought about that. But David and I have always been close and I'm going to tell him that David just ended a relationship and was planning on taking that person. Now he doesn't want to take just any old fling. Trust me, Jeff won't question it."

"I guess you've got it all figured out."

I thought about how deceitful I must look to her.

"Steph, please don't think I'm a pro at this. I've *never* done this before, and truly, the last thing I want to do is hurt Jeff. Or anybody, for that matter. But I can't deny what I feel for you and I want to spend time exploring these feelings. I really don't like lying." I added jokingly, "Lies are so hard to remember."

Steph ordered another cup of coffee, exceeding her two-limit maximum. "I believe you, Kyla. You don't have to explain yourself. I can tell this isn't your usual nature. And I'm glad you want me to go with you. We'll have a great time."

"Your mom will keep Jaron?"

"Of course. But I'm not lying to anyone I know. I don't have to keep secrets."

Okay, she put a guilt trip on me with that one.

"I'll call and make the arrangements and call you later this week with all the details."

After saying our good-byes, I was getting in my car when she asked a question.

"Hey, what about David? Will he be game?"

"It's already worked out!"

She smiled at me in wonder, blew me a kiss, and got in her car. I couldn't help but laugh as I recalled the conversation I'd had with David last week after I finally decided to ask Stephanie to go on the trip with me.

"David, I need a huge favor," I said after he answered the phone.

"What is it, honey child?" he asked in his high-pitched voice, practically singing the words to me (yes, he really does talk like that).

I cleared my throat. "I won this trip to Nassau—" I was cut off by his screams of excitement. "You finished?" I playfully asked him.

"Girl, hot fun in the sun!"

I could hear his fingers snapping. He killed me sometimes.

"Well, I need you to pretend that you won the trip and that you're taking me with you."

"*Whaaaaaaaaat?* What do you have up your skinny sleeve, Miss Thang?"

"There's someone I want to take, but I can't let anyone know," I said.

"Don't tell me you're doing the nasty with somebody other than that fine species of a man you already have," David said.

"No, I'm not doing the nasty with anyone, David. But I want to take a girlfriend of mine."

"And what's the problem, sugar?"

I didn't respond, hoping he would get the hint. But being David, I should have known that even if he did get a clue, he wasn't going to let me know. Since he was so outspoken, direct and in your face, he preferred everyone else to be the same with him.

"Dammit, David," I said, frustrated.

"Girlfriend, don't go getting all flustered. You called me, remember?"

Fine.

I blurted out all the confusion, anxiety, enthusiasm, and passion I had been holding in for weeks. "I met this woman in class, David, and she makes me feel emotions I've never felt before. We've gotten close, and I want to take her with me. And I know that no one will understand why I chose to take this brand-new friend over Jeff, Tori, V, Yvonne, and Mom, you know what I'm saying?"

There was a short silence.

"My baby girl is finally coming out," he said proudly, like I had just aced a math test I had been studying for twenty-six years.

"What are you talking about? I didn't say I was gay."

"So classic you are, baby girl. The first stage is denial. Go ahead and say or don't say whatever you want, Papa knows the truth, honey. For every openly gay person in the family, there's always another in hiding." He laughed at his remark.

"What are you talking about?" I asked him.

"Kyla baby, when you and I used to play Barbies, why did I always have to change Barbie's clothes? You were so embarrassed to look at the naked plastic doll. Two, re-member Ms. Peters, Mrs. Bruce, and Mrs. Hartman? Hell, you had a crush on just about every female teacher you had! You hated your male teachers but adored the women."

"I really don't think that qualifies, David," I said, deny-ing I had been a closeted lesbian my whole life because I preferred female teachers.

"May be minor, but it counts. And let's not forget about Miss Stacey. You walked around like your pet died after she got sent away."

"I don't know, David. This is all so new to me." I thought about Stephanie's smile. "But it feels *so* good."

"Honey, I don't know what a woman feels like, but it *does* feel good to let your true self shine."

"That's the problem. I don't know if this is really me. I'm so confused," I said, sadly.

"I understand, Kyla. You're a late bloomer, but you'll come around."

"How can you be so sure when *I* don't even know?"

"Trust me, baby girl. Now tell me all about this wonder woman. She must be all that and then some if she drew your attention away from Jeff."

I told him all about Stephanie and I sounded like a girl struck by Cupid's arrow. "I can barely explain it, David. It's not like I went looking for something in her to be at-tracted to; it just happened. Like I couldn't even control it. I literally felt a pull toward her," I explained.

"I'll do this for you, Kyla," David said. "I'll plan a get-away of my own at the same time. But I have to tell you,

you don't want to keep up this facade too long. It's not fair
to you, and most importantly, Jeff and Stephanie. You're
setting someone up to get their feelings hurt. Take this
time to explore your feelings but know that eventually
you're going to have to make a decision."

"Thanks, David. I appreciate it."

"No thing, pumpkin. I'm glad you told me. Don't think
twice about calling me whenever something is on your
mind. And trust me, sweetheart, you're about to have
plenty on your mind."

"Tell me about it," I said. "I already can't keep my head
on straight. But I'm going to sort it out."

"Good for you, darling. Better late than never. I'll talk
to you soon. Smooches!"

He smacked the phone with his lips and hung up.
That's my David. I knew he would come through for me.

I called the travel agency as soon as I got home from
breakfast and made all the arrangements. We had a char-
ter flight at 6:00 AM the Friday morning after Thanksgiving and we were staying at the luxurious Atlantis Hotel on
Paradise Island.

As I stared at the pictures of the sparkling blue waters
and white sandy beaches, I wondered what I was going to
do with myself over the next four weeks. The anticipation
was more than I could bear. It was like I'd opened my mail-
box and finally received my million-dollar check from Ed
McMahon. Only, I couldn't cash the damn thing because
it was postdated.

PART 2

PAIN

9

I stood on the French balcony of our room in the royal tower of the Atlantis Hotel and breathed in the hot, salty air. I stared ahead at waves of endless ocean that lapped at the shore upon arrival. Below, at the pool, vacationers gathered at the bar sipping tropical mixed drinks, while others browned their skin under the steamy sun. Several children played Marco Polo with a beach ball in the pool while their parents stole quiet moments in the whirlpool. They must be hot as hell.

Stephanie came out and stood next to me, her skin glowing under the sun. We looked around Paradise Island in silence, elated that we were there. Elation wasn't the only emotion I was feeling, though. My stomach was a bundle of knots, twisting nervousness and excitement together.

It was our first of four days there, and you would have thought I was going away for two weeks by the way I shopped online before the trip. Because we were on the edge of winter, I had a slightly difficult time finding what I needed. But I ended up with seven pairs of shorts, nine tank tops in sassy, summer styles, five summer dresses, four bikinis, and too many pairs of sandals and sunglasses to count. Of course, I bought all new underwear, a definite with any trip.

I intentionally left my camera behind, although I hated to. There could be no evidence of this trip with David to be found. I hadn't yet figured out how to explain the reason I didn't purchase a one-use camera while I was here. I'd get creative later.

Steph broke into my thoughts.

"What would you like to do first?" she asked me.

I looked at my watch. It was 12:30 PM. We had only been in our room one hour, and we had the next four days entirely to each other.

"How about changing into swimsuits and going down to the beach?" I suggested. "The waters looked so inviting."

"Sounds cool to me. Do you Jet Ski?"

"I've only been once, and I was in the back. Why? You want to take me for a ride?" I asked.

"I sure do."

Her eyes sparkled, and I understood the true meaning behind her words. Just the thought made my knees quiver.

I watched Steph from the balcony doors as she went back inside, took off all of her clothes, and dug through her suitcase for a swimsuit, retrieving an orange two-piece. Steph's naked body was strong and fit with a smooth layer of skin covering her toned muscle. Light brown freckles splashed against her back. Her breasts were full, with small brown nipples that stood firm. Her waist slimmed, leading to curvy hips and healthy thighs. Steph's body was tantalizing, exceeding all that I had imagined it to be.

I figured it was now or never, and now was not the time to be shy. I followed her back inside and took my clothes off, hardly able to unbutton my shirt because my hands were shaking so badly. She was pleasantly surprised when I entered, and made her way toward me so I could tie the strings of her bikini. My heart was racing like I had just run five miles at top speed.

Both of us had our hair French-braided to the back with wooden beads that clicked with our every head movement. I lifted her braids in order to link the orange strings together in a bow.

"Here," she said, handing me sun protection lotion.

I massaged the cream into the skin on her back, and she stood still, enjoying my touch. Once I dressed in my own bikini, she returned the favor, and my body caught on fire, even in the air-conditioned room. She tested my personal space and closed in so I could feel her nipples graze the skin on my back. I moaned from this simple pleasure and quickly got embarrassed.

I turned around to face her and couldn't hide the yearning in my eyes. We stood face to face and eye to eye, and I had never felt so sexy and alive in my life. Nor had I ever found someone so desirable.

She reached and stroked my lips with her thumb before placing her soft, moist lips on mine. Her kiss was soft and tender, yet purposeful. It said she had been waiting for this moment just as long as I had been. The tips of our tongues met, and twisted, one on top of the other. She reached for my waist and squeezed the softness of my skin. I felt like I had been kissed for the very first time.

She parted from me, searching my face for a reaction. I leaned forward and kissed her once again, a sign of the contentment and pleasure I felt on the inside. She too seemed pleased.

We grabbed our straw bags, a pair of sunglasses each, and headed to the beach.

"This is so beautiful," she said, admiring what looked like heaven on earth.

"It is," I said in agreement. "And I'm so glad I have you to share it with."

She twisted her pinky finger in mine. "Me too."

Yep, this is what I needed. I felt like we were a couple, walking along the beach enjoying each other's company. This time would allow me to determine just what this nagging at my heart was all about.

We spent the next hour with my arms wrapped tightly around her waist as we rode the Jet Ski. She took on each wave fearlessly. I was having a blast, even though my eyes burned as saltwater splashed underneath my new sunglasses and snot ran out of my nose. We tipped over a couple of times but quickly hopped back on to resume our water adventure. I was having the time of my life.

Our skin turned golden brown under the sun. The tan only made Steph's eyes more piercing when she removed her sunglasses. We returned the Jet Ski, vowing to make one more trip before we left, and headed to the bar after rinsing off. We ordered Bahama mamas and sprawled on two lounge chairs nearby.

"Whew, that was exhausting," I said once I laid down.

She quickly sat upright and cocked her head in my direction like she couldn't believe what she'd just heard. "I didn't see you doing any work, missy. You got a free ride."

I laughed. "It was good too. I take it you've done this before," I said.

"Yes, I took a couple of trips to Florida with Michelle, and we spent some time in the Keys. I've gone out on Lake Michigan a couple of times too, but the experience isn't quite the same. I can't wait to take Jaron."

"I'm sure he would love it. I'm hooked already," I said.

"I've got a few more tricks up my sleeve," she said, mischievously.

She was laying it on thick now, and I was loving it. We relaxed and finished our drinks before heading to the Lagoon Bar for lunch. We settled on deli sandwiches and potato chips, saving our appetites for a big dinner that night of steak and shrimp.

"Do you feel guilty yet?" she asked out of nowhere.

I thought for a moment. "In all honesty, no, I don't. I wish I didn't have to see you like this under these secretive circumstances, but I wanted to be with you. I *do* feel guilty for not feeling guilty, if that makes sense."

"Guilty pleasure," she said.

"Have you ever dated a woman that had a boyfriend before?" I asked her.

"Sure, back in the day when I wasn't looking for a relationship. Then I made it a rule not to do that anymore." She shrugged her shoulders. "I see all rules are meant to be broken sometimes."

"Do *you* feel guilty?" I asked curiously.

"I don't like to be deceptive, Kyla. So, yes, I'll feel guilty when I see Jeff again."

"David told me that this is unfair to you and to Jeff."

"You don't think it is?" she asked, like I better say yes.

"Yes, I know it is." I paused. "So if I know it's unfair and so do you, then why did you agree to come?"

She leaned back in her chair and thought for a moment. "Have you ever met someone and felt like you had an immediate connection with that person? A vibe that tells you this person is special? I felt that way the first day in class. And I'm not the kind of person to ignore that kind of energy. I had to get to know you, to see if I was right."

"And?"

"I was," she said.

"I feel the same way," I agreed, surprising myself by opening up. "I don't normally let people get close to me, but you're different. I don't feel like you'd do anything to hurt me. The way I've felt over the last three months is like nothing I've ever felt before. I feel so close to you; you're so much more than just a friend. It's confusing because I've never wanted to be with another woman before, but I think about you all the time and I miss you when I don't see you or talk to you. I want to be near you and smell you. It's all so new to me, and I don't know what to do."

"Well, what are you more confused about? The fact that you have feelings for someone else, or that the someone else is a woman?"

I hadn't really thought about that. What would I do if I'd had feelings for another man? For some reason, that didn't even seem like a possibility. No man had ever made me feel the way Steph made me feel inside. But I don't know if that's because I normally had my guard up with men. No one, not even Jeff, had the keys to unlock every door in my heart. But Steph was opening doors that I thought I had locked and thrown away the keys.

"That thought hasn't even crossed my mind. But maybe it's a combination of both, Steph," I answered. "I have strong feelings for someone who happens to be a woman. I'm twenty-six years old, so why now after all these years? It makes no sense to me. David is convinced that I've been gay my whole life."

"What, you think you suddenly wake up one day and you're gay?"

"Well, yeah, I guess. What else could it be for me? I've never been involved with a woman before. I've always been straight."

"You don't think there's a chance that you've been gay all along but didn't acknowledge it? Or at least had a small attraction toward women that you just didn't act upon?"

"I don't know," I answered. I was feeling pressured again to act like I had been a lesbian all my life.

"Kyla, most people in their right minds wouldn't *choose*

to be gay. It's hard as hell. And even though society is slowly progressing, we still have a long way to go. Imagine people thinking you're perverted just because you're gay. Or that you want to screw every woman with two legs because you're gay. People dislike you, make harsh judgments, and may even find you disgusting, just because you're gay. Trust me, no one would go through this shit if it wasn't real."

"You included?" I asked.

"Hell, yeah! I'm very happy and comfortable in the skin I'm in, but it hasn't always been that way. Coming out to my mother, grandmother, and sister was the hardest, but I did it at a young age, so the shock wore off long ago. Jaron has always grown up around women and spent a few of his younger years with me and Michelle as a family. Right now he doesn't question it, but I fear what he may have to go through as he gets older and his friends recognize that he has a gay mother. Kids and their parents can be cruel."

"I agree. It might be difficult for him. How are you going to prepare him for the criticism?"

She sighed. "I can only love him the best I can and help him to be a strong person. I hope to show him that love has no barriers. Gay or straight, white or black, whatever. We should all have the right to love whoever we choose, as long as it's not hurting anyone."

I admired her confidence and determination. She was so secure in herself and I wished I could be that way. At that moment, I felt the complete opposite. Like a bird trying to spread its wings and fly for the first time.

"Won't you miss out on being married?"

"I can get married," she answered quickly.

"You'd marry a woman?"

"Surely not a man," she said, laughing.

"But it's not legal, is it?"

"No, but I could have a commitment ceremony. There are some pastors who will perform ceremonies for same-sex couples. I've been to a couple of weddings, and it's no different, besides the obvious, of course."

"You mean one woman wears a tux?" I questioned.

She moaned at my ignorance. "Not always. Some women are more comfortable in men's clothing, so in those instances, yes. But I've seen two women both in dresses too."

I pictured Steph and me at the altar and wondered who would wear the tuxedo.

"Who would wear the tux if you got married?" I asked her.

"Girl, I just said it's not a written rule. Hell, the marriage isn't even legal. It all depends on the woman and her own style. If I married a stud—you know what a stud is, right?" She observed my expressionless stare. "A stud is a female with masculine qualities," she explained. "Anyway, if she wore a suit that would be fine. But if I marry a fish, then she'd probably wear a dress."

"Fish? What in the hell is a fish?" I asked, scrunching my nose.

"A feminine lesbian."

"I wouldn't want to be called a fish. That sounds nasty as hell," I said.

"Kind of. But most lesbians don't take offense to it."

"So you're a fish?" I asked her.

"Well, I'm not a stud or even a soft stud. I'm a lipstick lesbian. That's another term for feminine lesbians."

"Should I be writing this down?"

"Yes, I'm giving you a quiz later," she teased.

"Do you have a preference in your type of woman?" I asked, comparing myself to Michelle in my head.

"I usually prefer more feminine women, but my high school sweetheart was a soft stud. Some studs prefer to

take on a more masculine, aggressive role, but underneath, we're all women. I, personally, have never had the
male and female roles in my relationships. I hate when
people ask me that."

"What?"

"Who's the man?"

I was *so* glad she said that because that surely was my
next question. Still, you'd assume one person would be
more dominating and the other more submissive, right? I
had to know.

"So who takes out the garbage and cleans and cooks if
there's no man or woman?" I couldn't help but ask.

She clicked her teeth and tapped her fingers one by
one on the table. I figured she was counting to ten and
trying not to strangle me for what must have been a stupid
question.

"You're saying you've never taken out the garbage? Or
Jeff has never cleaned the house? Just as in any other relationship, if one partner enjoys cooking, he or she may do
a lot of cooking. But that doesn't mean that he or she is
the other person's servant. Same with gay relationships. If
I'm good at fixing the clogged drain in the sink, it doesn't
mean that I'm the 'man.' I'm just good at fixing things."

"Okay, I didn't know," I said after her scolding.

"I know you don't know, Ky. I'm schooling you so you
don't have to go around asking anybody else these crazy-
ass questions. I want you to understand."

"What else can you school me on?" I asked, flirting with
her.

"You sure you're ready for the big lesson? I can teach
you any and everything you want to know. I'm all yours,"
she said, seductively. She twisted in her chair, allowing her
sarong to fall open, displaying her firm, sexy legs.

Wetness gathered between my legs and I got nervous

again. "Do you want to take a quick nap before dinner?" I asked.

"For sure," she said, hopping up from her chair and then helping me up from mine.

We went back to our room and were asleep within ten minutes. The sun, heat, and water workout had taken its toll.

When I opened my eyes an hour and a half later, Steph was facing me, eyes wide open, staring at me.

"Did my snoring wake you up?" I asked, noticing my mouth was wide open when I woke up.

"No, I was watching you sleep. You look so peaceful," she said.

"I've been known to drool and snore and I know that's not cute," I said as I wiped the corners of my mouth, just in case.

"You look beautiful as usual," she said.

We looked into each other's eyes for what felt like eternity. I wished it were. She studied my hairline, my eyebrows, my nose, and my lips. I watched her examine me, knowing she was wondering what she was going to do with me. Her eyes seemed filled with joy and uncertainty, intertwined. Joy for our time together, uncertainty of what would happen when we returned back home.

"We better get ready for dinner," I finally said.

After showering, I slid on a burnt orange minidress with spaghetti straps and low V-neck in the front. I found silver and orange seashell earrings and a bracelet at the boutique where I got my hair braided. The poor woman who worked behind the counter looked like she had used the salon services one too many times. The child's hair was about as long as my pinky fingernail for a good inch around her hairline. It took everything in me not to run out of there when I saw her.

Steph's dress was a black number falling just below her

knees with the entire back open, revealing the peace sign tattoo at the small of her back. It was quite sexy on her, especially with the black sandal heels that caressed her feet.

We went down to the Bahamian Club and were able to get a table, even though we hadn't made reservations. The place was filled with vacationers of every race, age, and sex, and the atmosphere was mellow cool.

"What shall we toast to?" Steph asked when our white wines arrived.

"Let's toast to us and the quality time we're able to spend together this weekend. And that we still get good grades even though we're missing class Monday morning." I laughed.

"To us," we chimed and clinked our glasses together.

Over dinner Steph asked about Vanessa. "How did the interview go? I wish I hadn't missed it."

"It was fantastic," I said after finishing a bite of medium-well steak. "I recorded it, so I'll lend you the tape. She was so good, and the interview was emotional for everyone. Roger ended up going to the interview with her, but she told us all the behind-the-scenes info. Mr. Davis's wife never betrayed him all the years he was incarcerated and believed in his innocence the whole time. She was always devoted to his case and helping him obtain his freedom. He cried, she cried, the kids cried. Vanessa got emotional. Girl, it was heart-wrenching. I think she's on her way to being much more than a reporter."

"Good for her. She deserves it. How are her wedding plans coming?"

"Once she and Roger decided to ignore what everyone else wanted them to do, plans started flowing smoothly. Final fittings for the dresses are right before Christmas. I'm happy for them. They're so compatible."

"I was watching them that night on the cruise, and they do look happy. So do you and Jeff," she commented.

I didn't even bother to respond. What was I supposed to say to that? And why was she bringing him up again? I was having such a good time and I wasn't interested in talking about Jeff. I didn't know if that was a good thing or a bad thing.

"Let's go dancing after dinner," I said, changing the subject like I always did when I didn't want to talk about something. She didn't pursue the topic either.

We asked our cute, caramel-colored waitress if she knew of a club nearby with good music. Janila was extra friendly with us, making sure that we were well taken care of, bending over backward to check on us about every five minutes. Steph figured she must have been "family." I didn't even ask what she meant by that. But Janila told us about a place down the road that vacationers frequented and enjoyed the reggae music.

We took a cab over and walked into a dark, smoky joint with a dance floor packed with what looked like every single person in the place. Men and women were bumping and grinding to the funky beat played by the band onstage. The two of us didn't waste a minute before joining the others on the floor.

We weren't the only female couple on the floor, so we fit right in. I tried to keep up with Steph as she swiveled and circled her hips to the music, making love with the loud drumbeat. But I started to mess up, concentrating too much on her.

She noticed my stuttering feet and reached over and grabbed both my hands and pulled me close. She turned me around so my backside was against her front. She pressed her hips into mine so I could feel her movements as I rotated my body with hers. Her hands were at my sides for guidance. I covered her hands with mine and stroked them as we let the music take over our bodies. It felt like we had become one with the music and the dance floor, all combined into one blazing frenzy. We danced several more songs before getting ice water at the bar.

"Thanks for the lesson," I said, drinking the water like it was the first drink I had all day.

"No thing. I love to dance," she said.

"I can tell. You can turn anyone on just by the way you dance," I told her.

She leaned forward and looked me straight in the eye.

"Is it working on *you?*"

"You don't even have to try. You already got me."

"Let's go," she said, getting off her bar stool.

We took our shoes off and raced back to the hotel, running from headlights to avoid getting hit and stubbing our toes on pebbles in the road. Of course, those strong thighs of hers led the race all the way back to our room. We were like little kids playing tag, laughing all the way. Inside the room, I leaned against the wall, hand against my chest, and tried to catch my breath.

"You win," I said, sounding like I was about to have an asthma attack. You'd think those Monday-morning workouts would have prepared me for events such as these.

"What's my prize?" she asked.

"Come and see," I answered, trying not to sound anxious.

She dropped her shoes on the floor and slowly walked toward me, never taking her eyes from mine. Stopping in front of me, she traced her finger around my hairline and over my eyebrows down to my lips, the same route she had taken earlier with her eyes. She leaned forward and kissed me gently, then deeply and passionately. Her right hand caressed my ear, neck, and shoulder. Her mouth followed suit, sucking my earlobe, kissing my neck, down to my shoulder.

Softly she tasted my skin, dancing her tongue on my body. She slipped my dress straps down and let my dress fall to the floor. Again, she used her fingers to trace over my nipples, massaging them until they stood erect. I moaned with pleasure as she took each breast in her mouth, circling each nipple tenderly with her tongue.

I reached behind her and untied the string that held her dress up. She backed away, stepped out of the dress and walked me to the bed. I laid on my back and stretched my arms upward as she kissed my ankles, my calves, knees, and thighs. She lingered on my belly, not missing an inch, before making her way back to my breasts, and finally bringing her lips back to mine. We kissed as she placed her body on mine, pressing her breasts against mine, grinding her hips into me.

She placed one, then two fingers inside me.

"Oh, Stephanie . . ." I whispered between kisses.

In and out, her fingers played with my insides, going deep into places that made me scream with pleasure. She removed her lips from mine and lowered herself, positioning her head between my thighs. She showered my thighs with kisses and tongue caresses before tasting the juices that flowed from my body. She dove inside, absorbing all I had to offer.

She lifted my hood, exposing my clit, and licked me expertly, until I felt butterflies all over my body. The electrifying sensations sent tingles from head to toe. I laid with my body shaking, savoring the pleasure she brought to me.

I took her head in my hands, bringing her up to my face. I wanted to touch her, taste her and please her. I flipped her over and straddled her from behind. I ran my fingernails up and down her spine, bending over and kissing every place I touched. I kissed the back of her ears, the slope of her neck down to the tattoo on the small of

her back. I reached for her warmth, excited by the wetness that engulfed my fingers. Her muscles contracted,
asking me to go deeper. I rubbed her insides and felt her
hips circle in motion.

I stayed inside until I felt her rush over my fingers and
heard her screams of delight as her body twitched under
mine.

She turned over and released my fingers. I stared into
her flushed face and put my fingers in my mouth, tasting
her sweetness. I took her in my arms and hugged her
tightly. For the first time ever, my spirit felt freed.

10

Jeff and I walked through the crowded, brightly-lit mall surrounded by Christmas trees draped in red and gold garland with shining white lights. A long line of anxiously waiting children stood to tell Santa if they had been good or bad, while their parents stood close by with cameras and camcorders. "White Christmas" and "Silent Night" replaced the usual elevator music heard as we ventured in and out of stores. Bells could be heard as men and women from the Salvation Army stood with their money bins, hoping for donations.

I'd normally be among the throngs of people crowding the malls and department stores the day after Thanksgiving, but of course I was occupied at that time. The remainder of my trip with Steph had been pure romantic bliss. We'd spent hours on the beach, walking and talking and stealing kisses whenever we could. Evenings were spent getting dressed up for candlelit dinners under the stars while listening to light jazz played by live bands. Each night we spent hours making love, wishing time could stand still and we could hold each other forever. Thoughts of home, school, and Jeff were cast aside; our entire focus was on one another.

David had met us at the airport and took Stephanie to her mom's house before driving me home. He looked refreshed from his weekend stay in Miami with John, an old flame of his that moved to Orlando after stirring up controversy in the city for having an affair with a married judge. The judge, last I heard, left the wife and kids behind and headed to good old San Francisco for a new life.

"Honey girl, what are you going to do?" David asked me after seeing the pained look on my face when I had to say good-bye to Steph.

"David," I said, trying not to cry, "I've just spent the best weekend of my life with one of the most wonderful people I've ever met. I have no idea what I'm going to do."

He grabbed my hand and held it. "Whatever you do, Ky, make sure you're able to be happy with your decision. *You* are the most important person that has to live with the decision for the rest of your life. I'm by your side either way, but I don't want you to regret anything you decide to do."

I squeezed his hand and kissed it. "I knew I could count on you, David," I said.

We spent the rest of the ride corroborating our stories. Hopefully our trip would no longer be the main topic of conversation by the next family gathering at Christmas. I couldn't stomach the thought of standing in front of the entire family recounting fables of a trip that never occurred. At least the way they believed it to be.

"What are you going to buy Yvonne this year?" Jeff asked, bringing me back to the moment.

"Well, now that she's getting a little booty on a regular basis, I'm going to get her a set of sexy pajamas. That way it will be a gift for her *and* Byron."

"I don't know if I want to be a part of that shopping selection," he said jokingly. "I'll leave that visual alone. Who else can we focus on today?"

"Let's do your shopping," I offered. "I'll do mine at the store next week."

Jeff headed straight for RadioShack, knowing he could do most of his shopping in that one store. He picked out a two-way pager for his brother, a cell phone and carrying case for his mom, and a digital camera for his dad. He didn't have any nieces or nephews yet, so that pretty much summed up his Christmas shopping.

"What about me?" I asked, batting my eyes. I was trying so hard to remain my usual self with him, but it had gotten difficult.

He grinned. "I already took care of you, babe. While you were gone getting tan in the sun, I got your Christmas gift."

Great. I didn't ask any more questions.

It was nearing 7:00 PM and, even though we were tired from walking, we decided to head downtown to Winterfest for ice-skating. It was the first weekend in December and my only Saturday off until the thirty-first, so I wanted to take advantage of the free time.

The rink was so brightly lit that it hardly seemed dark outside. There were a few pros on the rink, dressed in flared miniskirts with matching sweaters and hats, skating on one leg, the other gracefully holding its position in the air behind them. Most people were like me and Jeff, though. We knew how to ice-skate cautiously without falling down. But then there were those that I feared: the few that skated, slid, lost control, and fell. I avoided those people the way you run from a bee to avoid getting stung.

We skated around and around, laughing and holding hands, as our noses turned red in the cold night air. When we broke for hot chocolate, I heard a young voice call my name.

"Kyla!"

I turned around and saw a handsome little face blushing at me a few feet away. His mom suddenly jerked her head in my direction with widened eyes. I stared into the face I had been longing for the entire week.

Jaron ran over to me and wrapped his arms around my waist. I hugged him back.

"Hello, mister! I've missed you!" I said to him.

He smiled at the floor and didn't seem to know what to say. Then he remembered something. So did I. And so did Steph, all at the same time. She came running up behind him.

"How was the Bahamas? My mom said—"

"Hey, Jeff. Hey, girl," Steph interrupted. "Fancy meeting you here."

My body burned with fear. I stood frozen, unable to respond. I may as well have had *guilty* blaring in block red letters across my forehead.

Jeff glanced at me, staring into my cup of hot chocolate. "Hi, Stephanie. How have you been?" he asked her.

"Fine, thanks." She turned to Jaron. "Jaron, go finish putting your skates on. I'll be there in a minute."

Jaron waved at me and Jeff and went back to his bench. Would Jeff notice her tanned golden brown skin also? I was so glad she had taken her braids down, allowing her hair to fall into long, kinky waves.

"It's just the two of you?" Jeff asked.

"Yes, just me and my boy," she said.

I could feel her eyes look in my direction, but I was still mesmerized by the steam drifting up from my styrofoam cup.

"No date tonight either? Don't tell me Ms. Matchmaker

hasn't tried to set you up yet," Jeff kidded. He put his arm around my shoulder and tried to shake me alive. I just wanted to sink into the floor.

"No, she knows better than that." Steph tried to joke back, but it came out a little too serious.

An awkward silence followed.

"Well, I'm going to hit the rink. Are you leaving?" she asked, almost hopefully.

"I'm ready," I finally said to some spot on the wall over Stephanie's shoulder.

Jeff looked at me, confused. "All righty, then. Take care, Steph," he said.

"See you," she said.

I managed to lift my feet from their nailed positions on the floor.

"Are you okay?" Jeff asked once we were inside his new Toyota Sequoia.

"Uh-huh," I lied.

He sighed, knowing I was holding something in as usual. Only, this time, I knew he couldn't even begin to imagine what it was.

"Did you two have a falling-out or something?" he pressed.

"No, not at all. You know Steph is cool." I couldn't even think of a legitimate reason for treating her like a stranger.

"Then why are you acting like you've just seen a ghost?"

"I don't know. I mean, I just don't feel well all of the sudden." Now *that* wasn't a lie.

"You want me to take you home?"

"Yes, please."

I stared out of the window, not liking the way I was feeling inside. Stephanie and David were right. I couldn't do this. I couldn't live two lives.

Four months ago I had a boyfriend that loved me inside out. And I still did. But at this moment, I no longer felt the same way he did. Now I had to put forth effort to focus on him and only him when we were together. Now I had to concentrate on *his* face and *his* lips when he kissed me.

I avoided making love with him all week because I wanted Steph's touch and Steph's kisses to linger on my skin and in my memories.

I didn't know how much longer he would go without feeling insecure or suspicious. The last thing I wanted to do was insult his masculinity. But was I able to move past Stephanie and pretend like she never happened and my feelings for her never surfaced? Could I walk away from the craving in my heart that yearned for her whenever we were apart? If I chose her, could I handle the scrutiny I would endure if I entered a relationship with a woman and became the parent of a child in a lesbian relationship? So many questions swam through my head in thunderous waves, forcing me to take way more Advil than the recommended dosage.

Jeff parked his truck outside my apartment and turned off the engine. I sensed he wanted to come inside. I grabbed my purse and looked at him, hoping my face wouldn't reveal my thoughts. I tipped my head sideways, inviting him in.

I wasn't in the mood for him to kiss me, caress me, or even try to please me. I wanted him to do what he had to do and leave me to my thoughts. He gave up on foreplay, once he realized I wasn't responding to his efforts. He took longer than usual to finish the job. Probably because I laid there, motionless, tensing up with every stroke.

"Mmm, Kyla, I love you," he shouted as he came.

I stared at my ceiling fan, waiting for him to get off of me.

"Are you sure you're all right?" he asked after rolling over to his side of my bed.

"I said I wasn't feeling well," I snapped. I didn't mean to, but I couldn't help it.

"It's more than that, Ky," he said, sitting up on his elbow. "You've seemed so far away the last few days. When I talk to you it seems like you're only half listening. You look at me like you're looking right through me at something behind me. Did I do something?"

He was taking my coldness toward him and blaming it on himself. I should have known all he would think was that *he* had done something wrong. I wanted to convince him that it wasn't him, that it was me, but how could I do that without telling on myself?

"I'm sorry, Jeff. I have a lot on my mind with the end of the semester coming up and Christmas and work hours. I feel a little stressed." That was the understatement of the year.

He wrapped his arms around me with his wet penis pressed against my hip.

"Don't wear yourself out, Ky. Maybe you should take the next semester off and take a break."

"Jeff, I've been in school too many years as it is," I said defensively. "Now that I found a career I want to pursue, I don't have any time to waste!" My voice cracked, displaying my frustration.

"Okay, okay, it was just a suggestion. Damn."

He let me go, irritated by my attitude. We both got up at the same time to go shower, but once he noticed my movement, he laid back down and turned his back.

I lingered in the hot shower, wondering what Stephanie was doing. Was she angry with me? Or was she hurt by seeing Jeff and me together? *She must think I'm such a slut.* Or maybe *I* felt like one at that moment. These thoughts tortured my brain and settled on my heart, weighing it down like a ton of bricks. I let the water run down my face to wash my tears down the drain before getting into bed with the man I used to believe could love me like no one else.

* * *

For the first time since I couldn't even remember when, I skipped my Monday-morning workout. Instead of exercising and energizing myself for the week, I stayed in bed, sleeping, believing the extra sleep would help me for the busy days that lay ahead of me. Deep inside I knew I just didn't want to look Tori and Vanessa in their eyes and lie to them about the adventures of my trip.

I looked out of the window when I finally rolled out of bed. The weatherman's prediction was correct for once. A blanket of sparkling snow lay across the ground. Just what I needed on an already sluggish Monday morning. I picked up my receiver and turned the ringer back on. I didn't even bother to check my messages. I could already hear Tori and Vanessa yelling into my voice mail asking where in the hell I was.

I double-checked my calendar to see when my period was due. Was I destined to remain in this PMS funk I had been in since Saturday night? Nope, I wasn't due for another twelve days. Couldn't blame it on hormones. I showered, dressed warm, grabbed my backpack with unfinished homework, and headed to school on barely shoveled and salted roads.

Stephanie was sitting in class reading a book when I arrived. She was never this early.

"Good morning," I said as casually as I could.

She looked up at me but didn't say anything. She turned back to her book. Shit, she was mad.

"You knew this was going to happen, didn't you?" she asked without looking up from her book. "Hell, I knew it was going to happen and I did it anyway." She shook her head.

"What?" I asked her.

She turned to me with a strained look on her face. "My feelings are hurt, Kyla," she said softly.

"I'm sorry, Steph. I don't want to hurt your feelings. I've felt awful since I saw you Saturday."

She turned back to the pages in her book.

"I'm not mad at you, Kyla," she explained in a hushed voice. "Nothing has happened between us that I didn't want to happen, so I'm not pointing the finger at you. But I've been in this life too long to resort to sneaking around to spend time with someone. I'm looking to love someone, Ky. *Openly.* I'm not trying to pressure you and tell you to give up your life today, because that's a lot to ask. But I'm not interested in being your mistress. That's a role I'm not willing to play."

Mr. Jelenchick started our classroom discussion, giving me time to think about what she said. In one week we had gone from looking passionately into each other's eyes, to not being able to look eye to eye at all.

I didn't know what to do. Well, maybe that wasn't altogether true. I knew what I wanted to do, but I was scared to death. My heart was open wide, screaming at me to love her and only her. My brain was fighting fiercely, telling me to think rationally. Give up a man that any woman would kill to have? Give up the chance to have the all-American dream? But whose dream was it? Mine or the one society created for me? Didn't I deserve happiness in any form it came?

But if I chose Steph, I would be labeled. I would be different. I couldn't talk about what my family did over the weekend with coworkers without wondering what others might think. I couldn't bring my girlfriend to work functions without stares and whispers. And in most companies I couldn't even add her to my medical insurance if we lived as a family.

"Let's go to my car," Steph said after class.

Once inside, she immediately wrapped her arms around me and hugged me.

"I want to tell you something," she said, still embracing me. "I'm in too deep, Ky. I have a weakness for smart, beautiful, sweet, kindhearted women. I've only come across two women that have made me weak in the knees. Michelle . . ." She broke the hug and looked at me. "And you."

I anticipated what she would say next and my heart soared from my chest to the middle of my throat.

"That's why I can't share you," she concluded.

My heart sank back down to the pit of my stomach.

"The longer we go on like this, the more I'll get wrapped up in you. I can't put myself out there like that."

"I'm not trying to hurt you, Steph."

"I understand that, but you keep saying that like you saying it is going to prevent it from happening. Do you really think either one of us will be happy trying to be together in this kind of situation? I want more than that and so should you. And don't forget that there's another person's feelings involved also. It's obvious how much Jeff loves you, Kyla. Don't string him along either."

I fought back my tears.

"What are you asking me to do?"

"I want you to look at your life and think about what you want out of it and what you're willing to do to achieve happiness. I want you to be happy, and if that includes me, then I'm here. If it doesn't, then I'll deal with that. I knew what I was getting into when this started"

I leaned forward and kissed her. Small pecks on her top lip, then her bottom lip, until our mouths opened for deeper, lingering kisses. I didn't care if anyone saw what we were doing. I only focused on her and the love I wanted to shower her with. It felt like she was leaving me, and I didn't want that to happen.

"You better go, Kyla. I'm tempted to take you home for a romp in the sack," she said, half jokingly.

"Okay," I said hopefully.

"Oh no," she responded too quickly.

"Breakfast?" I felt like I was begging.

She shook her head no. "I'm going to stay here and start preparing for my finals."

"Why do I feel like this is good-bye?" I asked.

"It's not good-bye," she said as she wiped smeared lipstick off of my chin. "It's *I'll talk to you later.*"

We got out of the car and hugged again. I walked back to my car wondering what I had done to get in this position. Was I being tested with temptation? If so, I got a big, fat-ass F. I stopped and turned around to look back at her. She was still standing next to her car, watching me walk away. She pressed two fingers against her lips and held them up to me. I did the same and turned my back to the first person that had opened my heart to honest, true love.

11

I was putting a Donna Karan sweater on a mannequin when a body closed in on my space.

"What up, girl?"

I turned around and stood facing a smiling Juan, Tori's disrespectful-ass date from the boat cruise.

"Hi," I said, and turned back around. I wasn't in the mood for his shenanigans.

"How have you been?"

"Fine, thank you." I still didn't turn back around to look at him. But I could feel his piercing stare.

"How's your girl doing?" he asked.

"Tori is fine. I'll make sure to tell her I saw you," I answered.

"No, not Tori. How's *your* girl doing?"

I spun around. "What are you talking about?"

"You know. Stephanie."

"What about her?" I asked.

"Don't play dumb with me. I know all about your girl. She must not have recognized me. I weighed a lot more in high school."

"So?"

"We went to high school together," he said, smirking at me.

"And?"

"I know she likes eatin' pussy just as much as I do. Has she turned you out yet?"

My jaw fell open, a blatant confession of guilt. I didn't know what to say. "Fuck you, Juan," was all that came out.

"Yeah, would be nice, but you're probably not interested," he said with a devilish laugh.

I started to walk away before my coworkers caught wind of the conversation.

"I was just fuckin' around with her that night," he continued, his voice rising. "I knew she wasn't down. I tried to explain to Tori, but she didn't want to hear it. Most of all, she didn't want to hear that her best friend was hanging around with a dyke."

I walked faster toward the fitting room, hoping he wouldn't follow me. I went into one of the stalls and closed the door, covering my face in my hands. So that was it. Tori knew about Steph this whole time but didn't tell me. That explained her funky-ass attitude after the cruise. I wondered why she just didn't come out and say it. She had never been one to eat her words before. But at the same time, I was glad she didn't. I wasn't sure if I should ask her about it. If I did, then that opened up another conversation I didn't think I was ready for.

One thing I *did* know was I was tired of walking around feeling like I was hiding something. I needed to talk to somebody. I went to the break room and picked up the phone.

"Hey, Ma," I said when Gladyce answered.

"Hey, baby. I was just thinking about you," she said.

"Really?"

"Yes, you've been on my mind. How are you?" She sounded concerned. Must be mother's instinct.

"Can I come by tonight?" I asked without answering her question.

"Of course, baby. I'll make you some lasagna, okay?"

She said that like lasagna was something you just slapped together like a ham sandwich.

"I'll be there around eight."

I hung up and called Jeff to cancel our movie date. At that moment, all I needed and wanted was a little comfort from my mother.

The house smelled delicious when Gladyce let me in. She made me feel extra special by setting some of her best dinnerware on the dining room table with the chandelier lights on low. Of course she had a Best of Gladys Knight and the Pips CD playing in the background. She prayed that our food was nourishing to our bodies, and we began to fill our bellies with lasagna, salad, and garlic bread, which we washed down with Merlot.

"Ma, how do you and Dad remain such good friends?" I started the conversation.

"We spent a lot of years together in love, raising a family. We built a solid foundation that wasn't broken, even when we got divorced," she said.

"So why get divorced? I mean, you don't act any differently toward one another."

"Yes, one might say that. Your father and I didn't have a nasty divorce. There was no infidelity, no lies, and no abuse. But the love we once shared was no longer there. I'll put it this way, we loved each other, but we were no longer *in* love. We were comfortable, but baby, sometimes that's not enough."

There was that *comfortable* word again.

"But what are you doing different? Neither one of you seems to be dating."

"Honey, what does that have to do with us being

friends? I love your father and he'll always be close to me. You and Yvonne may be adults, but unless we get to a point where we feel someone else needs to be brought into the picture, your dad and I have decided to keep our private lives just that. I told him not to bring just any old floozy around my daughters after that last stunt he pulled. Now, did you come here to talk to me about your father, or is something else on your mind?"

I didn't know where to start. I wasn't about to tell her the real deal with Stephanie before I knew just how I was going to handle that situation myself.

"It's Jeff," I started. "Lately I've been unsure about my feelings for him. I know I love him and he treats me well, but there's something missing. I don't feel like he completes me."

I know I sounded like Tom Cruise from Jerry Maguire, but that was my best example.

"You're saying he's not your soul mate?" she asked.

"I guess. If there is such a person," I wondered out loud.

"Kyla, I believe everyone has someone out there who *would* be their perfect match. But the chances of finding your true soul mate are slim to none. What most of us do is make the best relationship out of the one we have. It's about how determined each person is to make it work. However, if you do find your soul mate, trust me, you'll know."

"How?"

"I can only imagine that you would feel a connection with that person that you haven't felt with anyone else before. A feeling that you're *meant* to be with that one person."

She paused and stared at me, trying to figure out what was going on in her daughter's head. "Is there something you want to tell me?" she pried.

I sighed. I couldn't possibly tell my mother I thought I

was gay. That I was contemplating altering my entire life for a woman I hadn't known very long. "I'm feeling confused, and I want to make sure Jeff is really the one for me before we continue in a relationship together."

"Well, Christmas is next week, so you better get to thinking," she said.

"What does Christmas have to do with it?" I asked.

She hopped out of her chair. "Nothing. It's just the holidays and all."

Okay, and?

She started clearing the plates and went into the kitchen before I could challenge her. I sat at the table wishing I could open up and share my true feelings with her. Would she be mad? Hurt? Disappointed? Or would she be liberal and open-minded? I figured I could tell a little bit of my story without letting her know I was referring to Stephanie.

"What would you say if I told you that I have feelings for someone else?" I asked when Gladyce returned from the kitchen.

She responded like she had been waiting for me to get to the point the entire time. "Kyla, whether you're single or married, there's always going to be people that cross your path that you find intriguing and attractive. It's natural and it happens. It's what you do with those feelings that matters most. You can love and respect the person you're with enough to ignore what you feel and let it pass. Because it *will* pass, Kyla. Or you can act on your feelings and then you're in a whole new ballgame. And know that in that game, somebody is going to lose, and it just might be you."

She sat back down at the table. "Are you going to tell me about this person?"

I knew she'd ask. "No."

"I can't lie to you, Kyla," she said, losing some of the tenderness in her voice. "I love Jeff and I think he's a wonderful man. Don't go making any hasty decisions that you'll regret later."

Okay, it was time to go. I wanted to talk to her, but I didn't want to hear a lecture either. I guess the truth hurts. I decided to change the subject to something more positive.

"So who is all coming by for Christmas?" I asked.

Gladyce let it go. "Seems like everybody, your Aunt Shari and David of course. Catrina and Brianna can't make it because they're going to Atlanta to visit John's parents. Your dad will come by for a while, and your sister is bringing Byron. Your grandaddy and grandma are bringing my Aunt Pearl in from Memphis. And you know Jeff's family is coming this year. It's going to be a full house."

"I'll be by the night before to help you get all set up. Who's helping with the food?"

"Aunt Shari. Most everyone offered to bring a dish, but you know how I am about other people's cookin'."

Gladyce loved her kitchen. I learned how to cook from her, mainly by watching, because she never wanted me in the kitchen interfering with her creations. I gave Gladyce a tight hug.

"Thanks for listening," I said.

She twisted her fingers through my curled hair like I was a little girl. "Any time, baby. Be careful, Kyla. Don't let a good thing slip away from you."

I knew she was talking about Jeff, but I was thinking about Steph. I picked up my cell phone and dialed her number as soon as I was in my car and down the street from Gladyce's house. I knew she had been watching me drive away.

"Hello," Steph answered sleepily.

I looked at the clock and realized it was after ten.

"Hey, Steph, it's Kyla."

"Hey," she said, trying to perk up.

"I know it's late, but I want to know if I can come by."

I bit my lip, knowing she was about to say no or would give me a long enough pause to let me know she didn't want my company. Instead, she answered right away.

"Sure. You're on your way now?"

"Yes, I can be there in ten minutes."

"Okay."

We hung up and I pulled to the side of the road. I blew my breath into my hand and tested for garlic. I sprayed spearmint Binaca in my mouth and covered the shine on my face with powder. I didn't put on any lip gloss this time because I didn't want to look like I was trying too hard to keep her. It felt like so much had changed between us in such a short time.

We had only seen and spoken to each other during our last two classes, and since our final had been a paper that we already turned in, I wasn't going to see her unless I asked. I missed her terribly, but hadn't been selfish enough to call her up until this point.

She answered the door in black satin pajamas and leopard print slippers. Her hair was pulled back into her signature ponytail, but I could tell from the imprint on her forehead that she had just removed a scarf. She took my coat and hung it in the closet. I hoped that meant I could stay a while.

"Are you all ready for Christmas?" I asked, admiring her tree decorated with ornaments made by Jaron.

"Yes, I finished my shopping earlier this week. Are you?"

"Yeah, I'm done. I shop at the store and usually have my gifts figured out way before Christmas. Speaking of the store, I had a visitor today."

"Who?"

"Juan," I said.

"Don't tell me he was hitting on you now," she said, exasperated by the audacity of men.

"No," I answered. "Actually, it turns out that you and Juan went to high school together. He said he was heavier back then."

She sat for a moment, trying to remember.

"Juan? Juan Valesco?" She slapped her hand to her forehead. "Holy shit! He looks different. Hell, no, I didn't recognize his ass! He was a good three hundred pounds in high school. Damn!"

"That explains Tori's problem after the cruise. He told her about you," I said.

"I guess the kids were smarter than I thought back then," she said, finally sitting down on the love seat.

I followed.

"So she doesn't like lesbians, huh?" Steph asked.

Honestly, I had no idea. "I don't know. We've never talked about it. She could be homophobic, but I really can't say."

"I would assume she is, Kyla, or she wouldn't have reacted the way she did," Steph said in a tone that meant I needed to wise up. I had to trust her on that since she had more experience in this than I did. "Are you going to tell her you saw Juan?"

"I haven't decided. What do you think?"

"Girl, that's *your* friend and it's up to you. I don't want a twenty-year friendship ruined over me."

"It won't be over you. It would be over her closed mind," I said.

She nodded her head in agreement. "How is everything going?" she asked.

"Fine," I lied. Then *I* added, "I miss you."

"I have something for you," she said, getting up and going to the Christmas tree. She found a small box buried under all the large boxes filled with Jaron's gifts. "I hope you like it," she said.

"But I didn't bring your gift with me," I said as she handed me the box wrapped in sparkling gold paper.

"That's okay. I missed you too, and you being here is enough."

I opened the box and pulled out a silver necklace and cross, almost identical to the gold one of my mother's.

"It's beautiful," I said, overcome with emotion.

"I noticed your mom's necklace and thought about how nice the same one would look around your neck."

I handed the necklace to her and turned my back so she could put it on me. I went to the mirror and stroked the cross that hung between my collarbones.

"Thank you so much," I said, giving her a hug.

When she sat back down, I laid my head in her lap and inhaled scented skin between her button openings. She ran her fingers through my hair, gently massaging my scalp. I unbuttoned one, then two buttons and kissed her belly. My tongue fluttered against her skin, up and down and in circles.

She leaned forward and whispered, "Come on," in my ear. She took my hand and led me into her bedroom, closing the door behind us.

She took off her pajama bottoms, revealing her mound of short, silky-smooth hair. She unbuttoned my pants and lowered my underwear for me to step out of. She laid me on the bed and positioned herself between my legs, our thighs intertwined. She grinded against me. I moved my hips to her motion and our bodies rubbed each other, sending sensations up and down my skin and between my legs.

My heart rate heightened and my eyes closed. Never before had I imagined such an experience with a woman. Our moistures mixed as we pressed against one another until neither of us could contain ourselves. We came together.

She rolled over and wiped the sweat under her ponytail. "Whew! I needed that. You can go now," she said playfully.

I picked up a pillow and hit her upside her head. She reached behind her to snatch a pillow and hit me back. We took turns getting shots in at one another until we both lay exhausted on the bed. I took her hand in mine, and we fell asleep lying on our backs holding hands.

Steph woke me up at 5:30 AM, before Jaron had to get up for school. Quickly I got dressed, and as I was sliding into my boots, she knelt in front of me.

"I'm glad you came over last night," she confessed. "You're so hard to resist, and it's hard to stay away from something that feels so right. But I'm not taking back anything I said to you before."

"Okay," was all I could say. I wanted to take her in my arms and tell her I never wanted to let her go. "Can I see you before Christmas?" I asked her.

She sighed impatiently like I had ignored what she'd just said. I guess I did.

"Kyla, there's nothing more I would like than to see you every day before and after Christmas, but that's not going to happen. It's hard enough to say good-bye to you now, and I know it would only get harder and harder each time I see you. If you and I aren't going to be, then one of us has to be strong. You already make me feel so weak."

"But I didn't say we weren't going to be," I protested.

"You haven't said we are either." She looked in my eyes for a response, but I had none.

I put on my coat, and she walked me to the door.

"When and if you're ready, let me know." Steph said. Then she added firmly, "Just don't take too long."

I drove home hoping Jeff hadn't called late last night to find me not there. I didn't know what to do about Jeff and, I was driving myself crazy thinking about it. My mind was like a scratched record, replaying my worries over and over in my head.

I felt like Steph had warned me again. She hadn't given me an ultimatum, but she'd made her point clear. She wasn't going to sit around and wait for me, and I didn't blame her. So I gave *myself* an ultimatum to make a decision by New Year's eve. I couldn't continue to drag out my confusion or Steph's hurt forever. Or continue to deceive Jeff. I wasn't being true to them or myself by keeping up this threesome.

I wondered if I needed to see a psychologist. I wasn't sure I could dig deep enough to determine if I was a true lesbian by myself. If I didn't see a shrink in the next nine days, I'd settle for the next best thing: David.

I called him when I got home at 6:15 that morning. I asked him if he could meet me at Gladyce's house on Christmas Eve so we could talk.

"No problem," he said sleepily, but with concern in his voice.

I hung up feeling slightly better and wished for a sign. Could I walk outside and look in the sky and see *him* and *her* written in the clouds with a check mark underneath one of them? Or couldn't I trip and fall, bump my head, and the answer would be clear as day when I came to my senses?

I laid down for a quick nap, waiting for my answer to reveal itself to me. I fell asleep to the sound of my downstairs neighbors' headboard banging repetitiously against the wall. He moaned and she screamed until their excitement drowned out the banging and eventually calmed to a quiet aftermath.

That same thrill ride I had shared with both Jeff and Stephanie. Now I needed to determine whose ride I wanted to coast on for the rest of my life.

12

I was sitting on the floor of the bedroom that Yvonne and I shared as children, later to become my room alone. A poster of Prince lying in a bathtub with his curly hair covering one eye hung on the closet door. Yvonne and I fought over that poster, like bitches over a pimp, when she turned twelve and moved into the room next door. With the help of Gladyce's intervention, I eventually won the tug-of-war.

David was sitting cross-legged in front of me and massaging my hands and fingers with lotion before finishing my manicure. He'd loved polishing my nails since I was about six years old. You could still see the faint pink spill stains on the light blue carpeting if you stared hard enough.

"What do you think the family would say if I told them about Steph?" I asked David.

"Lucky for you, girl. I already took the stigma of homosexuality out of the family. Everyone would be shocked all right, but it might not be as bad as you think. There would be an adjustment period, but I don't think you would turn into the black sheep of the family.

"Honey child, look at me," he continued, running his fingers over his platinum blond Sisqó hairdo. "I fit every gay stereotype there is and our family loves me just as I am."

"Can you picture me bringing Steph and Jaron to Christmas dinner as a family?" I asked, laughing at my question.

"Yes, I can," he responded seriously. "The question is, can *you?*"

I was tired of asking myself questions. I felt like my heart already knew the answers, but I wanted to do the right thing. But was it the right thing for me or for everyone else?

"You know what else you have to think about?" David asked. "What would you do if your relationship with Stephanie didn't work out? I'm not wishing that on you, but keep it in mind, sweetie. Would you go back to dating men or be a full-blown lesbian? You'd never be able to go back and erase the fact that you once had a relationship with a woman. It'll follow you forever."

Good question. I hadn't thought about that. Would I go back to men? Or was I bisexual? I remembered a girl from one of my women's studies classes who identified herself as bisexual. She said she was looking for love and didn't care if it came in the form of a man or a woman. No, I didn't think I felt that way.

David picked up an emery board and squarely shaped my natural nails.

"Are you in love, Kyla?" David asked.

I didn't hesitate. "I think I am, David. I love everything about Steph. The friend she is, the mother she is, the lover in her, the career woman. I feel like I can share anything and everything there is about me with her and never have to pretend to be something I'm not. I feel like I could look into her eyes forever and it would always feel like it was the very first time."

"Hmph. Sounds like you know what to do, honey, you just need the courage."

We heard a creak at the door and fell silent. Then there was a knock and Yvonne walked in.

"Hey, what's up?" she asked casually, though she had that same guilty look on her face from childhood when she used to eavesdrop on David and me.

"What are you two talking about?" she asked, looking at me, knowing good and well she heard.

I could lie and she would know I was lying. Or I could tell the truth and start the process of filling my family in on my newfound revelation.

"We were talking about love," I answered, beating around the bush, something I was fairly good at.

"Who's in love?" she asked.

"We all are, aren't we?" I asked, hoping the subject would change to Byron.

She forgot about me so fast and started in on Byron that I *knew* the girl was sprung.

"He's so wonderful. It took long enough for me to hook up with someone, but he was worth the wait," she said, clasping her hands together with that dreamy look in her eyes that is usually only seen in movies.

"I'm happy for you, Yvonne. He's a really nice person," I said, grateful she accepted the bait.

"Yes, he is," she said. "I just can't wait until his divorce is final."

David stopped filing my nails and looked at me before we both turned to Yvonne.

"What?" I asked in shock.

"Rewind that tape, honey! What did you say?" David asked with a hand on his hip.

"He and his wife separated about six months ago and he's in the process of filing for a divorce," Yvonne answered nonchalantly.

"Girlfriend, has he actually filed yet?" David asked.

"Well, no, he's still looking for an attorney."

"Sugar, divorce attorneys are *not* hard to find. Just open the yellow pages and point," David said, demonstrating by pointing his finger.

"He said he wants to find a good one." She thought for a moment. "But it's not like they have a lot to fight over. They don't have any kids or own a house," Yvonne said, suddenly sounding curious.

"Why are they getting divorced?" I wanted to know.

"He said they want different futures," she said. "They got married right after college and spent the next few years trying to get financially stable, but he says she doesn't know the meaning of the word *budget*. He's not a tightwad, although being a financial advisor makes him value every dollar. Anyway," she exhaled. "His wife is ready to move to the next phase and start a family, but he wants to save money, buy a house, travel, and wait until he's sure he's ready to be a father."

"Are they sure that's grounds for divorce? It sounds like they might be able to work it out through counseling," I said.

"They tried counseling right before he moved out. They still decided to separate," she replied.

"Be careful," I warned. "Don't get all wrapped up for him to turn around and go back to his wife. You could be a temporary fill-in."

David snapped his fingers in the air. "I know that's right. You're on the rebound, girl," he said.

Now I wished I hadn't gotten her that sexy nightgown with the matching furry, high-heeled slippers.

Yvonne frowned her face at us. "He's coming tomorrow, so don't treat him funny. I know he's going to divorce her," she said in Byron's defense.

"Do Mom and Dad know?" I asked her.

"No! And keep it that way. We *both* can keep secrets, can't we?" she said, looking me in the eye. She was turning the conversation back to me and I wasn't playing into it.

At that moment, David was my only confidant. He put the last finishing coat of really red on my pinky fingernail.

"Blow, darling. And don't mess them babies up," he instructed me. Then he proceeded to paint his own nails the same color.

We all left around midnight. The house was beautifully decorated with strings of white lights twirled through Gladyce's five floor plants. I had hung red, gold, and green garland at the ceiling in half circles, making a wall trim in Christmas colors. Red cinnamon candles were placed on the coffee table, the stereo speakers, the bookcase, and anything with a flat surface. At Gladyce's request I spread gold glitter on her tan carpeting for a shimmer effect, but I had the feeling she wouldn't do that again after cleanup.

Again, I waited until I had driven down the street before calling Steph from my car.

"Merry Christmas," I said cheerfully.

"Back to you," she said, sounding wide awake.

"Can I come by and bring you and Jaron's gifts?"

"I didn't think I would see you until after the new year."

"I can't wait that long, Steph. Plus, I want you to have the gifts before Christmas, not after."

She pretended to sound irritated by my persistence, but I could feel her smile through the phone. "Okay, come on," she said.

David pulled up next to me at a stoplight just as I was hanging up my cell phone.

"Stephanie or Jeff?" he inquired after lowering his window.

"You don't have to ask, do you?" I replied.

We laughed, though the look in his eyes seemed like

sorrow for Jeff. A pang of guilt skyrocketed through me, yet I continued on to Steph's apartment.

Her place smelled like a bakery when I walked in. And she looked like Betty Crocker in an apron and cooking gloves.

"Smells delicious," I said, inhaling the scent as I took my coat off.

"I've made three cakes and the last one is in the oven," she said.

She led me into the kitchen and proudly displayed her German chocolate cake, pound cake, and lemon cake with chocolate icing. She pointed to the oven.

"This one here is a ginger cake," she said. She took her gloves off and swiped her finger around the mixing bowl. She put her finger in my mouth for a taste. "You like?" she asked.

"Very much," I murmured without letting her finger go. She allowed my tongue to linger for a moment before snatching her finger back.

"No. No more booty calls," she said, smiling.

I reached in my pocket and pulled out an unwrapped bracelet.

She squealed in delight when she saw it.

"Kyla! When did you get this?"

"While you were sleeping, I went down and talked to the concierge and one of them picked it up for me."

The bracelet was handcrafted, made of sterling silver bands and beads with a single onyx stone in the middle. She had seen the bracelet at a gift shop when we were in Nassau and drooled over it for at least ten minutes. Instead of purchasing it, she opted to purchase a gift for Jaron.

She threw her arms around my neck and jumped up and wrapped her legs around my waist. She kissed me over and over, telling me, "Thank you" in between smacks.

In an attempt to prove my strength, I tried to hold her up while kissing her back, but my arms gave in and we fell to the floor. We rolled around laughing and making so much noise that I was sure Jaron would wake up and the cake would fall. I laid on her and stretched her arms above her head and put the bracelet on her right wrist.

I hoped to make love to her right there on her kitchen floor. But I would honor her request. I didn't want her to feel like I was using her for the good sex we shared. Still, I pressed my body into hers to see if I could get a reaction. She closed her eyes and grinded long enough to get my panties dripping wet and then stopped abruptly.

"What did I tell you, Kyla?" she said, trying to sound stern, but her eyes were filled with pleasure.

"Okay, I'll behave," I said.

I got up and pulled her up with both hands. I kissed her and got my coat on.

"I better get some rest. Tomorrow will be a busy day for both of us," I said.

"I'll be thinking about you," she admitted.

"And I'll be thinking about you," I said. "I'll call you the day after tomorrow. Bye, sweetie."

She blushed at my words and it was so adorable.

After I left Steph's, my cell phone started ringing as soon as I got in the car.

"Hey, I'm outside your apartment. Where are you?" Jeff asked. I was just about to lie, but he kept on. "I called your mom and she said you left about an hour ago."

"I just dropped Jaron's gift over by Stephanie's. I wanted to make sure he had it on Christmas morning."

"Oh."

"Are you going to wait for me?" I asked.

"I'll be right here," he said impatiently.

I hurried home and pulled up next to his truck.

"What's that on your clothes?" he asked after we were

inside and I took my coat off. I looked down and saw stripes of chocolate on my jeans that must have come from Steph's apron. I hadn't even noticed.

"She was baking cakes and I must have gotten dirty," I explained.

"How?"

"I don't know."

He stood there looking at me, I guess waiting for a better explanation. I wondered if he was beginning to speculate about the depth of our friendship.

"I'm tired. Let's go to bed," I suggested.

As usual, he dropped the subject and followed me into the bedroom, telling me about his evening at his parents. His brother had made a major announcement that his girlfriend was pregnant. Kent first mentioned it to Jeff a couple of months ago but had him swear to secrecy.

"I would have told you, but you don't always keep secrets very well," he said, eyeing me curiously.

"Are they going to get married?" I asked him.

"That was my mom and dad's first question too. Kent and Kendra don't want to rush and get married just because she's pregnant. And I agree, it's their decision."

"I'm surprised she doesn't want to get married. She's older than him, isn't she?"

"Yeah, she's thirty-one, but she has an eleven-year-old daughter and she's been married and divorced already. I guess her parents sent her to the courthouse the first time, so she's in no hurry to rush to make that same mistake again."

"Well, she already went and got pregnant, didn't she?"

He looked at me like that wasn't a very nice thing to say. I tried to clean it up.

"So you're going to be an uncle. Are you excited?" I asked him.

"Hell, yeah! If I like it enough, I'll have to make some

rug rats of my own," he said, smacking my behind as I put on my nightshirt.

I changed the subject to Byron, telling Jeff I couldn't believe Yvonne had gone and gotten herself mixed up with someone who already had somebody. Then I shut my ass up as soon as I thought about Steph's involvement with me.

"I can talk to him tomorrow and see where he's coming from," Jeff offered.

"Oh, no. My parents don't know, so you can't bring up the topic."

Plus, if Jeff spilled the beans and Yvonne found out, she might resort to letting out my little secret. I couldn't chance that.

We got into bed and he wrapped his big body around mine, and I pretended to fall asleep immediately. He kissed my forehead and it wasn't until I felt his body ease away into dreamland that I allowed my body to relax and drift off to sleep myself.

Gladyce's home was filled with Christmas merriment as the BeBe and CeCe Winans *First Christmas* CD played through the stereo speakers. Everyone had feasted on ham, greens, chicken, dressing, green beans, and potato salad; and those were just a few items on the menu.

My grandma and grandpa, who I generally spend time with only when I visit their suburban retirement community, sat in the leather recliners on opposite sides of the Christmas tree, each sharing family stories and doling out years of wisdom when asked for advice from the younger generations. Aunt Pearl found joy in the company of her sister and brother-in-law and other members of the family that she didn't get to see on a regular basis. Mr. and Mrs. Oldham, Kent, Kendra, and her daughter blended well with my family, cracking jokes and interacting with everyone there. Being a beautician, Kendra took a special liking to David, who reminded her of two of the hairstylists in the salon that she owned. Byron handed out business cards to all in attendance, assuring them a prosperous future if trusted with their finances. And Aunt Shari was Gladyce's partner and aide, helping serve dishes, keeping glasses full, and making sure guests were comfortable, all while trying to keep gold sparkle off of plates, out of children's hair, and removed from clothing. She fussed at her sister all evening, questioning why she would do such a thing as place glitter on her carpeting.

I was headed back into the kitchen for my third helping of macaroni and cheese when the doorbell rang.

"I'll get it," I yelled over the music and chatter and went to answer the door. Three familiar faces smiled brightly at me when I opened the door. "What a nice surprise," I said, giving Tori, Vanessa, and Roger each a hug. "What are you doing here?"

"What? We can't come see our best friend on Christmas?" Tori asked.

"I don't remember inviting you," I said sarcastically. "But I'm glad you're here," I added.

"Look who's here," I yelled at everyone as I walked the group into the living room. No one seemed surprised by their entrance.

"Right on time, we were just about to open gifts," Gladyce announced with a little too much enthusiasm.

David, dressed in tight black leather pants, a red sweater (to match the nails), and a Santa Claus hat, handed his gifts out first. I opened my box to find a poem written on a mirrored wall hanging. It read:

> *Let's treasure each moment that we have,*
> *because tomorrow is not guaranteed.*
> *Let's not waste our lives in fear or anger or pain,*

but break free of all constrictions
to live in a way that fulfills us.
Let's express what we feel we need to,
and do the things that reward us.
Life is too short to waste,
and time can never be recaptured.

Engraved on the back he quoted William Shakespeare:

This above all: to thine own self be true.
To my baby girl, much happiness and success in school,
career, and love. David

"Thank you, David," I said, kissing his lips flavored with strawberry gloss. I don't think anyone else in the room knew how special those words were to me. No one had any idea that I was internally tearing myself apart struggling to figure out just what it was I needed to be happy and what my true self was.

We continued with our gift opening and I hated to give Yvonne her gift. Jeff and I shared a knowing look when Yvonne whispered something in Byron's ear and you could practically see his dick get hard through his pants.

I gave Jeff his gift of three books by Michael Baisden, a money clip engraved with his initials, and two floor tickets to the Bucks vs. Lakers game in the spring. I did some serious groveling with a VP at the store and got the floor seats. Jeff shook his fist in the air like Arsenio did when he was famous back in the nineties. I knew he would love the tickets the most. Who wouldn't want to see Shaq and Kobe work their magic on the floor?

"So, Kyla, does this mean he has to take you to the game?" Roger asked, stepping close to Jeff like he was his best buddy in the world.

"No, he can take whomever he chooses. I don't want to go," I replied.

"All right!" They knocked fists together, confirming their date.

Jeff stood up and asked for everyone's attention. Gladyce hurriedly turned the music down as Jeff took the spotlight and started talking in her direction. I sat down, slightly confused by what he needed to say to everybody.

"First, I want to thank Ms. Thomas for opening her home to me and my family and allowing us to share this joyous holiday with you all," Jeff stated. "You and Mr. Thomas have always made me feel welcome from day one and I appreciate that." He looked around the room of smiling faces. "I know everyone in the room knows how much Kyla means to me and how much I love her. That's why I wanted everyone to be here for this moment."

I looked at Tori and Vanessa beaming at me, looking giddy as hell. Jeff walked over to the chair I was sitting in and knelt on one knee. *Oh shit!* I saw David's jaw fall open out of the corner of my eye.

"Kyla, there's nothing I wouldn't do for you to make you happy," Jeff said on bended knee. "You know that. All you ever have to do is ask. I'm here for you today, tomorrow, and I want to be here for you the rest of my life if you'll let me."

He reached in his pocket and pulled out a sparkling ring. He took my left hand in his and held the ring in front of my fourth finger. "Will you marry me, Kyla?"

My eyes watered and I couldn't control the tears that rolled down my cheeks. I looked at David, who understood the true meaning behind my tears. His eyes glistened with his own tears as he felt my pain. I looked at Gladyce for help, but she ignored my plea. I looked around the room of faces filled with anticipation and knew this was neither the time nor the place for debate. Finally, I looked into the eyes of the man who had just declared his love for me in front of our families and friends. His face beamed with happiness.

"Yes," I whispered, and the room erupted with cheers.

He slid the platinum, three-karat marquis ring on my finger and kissed the tears off my face.

"I love you," he whispered to me and only me.

"I love you too," I said as more tears began to fall.

All the women rushed to give me hugs and admire the ring.

"God *damn!*" That was Tori. She quickly apologized to the elders in the room.

"You put my ring to shame," Vanessa said in a low voice, then looking for Roger to be sure he didn't overhear her comment.

Jeff's parents gave me hugs and officially welcomed me into the family. My dad gave me a big bear hug, and I wanted nothing more than to cry like a baby in his arms.

"My baby," my dad said without finishing his sentence. He kissed my cheek, and I caught him wiping a tear away before it could fall.

Gladyce hugged me and whispered in my ear. "You've got a wonderful man right here, Kyla. Don't forget that." She spoke the same words she said three days prior to the momentous occasion.

Suddenly I realized that everyone had been in on this except me and David. That's why Gladyce was adamant that I straighten up before Christmas day. That's what Vanessa hinted at when we were trying on dresses. And this ring was what Jeff purchased for me while I was busy falling in love with someone else.

"Let's go fix that makeup, girl," David said and grabbed my hand, leading me to the bathroom at the end of the hall, next to the staircase leading to the second level. He closed the door behind us.

"Are you okay?" he asked, holding my face in his smooth hands.

"Oh, David, what am I going to do now?" I asked.

"Child, I don't know, but whatever it is, you better do it quickly."

"Did you see the look on his face? I can't break his heart."

"Baby girl, if you believe you can be happy with him the rest of your life, then do it," he advised in a hushed tone. "Walk away from Stephanie and move forward if you're going to commit to the life Jeff wants to have with you. If you have *any* doubt, then don't marry him. You would be depriving both of you from true happiness."

"What do you think I should do?" I pleaded. I desperately needed someone to tell me the answer.

"You know I'm not going to make the decision for you, Ky. It's your life."

I took a handful of Kleenex and wiped my eyes and blew my nose. David reapplied my mascara because my hands were shaking too badly to do it myself. I tried my best to turn my sad tears into happy tears when I walked back into the room filled with celebration. Everyone was talking about Vanessa and Roger's upcoming wedding on Saturday.

"What a way to bring in the New Year," my dad was saying. He spotted me returning to the room. "And as soon as these two lovebirds set a date, we'll be starting the process all over again," he said, putting his long arms around me and Jeff.

Everyone grinned while my stomach did a triple somersault and backflip.

"Ky," Vanessa said, rescuing me, "your dress and shoes are in the car. Let's go get them."

The fresh air breathed on my face like a freezer door had been opened. I inhaled and let the cold air flow through my nose and into my lungs, sending a chill down my spine.

"You knew about this, huh?" I asked her.

"Girl, yes. We've been holding it in for three months. Jeff told Roger he was going to propose, and I promised not to tell. He bought the ring while you were in the beautiful Bahamas, which I still can't believe you forgot your disposable camera in your room. Anyway, I'm so happy for you, Ky. You and Jeff make such a good couple."

She looked at me and waited for a response, but I just stared into the sky at the Big Dipper.

"Talk to me, Ky," she said. "I've known you too long not to know when something is bothering you."

I wanted to tell her that I was in love with someone else and that someone was Stephanie. And that I wanted to leave my life behind and run away with her. That with each passing day I was slipping farther and farther away from Jeff into her waiting arms.

"I'm fine," I said.

We transferred my dress and shoes from Roger's car to mine and went back inside. The rest of the evening was spent playing Guesstures, the nineties' commercialized version of Charades. Eventually we reverted back to the old-fashioned playing method, indicating whether we were doing a movie, TV show, or song by motions with hands, holding up fingers to tell the number of words and syllables. I temporarily moved every worry from the forefront of my mind to a dark space in the corner for overnight storage. I drank hot chocolate and laughed with the people I held closest to my heart. For just a short while, I felt happy and carefree. A feeling I hadn't known since I'd left the Bahamas.

I had zero energy when I got up at the crack of dawn the next morning, though I was due to greet all the hun-

gry after-Christmas-sale shoppers that would burst through
the door at 7:00 AM, like they hadn't spent enough of their
money the few weeks before.

I untangled myself from Jeff's arms and took a shower.
When I sniffed the soap for a sudden burst of energy like
the commercial suggested, I was disheartened when it didn't
happen. I walked back into the room to find a cheery face
peeking from underneath my comforter.

"Go back to sleep. I didn't want to wake you," I told Jeff.

"I will after you leave. I like what I see right now," he
said, referring to my naked body.

In the past I would have taken this opportunity to do a
quick dance or model my tits and ass for him, but I wasn't
feeling it anymore.

"When do you want to move in?" he asked.

I almost poked a hole in my pantyhose when he asked
that question. Damn, did we have to have this conversation already?

"I'm just as anxious as you are to move on with the future," I said. "But can we hold off making plans until after
the New Year? The next few days are going to be hectic
with work and the wedding."

Truth was, I needed time to gather my thoughts and
figure out what I was going to do. We could have that conversation later. If at all.

"Okay, but you *are* going to move into my place, right?
We can't be like Roger and Vanessa, moving on the weekend after the wedding and *then* going on the honeymoon."

"Your place is bigger than mine," was all I said.

He was satisfied with that response and nestled his head
back into the pillow.

I finished dressing so fast, you would have thought I was
going to get a $10,000 raise if I'd made it to work on time.
In actuality, I felt like the walls in the room were closing in

on me and I was going to suffocate. I ran my finger over his head, kissed him good-bye and darted out the door.

Finally, I exhaled once I was in my car and checked the voice mail messages on my cell phone while the car warmed up. The first was from Vanessa. She was up in the middle of the night trying to finish table gifts and she needed help if they were going to be finished in time for the wedding. She wanted the bridesmaids to help Friday after the rehearsal.

The second message was from Stephanie around three in the morning. "*Hey, Ky, it's me. I hope you had as great of a Christmas as I did. Umm . . . I missed you today and I want to know if I can see you tomorrow night, which will probably be tonight by the time you get this message. Anyway, I'm trying to pretend like I don't want or need you but the truth is, right now, I'll take whatever I can get. Call me and let me know if we can get together.*"

Three times I played her message, soaking in the sexiness and vulnerability in her voice with each listen. It was only 6:30 AM and I didn't want to wake her, so I decided to call her later.

Just as I expected, there was a line of shoppers waiting when I arrived. I quickly ran to my department, got the register drawers together and braced myself for a busy day. *At least the fast pace would help the time pass by quickly.*

I didn't realize so much time would be occupied with my coworkers gawking at my ring and celebrating an uncertain engagement. At lunchtime I excused myself from a group of women who were graciously giving me their ideas on everything from setting the date to locations for the reception, and where to get the best deal on invitations. I could see why Vanessa was ready to elope at one point.

"Hey, sweetness," I said when I broke away and had a moment to call Steph.

"Hey to you," she said.

"I got your message."

"Can I see you today?" She didn't waste any time.

"I get off at four. I can come by afterward. Is there something you want to tell me?" I asked.

"I just want to see your face. Is that all right?"

I knew she could hear me smiling through the phone.

"It's more than all right," I said.

"Jaron won't be here, but he told me to thank you for his video game."

"Good, I'm glad he liked it. I'll see you soon."

I hung up the phone wondering how in the hell I was going to tell her about the engagement ring. I knew telling her was the right thing to do, but I was scared I was going to lose her until I broke it off. If I broke it off.

The sight of Stephanie opening her door in a black corset, black thongs, and a garter belt with fishnet stockings and patent leather pumps was enough to make my heart stop. Her skin shimmered in sparkling gold body dust from her neck to her feet. Her hair hung in large, spiral curls, and she wore only black eyeliner with red lipstick. She looked like she could take Tyra Banks's job any day of the week.

She stepped back and extended her arm in a welcome pose. The smell of chocolate cake filled the air.

"Happy anniversary," she said.

"Huh?"

She leaned forward and planted her sensuous lips on mine.

"Four months ago you walked into my life and turned it upside down," she said.

Man, she took the words right out of my mouth. My life would surely never be the same.

"Well, are you going to stay or what?" she asked, reaching for my coat.

As I took my gloves off, I carefully slid the engagement ring off of my finger and let it fall into my glove. I shoved the gloves in my pocket before handing her the wool garment. As beautiful and happy as she looked, I couldn't shock her with the news of my questionable engagement.

She took my hand and walked me into the kitchen. The table was set for two and placed in the center was a homemade chocolate cake with chocolate frosting. She had written *Happy Anniversary* in yellow. Tears welled in my eyes at her thoughtfulness.

"Thank you, Steph. You're so sweet," I said, smiling.

She pulled me close and held me in her arms. "I want you to know how much you mean to me, Kyla. We haven't known each other very long, but time doesn't matter to me. Being with you felt right from the very beginning. I know this isn't an ideal situation for either of us, but I'm going to treasure any time we have together. I don't believe in coincidences, and I know in my heart that you came into my life for a reason."

I wanted to say something, but I was overcome with guilt. Some people yearned a lifetime for the love and affection I received from both Stephanie and Jeff. And there I was, selfishly soaking up all their love without being able to give 100 percent back to either one of them.

"Can we finish what we started the other night?" she asked, kissing my neck.

Her hair grazed my skin like butterfly kisses across my face. My body craved hers, and although I knew I should stop, I couldn't resist her. I leaned her against the kitchen counter and caressed her breasts in each hand. I teased each nipple until they stood hard and erect beneath the tight corset. I lowered myself to my knees and unsnapped her garter, then lowered her thongs and nibbled her thighs until the heat from her body told me she was ready.

She spread her legs to let me in, and I took a mouthful of her juices, savoring the flavor as she dripped down the corners of my mouth.

"Ahhh . . ." she cried out, tilting her head upward to the ceiling. She held the back of my head, guiding me, leading me to her spot. My tongue flickered wherever she led me until her thighs tightened and I felt her love come down.

My knees cracked loudly as I stood up, making us laugh, which caused a release of air from her wet pussy, making a noise as if she had passed gas. Some have termed this uncontrollable, embarrassing act a "coochie fart." That's when we doubled over with laughter, hardly able to catch our breaths. We didn't stop until we were on the floor with tears rolling down our faces and our stomachs hurting to the point where we couldn't laugh anymore.

"Oh, Kyla, I love you," she said behind her tears.

"I love you too, Stephanie," I said with certainty.

It was finally out and it felt so good, like that two-ton brick on my shoulder had finally been lifted. She rolled on top of me.

"How much?" she asked.

"More than I ever could have imagined," I answered honestly.

She kissed me quickly and hopped to her feet. "Let's eat!"

We gobbled down cake and vanilla ice cream while she told me about Christmas at her mom's. Her mom had never remarried since her dad died, and this Christmas was the first time she'd invited a man over.

"After eighteen years?" I asked in amazement.

"Girl, can you imagine? I encouraged her to date so many times, but she compared everyone to my dad. This man seems really nice. He has two adult children, a son and a daughter, but they both left the city for college and never looked back. His wife died of cancer three years ago, so he and my mom can relate. I like him."

"I'm glad to hear it," I said as I swirled my ice cream in circles, trying to figure out how to tell her about the ring. She opened the door for me.

"So, I hate to ask, but what did Jeff get you for Christmas?"

I continued to play with my ice cream, imagining I was the spoon, spinning around and around but going nowhere. One tear fell into my bowl of slop.

Steph reached out and touched my arm. "What's wrong, Ky?" she asked with concern.

I stuttered over my words, trying to get them out. My heart was pounding so loud that I could hardly hear myself speak.

"Jeff proposed yesterday. He gave me an engagement ring."

I looked into her eyes and watched her expression change from shock to pure anger. The eyes that normally twinkled at me glared at me with such rage that I got scared. She pushed her chair back and stood up, throwing her bowl and spoon into the sink, splattering white dots on her cream kitchen walls.

"Why didn't you tell me?" she yelled at me.

"I just did," I said, knowing I had been a coward for not telling her when I first arrived.

"Yeah, you wait until I pour my heart out to you, you get a piece of ass, and then you throw this shit at me?" Her breathing became heavy as I watched her chest rise and fall with each gust of rage bursting through her system.

She put her fingers to her temples and shook her head in disbelief.

"I don't believe this," she repeated over and over. Suddenly she grabbed my left hand.

"Where's the ring?"

"In my glove," I said, tears of shame falling despite my attempt to hold them in.

She threw my hand back at me. "You took the fuckin' ring off on purpose? What in the hell is that all about, Kyla? I don't have time for these fuckin' games! You should have come here and been a woman and told me the truth! Or better yet, if you're getting married, you shouldn't have come at all!"

"Why is it so different now than it was two days ago? I was cheating on him then too." I was whining, trying to plead my case, even though I was the guilty party.

Steph threw her hands up in the air. "I didn't say this was right, Kyla. I know good and goddamn well it's not! But you could have spared both of us the heartache of professing our love for one another if you're getting married! Damn! At least two days ago I had a glimmer of hope that there was a chance we could be together."

Her head fell into her hands and her anger turned to hurt as she started to cry. "Now there's no chance at all," she said.

I stood and reached to embrace her, but she swept past me and went into her room, locking the door behind her. I waited outside her door wishing I could reach in my chest and take my heart out to ease the pain. I banged on her door, pleading with her to let me in.

"Stephanie, please," I said between sobs. "I'm so sorry."

She answered me with silence. I sat on the floor and leaned against the door, praying she would let me in. I cried. I cried until my body shook, and my throat tightened until I could hardly breathe. I was losing the one person I had allowed myself to love completely. The one person who filled the questionable void left unanswered for so many years.

I finally heard movement in her room and I jumped up

as Steph opened the door just enough to expose half of her body. Her eyes were red and her face was blotchy. She spoke calmly and evenly.

"I love you, Kyla. And I'd be lying if I said I wasn't silently wishing you'd choose me. But now I know that's not going to happen. I've already crossed lines I never intended, and being with a married woman is something I sure as hell am not about to do. If you're going to be with Jeff, then be with him and only him. Keep me out of it. But before you make that decision, I suggest you do some soul-searching. If you truly loved him, you wouldn't have strayed so easily. Be honest with yourself and be honest with him." With that, she closed the door.

I called for her over and over but she ignored me. Eventually she turned her radio on so loud that it drowned out the sound of my voice. I got the hint.

I went to the closet and retrieved my coat. I placed the ring back on my finger and stared back toward the bedroom door, hoping she'd run out and tell me she couldn't live her life without me. If that happened, I would no longer question what I should do. That would be the answer I was waiting for. However, I knew that was too easy. I had to make this decision for myself.

13

After I rolled from underneath my bedspread and stuck my head out, I squinted at the clock until my vision focused on the red numbers. It was 8:20 AM and I desperately needed two more hours of sleep. But sleep would only be a dream, considering I was already behind schedule and due at the hair salon in forty minutes.

I scrunched my face at the sunlight peeking through my window blinds when I sat up. My mouth was sticky and my forehead throbbed, reminding me of the three too many shots of tequila I had the night before.

My dear Vanessa didn't want a bridal shower; she said that marrying the man of her dreams amongst friends and family on New Year's eve was celebration enough. The rest of us didn't agree with that fairy-tale, la-la land shit. She needed to go out like a champ, so Tori and I, along with Vanessa's sister, Chavon, and Roger's sister, Monica, who was in town from the ATL, finished the table gifts in less than hour and insisted on taking Vanessa out, in honor of her last day as a single woman.

Tori knew just the club to take us to. At first, Vanessa

was bashful and hid behind Tori, who of course went broke handing out dollar bills, but we all eased up after the first round of Long Island iced teas. And then came the shots. You couldn't hold Vanessa down after that. She was all over the dancers like the old lady in the front row at the Apollo. Once word got around to the dancers that she was getting married the next day, all eyes and bodies were on our group.

I didn't mind admiring the dancers, as long as they didn't touch me. However, one greasy, sweaty dancer who went by the name Long John (how original) felt the need to come grind his dick in my face. I wanted to punch him in the stomach and kick him in the nuts, but I refrained myself, not wanting to get us thrown out and all. Instead, I told him to get his funky ass off of me and he did. No one bothered me the rest of the night, and I had a fabulous time.

Tori had to call Malik to come and pick us up because we were all too lit to drive. He brought one of his boys to drive her car back home. Malik dropped each of us off and made sure we each got safely inside. I was happy that he and Tori were still going strong. Looked like she finally found a winner.

When I looked in the mirror, I prayed that Vanessa didn't look as bad as I did. I showered quickly and poured half my bottle of Visine into my eyes. I threw on a flannel sweatsuit, a baseball cap, and headed to the salon.

It was a mild winter day, with a temperature in the thirties, and the sun was shining brightly. I believed the winter break was especially for Roger and Vanessa.

After stopping at McDonald's for coffee, I arrived at Martha's hair salon just as Monica was getting out of the chair. Her shoulder-length hair was pinned up in the back with a flock of curls hanging down the right side of her lightly freckled face. One wispy curl hung next to her left ear with a few more sprinkled around her neckline. I assumed we'd all be getting the same hairdo, except for Tori, who would sport her usual Halle style.

I rested my eyes the whole time I got my hair washed, dried, and curled. I was so glad Monica stayed and talked to Camille as she did my hair, so I could have a few more minutes of rest.

Tori and Vanessa came in just when the curling iron left my head for the last time. Vanessa had the glow of a pregnant woman, with her eyes sparkling brightly and her white teeth on display nonstop. Her jaws were going to be sore by the end of the day if she kept it up.

"Do you have any last-minute runs you need me to make?" I asked her when I got out of the chair and hugged her.

She continued to talk through her smile. "No, you would think I had planned this wedding for years because everything is set. The decorations are going up as we speak. The band is arriving before the ceremony, so jazz can be played while we take pictures. Appetizers will be available for guests at that time also. I can't have people staring at the ceiling while we all take pictures. After that, we'll have the toast, dinner, and cake. And then the party is on!"

She was so hyper that she reminded me of a little kid who needed a double shot of Ritalin. I stayed and talked with them, since the ceremony wasn't until 2:00.

Tori delighted us with one of her infamous sex stories. Just about the whole salon had their ears tuned in. Apparently Malik had rocked her world last night.

"How could you even function?" I asked her.

"Girl, you know my stuff never gets tired. He was lapping up this drunk pussy like a starving man!"

She slapped five with Camille while the rest of us lowered our heads. The girl could be so uncouth sometimes.

"Oh, Ky," Vanessa said, "guess who we saw this morning?"

"I'm too tired to guess, Vanessa. Who?"

"Stephanie. We were at a stoplight together."

"Speaking of pussy . . ." Tori muttered quietly.

I shot a look at her. "What?"

"Nothing. You ready to talk yet?" Tori asked.

"Not today, Tori, okay? This is not the day," I said.

"Whatever," she said and went to admiring her short curls.

Couldn't she just set the bitch in her aside for one day? Everyone exchanged questioning looks, wondering what our words were about.

"Anyway, I asked her to come to the wedding. How come you didn't invite her?" Vanessa asked.

"I'm not getting married today," I said, trying to joke with her.

"I know." She giggled. "You should have reminded me to send her an invitation, though."

I waited for her to tell me Steph's response, but she was preparing to get her hair washed.

"Well, did she say she was coming?" I tried too hard to sound casual.

"She said she might. Her son has a basketball game at noon, so she didn't know if she had time."

I hadn't talked to Steph since she found out about the engagement. I yearned for her every waking moment, but I couldn't go back to her unless I was one hundred percent sure I could have a relationship with her—and I wasn't. I was too scared to leave my comfort zone and risk the chance of losing my family and friends. David's words constantly echoed in my head. If I chose to enter a relationship with a woman, my life would never be the same, whether the relationship worked or not. I couldn't chance being labeled the girl who let a good man go because she thought she was a dyke for a minute.

I broke from my daze and found Tori smirking at me. I ignored her and studied the French manicured nails I'd had done the day before.

Chavon walked in looking freshly painted as usual. She had been selling beauty products for six years and refused to step foot out of her house without looking like she was running for Miss America. "How am I supposed to recruit other women if I come out of the house half-steppin'?" she would say when asked why she put on a full face of makeup to go to the corner store. We didn't talk badly about the girl, though, because she was driving around in a free car, making some serious money.

"Are my models ready?" Chavon asked.

We looked at one another trying to figure out who did the last cover of *Vogue*. Wasn't me.

"I'll go first," Monica volunteered.

"There's a room in the back by the manicurist that you can use," Camille offered.

The two of them strutted off, which left Tori and me watching Vanessa's head move from side to side as Camille ran the blow-dryer through her freshly trimmed hair.

"So how come you really didn't invite her?" Tori asked me.

I let out a deep breath because I just wasn't in the mood for her. I only wanted to celebrate the marriage of one of my best friends without a fight with the other.

"Like I said, it's Vanessa's wedding, not mine."

"So you're inviting her to yours then?" she asked sarcastically.

She got me with that one, and I sat silent. She kept on.

"You haven't mentioned her much lately. Why not?" Tori picked.

"School's out. We haven't talked much," I answered.

"Yeah, right," she said, cutting her eyes at me.

I slammed down the magazine I had been pretending to read and leaned forward, close to her face.

"What is it that you want me to say, Tori?"

"Tell me the goddamn truth, that's what I want to hear," she said back.

"Fine. Is it that serious that I tell you she's a lesbian? A dyke, fag, gay, whatever you want to call her. What in the fuck is up with the twenty questions? I know you already know, so quit playing these tired-ass games with me." I spoke in a soft voice but in a tone that let her know she was pushing me.

She leaned back in her chair, somewhat satisfied. "Is that all there is to tell me? There's nothing else you want to confess?"

I stared at her, trying to figure out if this was truly my best friend of twenty years. I had seen this side of Tori before, but never directed at *me*.

"You know, Ky," she continued, hissing through her teeth, "I have an image to keep. I run one of the hottest restaurants in the city, and while dykes and fags may frequent my place, I don't want to associate with them on a personal level. You understand what I'm saying? I like dick way too much for people to think otherwise, because my best friend is hooked up with a fuckin' dyke."

Each word cut into my soul like razor blades. My eyes watered, but I refused to let the tears fall and show my weakness. Or an admission of guilt. That's when I realized that I would lose my friend if she knew my intimate feelings for Steph. I didn't want to lose Tori or our relationship after all these years, but knowing she'd drop me for the sake of her image hurt me.

The blow-dryer turned off, ending our conversation. I quickly got up and went into the bathroom, sat on the toilet and wiped the tears I finally let fall. I felt Stephanie's pain and all she had to endure in a struggle just to be herself. Surely, she had come across more than one Tori in her lifetime.

I took out my cell phone to call Stephanie and tell her I loved her and admired her strength and wished I could be as courageous as she was. Then there was a knock at the door.

"Kyla, darling, did you fall in?" Chavon sang high-pitched and off-key.

I put my phone back in my purse and squeezed the remaining half of Visine into my eyes. I opened the door to Mary Kay's African-American clone.

"You're next," she squealed.

I flashed my most convincing smile and stepped out of the bathroom, determined to make my best friend's wedding the happiest it could be.

I stood in front of a room of nearly three hundred familiar and not-so-familiar faces. There were several well-known local celebrities present, including TV anchormen and anchorwomen, along with the mayor, the police chief, and fire chief. All, like us, were there to watch their friends unite in marriage.

Since the wedding was not held in traditional church style, mine and Jeff's parents were seated at a table with Yvonne (yes, she brought Byron). Vanessa and Roger's parents and families had their respective tables on opposite sides of the aisle that divided the room.

Vanessa was stunning—her skin smooth, her makeup perfected, her hair lustrous. She wore an A-line floor-length ivory dress, with short sleeves and a scoop neck in the front and back. A tiara of pearls and rhinestones wrapped the bun in her hair with an attached veil that flowed down her back. Her ears and neck glittered with the diamond and pearl earrings and necklace her grandmother had given her mother at her wedding, which now had been passed down to Vanessa.

Every face beamed as Roger and Vanessa exchanged personally written vows. The exchange was not typical in which the bride cried and choked over her words. Vanessa stood beautiful, proud, and composed as she lovingly told her soon-to-be husband that she would be honored to spend the rest of her life with him. Roger, on the other hand, shed several tears as he looked into Vanessa's eyes and placed the ring on her finger.

The entire wedding party was teary-eyed when the pastor announced the official union of Mr. and Mrs. Roger Mitchell and the groom was given permission to kiss his new bride. Everyone cheered as they headed down the aisle toward the back of the room with the wedding party following. I walked toward a super-handsome Jeff in a black tux and red vest and silently envisioned our own wedding day as we walked to "This Is My Promise" by the Temptations.

Vanessa decided against a receiving line, since the reception immediately followed the ceremony. Attendees were instructed to take pictures with the one-use cameras while the wedding party took time to take pictures with the photographer. After the wedding party departed into the outside corridor, the waitstaff immediately tended to guests, taking drink orders and placing hors d'oeuvres on each table.

Chavon took a moment to touch up Monica's makeup, while the remaining bridesmaids waited our turn. I stood aside and watched the first set of photos as the groomsmen hovered around Vanessa, with Roger right by her side.

Suddenly, Vanessa waved at someone and then looked at me and pointed. I spun on my heels to find Stephanie waving at Vanessa. She was dressed in a black pantsuit with a red blouse, resembling the groomsmen.

My immediate reaction was to turn back around because the sight of her made my stomach drop like the first time. But my feet stood still. We blankly stared at one another for what felt like eternity. I walked to her and gazed into the eyes I had grown to love. I didn't know if the wetness in her eyes was from the emotional ceremony or from seeing Jeff and I walk down the aisle together. I felt my heartache flare up again.

She reached in her purse and pulled out her keys. "Can you tell Vanessa I couldn't stay?" she asked.

"Sure, I'll let her know," I said.

She looked at the floor and then reached for my left hand. She stroked the sparkling diamond on my finger and squeezed my fingers tightly.

I squeezed back but wanted more. I wrapped my arms around her, closed my eyes, and pretended we were back on the beach, embracing one another under the moonlight.

"You looked beautiful up there," she said.

"Thank you," I said, choking over the lump in my throat.

She cleared her throat as well, and I felt a tear drop on my shoulder. She backed away and forced the million-dollar smile I loved so much.

"Be happy, Kyla. Follow only what your heart tells you." With that, she gave my hand one last squeeze, and the one person who held my heart in the palm of her hand walked out the door.

I stood there emotionally paralyzed, not knowing whether to run after her or lock the door behind her forever. I looked at my ring shimmering in the light and thought about Jeff. My friends and family were waiting for me to join in on today's wedding and New Year's eve celebrations.

Speaking of New Year's eve, I remembered my resolution to make a decision by midnight and laughed out loud. I was no closer to making a decision than I was to walking across the stage and receiving my degree. Instead, I decided, as I dried my eyes, I would smile big for the camera, toast the union of two friends, sip *a lot* of champagne, and dance the night away.

I straightened my dress, ignored the disgusted frown Tori shot in my direction, and joined the rest of the wedding party as they gathered together for a group photo.

The hell with New Year resolutions; they never last anyway.

Epilogue

August 2003

I was sitting at the bar sipping a blue motherfucker and watching the women mingle through the smoky club. Friday was ladies' night at the Bar Code, better known as Traxx during the week, and this place had quickly become one of my favorite places to be.

"You need anything else, baby?" Sharice, the slim, sexy-ass bartender asked me.

"No, sweetie, I'm good," I said.

"Well, if you need *anything* else, you let me know." She slid a piece of paper to me.

I looked at the 404 area code and digits and smiled. "Of course."

I smashed my cigarette into the ashtray and cursed the day I started that nasty-ass habit. I slid off the bar stool and made my way to the edge of the dance floor, saying hello to several women I had grown to know in more ways than one. I stopped to hug Donna, a super-femme woman with a body so sweet, I just had to taste it on a regular basis. But I hadn't yet decided if she was the chosen one for the night.

Atlanta sure was an eye-opener for a Midwest girl like myself. I've been down here a little over a year now. I headed out three weeks after I graduated with my business degree. After all those years, can you believe I settled on business? But the thought of taking classes with Stephanie and seeing her on a regular basis was more than I could handle. So I talked myself into a new major, and a new school with an accelerated program that helped me achieve my much anticipated degree in nine short months.

I still think about Steph every day and hope that all is well with her and Jaron. From what I heard, she recently graduated from the university and accepted a position as a counselor in one of the public high schools. She moved back to the east side and purchased a home with Michelle, who came back to town shortly after my engagement to Jeff.

By the time I called off my wedding to Jeff, realizing I needed Steph in my life on a full-time basis, it was too late. Her love and her relationship with Michelle had rekindled and that left no room for me. I was ass out. No man. No woman. And a shitload of people waiting for an explanation.

After Vanessa and Roger's wedding a few years ago, I spent the next four weeks in complete shambles. Sleeping became an activity I stumbled upon only when my mind tired of the *what-if's, should I's,* and *no, I can't's.* Eating was a motion acted out only when Jeff showed up at my door with carryout, or Gladyce sent a plate of home-cooked food over by way of Yvonne or my dad.

The years I had put into the department store were near termination as one sick day followed another. And school became a hellish game of duck and dodge as I avoided any contact with Stephanie. I feared our meeting would end in her dismissing me out of her life completely.

The first few times I saw her I'd take cover behind a pillar, or post myself behind a cracked door and watch her as she walked by, studied from a book, or chatted with a classmate. She smiled and looked happy, but the sparkle in her eyes had temporarily faded and was replaced with a shadow of sorrow at the loss of the love we shared. Due to my deteriorating ability to cope with my surroundings, I remained in an oblivious state even when the shine in her eyes began to glow again. Even when I'd see her grinning while murmuring private words into her cell phone. I was blind to the heartache I was soon to encounter.

It took me eight weeks and two days to make the decision that would change the course of my life forever. And ever. And ever. That morning I awoke with a burst of energy I hadn't felt for months. I could hardly contain my excitement as I gaily swept through my morning routine of preparing myself for a boring Wednesday morning class and an even more uneventful afternoon cleaning fitting rooms, decorating mannequins with the latest "jones" of New York fashions, and assisting hungry customers desperately seeking the best deal from the annual Presidents' Day sale. But nothing could sour my mood as I loudly sang along with radio tunes while driving myself (uninvited) to Steph's apartment. When "If Ever You're in My Arms Again" drifted through the car speakers, I knew it was confirmation that declaring my love for Steph was the right decision. I mean, surely that was a sign, right?

I pulled into the parking lot of Steph's complex feeling more confident than Michael Jordan shooting a game-winning three-pointer. There was just no way I could lose

Steph. Continuing to hum Peabo's song, I got out of the car and walked to apartment 102. *Ding,* the bell chimed inside.

Heels clacked against the linoleum floor and a very stunned Stephanie Coleman opened the door. Geared up in a suit the CEO of her own company might wear, she looked amazing. No longer sporting her signature pony-tail, her straightened locks hung freely in cascading layers, with wisps down the sides of her face, and flowing down her back (apparently I failed to acknowledge the "new at-titude" hairdo as well). Steph's mouth instantly fell open, though she quickly gained composure and smiled at me.

"Hey, Kyla," she said, and then swallowed hard. "What brings you here?"

Standing erect with my hands at my side, you would have thought I was standing in formation before my supe-rior officer after going AWOL for eight weeks.

"Well, I came to see you," I said. In response I thought I saw an *I know that* look flash across her face. "Can I come in?" I asked.

Still leaning against the door, Steph turned around as if waiting for the living room to grant its permission. "Um, sure, I have a couple of minutes," she said, stepping aside to let me in.

Freshly brewed coffee alerted my senses and got my blood flowing. This was it! The climactic finale of my jour-ney to self-discovery . . .

"Have a seat," she said, leading me to the brown leather couch we had held so many intimate conversations on. Sit-ting there once again brought back a surge of emotions I could no longer contain. The familiar smell of her per-fume created a burning desire in me to hold her once again. For a moment I saw us making love on the couch, just five minutes into the future.

Her concerned expression snapped me out of my brief daydream and assured me that she was anxiously awaiting an explanation for my presence.

A memorized and rehearsed speech sat on the tip of my tongue, waiting its departure from my lips. Patiently she sat beside me, hands in her lap, eyes pouring into my soul.

"Steph, I came to see you today because I have something to tell you," I said.

Silence.

"Six months ago I never would have imagined sitting across from such a beautiful, kind, loving person. I never would have imagined opening my heart so completely. And now I'm willing and ready to let go of all fears, doubts, and worries about sharing a life with you. I miss you and I want you back in my life. I'm ready, Steph. I'm ready to love you openly and honestly," I said confidently.

I reached and placed my hands on top of her trembling hands. Her face softened, and an agonizing look of grief covered her face.

"Kyla—" she said softly.

Jingling keys and a sudden opening of the front door interrupted her reply.

"You know who forgot his book bag again," the hurried woman said loudly, barely glancing up as she stepped inside the foyer.

"Oh . . ." she said, finally noticing Steph and me sitting barely breathing, on the couch (or maybe I was the only one holding my breath).

Steph immediately stood up, hopelessly perplexed by her sudden predicament.

My head darted toward the silver-framed photo to my left. Several months prior, Steph had told me the story behind the four lovely women smiling for the camera. Although her hair had grown into a short bob, and she was dressed in a winter warm-up suit, as opposed to the evening gown donned in the picture, there was no question that this woman before me was Michelle, Steph's one and only true love.

"I'll get it," Steph said, racing in the direction of Jaron's room.

Michelle and I were silent, although the pounding of my heart seemed deafening, if to my ears only. During my time of contemplation, weighing the pros, cons, and what-if's, this dilemma here had not once crossed my mind. Never had Michelle even been a thought.

Steph returned with Jaron's backpack and handed it to Michelle, who quickly took the bag. Without words, their eyes exchanged a conversation that I later interpreted as:

> *Michelle: Is that Kyla?*
> *Steph: Yes.*
> *Michelle: Why is she here?*
> *Steph: (painful blank stare)*
> *Michelle: Because she wants you back?*
> *Steph: Yes.*
> *Michelle: We'll talk later.*
> *Steph: Yes, we will.*
> *Michelle: I love you.*
> *Steph: I love you too.*

After an empathetic glance in my direction, Michelle walked out. Steph slowly closed the door behind her, and then turned to face me. *Stunned* would have been a kind definition to describe what I felt at that moment. The self-assured demeanor I held only minutes earlier was replaced by a searing hot flash through my entire body. Burning cheeks revealed my embarrassment and disappointment.

"Kyla, I'm sorry," Steph said as she made her way back to my side. Her slender fingers reached for my face and caressed my cheek.

So badly I wanted to cry, but merely closed my eyes for a moment, and savored her soft strokes to my skin.

"About a week after Vanessa's wedding I got a phone call from Michelle completely out of the blue," she explained. "She asked me if it would be all right if she came to visit, and of course I couldn't say no. She stayed for about a week, and we caught up on all that happened to us over the past two years. Just like me, she hadn't had any luck finding a successful relationship either."

I knew that wasn't necessarily a dig at me, but it still stung a little.

"I told her all about you and how much I truly hoped we could be together. She listened to me, Kyla, and it felt so good to be able to talk to someone about us. I couldn't tell anyone about you because of your situation. It was eating me up inside. After she left I was so torn. A part of me wanted to ask her to stay, but another part prayed for a miracle with you." Tears threatened to fall from the corners of her eyes as she paused. "But you didn't call. I never saw you at school. You just . . . disappeared. After a while I assumed you must have decided to get married. I didn't know what else to think. And then I realized that I must have been given a second chance with Michelle. I didn't want to lose her again." She stared deeply into my eyes. "I didn't want to lose love again either. Please understand."

Although I understood, the regret I felt dominated my emotions. Had I not waited eight weeks and two days, perhaps this episode wouldn't have occurred. Had I gotten the courage to reveal what was in my heart sooner, then maybe, just maybe, it would have been me taking Jaron to school and not Michelle. But apparently Steph and Michelle were meant to be. Was I jealous? Hell, yes. There sat a woman I was ready to alter my entire life for, and she had fallen back in love with someone else.

"I understand, Steph," I said standing up and gathering my purse. "I'm happy for you. For the both of you," I managed, hoping I was convincing.

Steph stood also, an awkward, slow rise, as if debating her next move.

My head lowered in defeat; I was motionless, not wanting to leave, but knowing I couldn't stay. "I guess I better go." I struggled, unsure how to say good-bye. But then she was there. Right in front of me. So close I could feel her chest rise and fall with each breath. She wrapped her hand around my neck and leaned her forehead against mine. I closed my eyes when she kissed me. A tender kiss on my lips. I welcomed her lips on mine, though I was too afraid to kiss her back. She pressed against me, and then parted.

"I'm going to miss you, Stephanie," I whispered, tousling strands of her hair between my fingers.

She opened her mouth to respond, but I held my hand over her lips. The compassion and sorrow in her eyes spoke words she need not speak. Finally, her eyes lingered in the direction of the door, an indication of her concern that at any time, the love of her life would be returning.

Together we walked to the door, a melancholy aura following us. We shared a brief hug, and I inhaled the delicate scent of her skin once more.

"Good-bye, Stephanie," I said, biting my bottom lip in an effort to hold back my tears just a few minutes longer.

"Good-bye, Kyla," she said, and then turned her eyes to the floor to hide her own tears.

I was halfway down the walkway when Steph called for me.

"Ky!"

I turned on my three-inch knee-high boots.

"Does Jeff know?" she asked.

"Yes," I said, and smiled sadly. "Yes, he does."

A brief gaze lingered between us before Steph nodded gently and slowly closed the door. When I think about it now, I'm not sure just how long I stood there staring at that closed door. Perhaps I was in temporary shock. Total disbelief. Or complete bewilderment about what in the hell was going to happen to my life from that moment forward.

Only two days prior I had gathered my closest loved ones into my mother's home, in similar fashion as we had congregated on Christmas day when Jeff proposed to me. My mother, father, Yvonne, best friends Tori and Vanessa, and my fiancé Jeff sat throughout the living room while I took center stage. David, my lifesaver, stood just a few steps to my side, possibly ready to catch me fall if I fainted from an anxiety attack. Even with the seriousness of the event, I nearly chuckled at a passing thought. *I bet they think I'm pregnant.* No, that would've been *good* news compared to what I was about to announce.

"Um, well," I started, "I brought you all here because I love each of you, and I need to share something important." I glanced back at David, who gestured for me to continue. Even though I knew I should have been a bit more tactful, nerves got the best of me. "I can't get married."

Three individual gasps escaped loudly from my mother, Yvonne, and Vanessa. My father appeared terribly concerned, as a troubled frown formed between his eyebrows. Tori groaned irritably. Jeff tried to remain expressionless, but couldn't conceal his building indignation.

I sighed heavily and willed every ounce of courage in my body upward to my lips. "I'm in love with someone else," I said.

In an instant Jeff was on his feet, his arm grasped tightly

around mine as he led me to the spare room across the
hall, closing the door to the buzzing chatter we left behind. Tension engulfed the small room as Jeff paced back
and forth, occasionally glancing at me and shaking his
head. The dark purple wallpaper surrounded us, its darkness closing in on me as if I had reached the end of a tunnel of no escape. Because the space was no longer the
guest bedroom for visiting family members, boxes of old
clothing rested in the corner, awaiting delivery to Good-
will. Unused items were scattered throughout—a turntable
and floor speakers, a wooden rocking chair, and my mother's
sewing machine sat dusty in a corner of the room. As a child
I'd watch, fascinated, as the hole in the skinned knee of my
jeans miraculously disappeared under my mother's care.
Oh, the simplicities in finding joy as a child—how I wished
it were still so easy.

"Jeff, I can explain," I offered.

He held up his hand to stop me. "You've said enough already, Kyla. It's my turn now."

He stopped pacing and stood directly in front of me,
glaring at me, not more than a few inches from my face.
"It's because of her, right?" he snarled.

I gasped for breath so loudly, you'd have thought I had
been punched in the stomach. If only David were there to
catch me at that moment. I stumbled a few steps backward, balancing myself against the closed door.

"Did you think I didn't know, Kyla? Did you really think
that?" he yelled in my face.

I didn't answer, nor did he expect one.

"I know you better than you think I do, Kyla. I know
what makes you happy. I know what makes you sad. I feel
you, Kyla."

I lowered my head in shame, but his pressing finger
against my chin lifted my head up, forcing me to look into

his pained, but angered eyes. He commanded my attention.

"You changed on me. I had to know why," he explained. "One night I was talking to Kent about our wedding and I told him that I thought you were beginning to have doubts. He asked me had you started to behave differently and I said yes. The more I thought about it, I realized you started to act differently after she entered your life. *Our* lives," he emphasized. "Did you think I wouldn't find out she's a lesbian? That shit didn't matter to me, Ky. Don't you know me better than that? But the fact that you kept that piece of information from me was all I needed to know."

The finger against my chin moved to wipe away the tears that fell from my eyes. "Why didn't you come to me? You don't think we could have talked about this?" he asked empathetically. Then he switched gears. "And now you want to throw everything away without the decency of discussing it with me first? You just treat me like everybody else and tell me right along with the rest of your family? You weren't marrying them, Ky, you were marrying me. You went about this the wrong way. This is bullshit."

He reached for the doorknob behind me.

"Wait," I said, taking his hand away. "Can I explain?"

He thought for a moment, I suppose questioning whether or not an accounting of the previous six months would help if the end result was the same. Staring at me, seething in silence, he waited for me to go on.

"I don't even know how this happened, Jeff," I began, attempting to speak between the spasms in my chest. "It all went so fast. She and I just clicked right from the start. It was fun having her in my class and hanging out with her after school. The more I got to know her, the closer I felt to her, and all these emotions I didn't even know existed started surfacing. I started thinking about her in ways that were beyond friendship. I was so confused, Jeff . . . so confused about what to do with my feelings. All my life I've only desired men. And now one person has changed that," I said, staring at the hardwood floor.

He laughed at me. "Now you think you're gay, Kyla? You've know this woman for six months. Six months! You're ready to fuck up what we have, what we could have, for her?" he asked, fear and disgust of my upcoming answer showing on his face.

"I'm sorry, Jeff," I said, more tears stinging my eyes. "Believe me, I wouldn't be doing this if I didn't know it was right for me."

"Right for you? What about us, Ky? What about the life I have planned for me and you?"

"Please don't make me feel guilty, Jeff. Please. I am doing this for us. If I didn't make this decision, I'd be living the rest of my life wondering what may have been. You don't want a wife who will always be questioning whether or not she made the right decision, do you? That wouldn't be fair to either of us."

"Your love for me isn't strong enough to choose me? After all we've shared you want to give it up for a woman you barely know? I don't get it."

"That's the thing, Jeff, I do know her. I feel like I've known her forever. Like I said, we've gotten close," I hinted, not knowing how detailed I'd have to be for him to understand how strongly I felt.

"Hold up, hold up! You're trying to tell me that you slept with her? You fucked around with her while you were with me?" he yelled. "All this time I sat back and watched and waited for you to sort this out. When you pulled away from me, I knew it had to do with her. But I still trusted you enough not to be fucking around, laying up under somebody else, I don't care if she is a goddamn woman! You're still my woman. What the fuck? I haven't done shit to you to deserve this, Kyla."

"Jeff, I had to sleep with her to know if what I felt was real," I explained, an unsuitable defense in his eyes.

"Spare me this bullshit, Kyla. For real. Just tell me one thing—do you love her?"

I hesitated, closed my eyes, and sighed; my answer would permanently redirect the course of my life.

"Yes, I do," I answered honestly.

"I hope you realize what you're doing, Kyla."

I didn't respond, just moved aside, and he walked out of the door.

Only after I was sure he left, did I return to the living room. Tori, Vanessa, and David were gone, leaving me confronted with the confused faces of my parents and sister. Of course Yvonne was more baffled by the fact that I actually chose Steph over Jeff, considering she was already aware of my relationship with Steph when she overheard the conversation I had with David about falling in love with her. My mother, who knew there was "someone else," nearly doubled over in what appeared to be excruciating pain when she learned that the someone else was the woman she'd welcomed into her home a few months before. My gracious father, who I will forever appreciate for that moment, although clearly disappointed, simply hugged me and held me in his arms until the tears subsided.

While driving home, my mother's words played repeatedly through my mind. *"You've just made the biggest mistake of your life,"* she'd warned. Had I? I needed to pull the car to the side of the road twice, just to gain composure and ease the shaky nerves racing through my body.

A nervous voice mail message from Vanessa greeted me once I got home that evening. *Um, Ky, it's me. Uh, Jeff called and asked me to come pick up your things from his place tomor-*

row, so, um, that's what I'm going to do. Just call me when I can bring them to you. Call me anyway. A pause followed and I thought she was about to hang up, but she added, *I love you, Ky.*

The next voice message, which was from Tori, still haunts me to this day. She called me every degrading and derogatory euphemism for lesbian ever devised, and others created from her perverted imagination. By the time she referred to me as a "carpet-munching, fish-eating, pussy-licking, stank-ass dyke," I hit the erase button and cried again, surprised I still had any tears left at all.

I never saw Jeff or Steph again before I moved to Atlanta. After Jeff left my mother's house that day, he made it clear to me through an e-mail that under no circumstances was I to contact him for any reason whatsoever. He assured me that although he was hurt that I left him for a woman, he was most angry that I left him at all.

It was difficult not to call him, or even respond to his e-mail. I desperately wanted him to know how sorry I was. But I could apologize a hundred times over and the result would still be the same. Stephanie was who I wanted.

After Steph crushed my dreams of a blissful life together just two days later, I resumed my bedridden state for a week. Incessant worries of whether or not I had done the right thing drove me near insanity. I had lost two people who both were so willing to sacrifice their self-respect and allow me time to figure out what I wanted. Jeff, who, without my knowledge, patiently watched me fall for a woman, yet believed in me and our love enough to concede to the moment, faithful that it would pass. Steph, against her own conviction, submitted to falling in love with a woman in love with a man, a place she had vowed never to find herself. I could only hope they both would forgive me for the heartache I caused them.

Vanessa continued to offer her friendship, though my

grief and embarrassment shielded me from the outside world. Just David was granted access to my pain, confusion, doubt, and finally, resolution of what lay ahead for me. Only after a week of intense crying sessions, agonizing soul-searching, and foot-stomping anger toward myself was I able to conclude the following: the euphoria I felt in the presence of Stephanie was like none I had ever experienced. Not with Jeff nor with any other man prior to him. I concluded that in order to understand the depth to which those emotions derived, I needed to further explore relationships with other women. I was so scared! I hadn't known any lesbians before Steph. *How would it feel to touch a woman that was not her?*

At David's urging, he and I attended the annual black pride gathering in Atlanta that fall, him believing that by my submerging myself into a sea of lesbian women, I would overcome my fear of testing a relationship with a woman other than Stephanie.

David accompanied me to a party the first night we were there, and didn't need to chaperone me anymore after that. From the moment I stepped inside the door, I was overwhelmed with a sense of belonging. Surrounded by other women loving women felt right for me. It was comfortable, and I knew in an instant that was where I wanted to be. That weekend I experienced highs of emotional freedom so extreme that denying my longing and loving for a woman would have been impossible. During our thirteen-hour ride home, I expressed my desire to David about a move to Atlanta. Tired of the hometown scene himself, he asked to come along. And from there it went.

Of all folks to run into before I left, Tori had to be the one. With seven days in a week and fifty-two of them throughout the year, I'm mystified by the fact that both Tori and I wound up at the gym to cancel our memberships at the same time. Fate just had to try to knock me down one more time. I hadn't been to the gym since Christmastime, and I was unsure whether or not Tori and Vanessa had continued the Monday-morning workout routine until that unfortunate day. As soon as I exited the elevator, I saw her leaning against the counter, fussing with a young lady about a refund she felt was owed to her.

"Fuck it, I don't want your money. Just cancel me then," she said angrily, and turned her back to the girl.

When her eyes met mine, she groaned in disgust, not at all as caught off guard as I was by our unexpected encounter. "This is half the reason I don't want to come here anymore. Can't even go in the locker room without feeling like I'm being molested," she said, talking to the confused girl, but staring at me. "All these lesbians running around here, I can't shower without watching my back."

At mention of the *L* word, all heads in earshot turned in our direction, focusing on the person to whom Tori's words were geared: me. I quickly attempted to conceal the panic rising inside of me and gained my composure. I couldn't allow Tori's vicious behavior to rile me up. Curious eyes followed me as I walked to the counter, all the while Tori continued to spit nasty comments in my favor. Choosing to ignore her, I asked the flustered young lady for the papers to cancel my membership.

"Not enough pussy in here for you, Kyla?" Tori asked.

Was I being a coward by not responding to her attack? If so, I didn't care. I had developed enough respect for myself not to act a fool with Tori or anyone else about my sexuality. She could make an ass out of herself on her own. But, damn, I never knew my being a lesbian would cause such a stir in people.

My relationship with Gladyce was slowly coming around. We talked on the phone on a regular basis, but the conversation almost always reverted to her checking to see if I'd gotten back "right" yet. My dad had been down to visit me on several occasions, continuing to love me no matter whom I love in my bedroom. And, Yvonne, that girl married Byron after all. Just before I hit the road with my U-Haul, I was maid of honor in my baby sister's wedding. She was pregnant with their first child now. Guess he wasn't so fearful of becoming a father after all.

Vanessa and Roger finally moved to Chicago where she was an anchorwoman in the prime-time slot for the highest rated channel in the city. And, Tori, well, my girl was serious. She cut all ties with me like she never even knew me. I haven't seen nor spoken to her since our incident at the gym. I guess there's no way around it. Some people just aren't cool with gay people, no matter who they are.

I still don't talk to Jeff often. We drop each other an e-mail every once in a while just as a courtesy check-in, but that may be coming to a halt very soon. Gladyce informed me that he's chosen a new bride and is due to get married next year. And with all my heart, I hope he's found the happiness he deserves.

I was finishing my drink when my cell phone started vibrating. I reached in my purse and looked at the glowing blue screen in the dim light. *Quit standing there and bring your ass over here* the letters in the text message said to me.

I looked around and saw Angie, standing in the corner of the club dressed in khaki shorts and a white T-shirt, her cell phone in her hand. Angie was a soft stud, one of the first I met when I got here. Cute as hell, though she wore no makeup except for the occasional mascara and clear lip gloss for special events like black pride. But the girl knew how to *work it*. I damn near went into convulsions just by the girl's touch. Yep, she was the one for tonight.

I'll be there in 25 I typed back to her. She nodded her

head and went out the door. I stepped into the bathroom and unpinned my hair, letting it fall past my shoulders. Angie was good for grabbing a girl's hair when she was . . . well, never mind.

I went outside and absorbed the humid night air. I got into my convertible Mustang and blasted a Maxwell CD as I took 85 South to Angie's apartment in East Point. This was just what I needed after working sixty hours this week at Rich's, where I'm a buyer (all those years at the department store finally paid off). My body needed some attention and a little somethin'-somethin' to help me unwind. Yeah, this shit was about to be *on* tonight!